accomplishments. His telling of up-close-and-personal experiences covering his many years in the business gives the reader a front row seat to how it really was during advertising's Golden Age (or Wonder Years)."

JIM LAVELLE, Chairman/CEO, Lightbeam Energy, Inc.; founder, Chairman/CEO Cotelligent, Inc.

"Fred Goldberg was a force of nature. He was more driven—and more focused—than anyone I ever met. He worked harder, he worked longer, he worked smarter than anyone else. He sought—and passionately supported—breakthrough concepts on every project in which he was involved, every bit as much as does the most gifted creative director."

JOHN FERRELL, Former Chief Creative Officer, Hill Holliday New York; Creative Director, Young & Rubicam

"It's insane to think that Fred could have worked on Apple, Cisco, Dell, Kia, Intel, Rice-A-Roni, General Foods, Puerto Rico and Gallo . . . and lived to tell about it. And who wouldn't want to read a book from the man who told a twenty-four-year-old Michael Dell he needed a girlfriend."

MIKE MASSARO, former COO, Goldberg Moser O'Neill

"Fred Goldberg has written the book on what really happens in advertising. And it isn't pretty."

BRIAN O'NEILL, former Creative Director, Goldberg Moser O'Neill

"When Fred arrived at Young & Rubicam, it was not long before it became obvious that he had a passion for the advertising business, recognizing the challenge of making disparate elements work together, and knowing that whatever anguish was involved, it was all worthwhile to produce a great end product."

JOHN MCMENNAMIN, former Vice President, International Marketing, Max Factor; VP, Marketing Services, Carnation/Nestle USA

"The truth about the advertising business from an insider who knows its insanity—he was a significant part of it. He did it all and tells his story in typical Fred fashion: no punches are pulled in his description of the business and people in it."

RICHARD GREENE, Greene Radovsky Maloney Share & Hennigh

"3M saw in Fred a person who would challenge them and stand up for the best creative rather than a middle-of-the-road approach that might achieve consensus."

RICK KURZ, former President, Consulting, Marketing Corporation of America; President, Somerset Wines; Director of Marketing and Advertising, E & J Gallo Winery

"Fred had the passion, intelligence, and creativity to change things. And the balls to put honesty before convenience. He is one of the best ad men I have had the honor of working with."

FLOYD MILLER, founder and CEO, Miller/Kadanoff

"Fred always could see farther down the road than anyone else in the room. Riding his coat-tails was the best and the most fun ride, ever. I was honored to be his client—twice."

ROBERT CUDD, former VP, Marketing and Editorial, Fatbrain.com

"Fred Goldberg is a brilliant ad man! The very best strategic thinker and leader that I have ever been around. His book is a must read for all advertising people!"

DOUG SHERFEY, former Executive Director, Advertising and Public Relations, John Ascuaga's Resort Hotel Casino, Reno

"The creators of the TV series Mad Men needed Fred Goldberg as a creative consultant to capture just how 'mad' the advertising world has been over the years."

JOHN RACZKA, VP, Entertainment Development, Melco Crown Entertainment

"Of all the Mad Men I worked with, Fred Goldberg was the maddest of them all. Responsible for driving many legendary campaigns, he gives an entertaining account of his thirty years in the biz. Always opinionated and never boring, Fred played the game well, never forgot a friend or an adversary, and ended up with all the marbles."

RICK HERRICK, founding partner, SALT Branding

THE INSANITY OF ADVERTISING

THE INSANITY OF ADVERTISING
MEMOIRS OF A MAD MAN

Fred S. Goldberg

Grateful acknowledgement to Getty Images for permission
to use the following photographs: page 34, photo by Bill Ray;
pages 102, photo by Marilyn K. Yee; page 134, photo by AFP;
page 192, photo by Rabbani and Solimene Photography; page
199, photo by Dave M. Benett

Library of Congress Cataloging-in-Publication Data on file
with the Publisher

Council Oak Books, LLC
2822 Van Ness Avenue, San Francisco, CA 94109

www.counciloakbooks.com
www.theinsanityofadvertising.com

ISBN 978-1-5717-8321-9

Printed in Canada
10 9 8 7 6 5 4 3 2 1

Distributed by Publishers Group West

THIS BOOK IS DEDICATED TO my three girls who somehow put up with my commitment to the business of advertising, which took us from Madison Avenue to the wild West and spanned more than three decades.

My wife Jeri lived with the business every day . . . and night. Both of my daughters, Robin and Susanne, tasted what working in the ad business was like, vicariously and actually. They made me very proud of the fine jobs they each did during the time they spent in it.

Somehow we emerged a reasonably sane family despite the insanity of the ad business.

With love and affection, I give an enormous thank you to Jeri and my daughters for their patience and understanding and just for being who they are.

The book can provide anyone remotely interested in advertising a real-life, inside look at the workings and issues of the business. It is also a management primer for dealing with many of the everyday situations that arise in the business world. Moreover, it's entertaining and fun and so surprising that you will very often find yourself saying to yourself, *No way! Oh, my God!* And, *Shut up!*

Finally, I hope that this memoir will offer a legacy for my grandchildren, Cory, Alison, Jack, and Charlotte, and that they will gain some understanding of what their Grandpa Fred did with his life—and maybe it will provide some inspiration and motivation for each of them.

"Time spent in the advertising business seems to create a permanent deformity like the Chinese habit of foot binding."

—*Dean Acheson*

CONTENTS

PART II: THE BELIEFS, THE OBSERVATIONS, THE DERANGEMENTS

INTRODUCTION

insane (adj.) 1. being afflicted by or manifesting unsoundness
of mind or an inability to control one's rational processes

EVERYONE LOVES THE ADVERTISING BUSINESS. Or thinks they do.

That's why traditionally there were never enough jobs to fill the demand. The draw is the perceived excitement, the high profile and visibility, the creativity, the glamour, the fun. Many of the things that make the business bad are also what make it attractive. There are so many unexpected happenings and tons of challenges; there is an exciting uncertainty inherent in the constant ups and downs. The world can be different every working day.

And, your mother gets to see what you do for a living by watching television.

But few people realize that the business is often a grind and a difficult one to navigate. There is an essential need to always keep bringing in new business and winning accounts to replace the ones that are leaving. There is the challenge of getting clients to maintain ad-spending commitments. Even before that, there is the task of developing and getting approval for the advertising, particularly if it's more creative advertising.

It is all a highly complicated and emotional process. And a high percentage of clients make it all the more so. It's been said that the business would be easy if it didn't have any clients. Or for that matter any employees. When you take a bird's-eye view of the entire "do funny" occupation, it very often looks and feels like a cuckoo's nest.

The advertising business is composed of a bunch of people who can be crazy at times. Some are crazy all the time. People you have working for you. People you work for who are your bosses and clients.

On the other hand there are some wonderful rewards in working in this nutty livelihood, but on balance it's definitely an off-balance place in which to make a career.

Delicious but wacky. Rewarding but it can drive you to drink. It's predictable but uncertain. Most people in it could use some therapy. Some people need it regularly. You might think of it as nutcracker suite.

Back when I started in the business at 285 Madison Avenue at Young & Rubicam (Y&R), the agency was rumored to have a rate of alcohol addiction that was twice the national average at the time. The business had the potential to drive people to drink, and I was told that the agency had gone to the extent of hiring a full-time person to counsel those individuals that had been identified as problem drinkers. I don't know if this was true because I never had the pleasure or need to meet this guy.

The Insanity of Advertising provides an authentic inside look at some surprising, often unbelievable situations and events that actually happened in working in advertising. My involvement spanned some 33 years. Some of my experiences are pretty; some pretty ugly.

The very first clue that I might end up in the advertising business occurred during an advertising course that I took during my last year at the University of Vermont. Heublein Inc. underwrote a contest to create a television commercial for one of their products, a cereal known as Maypo.

I submitted a campaign that had a professor cartoon character who was inevitably and persistently demanding his Maypo no matter the situation.

"I want my Maypo!"

"I want my Maypo!"

"I want my Maypo!"

I guess this turned out to be a pretty good idea since years later the same idea appeared for a television channel and became a great success, minus the professor.

"I want my MTV."

Oh, and I won a third place honorable mention in the ad contest.

Another early hint of my advertising and marketing prowess came during my very first job as a marketing analyst at P. Ballantine & Sons in Newark,

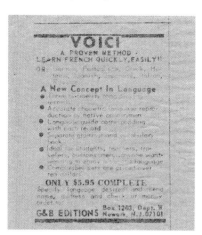

New Jersey, brewers of fine beer and ale. I wasn't really a "marketing analyst"; I was more like a clerk who punched an adding machine with sales figures from nine to five. It was not the most challenging situation.

So for a bit of added interest and sanity maintenance, the fellow who sat next to me, Mike Beder, and I decided to form a company, which we incorporated as G&B Editions (a foreshadow of GMO). We advertised two very different products before we closed our doors. The first was a set of Listen & Learn Language records, which offered recorded lessons for learning French, Spanish, Russian, and so on.

This was an excellent product to focus on since there weren't many other similar offerings at the time. Far more importantly, I was able to secure the product only as the orders were received, since my dad was then national sales director at Decca Records, which distributed these record albums.

The second product was for a sweatshirt with a Ballantine Beer self-opening can. Pop-tops were just being introduced in the industry, and they were a real innovation and attraction. Our sweatshirt had across the front "Be The First On Your Block To Wear A Self-Opening Can." And on the back was a big picture of the can and top itself.

Again this product was of interest since we did not have to lay out any money in advance for inventory. We could go down two floors to the Ballantine Store and buy the sweatshirts at the employee discount.

It was far from an elegant ad but we sold 40 Listen & Learn records, mostly French. Hebrew was our poorest seller: one order. And we didn't sell a single shirt and so decided to focus back on our regular day jobs.

And by the way it was absolutely no fun securing those albums from a Decca Record branch in Woodside, New York (we were in New Jersey); packing the individual orders; addressing and labeling them; schlepping them to the post office; adding postage; insuring them; and making sure each of the checks cleared before dropping the packages in the post.

But it was way easier than when my dad first started selling records in the 1930s. His territory consisted of Illinois, Michigan, Indiana, Wisconsin, and Ohio, and he sold and delivered records out of the trunk of his car.

I got promoted from analyst to supervisor and then to marketing research director, allowing me to become significantly more involved in things of a marketing and advertising nature.

During this time I received my first real insights into how many marketing and advertising decisions really work. Being in the marketing research department, we were investigating the development of a new package design, one that would be more attractive to consumers, stand out from the competition, reinforce the brands' perceived strengths, and so on.

We had spent considerable time and a large amount of money on a consumer survey to determine which of some 50 proposed label designs would best accomplish these objectives. Finally, we were ready to present our results to Ballantine's top management as to which would, in fact, be the most effective new design.

Our meeting was held at the brewery in Newark, New Jersey, in the executive boardroom. Present were all of Ballantine's senior management: heads of sales, production, finance, and even human resources. And of course, C. S. Badenhausen, the son of C. W. Badenhausen and president of the brewery. C.W., board chairman, was there as well.

We were careful in presenting our research methodology and the meticulous results. With 50-some label alternatives, this was a gargantuan effort. At the end it boiled down to the recommended two versions for the new label design, with a strong bias for one of the two based on the conclusive evidence from the consumer survey. The study had been carefully designed and was very considered marketing research conducted with hundreds and hundreds of actual Ballantine users as well as users of our two most direct competitors, Schaefer and Rheingold.

We finished our presentation and no one in the room said a word. Not a single thing. Then after a few minutes C. W., the old man, cleared his throat and kind of grunted. He was sitting at the head of the large conference table that dominated the room. All of his executives were sitting on each side of the table. The 50 or so new label designs for the cans were displayed on a rack that ran almost the entire length of one wall of the conference room.

C. W. had his hands clasped and his two index fingers touching one another, the ends of which were inserted into the bottom of the middle of his chin. His lips were kind of pursed and puckered, and his upper one was clearly overlapping his lower, giving his face a strange quizzical contemplative kind of look.

Finally, C. W. squinted and moved his hands, still clasped together, and pointed his two index fingers, still touching one another at their ends, toward the row of cans on the wall rack.

As he moved his two fingers slowly up and down, as if aiming a pistol, he pointed and said, "That one. That one there. That's the one."

And that was the one!

This became my first real insight and understanding as to how marketing decisions are really made in big corporations throughout America.

Around this same time, I got entrepreneurial yearnings again to try to do some direct marketing and formed a company on my own, which I called Carlisle Classics.

My initial product was a high-quality knockoff of a popular travel bag that you could carry instead of a briefcase or attaché. My wife's uncle, Mendel Krauser, was a luggage manufacturer and made the bag to my specs and as needed to fill my orders.

I created a small-space print ad to promote it and, after much analysis and introspection, placed it in the *New York Times* Shopping Section.

I sold about 60 bags out of the gate but discovered, again, that the amount of work involved in getting product, billing, packing, shipping, and waiting for checks to clear, which many didn't, was overwhelming, particularly since I was the only employee.

But this was the third foreshadowing of a possible career in the advertising business. The ad effort was not particularly clever, but it seemed to work.

It had as its headline, "This famous bag direct from the manufacturer . . . only $39."

I am quite confident that if circumstances had allowed me to continue to promote the bag, it would have proved a greater sales success.

And who would have known that this particular style of bag, a Ghurka, would become part of the dress code for many of the senior executives at Chiat/Day. Jay Chiat was disposed to carrying the real Ghurka (around $400 back then), an influence that translated downward in the organization, as we all seemed to end up with one.

This episode was great, too, since it allowed me to expand my in-depth experience in direct marketing, which came in handy years later when I won what was arguably the greatest direct marketer in the country: Dell Computer.

There is no question that advertising is an intellectually stimulating and phys-ically, psychologically, and emotionally exciting and satisfying business. It's a young business and young people keep you young. And on the edge. It is for these very same reasons, and others, that the business is exacting and insane.

The people in it are often weird and wacky but wonderful. I believe that a much higher percentage of smart and clever people enter the industry. But while creative people can be exceptionally talented, they can be totally oblivi-ous to the most obvious commonsense things or the world around them. Somehow these afflictions seem to trickle down and across everyone who works at an advertising agency.

Clients can be passionately committed to the need to advertise and yet be totally lacking in understanding anything at all about what makes for great advertising and how it is developed, how to encourage it, and what it looks like even when it is stood up on an easel in front of their noses.

There are so many forces, internal and external, that make the business a much more demanding one than most. It is a business that makes managing your own destiny very difficult.

At times the business can be characterized as bananas and demented and deranged and lunatic and unreasonable. And it is often each of these alone and all at once. So many things that happen are beyond controlling or plan-ning for and can be completely unexpected. The nest can be fouled and made even more cuckoo by the most experienced senior executives, or by clients who are entrepreneurs or directors on boards, and even by entire boards of directors.

If there is one thing this book demonstrates for sure, it is that while there is lots of room for accomplishing incredible and significant things in advertis-ing, and for having fun doing it, you are very often caught with inmates on the loose conspiring against you.

IT'S DIFFICULT TO ANTICIPATE THE UNANTICIPATED

For TakeCare, an HMO, we created a full-page newspaper ad that showed a large tongue depressor being held in a physician's hand with the headline, "If you think this makes you gag, wait until you see the bill."

A few newspaper readers called TakeCare headquarters complaining that the tongue depressor looked like a giant phallic symbol. That would be a penis. It wasn't proper, they said. It exposed children to a bad experience. I wondered how many children read the daily newspaper and the HMO ads.

There were some at TakeCare who were immediately concerned and wanted to pull the ad because of the complaints. But we were able to persuade them, Judd Jessup, CEO, Bob Fahlman, marketing VP, and Ruth Grossman, ad manager, all clients extraordinaire, to carry on with the ad and with the rest of the campaign. It turned out to be very effective. No guts, no glory.

A print ad for Gallo's E&J Brandy was nothing more than a photograph of a nicely lit bottle and an innocuous headline, "E&J Gallo Brandy."

Some people called Gallo and complained that there was a penis in the bottle. Say what? It happened that the lighting was a bit shadowy on one side of the bottle. Without any hesitation, Gallo ordered that the ad be pulled.

Moreover, there were some at the client who went on to accuse us at the agency of doing this on purpose, believing that the art director conspired with the photographer to shoot the bottle in such a way as to have the offensive image appear subliminally. Why? Simply to embarrass Gallo.

Who are these people that are looking so introspectively into ads? Don't they have anything else to do than cause serious headaches for advertising agencies? And why do the clients listen to them?

THE INMATES ARE PRONE TO SHOOTING THEMSELVES IN THEIR FEET

Chiat/Day San Francisco was trying to get included in an agency account review conducted by Airborne Express. The Chiat/Day general manager at the time sent a letter, along with some sample print and TV ads, to the VP of corporate marketing at Airborne Express, Ken McCumber.

He in turn sent a letter back, complimenting us on the impact that our package had had upon receipt, and then mentioned that we would never ever have a chance to work on the Airborne Express account.

Oops! We had sent our package via Federal Express.

Just after Chiat/Day purchased and merged with Mojo, an Australian ad agency, we kept up the tradition of sending out clever and arresting holiday cards to clients, employees, and others. That year's card was a traditional Christmas green and white with a touch of red, and a seasonal message on the front flap.

Here's the thing. Jingles were greatly frowned on throughout Chiat/Day and I don't believe the agency had ever used one in an ad.

But the ad agency that we had just purchased for millions and millions of dollars, Mojo, was started and built by two guys, Alan Morris and Allan Johnston, better known as Mo and Jo. Their success was attributed importantly to writing jingles and selling them to their clients. Many of the ads they did, for almost every account they represented, had a jingle. That was one of the main attractions of their agency.

In a stroke of incredible arrogance and insensitivity, you might say "uber-hubris," the Chiat Christmas card was able to ridicule the hundreds of people in every Mojo office around the world, all of whom were pretty proud of what they did for a living and all of whom had just come to work for Chiat/Day.

Merry Christmas and ho ho ho.

⊘ ⊘ ⊘

In 1989 Jay Chiat hired a keynote speaker to address the entire group of creative people from all of the Chiat/Day/Mojo offices around the world. Everyone was gathered in a banquet room in a hotel in Marina del Rey in Southern California for a two-day conference.

As you would expect, most if not all of these folks were liberal minded and leaned left, way left. So there was a considerable amount of wonder when Jay introduced the keynote speaker at the meeting: the man who had been president of the United States only a month earlier, giving his first "professional" paid speech since leaving office.

We all listened to Ronald Reagan give a 25-minute talk at a rumored cost to the agency of $150,000. Indeed he was a "great communicator." He touched on all those subjects close to his heart: strong defense, anti-abortion, low taxes, and the like. Conservatives and Republicans were few and far between in this audience but surprisingly nobody booed when it was

Ronald Reagan and me.

over. At the end the only thing heard was the sound of one hand clapping.

Clap! Clap!

What was he thinking? Jay, that is.

Maybe he thought that Reagan would recall the days when he had been a Democrat and the head of the Screen Actors Guild and had a considerably different value system. Or maybe he just wanted a photo of himself standing with Reagan like the one I got.

AD TALES . . . SHORT ONES!

Coca-Cola was one of our most important accounts at Goldberg Moser O'Neill. We represented several brands, including a new soft drink called Citra.

There was a famous story that circulated around this time about a large, highly respected Madison Avenue agency that while pitching the Pepsi-Cola account had served up Coca-Cola in the meeting. It turned out not to be a good meeting.

So when we got the Coca-Cola business, I issued explicit instructions to our office service people to henceforth serve only Coca-Cola.

Then one afternoon I walked into a meeting with Coca-Cola and there were six Dr. Peppers and six 7-Up cans staring at me on the back bar of our main conference room. When I asked for an explanation later, I was told that they thought as long as we didn't serve Pepsi-Cola, "anything else was OK."

The New York office of Chiat/Day had just won the American Express Gold Card account and was told absolutely not to say anything public about it yet. Just to make sure, someone from that office sent out an e-mail: "In most emphatic terms, we must not discuss our Amex appointment with anyone outside the agency."

She sent this "Amex Important" note to everyone in every one of the Chiat/Day/Mojo offices around the world.

Ssshhhhhhh!

Bialla & Associates, an executive recruitment firm based in Sausalito, California, sent a proposal to Jay Chiat asking whether he had any interest in participating in a confidential survey they would be conducting of the Chiat/Day/Mojo San Francisco office, of which I was the manager at the time.

"The project will be done with a high degree of confidentiality. Local management will not be aware of this study."

Jay forwarded the proposal to me with a yellow Post-it note attached asking sarcastically if I had any interest.

I wrote Vito Bialla asking whom his study would be conducted among and how much it would cost.

I never heard back from Vito.

⊘ ⊘ ⊘

YOU'RE IN A COMMUNICATION BUSINESS BUT PEOPLE DON'T COMMUNICATE

One of the brightest and hardest-working people I worked with, head of our MIS department, sent out this helpful e-mail to the organization on the Y2K situation, when the world's computers were at risk of not recognizing the millennium change.

> *Subject: Y2K–Laptop Computers–revised backup instructions*
>
> *Two points that need clarifying:*
>
> *1. Backup your documents to your I:/drive, not M:/Backup. M:/Backup doesn't exist.*
>
> *2. Make sure you backup your actual documents, not a shortcut to your My Documents folder. To do this, open your My Documents folder and drag the actual documents inside of it to your I:/drive.*
>
> > *Sorry for the confusion.*
> > *Jamie*

Well, that cleared it all up, didn't it? Now we knew exactly what to do.

⊘ ⊘ ⊘

COLLEAGUES ARE SUPPOSED TO HELP YOU, NOT HURT YOU

Chiat/Day/Mojo San Francisco was working with Doug Tompkins, founder of Esprit, the clothing manufacturer. We had been trying to get a larger assignment and were making progress.

Then *Ad Age* reported that Chiat/Day/Mojo New York was one of the agencies talking to Calvin Klein about their account. I sent a note off to Jane Newman, who was head of that office.

"Jane, what's going on? You know we have the Esprit business and are making progress toward gaining even more of it. Calvin is a conflict."

Her response came back in an e-mail: "Sorry. We aren't actually pitching . . . just meeting."

One of the outstanding features of our office space at 77 Maiden Lane, in the heart of San Francisco's Union Square, was the seventh floor area, which had a swanky penthouse that led to a outdoor rooftop garden deck with trees, benches, and even a barbecue.

The penthouse contained two bedrooms and two baths; a full kitchen; a dining room, which mostly served as a conference room; and a lavish living room area with a wood-burning fireplace. It was more of a showcase than a usable business conference room. We used it mainly to entertain and impress existing and would-be clients. And it was very impressive indeed.

At this time, we subleased some space to a sister agency, Anderson & Lembke, owned by Chiat/Day and run by an affable Swede named Hans Ullmark. They were housed on the second floor in relatively small but nice quarters.

One day Hans called and asked if he could use our penthouse. All they required was the afternoon the next day. Rosalinde Estes, my office manager, relayed the request to me and I asked her to find out specifically why Hans needed it.

It seems he wanted to impress a new business prospect, which happened to be the same one we were meeting with as well that very morning.

I called Hans and asked, "Are you serious?"

He said, "Yah!"

And I said, "Nah!"

⊘ ⊘ ⊘

CREATIVES CAN BE AFFLICTED

Early in my account management career, I was a young inexperienced account executive working on the Minute Rice account. I had worked with my client, General Foods, on establishing a strategy for the development of some new ads. Everyone on the agency account team agreed with the direction, and creative development had begun.

At the time, the creative director of Y&R was a guy named Tony Isidore. He was a well-respected creative talent, and the General Foods people particularly liked him and had made that broadly known. He was in charge of many of their brands, which the agency represented.

One day Tony called me down to his office and asked me to explain why we were doing ads against what he considered a stupid copy strategy. I explained the reasoning behind the direction.

Tony got angry. "It's all bullshit—we're not going to do it."

I said, "Yes we are, because everyone has long ago bought into this direction here and at the client, and they think it's the right thing to do."

Tony got angrier still. "I said we're not going to do it."

"We are going to do it."

"No we are not!"

With this, Tony got up and walked ominously from behind his desk toward me. He was a large, rotund, heavyset guy, with dark eyes, thick black hair, and big black bushy eyebrows. He reached toward me, if my memory serves me right (and it may not), and grabbed me with one hand on the seat of my pants and the other on the back of my suit collar. He lifted me about two feet off the ground and threw me out the door to his office. I landed on my backside.

I got up, my back and my backside hurting, but the level of my embarrassment and insult hurting more. I went to my office and sat down at my desk and festered.

After a few minutes, I picked up the phone and dialed Tony's extension.

"You've got a hell of a nerve. I don't give a shit that you're the creative director or who you think you are. I am going to report what you've done to management. And I am going to sue your ass for verbal and physical assault and battery. And not only that, I expect that you will get the creative team to complete the ads that are due in three days."

I slammed down the phone, not giving him a chance to respond. Adrenaline was shooting through my body. I was really angry and my ego had taken a brutal blow. And so had my suit jacket. I could hardly afford even a moderately expensive business suit at the time, and the collar had been twisted and ripped and would need to be replaced.

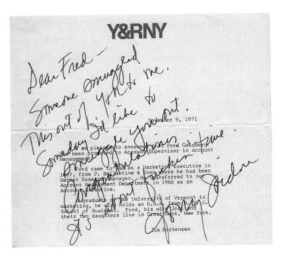

A few minutes went by and my phone rang and it was Tony.

"I'm sorry. We'll do the ads."

Now it's unlikely but possible that I dreamed this entire episode, but regardless of what happened or didn't happen, we lived happily together ever after. For the rest of my days at Y&R New York, I never ever had a problem with Tony Isidore. In fact I received preferential treatment henceforth.

Tony eventually left the agency, and a few years later when I was promoted to account supervisor, I received a handwritten note from him scribbled across the Y&R announcement of my promotion.

⊘ ⊘ ⊘

Brian O'Neill, Goldberg Moser O'Neill partner and creative director, was looking for a senior copywriter, and among the candidates was one particularly talented fellow. Brian flew him out from New York and he was in San Francisco for about a week.

Sometime later I was reviewing expense submissions, as was my habit, and came upon this guy's, which included flying first class to California and renting a Ferrari while he was in the Bay Area.

I raised my concerns to Brian and he in turn spoke with the candidate (although not quite in the way I did to Brian). The copywriter just didn't understand what the issue was. After all he was a gifted writer whom we were interested in, was he not?

Fortunately, we had him stay in our penthouse bedroom or I'm sure we would have sucked wind on a suite at the Campton Place hotel around the corner, or possibly the Presidential Suite at the St. Francis.

He ended up not joining us, as I recall, which may have been most fortunate in saving us from many future indiscretions, although we probably lost out on some really great ads.

⊘ ⊘ ⊘

One of the most talented creative people who ever worked for me was a copywriter who had a narrow sense of right or wrong in some matters.

He went to London to shoot some commercials but was in such a hurry that he left the country without checking the weather in the UK. It turned out to be cold and raining, and he didn't have a proper coat.

He had already decided to treat himself to an airline ticket that was substantially more costly than the one we had already secured for him. Wasn't it perfectly understandable that he wanted to fly on United Airlines so he could get the frequent flyer miles in his personal account?

And it was also understandable that he didn't want to go on a one-stop flight, which would have saved gobs more money for the client and ultimately the agency, since we had to eat the incremental costs of his flight and upgrade.

So, of course, it was understandable, too, that he purchased a jacket in London to keep warm upon his arrival there. It was Armani.

⊘ ⊘ ⊘

Rice-A-Roni was a valuable client and they so supported the new GMO agency. They believed and trusted us with a considerable amount of money by advancing our fees. In turn we were shooting a commercial for them, one that required a dish to be made that simulated the china used in the White House. Well, our TV producer went right out there to replicate the presidential plate, no doubt at the encouragement of the art director. So a beautiful rendition was prepared by a graphics and prop design company that had the eagles at the top and bottom and the stars and stripes around the edges.

It was a beautiful copy and only cost $1,353.13, including tax.

You can imagine that these trusting clients became a little less trusting.

When asked how one could spend this kind of money, there it was: conscious unconsciousness. At least the client provided the china dish. By the way, you couldn't see the eagles or the stars in the finished commercial. Unconscionable! Insane!

One of my associate creative directors agreed that a senior account person would review some rough cuts before they went to the client. This was a client that could easily get spooked.

It so happened that the account

person was on vacation when the rough cuts of the commercials were sent to him to review. And at the same time the associate creative director sent the rough cuts to the aforementioned skittish client, who predictably expressed a great deal of concern when he saw them. In fact, the rough cuts were virtually unintelligible as presented.

The senior account person asked the creative director, "Why in the world did you send them to the client after our agreement?"

His answer: "Because she asked to see them."

This response came just moments after he displayed that familiar surprised and quizzical look of conscious unconsciousness. A glazed-eyes blank stare into space.

CLIENTS CAN BE SURPRISINGLY SURPRISING

In 1981 Chiat/Day San Francisco had acquired the advertising part of Regis McKenna, which was a technology communications firm based in Silicon Valley. Among the technology accounts that came over to Chiat/Day was a chip manufacturer named Intel.

At the time, Intel's ad budget was around $3 million, but that was spread over 20-some separate divisions. All the media was run in mostly highly specialized vertical print magazines.

When we inherited the Intel account, we really didn't care what they made; we created great advertising for them. The work was almost all excellent.

We did one neat ad after the other. And we won a lot of awards for creative excellence. And Intel's business prospered.

I had only one meeting with then-CEO Andy Grove during our six-year relationship. It lasted 20 minutes, during which he told me that he didn't believe in advertising.

Regardless, I argued with him that he needed to spend more. At the time, Intel was spending something like one-tenth of 1 percent of their total sales. This was by any standard a meager and insufficient investment. And of course all of that was against very narrow vertical targets like original equipment manufacturers, the military, and the education markets.

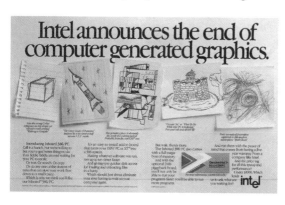

Several years later we were fired, but not too long after that the company started a branding campaign. "Intel Inside" was born as a way to get consumers to think about the quality of the chips contained inside all the personal computers that were beginning to be purchased en masse. This program later expanded to include reimbursements to PC manufacturers who displayed the Intel Inside logo in their ads and of course had to purchase Intel chips.

Intel became one of the largest advertisers in the world, reportedly spending up to a billion dollars a year. Andy surprised us all and had become a believer in advertising after all.

⊘ ⊘ ⊘

Games that you play on personal computers were becoming popular, although it was still an extremely narrow and limited market, and most of the games were difficult to play. At the time, the early 1980s, there weren't really that many PCs being used, particularly at home.

One day I received a call from Bob Botch, the marketing vice president at a company down in Silicon Valley named Epyx. They had a line of computer games, several of which were fairly popular. They wanted to talk to us about doing some advertising.

So I drove down with my creative director Ross Van Dusen to a meeting at their headquarters. It was a typical Silicon Valley prefabricated office structure with lots of offices and cubicles crammed inside what had started out as an empty shell. We met with Bob and he introduced us to the president, Mike Katz.

We had a very pleasant conversation, and as we concluded what was a successful meeting, we were offered a tour of the facility. The place wasn't all that busy. There were a small number of people and lots of empty cubicles and offices with no signs of life at most of them. However, we understood that they were growing and adding staff as need be.

After viewing the office space, we were led through a door to the rear of the facility, which they announced was the Epyx factory. We walked through a heavy steel door and into a cavernous warehouse. There were three or four huge roll-up garage doors across one side, typically used as bays for trucks making deliveries and/or picking up product for distribution. But there wasn't a truck to be seen anywhere.

In fact there wasn't a single person in sight in the entire humongous space. The place was absolutely clean and spotless. There wasn't even a gum wrapper in evidence on the floor. Nothing was in this huge space but air and the hollow sounds of our shoes walking on the cement floor.

Then we went around a corner and stood facing a 12-foot-long narrow table set against the wall with two of what looked like DVD machines on top. There were several piles of floppy discs 18 inches high on the right side and similar ones on the left. And there was a man, one man, standing in front of two black boxes. He was putting a disc into one of the black boxes with his right hand and removing a disc from the other black box with his left. He did this as if he were a robot. Put in a disc; take out a disc; put in a disc; take out a disc. Right, left, right, left.

What we were experiencing was the Epyx factory running at full production capacity. Right, left, right, left.

We did some really good ads for Epyx, which ran against a very limited market in enthusiast PC gaming magazines. Both Bob and Mike were a delight to work with. I did, however, make sure to collect our accounts receivable in an unusually timely manner.

⊘ ⊘ ⊘

Collagen Corporation was started by an entrepreneur named Howard Palefsky. He had discovered a substance made out of cow's collagen that could be injected into those little age lines and wrinkles that people so desperately want to get rid of as they grow older.

Collagen was a complicated account because the substance was considered a drug and as such required approvals from the FDA. This was true for the advertising and all of the marketing materials as well.

In addition the ads required getting approval from the television networks, which was made even more complicated because this was the first time that any product like this was to be advertised on television. Prescription drugs were not allowed, and this was considered one.

After many hours of negotiation we were successful in gaining approval to run both print and television ads. The idea of the campaign was to show side by side, before and after, pictures of an attractive woman who had received the Collagen treatments. These were not retouched in any way, and this was indicated in the ads. Of course it would have been an obvious no-no to do any retouching. But the comparison of before and after was quite remarkable, startling really. Not the most creative ad but it was powerful and persuasive stuff.

Surprisingly the ads were able to retain most of their integrity and were very good, considering all the different people that had to sign off on them. In situations like this, advertising generally gets sandpapered to death.

With approved ads in hand and a media plan in place, Collagen held a meeting to announce the program to all of its marketing and sales representatives. Howard Palefsky and his attractive marketing vice president Judy O'Shea organized and ran the meeting. Everyone gathered at the Hyatt Hotel in Incline Village up in North Lake Tahoe for the occasion. I attended with Jay Chiat, who seemed to be very friendly with the provocative Judy, possibly explaining why we had the small account.

There were maybe a hundred Collagen sales reps in attendance. These were the people who call on doctors to tell and sell them on using various drug products. Having this kind of a sales force was a common practice for drug companies then, and it represented a huge chunk of the cost of doing business. It was an essential marketing tool.

We walked into a large auditorium at the Hyatt, and there was Howard Palefsky up on the stage getting ready to start the meeting. He was shuffling some papers around on the podium. There was an exciting buzz throughout the room, as word had leaked out that some special news was to be announced.

We took a seat about a quarter of the way back from the stage and on the aisle. I gave a look around at the chattering crowd. I glanced from one rep to the next, to the next, and discovered that the place was filled with extraordinarily good-looking people, men and women ranging in age from maybe 30 to 45.

I learned later that Howard personally took part in the casting, I mean, the recruitment process of all the sales personnel. It made sense since you wanted to make an impression on your target audience, in this case a doctor. Why not have a good-looking man or woman as opposed to one who isn't. Moreover, since they were really selling a cosmetic product even though it required a procedure, why not make sure that the person delivering the sales pitch actually reflected the product benefit?

I thought it was a very clever and effective selling strategy. And it must have added a considerable interesting dimension to Howard's CEO duties. Months later I learned that Howard used another criterion to pick these salespeople. Everyone used or had to begin to use Collagen before they were hired to work for the company. Not only did they drink the "Kool-Aid"; they injected it. Howard insisted on it.

Brilliant!

THERE'S NO BUSINESS LIKE SHOW BUSINESS

I was manager of the Los Angeles Y&R office and in search of new business. The movie industry wasn't a high priority, although being in LA and all, it made sense to try to represent one or two studios. Movie accounts were exciting and glamorous, and it was a kick going to the studios sprinkled around LA and rubbing shoulders and eyeballs with the actors in the commissary.

Columbia Pictures announced that they were reviewing their advertising account. It so happened that the advertising director was named Fred Goldberg. This appeared to me to be an unrivaled opportunity.

And it so happened that Columbia had been running advertising for their blockbuster hit *Kramer vs. Kramer* and their other feature movies using a similar format for each.

I created a tease campaign with an ad that I ran in a variety of trade magazines, including a full page in *Variety* magazine, which everyone in Hollywood reads. The all-type ads used the identical typeface and format that the Columbia ads were using for their promotional materials, but I substituted *Goldberg vs. Goldberg* for *Kramer vs. Kramer*. Each movie and therefore each of my ads had the typeface they used for each of their movies.

Each ad used the sub-headlines that Columbia was actually using for each of their movies. "A Love Story" was for *A Love Story*, "Electric!" was for *Electric Horseman*, "It's Not Supposed to Happen Twice in Your Life" for *Chapter Two*, and so on. The double entendre of each of the sub-headlines as it related to the two of us working together was clever and attracted a lot of attention.

"Goldberg vs. Goldberg" A Love Story
"Goldberg vs. Goldberg" Electric!
"Goldberg vs. Goldberg" It's not supposed to happen twice in your life.

All the ads were run blind without identifying who was sponsoring the ad, so no one at Columbia knew who was running them until I sent a letter presenting Young & Rubicam as a candidate for their account. This was timed to the last ad: Goldberg vs. Goldberg: The Evidence Is In. That was a headline that they used for one of their most current films and which worked really well with my delivering a package to them.

"GOLDBERG VS. GOLDBERG"

It's not supposed to happen twice in your life.

The package contained a strong, well-thought-out and well-crafted letter and samples of our work. The letter ended by suggesting Y&R could offer Columbia something no other ad agency in the world could. Fred Goldberg.

We received a lot of favorable publicity and accolades for the effort when it became known what I did. Army Archerd, the famous Hollywood journalist, wrote about it in his column in *Variety*. *Ad Age* and *AdWeek* carried stories too.

The other Fred Goldberg called me with congratulations. I never got to pitch the account.

⊘ ⊘ ⊘

ADVERTISING REALLY DOES WORK

Some of the very best creative work that we did was the pro bono ads for the University of California, Berkeley. We only did one a year for 15 years, and it was always directed at trying to raise contributions for the university.

HELP US TIE A PROFESSOR TO THIS CHAIR.

U.C. BERKELEY

One day we received a letter from the UC Berkeley Foundation office that had been sent to them by a Mr. Hymen Shapiro. This gentleman had just received a check for $5,000 from a nephew who had borrowed the money 10 years earlier and from whom he had not heard a word in all that time.

Mr. Shapiro by chance had seen the 125-year anniversary report from the university lying face down on a table in front of him. One of our best ads for the university stared up at him from the back cover: "Help Us Tie a Professor to This Chair." The ad was seeking funding for an endowment.

Looking at the ad, Mr. Shapiro recalled that exactly 60 years earlier, on May 13, 1933, he had received his BS degree from Berkeley at the Greek Theatre. He further remembered that his niece's husband and their son had also received degrees from Berkeley.

He saw the ad and was moved by it. He sent the $5,000 check he had just received to the UC Berkeley Foundation as a gift.

⊘ ⊘ ⊘

During the O. J. Simpson murder trial, one of our media merchandising executives noticed that the TV cameras would regularly pull in and out with shots of Judge Lance Ito. As a result, any products sitting about on his bench would get some free name and package exposure. And it happened every three or four minutes during the trial.

During the circus of these court proceedings, one of the attorneys asked for a recess to get some pizza, and Judge Ito sarcastically asked for a broccoli pizza.

Susan Satmary Hirschhaut, head of our media merchandising department, jumped on this and sent off a package to the judge with some promotional materials for one of our clients, Mann's. They sold a product called Broccoli Wokly, precut prewashed broccoli heads. Ready to eat.

And sure enough one of the Broccoli Wokly coffee cups we had sent ended up sitting proudly on the judicial bench. So just about every time the camera slowly moved in for a close-up of Ito, it panned in and up and over the coffee cup with the Broccoli Wokly logo.

Subsequently we received a letter from the good judge asking for some more Wokly shirts. Extra large.

Unfortunately—or fortunately—Judge Ito will be remembered more for having presided over the acquittal of O. J. Simpson than as an endorser of Broccoli Wokly.

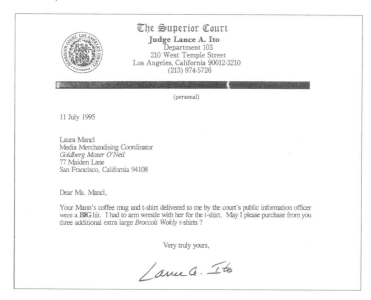

The Superior Court
Judge Lance A. Ito
Department 103
210 West Temple Street
Los Angeles, California 90012-3210
(213) 974-5726

(personal)

11 July 1995

Laura Mancl
Media Merchandising Coordinator
Goldberg Moser O'Neil
77 Maiden Lane
San Francisco, California 94108

Dear Ms. Mancl,

Your Mann's coffee mug and t-shirt delivered to me by the court's public information officer were a **BIG** hit. I had to arm wrestle with her for the t-shirt. May I please purchase from you three additional extra large *Broccoli Wokly* t-shirts ?

Very truly yours,

Lance A. Ito

GRATUITOUS GRATITUDE

Jay Chiat received the following Western Union Telegram on December 18, 1985: "1985 has been a challenging year for Apple in many ways. Needless to say, we have made it equally challenging for Chiat/Day. So, as we end another year of partnership, I'd like to wish you a happy holiday and a prosperous New Year. And although I can't be here to thank each of you personally for your tireless efforts on Apple's behalf, I would like to give each of you a gift of a crystal Apple mug that represents a small measure of our appreciation. Merry Christmas."

The telegram was from John Sculley, president and CEO. The crystal was a nice gesture, and his personal thanks for the "tireless efforts on Apple's behalf" were even more appreciated.

How Chiat/Day lost Apple. Again.

Every year for the past five years, as regular as ringworm in the summer, we've lost the Apple account.

A major crisis. A threat of review. Months with no weekends. Heartbreaks and breakdowns.

But, after all the rending of garments and gnashing of teeth, we'd win Apple back again. And get to run the wonderful work that's made us look like a great agency and Apple look like a great client.

Well, we finally lost Apple for real.

We worked harder than ever, but it didn't work. The work was better than ever, but it didn't work.

We lost. And it hurts.

Because there's something so wrenchingly unnatural about it all. The Apple of computers with the IBM of agencies?

Ah, well.

As the Buddhists say -- "A door opens, a door closes."

As the Jews say -- "Yeah, occasionally on your foot."

But who knows?

Maybe there's some IBM of computers out there looking for the Apple of ad agencies.

But not too long after this, Sculley successfully forced Apple's founder Steve Jobs out of the company he had created and built. Jobs was the guy who had brought him into Apple in the first place, asking him famously if he wanted to continue to sell sweet fizzy drinks at Pepsi-Cola or come to Apple and change the world. Sculley didn't do much to change the world, although he did change the world of Apple by getting rid of Steve Jobs.

He was determined to get rid of Chiat/Day as the agency for Apple as well. He invited BBDO New York, his previous agency at Pepsi-Cola, to solicit the account.

I helped Jay Chiat craft a letter to send to Sculley, arguing passionately and logically why we should be retained as the Apple agency after having endured a nine-week shoot-out with BBDO.

The day before the final meeting took place, Jay sent a memo to everyone at the agency thanking them for the pitch effort, and he attached what he referred to as the "longest letter I've ever sent." Which was the one I wrote and Jay signed and sent to Sculley.

It didn't take very long for the next memo from Jay, announcing to everyone that he had received a call from Sculley to "tell me Apple had decided to award its advertising account to BBDO."

After this, it was decided to run an ad in the *San Jose Mercury News,* the best vehicle to reach all of Silicon Valley business, including everyone at Apple. "How Chiat/Day lost Apple. Again."

Some people at Apple decided to respond with their own ad, which somehow found its way into *Advertising Age* but with some editing of the headline.

There must have been a few folks at Apple, besides Sculley, that didn't like Chiat/Day. Oh the emotional discomfort we could have saved if Sculley had only sent us a crystal ball instead of that crystal apple mug.

Fuck you, Chiat/Day. Seriously.

Congratulations. You think you're so smart. You really do. You think you won some big ones. You didn't.
You were wrong all along.
Apple doesn't stand for blondes with big hooters and a hammer.
Apple stands for middle managers. The kind you push off cliffs.
You said we could sell 128K Macs to business. Then you screwed up *Test Drive.*
You said you needed an Apple III *that worked* to shoot an ad. Did you have to take our only one?
You're washed up. Even Nike thinks so.
And what about your big ideas? What about double page ads in *The Wall Street Journal?* If that was so smart, how come you guys run single page ads *for yourselves* in *The Mercury News?*
No wonder we were losing money last year.
We won't even mention how you guys named and priced Lisa, then changed your mind after the Macintosh intro.
Listen. You're fired. And remember. We were real guys about it. We did the agency review dance.
Thank God we didn't blow a million bucks on Super Bowl '86.
And finally, just get one thing very straight. We don't need your kind of creative lunatics around here no more. Seriously.

P.S.— We want our hammer back.

⊘ ⊘ ⊘

Goldberg Moser O'Neill had been purchased by Interpublic's Lowe Group, which had Coca-Cola as a major account. Goldberg Moser O'Neill won a new product assignment, Citra, which was being confirmed to Frank Lowe, head of our new parent The Lowe Group, by senior Coca-Cola executive Ian Rowden.

The Coke executive noted in his letter how delighted he was with the prospect of working with "Goldman Moses O'Neil."

I know someone named Goldman, but I was Goldberg. And confusing Moser with Moses was understandable as Goldman was close enough to Goldberg to be from the same tribe.

But leaving off the second "l" in O'Neill was really inexcusable.

⊘ ⊘ ⊘

All these things—and so much more—are why the world of advertising is an insane place in which to make a career. The rest of this book is an even more introspective and candid look into some of the most colorful people with whom I have worked over the years, and some of the most colorful things these people did. Or didn't do, but should have.

Some of these people include Steve Jobs at Apple Computer, Larry Ellison at Oracle, John Chambers at Cisco, Michael Dell at Dell Computer, Les Crane, and John Wayne. And there are others who are less well known but contributed as much to the insanity of the business and also to the incredible rewards that can be found in working in it.

I had a hell of ride in the crazy ad business. These are my true, surprising, and sometimes titillating adventures.

The book is divided into two sections. The first focuses mostly on individual clients and people, traversing my ad world experience from its start in 1967 at Young & Rubicam in New York and ending with the sale of Goldberg Moser O'Neill to Interpublic Group (IPG) and finally the subsequent merger of the agency with Hill Holliday of Boston. This section is titled "The Harebrained, the Happenings, the History."

The second part has more of a philosophical bent to it. It includes my involvement and learned appreciation for architecture and interior design as it relates to the business; the vagaries of agency mergers; and selling great work, among other topics. This section is titled "The Beliefs, the Observations, the Derangements."

This book will take you from Madison Avenue to San Francisco by way of Los Angeles and Silicon Valley, with many unbelievable but real true-life occurrences in the business of advertising. There are insights and lessons to be learned about the ad biz along with inside observations and revelations about some well-known people and some not so.

Go ahead and jump in. You'll find the water is surprising, eye-opening, and fun. You may get wet laughing at some things and crying at others. The tears will not be from sorrow but rather stupefaction and bewilderment as to how one industry could spawn such an unfathomable level of ludicrousness, ineptitude, madness, and insanity.

THE HAREBRAINED,

THE HAPPENINGS,

THE HISTORY

PART I

CHAPTER 1

HOW THE COOKIE CRUMBLES

ONE OF THE MOST DIFFICULT THINGS about the advertising business is the resistance one gets to new ideas combined with the tendency of people to judge things that are different against a yardstick predicated on past experience.

In 1968, when I became an account executive, the very first account I was assigned at Young & Rubicam was a General Foods product called Whip 'n Chill. This was an ersatz powder concoction of mostly chemicals and preservatives, to which you added some milk or water, whipped up for a minute, and poured into pudding dishes and placed in the fridge. Voilà! Minutes later, out came a fabulous dessert that the whole family could enjoy and which they applauded.

Now you know why dads and kids were always shown applauding in those old food commercials. It was mandatory back then as an expression of appreciation and family love. Times have changed a bit.

Whip 'n Chill had been at one time an enormous success, albeit relatively short-lived. It had turned out to be a fad-type product. Now it was being purchased by a small remaining hard-core user base, and the client was only promoting it with a quarterly recipe ad and coupon in Sunday supplements. For example, to be used in a pie recipe.

The very first ad I had to present was a straight at you headline, "Whip 'n Chill Dessert Recipe," with a tasty photograph of a pie made with a package of Whip 'n Chill.

Bill Dordelman, my client, was the product manager for Whip 'n Chill. Bill was a very smart guy but tended to adhere to the party line. A very ambitious fellow who wanted to get promoted in the worst way and, I always believed, saw emulating past success as a critical part of his strategy. In fact, most of the folks who got promoted at General Foods in those days did the same thing for the same reason.

I quite easily received approval for the ad and with it a signed estimate to go and shoot the photography. It wasn't a huge challenge or decision. The ad had only the simple headline and a picture of a pie and a coupon for cents off.

At the shoot, the agency art director decided to do some experimenting, and instead of shooting the traditional food shot on a bright or white background, he chose to do it the other way around. I pointed out at the time what the client had approved and what he was expecting. Being a good account executive, I made sure we covered having the white background taken.

It turned out that there was no comparison between the final photographs. The dark background proved to be gorgeous. Much more attention getting, more mouthwatering, projecting far higher quality, and it made the pie look lip-smacking absolutely delicious. Hmmmm.

My next trip up to General Foods headquarters in White Plains was with the photographs under my arm. I arrived and took out the chromes from my portfolio bag and placed them on the light box without saying a word. They were the ones with the darker background.

Bill looked at them and looked at me and said, "It doesn't have a white background."

"That's right, but what do you think?"

"It doesn't have a white background."

"I know, but what do you think?"

"It doesn't have a white background."

"Yeah, I know, but what do you think about the way it looks?"

"It's got to have a white background."

I put the alternate version of the shot with the lighter background next to the first one on the light box.

"Bill, but it looks great and is much better than the traditional way of shooting this."

"Nah, it's got to have the light background. That's the way we do it. You're pretty new and maybe you don't know that."

I replied, "I don't agree."

I took down the chromes and packed up my bag and left and returned to the agency. I immediately went to the Y&R library and had the librarian help me find a range of recipe photographs from an array of upscale women's and fashion magazines. I pulled a dozen or so that were exquisite. I also identified about a dozen others that utilized the traditional light and white background photography. The darker ones truly made the food look sensational and much more inviting than those with a brighter and whiter background.

In addition I was able to retrieve some Starch readership scores, which clearly showed that women were more attentive to recipes that had the more inviting darker photography.

Then I convened a group of women who were bakers and all worked at the agency. I got them in a room and showed them the two photographs. It was no contest. The darker one was the winner hands down.

So, the next day I drove back up to White Plains. I met again with

Dordelman. First, I put the two photographs side by side on the light box. Then I laid out on the floor all the ads and editorial photos I had found from the magazines. Then I told him about the Starch results and finally the reactions from the women at the agency.

Bill said, "Let's go with the lighter background. That's what we agreed before we shot it. That's what we have done in the past. End of discussion."

At that very moment Bob Haynes, who was the group product manager, happened to be walking by Dordelman's office, and he popped his head in the door. He looked at the photos up on the light box and he looked at the magazine ads all over the floor.

And he asked, "What's up?"

Bill hesitated and then said, "We're trying to decide which photo to use."

Haynes said, "What's to decide? The darker one is clearly the better, more appetizing picture."

He turned and walked out of the office. I packed up all my materials and the photos and headed back to the agency. I had my first ad sold with a photo that I was quite proud of. And I created one pissed-off client I had to deal with from then on.

Fred, 1968.

But we had a much better ad, not a brilliant ad, but certainly better looking. And this was my first encounter with all the problems that an account person faces, and advertising agencies in general face, in trying to get advertisers to approve better, more inventive advertising.

A few years later, I was a somewhat more accomplished account person, now an account supervisor, in charge of the Jell-O Gelatin account at General Foods, which at the time was probably the most important assignment from this client. It was the oldest Y&R client, at almost 50 years with the agency.

There was a copywriter at Young & Rubicam New York named Mike Becker. Mike was quite a talented fellow and he was assigned to the Jell-O business at the same time as me. He was a good guy and we had a great relationship between our arguments. And he had a great and quite unique relationship with the client on the Jell-O business.

The client was a product manager by the name of Dick Mayer. He was a terrific guy and one of the very few executives at General Foods that had a sense of creativity, a willingness to try new things, and a set of balls.

Most all of the assistant product managers, associate product managers, product managers, and group product managers evaluated advertising in three stages: first on its legal merit, then on its strategic merit, and rarely, if ever, getting to the third, on its creative merit.

Dick was the exception. He did it the other way around. He was always looking out for an idea that could break through the usual mundane mess of advertising and marketing promotions, in this case holiday recipe ideas that filled the women's magazines at the holiday time of year.

Now Dick had made his bones on a General Food product called Dream Whip. This was another ersatz chemical-laden white powder that whipped up into a gooey sweet substance and was supposed to replicate real whipped cream. Its appeal lay in the fact that it was more convenient than using fresh cream. For a while, Dream Whip did very well as the convenient alternative, but it fell on hard times and was declining in popularity when Dick was assigned to it.

Well, he had a stroke of genius one day when he discovered that if you mixed this Dream Whip substance into a cake mix, it could make the cake marvelously higher than without it. All the cake-cooking research indicated that women craved a higher, taller end result. This idea turned the brand completely around and generated untold millions of dollars of unexpected revenue that General Foods added to its coffers.

Dick was a hero. He was given a huge bonus for his efforts on Dream Whip and was rewarded by being given the Jell-O Gelatin business to run, the most prestigious brand in the division.

This background is necessary because it was the reason that Dick believed he was the quintessential expert on selling baked goods to women all across America. He genuinely felt he knew everything about anything that had to do with recipe advertising but particularly dessert baking recipe advertising. After all, no one had had the success that he had with Dream Whip.

As it happened, we all had agreed on a strategy to promote a Jell-O cookie recipe for the holidays that year. The recipe called for using a box of Jell-O as an ingredient as well as a topping. The Jell-O made the cookies more moist and tasty and, when sprinkled, added attractive, festive red and green accents on the surface.

I was excited about this idea, which I thought strategically was a great concept. Using Jell-O in untraditional ways could conceivably broaden its usage dramatically, as just about every household in the country had a box of Jell-O waiting to be used. If we could get them to use it other than just as a wiggly, sweet, and cool dessert, that would be a positive thing for the business.

And Dream Whip and Dick Mayer had proven that it was possible to reposition products in this manner. Of course, Jell-O was even better known and used by far more households, and so it followed logically that this could be one very successful holiday promotion effort.

I was also excited about the ad that my copywriter, Mike Becker, had come up with. I grabbed it and set out to White Plains to present it to Dick and his brand management group. I had given considerable thought on what to say to convince them that this was a great ad and went over it in my mind during the 45-minute drive.

I started the meeting. Dick and his associate product manager and his assistant product manager were there. I did a little preamble set-up. And then I showed the ad. It was a rough comp but it was pretty simple: a headline and a photo of the cookies.

There was silence. Not even a whimper. The assistant brand manager was busy doodling on a pad and didn't look up. The associate brand manager was looking out the window at the leaves on the trees gently moving back and forth.

And Dick just sat there and kind of stared. Dick wore contact lenses, and back then you couldn't always tell exactly which way a person who wore contacts was looking. That was the case now.

So the silence went on for a minute or two. I didn't even get the usual: "That's interesting."

"That's interesting" is client speak for "It's not right," "It's not what I was expecting," "It's not what we agreed to," "It's not what I want." These are generally followed by a dissertation on everything that is wrong with the ad you've just presented.

They didn't respond because they had already designed the ad they wanted. And they thought we were going to present that ad. In their minds it was an easy assignment and didn't require much work or any creativity. Rather, utilize the same formula that had been so successful with Dream Whip. Show a plate of cookies made with Jell-O as an ingredient, with the recipe on one side, a cents-off coupon on the other, and a straight at you, hit 'em in the face between the eyes, nothing fancy headline like "Dream Whip Cake Recipe."

So what they were expecting was "Jell-O Cookie Recipe."

Instead, I was showing them what I believed was one of the best ads created since I had been on the account and even since I had joined Y&R. I thought it was one of the best ads I might ever be associated with.

The ad was simple but brilliant. It was clever. It was eye-catching. It made you smile. It made you get engaged with the message. It was what often makes an ad great. It made the familiar a bit strange. And the strange familiar.

The layout had as a visual a plate of cookies made with the Jell-O as an ingredient and topped with sprinkled dry Jell-O. It had a recipe on one side and a coupon on the other.

But it carried the headline "How to Make Jell-O That Crumbles."

What a smart attention-getting headline it was. Everyone expects Jell-O to wiggle, not crumble. So the reader's immediate reaction must be "Say what?"

But here I was talking to the "expert" on recipe advertising because he had turned around the Dream Whip business with ingredient ads that had headlines like "Dream Whip Cake Recipe."

After much debate and much discussion, over many days, we were at a stalemate. Dick Mayer wanted "Jell-O Cookie Recipe." I wanted "How to Make Jell-O That Crumbles."

In situations like this, where you come to a wall and can't climb over it, typically you generally seek another point of view. However, two things mitigated against going to Dick's boss: first, it wasn't a good thing to use this chip too often if you wanted to maintain any semblance of a working relationship; second, Dick happened to be a good friend of mine.

Nevertheless, I said, "Dick, we've been arguing over this too long. The deadline is upon us to close the ad. I want to take it to Hal for an opinion."

Dick just sat there with an expressionless look on his face. And his eyes had that faraway look. This time it wasn't just the contact lenses.

Even though Dick was confident in his position, no one likes to have an agency go around or above him in the corporate hierarchy. It signaled a lack of control, an unstable working relationship, and it said something about your management style and more.

But this one we were going to have to review with his boss, a fellow named Hal Scutt, and let him make the decision. I was prepared to take it even above Hal if need be, I felt so strongly about the work.

Dick set the meeting. I brought two comps. Except for the headline, the rest of the ads were identical. One had Dick's headline, "Jell-O Cookie Recipe," and one had mine, "How to Make Jell-O That Crumbles." I did my preamble; Dick did his and added a rebuttal to my arguments.

After listening to both of us and without hesitation, Hal said, "Let's go with the agency recommendation."

So we did. And I had one pissed-off client. And friend.

But I also had what turned out to be the number one, most read ad, according to Starch Reports, in *Reader's Digest*, *TV Guide*, and every other magazine where the ad ran, for the entire year.

Despite our disagreement, and it was one of very few that I had with Dick Mayer, he remained one of my very best clients and friends. As I look back, he was close to the "perfect" client and he would have relished working with a really creative agency.

A few years later, in 1974, when we were no longer working together, I received a letter from him when I became, as Alex Kroll, Y&R president, pointed out in the announcement, the youngest-ever senior vice president/ management supervisor. They took a really dramatic photo of me at the time. One that I very much cherished as I did the letter I received from Dick Mayer on the occasion. By then Dick had moved on from General Foods to a much more important position at Heublein Inc. and soon would become president of Kentucky Fried Chicken.

Unfortunately I never got to work with Dick again. As these things happen, we drifted apart over the years. I would have very much liked to have worked with him when I was at Chiat/Day or Goldberg Moser O'Neill. I know he would have enjoyed the experience, as would have I. And I am certain that together we would have been able to produce some brilliant things.

But we didn't, and that's the way the cookie crumbles.

CHAPTER 2

GET THE MONEY!

ONE OF THE MOST DIFFICULT PARTS of the ad business is collecting money that is due to you or, worse, money that you need to ask for in advance. Money is always a touchy subject, and for some clients, particularly those that may not have enough of it, asking for it is an affront. Many clients take this kind of request very personally. But one of the surest ways to jeopardize an ad agency financial position is to not be vigilant in this area.

In the summer of 1973 someone at the Young & Rubicam New York office took a call from AVCO Embassy Pictures, then located in Midtown Manhattan.

"Are we interested in doing some work for Joseph Levine, the producer?"

"That's Joseph E. Levine, who produced *The Graduate*. If you are interested, be over here in three hours."

Well, OK, but who will we send over there? Y&R didn't have too many accounts that resembled the entertainment business, much less the movie end of it.

Someone decided that Roby R. Harrington III, a senior executive, should be the designated batter, but with a name like his, they knew they might have to dig a little deeper.

So they found me . . . Freddy Goldberg. From Great Neck, Loooong Island.

That's Fred S. Goldberg. The one. The only.

I was still a pretty unique person in the account management department back then, circa 1970, with a relevant ethnic background (if you know what I mean). So, they had me and John Ferrell, a talented copywriter with whom I worked on some other accounts, provide some cover for Roby.

We three jumped in a cab and hightailed it over to AVCO Embassy's offices and soon got ushered into the office of the man himself, Joseph E. Levine. There he was, in all his splendor, suit and tie, a bit stocky, sitting behind a huge antique Louis XIV desk with a leather top and ornate gold filigree up and down the legs.

He was a short and squat man, maybe five feet four, and looked maybe 200-plus pounds, but he had a commanding presence behind that desk, which was situated about 40 feet from the entrance to the office. He wore black heavy horn-rimmed glasses. He actually looked like what I thought a Hollywood mogul for a major movie studio was supposed to look like.

I discovered that he was sitting on a raised platform about a foot off the ground. Just to his left stood an elaborate carved cane with what appeared to be a solid gold top, leaning against the desk, and to his right was a large console with a button for everyone of any import who worked there.

There were even buttons for those who had no import. When he wanted someone, he took one of his fingers and punched a button, it lit up, and he shouted into a speakerphone, "Get in here."

Maybe that's where the expression "pushing people's buttons" comes from. I'm not sure.

Joseph E. Levine pushing people's buttons.

As Roby R. Harrington III, John, and I first stepped into the office, Levine looked up from his desk and pointed at three chairs assembled before his throne, I mean desk. He said, "Have a seat."

He wasn't asking.

One of the chairs was placed directly in front and across from Levine, which Roby, our "key" person, took. John and I slipped into the remaining two chairs, which were set ever so discreetly slightly back a foot or so. Clearly whoever was supposed to be "in charge" from the agency was to make himself known by taking the frontward seat. Mr. Levine would then direct his remarks to that person.

Then Court was in session and Mr. Levine spoke.

"I made a movie, *The Day of the Dolphin*, with George C. Scott. Two other advertising agencies created advertising for it. Attendance stinks. The ads are not working. Do you think you can do something?"

Without missing a beat and not knowing a damn thing about the project, Roby R. Harrington III answered, "Yes, sir, definitely!"

Then he began to ask Levine some questions.

"Could you brief us on the strategy?"

"Is the problem a strategic one or an executional one?"

"What kind of budget do we have?"

"When do you need the creative?"

Now these were the kind of questions that were highly appropriate and appreciated in Cincinnati at Procter & Gamble, but not at AVCO Embassy in New York City.

Levine sat there with a funny look on his face and said, "What the fuck are you talking about? I thought you said you could do something. Mr. Roby, I need something FAST!"

I jumped in and said, "How soon can we have the film elements? When can we show you something?"

Levine looked over at me and responded, "Right now; two days."

Roby R. Harrington III started to open his mouth again and was about to protest that that kind of timing might be a problem when I asked, "Where's the film?"

Levine lifted his right arm and took one of his fingers, the index I believe, and punched one of the buttons next to him on the console. The light lit up and he shouted out, "Get in here!"

A minute later a tall gawky-looking fellow appeared at the door and stuck his head in but left his body outside the doorway. Turns out it was Levine's son.

Poor guy. But then he didn't have to work for his dad, did he? We learned later that his name was Richard, and he would end up working for his father for 20 years from the age of 16.

Levine bellowed, "Get the dolphin film for these boys!"

Richard made the mistake of beginning a protest that he was in the middle of something important when Levine reached over and grabbed his cane and slammed it against the console one, two, three times. Now he raised his voice even further and screamed, "Get the fucking film NOW!"

Richard left to get the fucking film.

The three of us were excused and left with instructions to pick up the film outside, and that's where the film stood when we got to the reception area.

Now it turns out that this was a full-length feature film and back then they used 35-millimeter film. So there were six, 18-inch-high, eight-inch-wide, hexagonal, shiny bright stainless steel canisters, each containing reels and reels, lined up in front of the reception desk.

Mike Nichols was the director of this film. It is customary for the director to have his own personal copy of the film that he shot. And it was the case here as well. The film that Richard Levine had given us, and we took back to the agency to cut apart to make commercials, was Nichols's personal copy. I heard later that when he found out, he was not a happy camper.

The three of us grabbed a canister with each arm and proceeded to schlep them to the elevator and then into a taxi. And I mean schlep, as each one of these things weighed at least 30 pounds. Now imagine a New York City yellow cab with its trunk completely filled up and part of the payload inside the cab itself, along with three grown men, as we headed back across town to the agency. It wasn't comfortable and it wasn't cool.

But John Ferrell thought it was and he was very excited. He hadn't done any movie work before and he just loved the idea of working with Levine and H-O-L-L-Y-W-O-O-D. When we arrived back at Y&R, John immediately took charge of the canisters, and the next time I saw him he had worked almost 24 hours straight with a favorite editor cutting together a :30 and a :60 spot.

These commercials were very different from the usual promotional movie advertising of the times and way different from what the two previous agencies had done for the movie.

The spots turned this essentially stupid plot of two dolphins who had been trained to blow up the United States presidential yacht into an exciting, entertaining, and even plausible storyline. The commercial was good, all the more so having been done virtually overnight.

So now it was Friday morning after the Wednesday afternoon when we had first met Joe. We marched back into his office, where a previously requested 3/4-inch video machine had been set up.

Roby decided not to join us this time. Good move. He figured it wasn't really his kind of client.

Levine was sitting in a chair in front of the television monitor when we entered. He didn't bother to say hello when we came in the room. All he said was "Let's see what you got."

Without a word John forced a smile and shoved the tape into the machine. He pressed the play button, raised the volume, and let the :60 version of our commercial run.

A very serious deep-voiced announcer opened over back-and-forth quick cuts between George C. Scott at the edge of a swimming pool and a dolphin.

There was a shot of Scott as the camera pulled in toward him and the announcer said, "This man trained a dolphin to kill the president of the United States."

Then you saw a shot of Scott leaning farther over the edge of the pool and speaking to a dolphin as if training him. He said, "Get B, find B."

The next shot cut away to a dolphin with a bomb strapped on its back swimming underwater. We cut away again to a shot of the dolphin's destination, which was a huge white yacht flying the presidential flag of the United States.

Throughout this sequence you heard a slow low sound, "Tick, tick, tick, tick." It was the bomb's timer that had been set.

Then you went underwater and saw the dolphin attaching a bomb with a magnetic strap to the underside of the ship. You heard a "clunk" as the bomb caught hold to the metal bottom of the boat.

After a long, slow, silent, seemingly endless pullback from the yacht, you saw and heard the ship explode with a resounding boom as the pieces of the ship went up and everywhere into the air. All of this took place in slow motion, so it was very visual and compelling. Building up to this moment was some underlying tense dramatic music, which went completely silent just as the ship blew up. And then there was total silence.

The pieces of the ship floated downward onto the ocean surface very slowly and gracefully and the announcer boomed out, "Joseph E. Levine presents George C. Scott in *The Day of the Dolphin.*"

Without a hesitation Levine boomed out, "I love it!"

He had a big smile on his face. He thought it was great. John and I were excited, as we had just done our first movie assignment and the client "loved it."

This was why it was so rewarding working with the people who ran companies and not with their minions. They made decisions and had opinions that they were not afraid to express. They also had the ultimate authority to say yes.

Joseph Levine turned out to be no different from all the others I got to work with over the years in this regard. But in some other regards, he was different.

Levine said he wanted to run it the following week. It was Friday and he wanted it on air on Monday, latest Tuesday. He wanted to put $500,000 in TV time behind it over the next two-week period. This was a relatively huge amount of money to be spent in such a short period of time.

As we left we promised to finish up the spots and be back to him with a media schedule that same afternoon. Before we left the AVCO offices I called Roby to let him know what had transpired. He was pleased.

Who knew whether we could even buy this much media at such a late date. Or any media for that matter.

We went back to the agency, and John went off to finish the commercials and I went off to the media department. I told them what the movie was about and talked a bit about to whom it might most appeal, and I asked that they put together whatever they could to start running the next week. No media plan, just gather as many spots as we could purchase against the intended audience.

After the expected antics and protestations about there being no media plan and needing more time and not being sure whether it could be done and on and on, I cajoled them to begin the buying process. I reminded them that there was a high sense of urgency so they should get back to me ASAP.

Returning to my office I sat down to contemplate it all. Clearly this was fun and it was exciting. I mean this guy was a key part of the Hollywood scene, a player, and we were right there with him.

And of course when you work with the top guy, you cut through all of the bullshit with the little people trying to second-guess their boss. This was a particularly sick part of the advertising business, and it was even more heightened in the movie industry, as I found out later on. But we didn't have to deal with that here.

It was highly rewarding hitting a home run the first time up at bat with this guy who was a legend. His greatest claim to fame was probably the movie *The Graduate*, with Dustin Hoffman and Anne Bancroft. He had a framed picture on his desk of Hoffman peering under Bancroft's naked leg, which had been used to promote the movie. But he had many others that he either produced or contributed financial backing to, which were notable as well, including *A Bridge Too Far*, *The Carpetbaggers*, *Harlow, Tattoo, Carnal Knowledge*, *The Producers*, *8½*, *Divorce Italian Style*, and *Two Women*. And the list went on.

His temper and eccentricities notwithstanding, these were fairly typical of what we've all read about movie industry people. His relationships with others in the industry were notable.

At this time in the business, an advertising agency would receive a 15 percent commission on the media placement. In this case that was $75,000 for essentially two or three days of work. Obviously all of this income dropped right to the bottom line as profit since we hired no extra people and incurred hardly any extra costs. John and I, with very little else, were able to put it together.

While I was thinking about this, the phone on my desk rang. I was surprised to hear the distinctive tone of none other than the president of Young & Rubicam, who had heard from Roby R. Harrington III what was going on.

Anyway it was Ed Ney, who offered in his distinctively gruff voice and in no uncertain terms that I should "get the money."

He sounded a little like Marlon Brando's Godfather. I know about these kinds of voices because I have one just like it. In college my nickname became "Sandpaper." I asked, "What money? What do you mean?"

What he meant was that I had to get a check for $500,000 from Levine before Y&R would commit to making the media buy. Why did I have this funny feeling that this was not going to be easy—and it wasn't.

I couldn't reach Levine that Friday afternoon but left a message with his secretary as to the situation and gave her my home phone number, which she then relayed to him. I also advised her that we were able to put together a very good media schedule that had been requested and which was being sent by courier as I spoke. And I advised her to please relay that I would appreciate a check for the media so we could move forward and make the media buy. I asked her to tell all of this to Levine to review as soon as she could.

The phone rang at my house early the next morning. My wife Jeri answered and told me that a Joseph Levine was on the phone. Uh oh!

I grabbed the phone and in my most confident voice said, "Hello, this is Fred Goldberg."

Then I heard the very same voice that had been shouting at Richard a few days before roar at me, "Do you know who the fuck I am? Do you know how much fucking money I am worth? What the fuck are you telling me? What's this crap about sending you a check?"

When he stopped his rant I calmly advised, "Mr. Levine, I am just a small cog in a big machine and can't do anything about this situation. I was given my orders from the head of the agency, who you are welcome to speak with if you like."

I successfully employed this same "small cog/big machine" argument many times over the years, having learned it right here on the combat field. I was just a messenger. Don't shoot the messenger. I even made up some higher-ups along the way. "Our bankers will not let us make such a large commitment." "Our financial vice president has very strict covenants as regards client receivables." "The media will not advance us this kind of credit." And so on.

That was the way it had to be since we had no prior relationship, there was no credit established, and we knew little about AVCO Embassy. Not to speak of the fact that we had no signed agreement of any kind. All of this I made up as I went along. It gave me some great practice in spontaneous lying.

"Mr. Levine, we can't run the spots unless we have the money up front to pay for the media."

He said, "Fuck you."

Click!

He hung up the phone on me. Jeri was standing next to me in our kitchen in Great Neck, New York, that day. She listened in some disbelief and shock to the entire conversation since I was holding the phone three feet from my ear to protect my hearing. She did have a smile on her face, however, and after the call wondered whether I really wanted to continue on in the advertising business.

Monday morning came and so did a special courier with a $500,000 check delivered to me at my desk. I told the media folks to make the buy and we moved forward to run the commercials.

The Day of the Dolphin was never a great box-office success but the advertising we did helped to generate some meaningful increases in attendance versus where it had been before we got involved. Our efforts resulted in Levine asking us to work on two additional films, one notable and one not: *A Bridge Too Far* and *Lucky Luciano*.

Neither of these was a great box-office success either and so ended my involvement with H-O-L-L-Y-W-O-O-D for the time being.

However, I did learn a valuable lesson from all this and made a point to never forget it. I even had a rubber stamp made to remind certain folks that worked for me from time to time. All it said was "GET THE MONEY." I used red ink in the pad and made frequent use of it on delinquent accounts receivable reports and memos.

"Puerto Rico,
You Lovely Island . . .
Island of tropical breezes.
Always the pineapples growing,
Always the coffee blossoms blowing . . ."

In 1971 I was the account supervisor on the Commonwealth of Puerto Rico account and had occasion to regularly fly down to San Juan, Puerto Rico, to visit with these clients. They were all government types, some elected, most given their jobs in return for favors and such. All bureaucrats.

Ed Ney, then president of Young & Rubicam, was close to the account, as was a fellow named Gary Hoyt. Gary was based in San Juan and close to the government and the governor of Puerto Rico, Don Luis A. Ferré. Gary was well known all over the island because he was a good-looking suntanned bon vivant kind of guy, and he had a 50-foot sailing vessel and was an Olympic-class sailor and respected for it.

One day we were to meet with Manny Casiano, who was what they called "The Administrator" for the government directly under Governor Ferré. He was the number two hombre. At the time they owed Young & Rubicam a lot of money, millions that had been advanced for media and production expenditures, and they were seriously behind in bringing these accounts receivable current, which was the reason for our meeting.

When we three arrived, we were ushered into a large conference room with expansive windows looking out across San Juan and to the ocean. There was a huge conference table and a long cabinet that ran the length of the table on one side of the room. We were told by the receptionist to make ourselves comfortable, which we did for the next several hours.

We waited and waited and waited. And as you can imagine, we had some conversation about this and about that during the wait. As time went by the conversation drifted to how rude and disrespectful it was to keep us waiting so long.

Ed Ney said, "This is getting to be a little ridiculous."

Gary Hoyt replied, "These guys are bureaucrats with tiny little minds."

Ed Ney: "Isn't there some way we can get them in here?"

Gary: "It's all part of their game. This is a power play. Who's more important? Us or them?"

Well, this discussion went back and forth between Ed and Gary for a while. The longer we waited, the more frustrated and vocal both men became. During all this, I was pacing around the table, over to the window, back to a chair, back over to the window, and so forth. I looked over just about everything and every square inch of that room, and at one point my eyes fixed up on the ceiling.

Lo and behold, buried in one of the recessed light fixtures was what appeared to be a microphone.

I waved my arms around over my head, held my hands up in a T toward Gary and Ed, and without saying anything pointed to the ceiling. Oops, it looked like we might have been monitored or recorded.

The three of us sat silently, each of us thinking back on what we might have said during the past few hours. It was not all flattering and certainly would not make for a positive meeting if they had heard any of it, particularly since we were there as money collectors.

Five minutes later, while we were all silently staring down at the tabletop contemplating the situation, into the room burst Manny Casiano, followed in short order by four of his appointees. One after the other after the other, each marched in behind the next.

Each had a similarly smug and bellicose look on his face. Each carried a black attaché case, which he placed on the long credenza behind their chairs and which he opened before sitting down and left open on the back bar. In several of the pouches in the lids sat dark, odd-shaped handles sticking upright. It occurred to us pretty quickly that each of those handles was likely attached to a barrel.

They all sat down simultaneously. And without a hello, without a how are you, without a how was the trip down, without an apology for being late and keeping us so long, Casiano asked, "Now, what is it you are here for?"

Of course, he knew well why we were there but this was all part of the script. He probably knew too that they had us off balance, having likely heard us stop talking after discovering what well might have been the microphone. We were even more off balance when they exposed the handles of the pistols they were packing.

I should explain in fairness that this was a time when one of the Puerto Rican political parties, the Independistas, was blowing up buildings in Puerto Rico and threatening to do so in Manhattan as well. They actually were able to place at least one bomb in a New York City high-rise, but it didn't go off. As a result, many of the people associated with the current administration went around carrying handguns.

Gary Hoyt did all the talking and expressed how supportive Young & Rubicam was of the administration and Governor Ferré, and all that they stood for. After six minutes of many platitudes and compliments, he got around to asking if they couldn't (please?) find a way to address the rather large outstanding balances that had been created and were substantially past due to the agency.

Casiano looked at Gary Hoyt and said, "We will see what we can do."

That's all that was said, by anyone. Just those seven words: we will see what we can do.

And with that the meeting was over, he stood up, and his four lieutenants stood up; and in unison they closed their attachés, clicked them locked, picked them up by the handles, and filed out of the room.

It was shortly thereafter that I called our travel agent to change my scheduled airline ticket. I had planned on flying back to New York with Bill Colon, one of the Puerto Rico clients who was based in Manhattan.

It took us another 12 months to collect the receivables. But we eventually got the money . . . all of it. Nonetheless, I never again flew on the same plane with any of these clients for the rest of my tenure on this account.

⊘ ⊘ ⊘

I had a client at Goldberg Moser O'Neill whose name was Les Crane. Les had been a well-known and popular radio personality in the 1950s and then on TV in the 1960s. He had some pretty spectacular moments in his career, including creating the Top 40 list of pop songs according to Casey Kasem, and getting some great guests to interview, like Bob Dylan, Richard Burton, Martin Luther King, George Wallace, Robert Kennedy, and others along the way. He was also known for having been married to the gorgeous red-headed actress Tina Louise for a few minutes.

When I caught up with Les in 1992, he owned and was running a company called Software Toolworks. He had somehow come upon a really fantastic product called the Miracle Piano Teaching System that he was about to launch.

We did some ingenious advertising for him for this product, creating a commercial where we filmed a bunch of kids in Petaluma, California, who had never played the piano. It followed them over a month's time from being given the product and learning how to play it and ending up giving a real-life concert on the Miracle Piano. This was reality TV way before its time.

Had it not been for foul-ups in the production of the product and in its shipping, it would have been an enormous success that Christmas. Regardless, it was still very successful.

After Les decided to part with us as his agency, he still owed us some money. I was pressing him to pay us and he was resisting. This is not an unusual happening with clients who at first seem to be your best pals but then show their truer colors later on, particularly when they no longer need or want you. Or when cash gets tight.

In fact, this is one of the most dangerous things in the advertising business and is ludicrous as well. The agency was required to, say, buy $5 million of media time for a client. The agency revenue from that buy would have been around $750,000, on which they might make 20 percent, or a $150,000 profit. However, the agency was mostly held responsible by the media for the $5 million, so if something were to happen with the client, it became a problem. It was a most risky bet: lay out $5 million to make $150,000. Some would say it was insane.

Les called me one day and said he wanted to have lunch. We agreed to get together at my favorite restaurant in Sausalito, Angelino's. We met, we talked, we ate, we talked, we finished, and finally Les said he wasn't going to pay the $100,000 fee he still owed us. He claimed he didn't like the work after all, even though he had previously approved it and applauded it and used it. By the way, the work had received all sorts of accolades and was truly wonderful and effective.

I said to Les, "But Les, you owe us that money."

"Maybe, but I'm not going to pay it."

"We'll have to sue you then and it will end up costing everyone more."

He said, "Sue me!"

So as I stood up to leave I said, "OK."

He remained sitting and looked up at me and said, "I'll give you $50,000."

I said, "OK."

With that I reached for the $63 check and consummated the lunch, which ended up being my most expensive client lunch ever, costing $50,063.

By odd coincidence, years later I ended up living in Belvedere, California, about a quarter mile down the same street from Les, who had built a beautiful contemporary house on the side of the hill there. Not by coincidence, he was in a dispute with his next-door neighbor and the town of Belvedere, over house construction matters.

Yes, getting the money out of clients for your work can be trying and difficult. With Worlds of Wonder we had to manage the accounts receivable on a daily basis and even so ended up suffering a serious loss.

While we managed our cash outlays and commitments on this client very carefully, with regular calls to the client, with automatic stops on further commitments, and even with securing letters of credit, in the end we still took it in the shorts. I personally was involved in reviewing this situation on an almost daily basis and was unable to prevent getting burned.

In addition, I personally took considerable added abuse from Jay Chiat over the matter. We got stuck holding the bag for some network television media buys to the tune of close to a million dollars. We were able to put back more than half of this onto the networks and so ended up having to eat around $400,000.

Now $400,000 is not a small sum to have to absorb, but to this day I don't understand why Jay was quite so upset except for the fact that he always liked to keep you on the defensive at all times. God knows, Jay spent this kind of money on a whim on so many occasions for some of the most ridiculous things. At least I thought so.

Yes, we had to write off the money, but over the three years that we worked for Worlds of Wonder, we had generated an extraordinary amount of income, the result of great work, which drove their sales and still further increases in the advertising budget. Everything was billed at a full 15 percent commission.

I felt the write-off was a reasonable cost of doing business and a minimum given the kinds of risks that we took and managed during our relationship with this client. No one seemed to remember that we had spent virtually nothing to win the account. The total out-of-pocket cost was a plane ticket for Guy Day from LA to San Francisco.

Our income amounted to $20,000,000. The write-off was $400,000. That's a 2 percent giveback. If we hadn't taken on the business, we would have lost $19,600,000 by my way of thinking.

When it comes to advertising, I have always felt that the biggest risk a client has is that their advertising is not being seen. The biggest risk an agency has is not seeing the money.

CHAPTER 3

THE DUKE AND I

IN 1975 BRISTOL-MYERS, the big pharmaceutical company, woke up to the fact that Tylenol analgesic from the Johnson & Johnson Company was eating not only their lunch but their entire portfolio of aspirin-based pain relievers, including Excedrin and Bufferin.

Tylenol was made with a generic ingredient called acetaminophen and was as effective as aspirin-based products but a whole lot gentler to the stomach. You may ask why you are suffering through a pharmacological lecture when we're supposed to be talking ads and advertising.

Well, at the time I was a young account supervisor assigned to the Excedrin account at the then prestigious advertising agency Young & Rubicam. I was successful at persuading Bristol-Myers to assign us their new competitive extra-strength nonaspirin analgesic, which was to be named Datril 500. We presented numerous campaigns to launch this important product, but alas in the end "cooler" heads of the client prevailed. Or should I say when the president of the company finally reviewed the recommended campaign, which had been approved by the advertising director and the marketing and sales director and the president of the products division, it was rejected in favor of what Dick Gelb felt was a far better idea.

His turned out to be a tried-and-true formula for the company. When you can't think of anything else to do, get a celebrity. And so it came to pass that Mr. Gelb's idea of getting a celebrity turned out to be getting John Wayne. Now John Wayne had never done any commercials to this point, although many people associate him strongly with the Great Western Savings work, which was done later. And it is important to note here that despite a rather exorbitant fee, Mr. Wayne (or rather "call me Duke") didn't really want to do these or any commercials for that matter. Nonetheless he was close to being completely broke, having to support several wives and families and cattle and boats and all.

So this story is how I, along with a group product manager fellow from Bristol-Myers named Eric Schulman, and a copy supervisor from Y&R named Eric Weber, spent five days with The Duke. At the end of the day, or week I should say, we collectively agreed that despite this man's accomplishments in the entertainment world, and his public persona, he indeed could make you puke.

We worked many months coming up with scripts that the agency creative director liked, the client liked, the network clearance folks liked, and which would seem at least somewhat probable coming out of the mouth of a folk hero like Wayne. Datril 500 was developed to be an extra-strength pain reliever, which was strong but, because it was made with the same ingredient as Tylenol (acetaminophen), gentle. Tough on pain, gentle on the stomach. And since John Wayne was a big, hulking, strong kind of a guy, who apparently had his gentle moments, this became the idea of the scripts. Datril 500, a strong but gentle pain reliever. Who else could better deliver this message than John Wayne?

Three wise men from New York City: Weber, Goldberg, and Shulman oy vey!

It came to pass that these commercials were to be shot in Monument Valley, Utah, and Flagstaff, Arizona. The thinking was that these were places that Wayne and anyone else could relate to. Big, open, grand scapes. The West. And it was felt that Wayne would be receptive to returning to that part of the country where he filmed one of his most famous movies with John Huston.

Now, Bristol-Myers, and particularly the products division, was notoriously known for spending the least amount of money they absolutely could on commercial television production, and everything else for that matter. They called it prudent, but it was often just plain cheap and shortsighted. No one would have known that from the Datril experience. They willingly put up whatever it took to get John Wayne, and it took a lot, $250,000, which at the time was a heck of lot. On top of which, shooting at two remote locations was extremely expensive, as was paying for all the incremental amenities that Wayne insisted upon.

Nevertheless, off we went to a little town in the middle of Arizona called Kayenta, the closest semi-civilized place to Monument Valley. Eric Weber and I flew into Phoenix and then had to board one of those pretend planes with one propeller to fly the rest of the way to Kayenta. No sooner had we landed and a dozen agency and production house people came scurrying up to advise us that Duke didn't like the scripts and wasn't going to do the commercials. We were to start shooting first thing in the morning and the meter for the production was close to $500,000 per day.

Before we could even check into the only hotel in Kayenta, a Holiday

Inn set among 50 trailers containing mostly real live Indians, we marched over to where John Wayne had set up his camp. This was actually an oversized Winnebago that had to be part of the deal in order to get him to do the commercials. We also had to pay all expenses for his 30-plus-years-younger live-in girlfriend to come along.

Into the camper Eric and I went and were greeted with "Who the hell are you sonnies?" Well, to be honest, we were two pretty young guys at the time, in our 20s, and we both looked even younger. But what was even more surprising I suppose to Wayne was that we were New Yorkers. And Jewish. Two young New York Jews about to tell John Wayne, probably the most right-wing ultra-conservative SOB I had ever been next to, that he had to use the existing scripts for the commercials.

We told Wayne who we were and what he had to do and he launched into an orbit of screaming and yelling. Most of this was the result of his not ever wanting to be involved with the stupid commercials to begin with, but alas he needed the money. He had a ranch with hundreds of heads of cattle that weren't going to get fed and a 125-foot converted WW II minesweeper docked in Newport Beach that needed 50,000 gallons of fuel to fill 'er up. And his live-in girlfriend.

After 30 minutes Wayne calmed down a bit and offered a compromise. He got up, went to his briefcase, and, voilà, out came his recommendation on how the scripts should be done. He had it typed out on his own personal stationery and proceeded to present the idea to the two of us.

Datril Commercial

The camera directions and stage directions for a one minute Datril commercial for me John Wayne. I suggest that we find a location on a hill so that when the zoom lens is used it will open up from a medium close shot to include the majesty of the snow-capped Olympics in the background. Now from the closer shot my dialogue will go as follows:

"A lot of you folks don't seem to cotton to my doing a little medicine show for Datril. I'm sorry about that. I believe in it. It's aspirin free and it works for me. But if you all don't want me spouting off about," then I reach for the bottle and pick it up and say, "This will be my last ad for Datril 500." I will look at the Datril bottle, shake my head in thought and look back and say, "Too bad. It's good medicine." And at that point the camera will pull back to the full shot with me a block away in the foreground with the bottle and behind us the snow-capped Olympic range, as the choral group harmonizes just three words, "Datril, Datril, Datril."

I mean don't pay any attention to my musical contribution here but I think this would make a most remembered commercial, but it would take a minute. I tried to cut it down, tried everything possible that I could do with it to give the same feeling to it and it's just impossible to do in less than a minute. Anyway there it is for your judgment. Thank you.

If we are to do the proposed half minute "I hear you friend" commercial, I suggest that if it is a lady with her children, that my line read something like "dear lady I sympathize with you, I raised 7 children and 21 grand kids."

John Wayne

We were stupefied by the utter lack of understanding or regard for the commercial development and approval process. He didn't give a damn about the required network clearance or the FTC copy clearance. Maybe he was mostly right since his script had no strategic relevance whatsoever and didn't require someone's approval. He suggested using the Mormon Tabernacle Choir for the music part. It was interesting that he proposed holding up the bottle of the product, a subject we will revisit later in this episode. But, the pièce de résistance was that we shoot with the snow-capped Olympic Mountains in the background. It apparently didn't matter that we were to start shooting the next day and we were in Kayenta, Arizona, about to travel the 30 miles to Monument Valley, the location of the first commercial.

We told Duke it wasn't going to work. We had to shoot the script exactly as it was written if for no other reasons, legal ones. He sat his six-foot-six or so frame down and said, "I'm going to call Leonard Goldstein." And he did right then. His live-in girlfriend/assistant put the call through. Leonard Goldstein was the chairman of ABC at the time and coincidentally was taping a special commemorative show in Wayne's honor the next week. Goldstein immediately took the call and listened to Wayne explain that he didn't understand why the commercial had to meet network clearance regulations and that he wanted to change them. Goldstein then advised Wayne that he had an early morning board meeting and would bring up the issue and get back to him. We all agreed, Wayne as well, to wait until the next morning but if the answer was negative to proceed with the script as is. The call came in the morning and Wayne reluctantly set out in his Winnebago to shoot the commercial with the original and approved script. As is.

It was 12, high noon. Bright sun, clear blue cloudless sky. The scope and grandeur of Monument Valley were breathtaking. There was all this red dirt and dust everywhere, immense rock formations and buttes all around us. The idea was to have Wayne stand with two of the most famous of these icons behind him in the distance, Right Mitten and Left Mitten, as they are called.

There were all these people, vehicles, and caterers belonging to the

production company, and a few Indians who actually lived out there watching this spectacle. There was the Winnebago parked with Wayne inside. There was a leather director's chair looking as though a branding iron had burned THE DUKE on the backside. There were the production and agency creative folks setting up the lighting and the place where Wayne was going to stand. We had arrived at 8 a.m. and they still weren't ready to call Wayne to start shooting at noon. It took four hours to figure out his spot and set up some light reflectors. Oh well. It was finally time to call out the man to read his lines.

They knocked on the door and called for The Duke. "We're ready for you, Duke." Duke appeared in the doorway of the Winnebago, which he literally entirely filled. But that was not as interesting as what Duke was wearing. The very same outfit that he wore in the film he shot in Monument Valley with John Huston back in God knows when. Leather pants, tan cowboy shirt, big ol' cowboy hat, and a purple scarf around his neck. This was actually a nice idea, I thought, but what was not such a nice idea was that he was wearing six-shooters. Yep! That's right, partner. There they were, one on either side. This was not in the agreed-to game plan. And this is where Eric Schulman made his presence known and exerted his influence as the client.

Before anyone could say hold on, Eric went running up to Wayne as he stepped down the stairs of the trailer. He pleaded with Duke. "You can't wear those guns."

Wayne looked at him for a moment or two and took his hand and turned it sort of inward and placed it on Eric's right cheek and proceeded to fling Eric to the left. Eric went tumbling into and over the red dirt and dust as Duke bellowed, "Get out of my way, sonny!"

I guess The Duke, having no respect at all for the client, wouldn't have made a good account executive.

Two days later at breakfast we received a lecture about gun control. There were probably 50 folks in the restaurant, and Duke sat down across from me and Eric Schulman and reached into his pocket and pulled out a letter that he then proceeded to read out loud so everyone in the place could hear. It was from a woman who had written Wayne about how she had been raped and that they hadn't had a gun around because of various controls in the state where she lived but wished she had had one. After reading this Wayne accused us easterners, because of our antigun mentality, of causing these kinds of things to happen. We just ate our scrambled eggs and sausage. And we watched every one of those people in the restaurant come up to Wayne with comments.

"Way to go, Duke, we love you."

"You are my hero."

"When are you gonna run for president?"

And so on.

The commercial was to be a full-length shot of The Duke, with the Left Mitten over one shoulder behind him and the Right Mitten over the other. There was a straight 22 seconds of dialogue that Wayne needed to read top to bottom. He lumbered over to the marker on the ground where he was supposed to stand. The director told Wayne to look right into the camera and on his cue deliver the script. They slated the take. The director said "Action." Wayne moved his hip to the left a bit, took a step forward and hit the mark, stared down the lens of the camera as it rolled, and delivered the approved script in exactly the allotted 22 seconds. And perfectly. They did seven more takes just for the hell of it but none equaled the first take, where The Duke had nailed it. Oh, and we ended up shooting The Duke from the waist up. Nobody ever knew he had those six-shooters. Don't know what he thought when he finally saw the finished spots. But then we didn't care at that point.

I guess that's what the best actors do best. And that's why they said Wayne was a great movie actor. He really knew how to make it happen once he got in front of that camera.

On the second or third day of shooting, The Duke was not feeling too well. We had traveled to Flagstaff, Arizona, to a magnificent ranch up in the mountains. The landscape was awesome, the poplar trees spectacular, but we were up over 10,000 feet and Wayne at the time had only one lung left. He was regularly sucking on an oxygen machine that was in his trailer. He was in a surly mood. And he was treating everybody like dog shit. Everyone, that is, except anyone from the public who was watching the goings-on. He always made sure to respect his fans.

The first commercial, as I already explained, had Wayne deliver 22 seconds of nonstop on-camera dialogue. He never showed or touched the product. The idea was to cut away at the end of the spot to the product package and tag line: Strong, but gentle. Of course it would have been much better to have Wayne hold up the package. It would have had far more impact and possibly add some credibility. But he refused to even touch the package on camera. This, despite the structure of the commercial that he had scripted for himself earlier. No one ever said celebrities had to be consistent.

Well, we were nearing the end of the shoot of the second commercial and I received an urgent call from New York. Turns out the very senior executives at Bristol-Myers had been thinking further about the commercials and they really felt that Wayne needed to hold the package when he delivered his lines. They had previously understood that he refused to do that. The caller who delivered this message to me was none other than Alex Kroll, then president of the Y&R New York office. I told Alex we already had the first commercial in the can and we were near completing the second.

He said to me, "Look, you get a shot of him on camera with the package."

To which I remember so clearly responding, "Alex, neither you, me, nor God could get him to hold up that package, but I'll give it a try."

We had a dummy package made up that was sitting on a fence post. And we were taking a break from shooting and I happened to be standing next to Duke. I nodded toward where the Datril 500 package was resting and said, "Duke, everything you've done has been really great but it would be simply terrific if we could get just one shot with you holding the pack up."

And with that I nodded toward the Datril package again, still resting on the post.

Duke turned to me and said, "OK, why don't you go over there and get that package and bring it over here and then bend over and I'll shove that pack so far up your ass you won't even feel it."

I looked at Wayne and said, "Duke, you mean you don't want to hold the package?"

He fired back at me. "Get the hell outta here, sonny."

And I did.

The Duke and Me in Monument Valley, Utah.

We returned to New York with the finished commercials. Bristol-Myers management was very pleased with the results, no package in Duke's hand notwithstanding. According to their process, they copy tested one of the spots and it did extremely well on recall, which is a measure of how many people actually remembered seeing the commercial. In fact it was the highest-scoring analgesic commercial they had tested to that point in time. There was just one problem. Nobody remembered what the product was or did.

All they remembered was The Duke.

CHAPTER 4

THE BRITISH ARE COMING!
THE BRITISH ARE COMING!

ONE OF THE MOST FASCINATING AND EXCITING CLIENTS I worked with was an English company called Marshall Cavendish. Two gentlemen, Peter and Patrick, had started a business in the UK and were expanding it around the world and now into the United States.

Peter Marshall and Patrick Cavendish had invented what were known in England as "part works." These were weekly magazines that over the course of 52 or 104 weeks built into an encyclopedia that you then stored in binders so that they became a reference.

Examples of the titles were *Story of Life*; *Man & Woman*, an exploration of sexuality and the sexes; *Animal Kingdom*; *All About Science*; *Golden Homes*; *Golden Hands*, about knitting and needlecraft; *Man, Myth, and Magic*; *World War II*; and *Life History of the U.S.*

There were a number of interesting things about this concept from a business standpoint and even more so from an advertising point of view. No one had ever done anything like this in the US.

The business was predicated on a model that required projecting and estimating the total number of copies that would be sold after receiving the results from the first introductory week or two. Failing to accurately predict these sales resulted in printing too many copies and ultimately in a money-losing proposition.

The business was also unusual in that the only advertising that was done was to promote the first issue of each magazine series. And that was it.

We were directed to use the existing commercials that had been developed in the UK, modifying them as little as possible. Sometimes we would be required to change only a few words and/or expressions that might not be understood in the US. Other times we shot some footage that would be dropped into the existing spots.

Of course this is not something most advertising agencies like to hear. They know their own culture and after all they are the "creative experts." They want to be left to develop and recommend what is best for the US market.

But this client had other beliefs and believed in formulas. Don't change anything that worked already. So most all of the creative work was nothing to speak of in terms of inventiveness. Only a very few times were we required to start development of a commercial from scratch, and as I recall these were not very successful in the marketplace. The commercials that actually worked the best were the modified versions of the English originals, and modified the least.

A second point about this business was that all of the advertising was placed over a 10-day period and was directed at selling as many issues of the first issue of the magazine as possible. The way the sales accumulated was that a certain percentage of those people who had bought the first issue would buy the next and so on. However, the number of people predictably dropped off week to week.

Another thing that was quite unique and remarkable was that since the entire budget, say $2 million or $2.5 million, would be spent over only 10 days, thousands and thousands of gross rating points were generated in a very short time. In effect this made Marshall Cavendish, if not the largest, one of the largest advertisers during the time they would have the commercials on air. No one in America who watched TV could miss seeing them, since Marshall Cavendish bought such a massive numbers of spots. There were times on some TV stations when a Marshall Cavendish commercial might appear every 10 minutes just about around the clock.

And that gets us to a final thing that was quite special and way ahead of its time. We were able to measure every sale, day by day, market by market, copy by copy.

Peter Marshall and Patrick Cavendish had sent another Brit over to the States to manage all this business. His name was Peter Godfrey and he was a perfectly coiffed blond, good-looking, persuasive, very bright person. He dressed very nattily and spoke with eloquence. I have found that many English businesspeople have this capability of sounding smart and eloquent although sometimes they may not be eloquent or smart at all, but this was not the case with Peter.

Peter in turn had hired a fellow to work with him. He was not so good-looking, considerably less persuasive, and not near as bright a guy. He wore suits that didn't quite fit and never seemed pressed, and he had a bunch of unruly hair that always looked like it needed washing and combing. He spoke with an English accent too, but it had a decidedly cockney twang. By coincidence his name was Bob Godfrey, no relation.

I wondered whether the fact that Peter Godfrey had hired Bob Godfrey had anything to do with Peter Marshall having hired Peter Godfrey. Probably not.

Regardless, neither of the Godfreys knew very much about the United States or the media market here when they arrived. But through incredible sheer tenacity and knowledge mining, they drilled down and pretty much changed the nature of buying media. At the time Young & Rubicam was one of the largest and most powerful media buyers in the country, and they learned a few things in the process of handling the Marshall Cavendish account.

What Marshall Cavendish was after was the absolute rock-bottom-line, downright lowest cost they could buy a TV spot for, with little regard for where or what time it would appear. This was heresy and anathema for traditional media people. Since Marshall Cavendish did not have national distribution, they only were interested in spot TV. Later on they did try to test some things in network TV but without much success.

The company believed that the media weight totally determined the success of the sale of the first issue of their magazines. It didn't matter in what kind of show the commercial ran, or where in the show it ran, or what audience the show might have appealed to. It didn't matter what station was being purchased either. The only thing that mattered was the cost per point. The lower the better.

It was a fascinating concept and one that no media person in the entire agency at Young & Rubicam endorsed. I suspect this would have been the same at all the other agencies in town too. I mean, most of them would lose their jobs if buying media were simply a matter of getting more spots.

Most of Peter and Bob's time was spent going from market to market, with and without the agency, meeting directly with TV station managers and salespeople. This occurred over the protestations of everyone in the media department at Y&R, from the buyers assigned to the account right up to the media director of the agency.

The Godfreys spent a lot of time going from one city to the next because a very important ingredient in making a magazine a sales success was to secure distribution in each market. At the time, in many markets, some people who had ties to organized crime syndicates controlled magazine distribution through retail racks. If you wanted your magazine displayed in a supermarket, you had to persuade these folks to take it on and put it there.

One time I accompanied Peter to New Orleans to visit a distributor. We arrived and introduced ourselves to the receptionist, who asked us to have a seat. About 15 minutes later she said we could go in as she reached under her desk and pressed a buzzer, which was connected to a door behind and to the right of her reception desk.

Peter and I went through the door, which closed behind us. In front of us was a long hall about 5 feet wide and maybe 40 feet long, at the end of which was another door. There was nothing else in this corridor. We walked toward the second door, our footsteps echoing off the walls. We reached the end and there was a button, which we pushed.

The door opened electronically into a huge office. Straight ahead of us sat a man who looked like a larger version of Burl Ives at his largest. There were piles of magazines on his expansive desk along with a number of phones. The room was kind of dim with fluorescent lights in the ceiling, some of which were flickering and some burned out. There wasn't a window in the room. And sitting around and standing around, some smoking, were six or seven men right out of central casting for *The Godfather*.

The big man at the desk looked up over his half-glasses but under the bushiest eyebrows I ever saw and bellowed, "Sit down!"

We took the two empty chairs just in front of his desk.

"What can I do for you?"

Peter did most of the talking. Every now and then I would add what I thought was an astute comment to the discussion. Basically the big man didn't understand the concept of part works and wasn't going to take on the distribution.

But both of us were really ballsy and in this guy's face and he liked it. Or maybe he couldn't believe it. At the time we didn't know that we were dealing with one of the more powerful underworld guys in Louisiana.

At the end of 45 minutes he said he liked us and he would take on the magazine. As it turned out he must have liked us a lot because the magazine ended up being placed in supermarkets like Piggly Wiggly right at the check-out counter. That space was reserved for high-velocity magazines like *People* and *Time*, which happened to have paid a handsome ransom to get that position. Marshall Cavendish didn't pay a dime.

We said thank you very much and left, waiting for someone to buzz open the innner door so we could walk back down the long empty corridor to the second door. There was no handle or button on the door. We looked at each other and stood there for a while noticing several video cameras above. Finally a buzzer sounded and the door opened and we walked back into the reception room. From there we went on to visit a number of TV stations in the New Orleans area, where we had equal success. New Orleans turned out to be a very high-selling market for the magazines.

Back in the early 1970s it was unheard of to have clients meet with media salesmen directly. Media-buying people mostly conducted their business of negotiation with their butts in their seats in their offices on Madison Avenue. Secondly, clients rarely talked to the TV stations.

In fact, over the years I found that most clients have very little real understanding of the media-buying process despite spending the lion's share of their advertising dollars buying media. Often it was viewed as a mundane part of the business and fairly rote. It is far from that.

Another thing that Peter and Bob did was insist on meeting with the Y&R media personnel before, during, and after every media buy that was made. For every market and for every magazine that they launched. Here again, it would have been extremely unusual for any client to meet directly with media-buying people. Clients hardly knew they existed.

One of the things that never failed to surprise me was how clients will argue about production estimates before they approve them. They will scrutinize every last detail and dollar and each line item, some even the amount they are being charged for the food that the production company might have included in the budget. I recall one client of mine who was completely bent out of shape over the $13 corned beef sandwiches from the Stage Deli that had been expensed to a production estimate for radio commercials done in Manhattan. He never let me forget about those sandwiches for the six years we worked together.

Yet, when it came to approving a multimillion-dollar media plan, most clients would spend far less time and would rarely drill down into the real nuts and bolts, market by market, station by station, spot by spot. But Peter and Bob did. And the media people didn't like it.

I worked on the Marshall Cavendish account for seven years and for the last few of those years had the good fortune to have a senior media person assigned who understood what these guys were trying to do and was willing to roll with them and their punches. His name was George Sharpe and he was one of the very best media people I ever worked with. He probably did more to save this client money than anyone else who ever worked on this business.

But despite George we still had a hell of a time containing and controlling these clients, who would show up unannounced just about anywhere and everywhere.

A Y&R media buyer could be negotiating a Marshall Cavendish buy with a Tulsa, Oklahoma, station and the station person would say, "Hey, there are two guys here in the lobby who claim they are with Marshall Cavendish and want to talk with my salespeople."

Or, "I already met with a Peter and Bob Godfrey several days ago and we signed a deal where they purchased $353,000 worth of media time."

More often than not, these two guys could end up getting lower prices than if the agency would have been left to their own design. This was a function of their persuasiveness and deal-making capability and an agency media person's general lack of motivation and desire to get the absolute lowest "rock bottom can't sell for less than that" cost.

The Godfreys would have me schedule a meeting before a media buy was to be made and insist that every buyer be in attendance so they could explain what they wanted out of the buy. More like what they expected. We did this on every media buy.

And since Ed Ney, who was then president of Y&R, had a relationship with Marshall and Cavendish themselves in the UK when he was in the international division, Peter and Bob insisted that he be present at many of these meetings as well. And if you ever wonder what really drives a big Madison Avenue advertising agency, this should clear it up for you. It's the money! Ed was fully cognizant of that. And Ed religiously attended these meeting when asked.

I was quite happy having Ed Ney involved. It increased the importance of the account at the agency enormously. Somehow people listened a little more when I spoke. It also gave me my second opportunity to be involved with the president of the agency, something that would not have likely happened.

I had already been involved with Ney on the Commonwealth of Puerto Rico business, again because of his connections in international and some relationships he had with the government people on the island. My work on that account somehow got me involved with the Marshall Cavendish business and I suspect that Ed Ney had something to say about that.

The Godfreys' penchant for surprise and for bloodless indifference to the most maligning and deleterious comments and accusations was something else. Maybe it was kind of a genetic thing found in Englishmen, as I had experienced some other Brits with the same attitude. Think Simon Cowell of *American Idol* fame. There was an absolute insensitivity to doing what they thought was necessary in order to drive down their media costs, including creating a competitive circus. Meaning: having other media-buying firms and/or other ad agencies make their proposals against ours.

Most of the time we were not aware that they were doing this, so it gave them a truly double-edged stick and schtick. Not only could they beat the agency up if they found a lower cost, or if the cost per point was lower, but they would actually use this to hammer down the cost of individual spots on specific shows even with a specific station. It was very ungentlemanly, and the stations didn't appreciate it either but they loved the extra revenue that this business generated.

Peter would say he didn't know that Bob had gotten another firm involved. Or Bob would say he didn't know that Peter had gotten another firm involved. What's that thing about some of the bloody English?

Y&R put up with this arrangement for a long time. And all the TV and radio stations that we dealt with did the same. Why? At the end of the day, if anyone asks, "It's about the money, stupid."

Think about it. Say you had a $3 million ad budget on Jell-O Pudding against which you had to allocate resources and people to service it for an entire year. It required meetings to discuss and debate this and to debate that. But with Marshall Cavendish, maybe you spent four or at most five weeks planning and making a media buy, and it was over and those resources could now be allocated elsewhere.

The fixes to the commercials could generally be made in a few days. That was it. At 15 percent back then, the $450,000 commission yielded gobs and gobs of profit to the agency for a few weeks of work, albeit intense work. No one was ever hired specifically for the account because of the downtimes. Rather, resources were drawn from other places. It was worth putting up with a lot. And the agency did.

But being put in the competitive situation with other firms was really kind of ugly and demotivating. Having the Godfreys assign "our" business to others and use the results as a whip on us wasn't nice. To my knowledge, the

Godfreys never did anything dishonest, but they were relentlessly driven to beat down the costs. All the costs. I personally spent ungodly amounts of time with and without George Sharpe putting together various briefs and analyses and defended our media costing structure and results to try to mitigate some of this.

They would ask a seemingly simple question like "What would Marshall Cavendish's savings be if we were to move into network utilization?" On the surface it would seem this could be answered fairly easily, but media is one of those really gray areas where no one concerned could agree on a given set of rules and assumptions upon which to generate an estimate and therefore provide an answer. And even when they did agree, the rules kept changing. How much daytime network was to be used in the mix? What quarter of the year would we use to generate the estimate? What day part mix should be employed? And on and on.

There was an unlimited number of variables and hence an unlimited number of answers to every question that the Godfreys would ask. And keep on asking they did.

At one point we agreed to go back and use historical data rather than try to predict what could happen in the future. I was extremely keen on this approach and decided that I would build a database of all the results for every part work on a market-by-market basis showing all the relevant historical actual data. This included such things as media dollars invested by day part, cost per gross rating point, cost per initial magazines sold, cost per total magazines sold, and so on.

I went even further and developed a mathematical model to project future sales of a part work after a sales trend had been developed for the initial few issues. The data helped determine print orders for future issues. Generally we were able to reasonably predict after 10 issues were distributed, and individual issue sales could be projected forward with a great deal of accuracy. My education at the University of Vermont had paid off although I received a 68 in statistics. I did much better with the same course later at the NYU Graduate School of Business, getting an A.

These computer applications became invaluable tools for us and for them, and it took me a huge amount of time to collect the data, program the system, and spit out the reports. But I felt it was worth it in answering many of the obscure and hypothetical questions that came up. And maybe more importantly it was something we "owned" at the agency that was of considerable value to Marshall Cavendish and I am certain helped in retaining the account through many storms and much rough water.

Believe it or not, I had a terrific relationship with Peter and Bob, but I couldn't stop them from going about their business the way they did. It was just business as usual for them.

However, it all came to a head one day in a meeting with both clients and all of our media-buying people who were assigned to the business. We were discussing an upcoming buy for a product called *Golden Hands*, a sewing and knitting magazine. Bob revealed some data from a competitive agency that he claimed indicated our cost per spot in several markets was out of line (i.e., too high). And for them "too high" could mean just a penny or two. In this case he indicated some much more radical differences.

The meeting ended with the threat of their pulling the buy and giving it to another agency. Subsequently I had a meeting with Ed Ney to post him on what was transpiring.

But it turned out that the client was right. Young & Rubicam had been delivering much higher media cost numbers (cost/point, cost/thousands) than the competitive agencies that Marshall Cavendish now included.

The question became why. And the answer turned out to be a dirty little secret part of the agency media-buying business that, if true, was not at all wholesome. It was rumored at the time that there had been some agreement made with one of the agency's largest accounts that the agency would not buy lower for any other client than the lowest cost that was being bought for this preferential client.

At the end of the day the agency met the costs that Marshall Cavendish had reviewed.

Toward the end of the 1970s it became a lot harder to successfully do what Marshall Cavendish had been doing. That is, using cheap gross rating points to drive awareness for each of the titles that it introduced. Media became more expensive. So did paper and printing. They made a decision to retrench back to England and Europe.

However, along came a fellow who had worked at an ad agency on the Marshall Cavendish business in the UK. He was actually a copywriter by trade. His name was Francis Wilkinson. Francis negotiated the rights to introduce a number of Marshall Cavendish titles in America after they had pulled out.

Francis turned out to be one of my best clients and friends. He was very bright and resourceful. He took over trying to resuscitate the Marshall Cavendish model in the United States.

He spent a great deal of time much like a vacuum, sucking up every bit of knowledge and understanding he could. I spent days providing all that I could to aid him in his learning process.

Francis already seemed to have been quite successful, having homes in London, Manhattan, Paris, and Bermuda. I had the pleasure of imparting my erudition to his learning bank at his New York townhouse, at another in Paris, and at his home in Bermuda. Never made it to the London one.

The New York townhouse was on the East Side in the most prestigious area in the 60s. A beautiful four-story walk-up. In Bermuda the house was set between the ocean and a lagoon on a point jutting out toward the ocean.

It was stunning, and my reward for joining him down there was bringing my wife with me and having a fantastic traditional English lunch of roast lamb and Yorkshire pudding. It was as delicious as the views we enjoyed.

My meeting in Paris went beyond if that were possible. We met; I taught. We had dinner with our wives at La Tour d'Argent, the purported oldest restaurant in Paris (1582), where they claim the fork was invented. However, according to my research it was invented in the Middle East in the year 1000. Regardless, they did serve a very special duck.

Not only did the duck come with its own pedigree tag but it was served three ways in three different sauces. It was delicious but resulted in some of us falling in love with the toilet bowl later in the evening. Rich, very rich. And you had to be very rich to eat at this restaurant, as it cost around $100 per person, 40 years ago.

Fortunately my expense account was able to handle the charges. Unfortunately all of my efforts to infuse Francis with everything we had done the previous seven years and more were not enough. Nor were his own intuitive and insightful efforts. The cost of media had grown to a level where there was simply no way to make the part work model work anymore.

Many years later I was living in Sausalito and running the Chiat/Day San Francisco office and bumped into Francis on the main drag in town. It turned out by coincidence he was now living in a rented house on the hill not far from my own home. We agreed to get together for dinner and did with our wives at a place called the Panama Hotel in San Rafael.

We very much enjoyed reminiscing about our past adventures together and hearing about plans that Francis had for another business. They soon moved from Sausalito and I never heard from Francis again.

CHAPTER 5

HANGING BY THE GALLOS

"THE AGENCY DOESN'T LISTEN."

"The agency doesn't get it."

"The agency doesn't hear what we told them!"

The E&J Gallo account was reputed to be the most difficult account in the world. And I am certain that it was, even having never worked on all the other accounts in the world (and that is not sour grapes). Trust me, though, it was not a lot of fun. Actually it was no fun whatsoever. Having an executive of any company screaming in your face that you don't listen and get it is hard.

Young & Rubicam first had the Gallo account in the early 1960s and lost it after four years. But then, they got it back at the end of the 1960s largely due to a creative fellow who was able to manage Ernest Gallo and his henchmen somewhat successfully, more successfully than most any other creative person who was ever involved with this crowd.

This was Hanley Norins, and in fact Y&R retained the business the second time around for almost 14 years largely because of him. Hanley was a very special and gifted man, with many unique talents. One day, however, he simply lost it with the Gallo gang and refused to work with them any longer.

I was sent out from Y&R New York in 1978 to "manage" the Gallo account. The agency was not doing particularly well at the time. I had run and worked on difficult accounts before but I had no idea that I was being sent on a suicide mission to California on Gallo.

I was able to sustain myself on the business for almost three years and was involved with some general office management matters as well during this time. I became seriously ill after trying very hard to effectively and logically manage the Gallo business. It turned out to be an impossible task. However, I am living proof that just about anything and everything you've ever heard about the Gallo business, the executives there and Ernest Gallo himself, is true. The folks that brought you the Spanish Inquisition could have learned much from these cannibals.

Though I suffered untold indignations, one of the best things that ever happened to me, careerwise and lifewise, was being assigned to the Gallo wine account out in "Go West, young man" California. It led me to opportunities that I otherwise never would have experienced. It also gave me an extra-special reserve of toughness that served me well going forward. Were it not for this, I might have called this chapter "Sour Grapes." Or you might have.

At the time, and 30-plus years later, the Gallo company reputation still swirls around advertising circles. Ernest and Julio have passed away; their legacy lives on. And, even after all these years I still suffer the pain and have the scars from working with them. Literally.

In 1977 the Gallo account was being managed, or rather the attempt was being made to manage it, by the Los Angeles office of Young & Rubicam. A fellow named Sid Marshall, then western regional director, had a philosophy of doing, casting, flinging, heaving, lobbing, shoving anything and everything at the account that he thought might keep them at bay, if only for even one more day.

The Gallo account was not unlike a *Wild Kingdom* documentary of a pack of raging wolves, with saliva dribbling from their snarling jaws and a mouth full of bared teeth. It was an ugly thing to run into.

Sid Marshall's strategy at Y&R LA worked for many years. It was never about managing the account forward. Rather it was about managing the account just to get to another meeting. When I arrived I became the latest comestible to be offered up by Y&R to the Gallo people. I was sent out from New York to "fix" the situation. I didn't anticipate that in accepting the Gallo assignment I might end up as roadkill.

Well-known San Francisco adman Hal Riney used to crow about his long-term relationship with the Gallo folks (I use the term "folks" extremely loosely, as they were far from folksy). Longer than any other agency, that being seven some years. Young & Rubicam actually held this dubious record of achievement. They had the account for a total of 18 years over two tours of duty.

I had faced numerous significant business challenges in my then relatively short career in the advertising world. But being involved with Ernest Gallo and his henchmen added an entirely new dimension to the word *challenge*. Actually *challenge* is not the right word at all. More like a situation of the absurd, the impossible, the insane, and the stupid.

Yes, stupid! *Webster*'s definition of which applies here beautifully. "Lacking in or exhibiting a lack of power to absorb ideas or impressions."

It was a crazy reality show of the preposterous and asinine. If a video cam had captured any of the proceedings, it would have made for a remarkable series of the irrational. It was real-life *Looney Tunes*. It was far more engaging and unbelievable than any of today's reality shows that frequent the airwaves and cable stations.

But there was a benefit. I was able to gather more bizarre stories to tell about my two-plus-year sentence than most people accumulate in a lifetime. And I have found that no matter where I go around the world, people are always fascinated hearing about the Gallos, particularly the bad, insane, and ugly parts, which are basically all the parts. Like the man said about chicken innards, "parts is parts."

The mandate from Gallo was to have a senior account person who had packaged goods experience assigned to their account. This is interesting. And may be a lesson here for many regarding the importance of a business school MBA and traditional training in the packaged goods industry. Later on I was also hired to run the Apple Computer account because the same requisite was made. "Get me a packaged goods person."

The advertising and marketing director at Gallo, a man named Walter Bregman, had previously been an account person at several big advertising agencies before joining Gallo. He had also worked at Procter & Gamble in high-level marketing jobs and became president of Playtex after leaving Gallo.

Wally had joined Gallo in 1974, just about five years before I arrived on the scene. Gallo had been a client at Leo Burnett in Chicago when he had worked there and he was fully aware of "their reputation as an impossible place to work."

Wally was quite a bright fellow who had an advanced and expansive mean streak, which he probably had not been able to put to full use in his previous employs. He didn't need to learn much from the Gallos. He came to the party and fit right into their "abuse" program.

Wally dreamed up the idea that somebody from the agency with some discipline in approaching the advertising and marketing issues that Gallo faced was required to run the account and might even help his situation in selling through various marketing programs. He was wrong, very wrong.

As far as I could see, Wally was an alpha dog in a pack of alpha dogs. He led and everyone else jumped in to devour the carcasses. I had the pleasure of working with Wally for only about a year.

After leaving Gallo, Wally bought a small hotel/resort somewhere in the Caribbean, which was never all that successful and was subsequently wiped out by a hurricane. I lost track of his whereabouts for a while and then came upon the book he wrote about his reminiscences in the ad business titled *Spray the Bear*. He devoted a fair amount of space to his Gallo years, but he never saw himself quite the way I, and others who had to work with him, did.

The higher-ups back at Y&R in New York (i.e., Alex Kroll, president), in all their wisdom, before setting their sights on me, sent out a fairly senior account person to fill Wally's request for a "proper" account man. Now, this account executive was a very personable guy who I think may have worked on a packaged goods account some time in his very long career at Y&R, for 20 minutes. He was not known for his business acumen on any important account that practiced packaged goods discipline, or any discipline, but rather for being very quick with a joke or two. He was more of a master of relationships type of guy. He knew the best restaurants, golf courses, whisky, and the like. None of which was relevant or applicable in any way to managing the Gallo account.

Critically, he couldn't have been more unfit to work with Wally Bregman, who was a smart, aggressive intellectual with real depth in marketing. Regardless, Y&R senior management had him fly out to meet with the Gallo folks.

This account executive was sent back to the Big Apple the very same day carrying a warning (i.e., threat) from Bregman, the CAD (chief alpha dog), and the rest of the pack. The message was clear. So much so that they didn't bother sending me out to "interview" as they had the last victim. They just sent me.

It's funny how this situation works in the advertising business. The same thing happened to me when I was hired at Chiat/Day to run Apple. They wanted a packaged goods person. They got one without ever meeting me beforehand. In advertising the reaction is often simply to give the client what he wants. In fact it's a lot better if you give the client what he wants, just before he knows he wants it. That's called intuitive and smart planning.

Truth be told, the only thing that the last account executive and Wally Bregman had in common was that they were Jewish. Other than that, there was nothing, not their experience, their clothes, their humor, their intellect, and so on. Ironically, I had no idea that he was Jewish until many years later. He didn't act or look the part and he certainly didn't seem to hold the values and/or morals that are common to many Jewish folks.

So that's how I became the next victim. Having had 13 years of concentrated packaged goods experience on accounts like Excedrin, Minute Rice, Jell-O, and others, I ended up with the misfortune of lasting northward of two very long years on the Gallo business. Think dog years.

My first visit to Gallo, located in Modesto, California, was highly illustrative. I flew out from New York. My gateway was San Francisco airport. Modesto was a solid 70-mph, 90-plus-minute, boring drive from San Francisco. This drive, which I took too many times to count, was very much like working on the Gallo business. You drive and drive and drive and seem never to reach your destination.

At this point I had not even met any of the various people working on the account teams, which were drawn from four different Y&R offices (San Francisco, Los Angeles, Chicago, New York). Gallo may well be where Y&R first learned the art of the "gang bang" approach to managing and presenting advertising to clients. Throw as many ads against a wall as you can and pray that something might stick. Very little ever did. But it took oodles of copywriters and art directors from all of these offices to fulfill the quantity required.

My inaugural arrival took place in the middle of the summer of 1977. It was hot! Modesto is in the California desert and it was 110 degrees that day. Gallo's headquarter offices were situated alongside one of their many manufacturing plants, in a contemporary concrete and glass Grecian kind of building (quite resembling a large mortuary, which is what it may well have been, where the living dead work and visit). It overlooked several dozen huge white fermenting tanks containing wine. Think Chevron.

As one approached the entrance to the administration building, it was extremely important to hop and skip and jump. This was to avoid stepping in the pies left all over the walks and steps and grass by the scores of peacocks roaming around the place dropping stuff wherever they pleased. I made it into the building with just a tiny bit stuck on one of my heels.

It was early in the morning and there were to be four separate advertising meetings during that day with the "Committee." The Committee was what they called a tight group of senior executives at Gallo. At the time it consisted of the aforementioned marketing and advertising director guy, Wally Bregman; a marketing research guy, Mike Boyd; a consultant type, Skip McLaughlin; one of Ernest's sons, David Gallo; Ernest's right-hand (and left-hand) man or consigliere, depending on your ethnic orientation, Albion Fenderson; sometimes an ex–Procter & Gamble guy named Pete Conway; and, of course, the celebrious man himself, Ernest. What they actually constituted was more like the Inquisition.

On some occasions the Committee would invite various product managers and assistant product managers who worked at the winery on whichever brand was under discussion into these meetings. I was in several meetings where they even brought in a bunch of college students they were interviewing for future employment, and had them participate in the "game" with the advertising agencies.

It occurred to me that they were hoping to see glimpses of each candidate's ability to dehumanize and insult the people who were trying to provide objective help and experienced advice. It was amazing how quickly that seemingly normal, innocent, and inexperienced people could become combative and evil when placed in this situation once they realized how the game was being played. Inevitably some of the best players at this game ended up getting hired and were able to help carry on the legacy.

I was in one meeting where they brought in a guy we had not heard of before. They didn't tell us anything and presented him as if he was taking over a key executive position. It so happened that this fellow had worked for Gallo years before and knew Ernest, the Committee, and the Gallo family quite well.

That particular day we were discussing what we were told was extremely confidential and not to be discussed outside the conference room. This guy sitting in the room that day, leading the meeting, turned out to be the head guy of direct competitor Seagram, Art Palombo.

Insipidity, confusion, irony, and Looney Tunes were always at play at

Gallo. It was a Machiavellian game. And with the incident with Art Palombo, it was no different. A few days after our meeting, a note was circulated to the entire Gallo organization. It went something like this: "Art Palombo joined us on Monday; I was fishing on Tuesday and when I returned from my trip I found he was gone. Ernest Gallo."

We didn't know who he was or why he was there and then only days later he was gone. His name was never mentioned again. Turns out, he actually had resigned from Seagram, where he had been executive vice president, and had joined Gallo, but after he arrived he was told he would be reporting to one of Ernest's sons, Joe Gallo.

Not happy about this, he asked Seagram for his old job back and they agreed to give it to him. He came back to Modesto, cleaned out his desk, got his clothes, which he had left behind, and ordered a limousine to take him to San Francisco airport, without ever saying a thing to anyone at Gallo. No one knew he was gone for good for at least an entire day.

But getting back to my very first day. As I mentioned, four Y&R offices were engaged in trying to feed this beast's insatiable appetite for creative work. I use the term "creative work" extremely loosely here. Just about anything that was concepted would qualify as fodder and feed, to dish out to this voracious monster. Strategy was a thing that did not concern them too much. In truth, all they really wanted was tonnage: lots and lots of ideas, black and white or color, with people and without, with copy and without, whatever. Completely and undeniably indiscriminate, so they could pick and choose what they liked from the bread basket that particular day.

"I'll have the sourdough."

"No, on second thought maybe the whole wheat."

"Then again, let me try that sesame bun."

"How about a croissant?"

"More please!"

"More please!"

Well, they never said "please."

The Y&R Los Angeles office was first into the ring that day and didn't disappoint. I met the agency group just minutes before they were to present print concepts for an E&J Brandy campaign. I hadn't seen the work that they were to present beforehand.

The meeting was extraordinary. The agency showed around 75 concepts for a print campaign. The print campaign was to be one ad. Each concept was "comped" up with actual photographs and overlaid set type. By the end of the meeting the conference room table, the walls, and even the floor were covered with all these concept ads.

Almost every one of these ads was a pun, with a photo of either the E&J bottle or a glass filled with the brandy. Some of the more "creative" ones had both the bottle and a glass. Or two. And a pun. The Gallo folks really really liked puns, such as "The Spirit of Christmas Present" or "Splendor in the Glass."

I hadn't a clue but the Committee was as impressed, as I learned later, as they generally ever were. After hours of discussion, which was mostly criticism, Albion Fenderson announced that they had a "possible interest" in one of the concepts. They had a possible interest in a single ad out of 75 presented. But, they wanted more time so they could think about it.

We broke for lunch and, to my surprise, I was invited to join the rest of the Committee to jitney over to a local restaurant, which if I remember correctly was called the Sun Dial. Gallo had its own small bus to shepherd its flock around Modesto. I could be wrong about the name, as I was wilting in the intense heat and not breathing too easily. The restaurant was nothing special except that when Ernest and the Committee walked in, everyone fell over backward to accommodate them.

"Good day, Mr. Gallo."

"Nice to see you today, Mr. Gallo."

"What a fine day it is, Mr. Gallo."

"Right this way, Mr. Gallo."

We were ushered into a simple but private rear room and I was told to sit directly across from Ernest. We actually had a pleasant conversation over some not very good fish. ("It's always fresh, but frozen in Modesto.") Ernest had left his Mr. Hyde outfit back at the office when he went to eat.

One time during my tenure on the account I had been invited to a private dinner at Ernest's home with Ed Ney (then Y&R CEO). You would never have known this was the same Mr. Hyde, I mean Mr. Gallo, who sat across the conference table at the winery. That night the three of us ate and had a jolly good time, while Ernest's wife scurried back and forth to the kitchen to offer this or that to try and please. They didn't seem to have any help. Ernest was a completely delightful host. Maybe food was the great calming influence in his life. The stomach is the path to the heart of a man?

At any rate, the most eventful thing at my lunch at the Sun Dial was watching Ernest drink a glass or two of white wine and start to fall asleep right there at the table. After finishing his meal, he had a cup of coffee, to which he added some white wine. Yucchh!

Not only did I learn about a new drink, a white wine coffee, but I learned it was not a good thing to have meetings with Ernest in the afternoon. Not only did he transform back to Dr. Jekyll, but he also spent most of the rest of the day in his chair in the conference room with his head tilted down. With his eyes shut. And, unlike the Japanese who do this kind of thing, Ernest was at times actually fast asleep, waking up every now and then with a grunt or two, to contribute a nasty criticism or comment or two.

I went through three more meetings that afternoon, each on a different Gallo brand. Different people from various Y&R offices presented. Every meeting had several themes in common. So much work was presented that it would have been difficult for even the most skilled advertising person to make intelligent decisions about any of the concepts. There was no inherent strategy that the work was developed against and therefore no way to judge whether it was strategically on message. Hence the ad concepts themselves were literally all over the map.

The work was always belittled and criticized. The agency people were always dressed down and abused and insulted by various members of the Committee. The agency people usually just sat there in a sort of stupor, with stoic faces, and let the verbal abuse roll over them like a wave, without saying a word.

A weird-ass fellow with a crooked eye most often led this advertising assessment hatchet process. His eyeball looked in a different direction from the other, always away from you, and the eye blinked in a bizarre manner as he spoke. He was kind of like a leadoff hitter in a baseball game trying to get on base or more appropriately make the first "hit." His blinking eye kept time with the intensity and anger of his remarks, as he told you how bad an idea was and what a piece of shit you were for bringing it to the meeting and wasting their precious time. This was Skip McLaughlin, who had been a fixture at Gallo for many years. He was a nasty dude and was respected and rewarded for it by Ernest.

There was one meeting where David Tree, Y&R LA creative director, and I were involved, which started just after lunch. It should have taken an hour, two at most. But the meeting ran on. And at this time, there was only one commercial flight out of Modesto to Los Angeles in the evening. United Airlines left at 6:30 and everyone at Gallo knew that, and they also knew that David wanted to get back for a special event he was involved with later that evening. Well, just to demonstrate what pricks they could be, they purposely kept the meeting going until 6, making sure we wouldn't be able to catch the last plane. And we didn't.

But David Tree was a bon vivant kind of guy, and he decided he was going to get back to LA no matter what. He chartered a small two-engine plane, which I made the mistake of agreeing to go on with him. It cost more than $1,000 and we hit a thunderstorm on the way down to Los Angeles. I thought the jig was up and I never flew on one of those small planes again. But David was able to make the last several hours of the party, the Gallo folks notwithstanding.

There are so many stories to tell of serving my time with these inmates. It's difficult to decide which are the most amusing and/or amazing. But a few stand out.

During my first six months we were trying to get approval for a commercial to support Gallo's Riesling. We had made many trips to Modesto with buckets of television storyboards and had finally received "interest" in one from the Committee, and then an actual approval to produce it.

It was a pretty commercial, to be shot in Hawaii, featuring a good-looking man and woman relaxing and playing around on a beach. There were intercuts of wine being drunk and food being eaten. The commercial didn't have any substantive underlying strategy or significant idea, but it contained beautiful shots of the landscape, the ocean, the food, and handsome people; and it had some nice music underneath it all. Of course, it featured the Gallo Riesling integrated here and there throughout the spot.

We were in Modesto to preproduce the commercial—that is, to get approval for every single last detail before we went off to shoot it on location. In my entire career, pre- and post-Gallo, I never ran a more intricate preproduction meeting. I had a fish on the line and was close to reeling it in, so I went out of my way to cover every last item.

We went over each and every frame in incredible detail with the full Committee and with Ernest participating grandly. Each nuance was covered as to the action and the propping and the like. Every aspect was reviewed, and it was expected that when we returned with the finished film, all the details would be reflected exactly as agreed in the meeting. And if the film didn't fulfill the agreements, Gallo had this funky habit of saying, "Well, we're not going to pay for it." But that only happened once to me, on my first day on the André Champagne account on a commercial that had been shot for a Thanksgiving promotion.

For the Riesling spot we had shipped up from LA to Modesto each and every item that was in each and every frame, and all of it was there in the conference room. I remember the big wooden crates that this stuff arrived in, as we had unpacked them in the room adjoining the main conference room. This was a complicated shoot and there were crates and crates of materials, including the plates, the food items, the flatware, the glasses, and more. There were alternate choices for each as well, so they could pick and choose, as was their custom.

I had flown in male and female models to display in the conference room, as well as to model the recommended clothes they could or would be wearing in the commercial. We had absolutely everything that you could imagine having to do with this production there for approval and for disapproval.

It had taken us six months to get the spot approved and I did not want to leave anything to chance. The meeting lasted the entire day. But Ernest was pleased. I actually saw him smiling at one point, as one of the very pretty female models came in wearing a proposed dress. He didn't say anything, but he lifted his right hand and raised his index finger and twirled it slowly in a counterclockwise circle, meaning that the model should turn around again. She did and, as she did, smiled at him. In turn, he smiled at her as she turned and he nodded his head ever so slowly up and down. Ernest was pleased, very pleased indeed, as all of this grandiloquent preparation had been done for His Excellency.

Part of this process had to do with the enthusiastic approval by Ernest and the Committee of one particular female model. We had shown several dozen casting videotapes of various male and female actors as candidates for the commercial. The Committee had reviewed the tapes over and over and over. In the end, they zeroed in on and approved a gal named Erin Gray, who had been at one time named the top model in New York by *Advertising Age* magazine. She was quite a stunning brunette. She was not a unanimous choice, however, but Ernest made the decision in the end.

There was much discussion at one point regarding the appropriate color of each model's hair but ultimately brown, as in Erin Gray, ruled the day. This despite a passionate argument made by a small minority in the room that the model's hair should match the color of the Riesling . . . that being yellow and logically therefore calling for a blonde.

It so happened that this very same week a new executive had arrived at Gallo who had been hired as the marketing director, replacing Wally Bregman. His name was Terry Laughren, and this was his first meeting with Ernest and the Committee. He wanted to impress!

For the most part he didn't get very much, if anything, that he argued for during the meeting. Frankly most of his discussion was quite lame, particularly so knowing that he had been an executive vice president at J. Walter Thompson advertising. He was in the minority arguing for the model's hair to match the wine, despite Erin Gray's breathtaking appearance and certain other attention-getting values.

The meeting ended on a very positive note and may have been my personal best meeting at Gallo, bar none. Some of us, including Terry Laughren, agreed to meet for dinner that evening. Also in attendance were the group product manager for the Riesling products, Lynn Jordon, and Gallo media director, Sue McClelland, along with a few other assorted Gallo people. Several folks from the agency joined me, but none of the Committee members were there.

We met at the most famous French restaurant in Modesto, called something like Coq au Vin. Actually it may have been the only French one. It served what French food might be like if prepared in the desert. Literally.

We were all seated at a large round table and I was across from Terry Laughren, when he suddenly made an announcement after several cocktails. HE was the marketing director and HE had decided that HE wanted to use a different model, a blonde model, in place of Erin Gray. All of us from the agency—David Tree, the creative director; Warren Lollich, an account supervisor; the television producer, whose name escapes me; and I—simultaneously said, "Terry, you do not want to do that."

A few drinks later Terry insisted on booking the blonde and unbooking the brunette right then. And we said in unison again, "Terry, you do not want to do that."

But Terry did want to do that. And he proceeded to order us to cancel Erin Gray and book the blonde.

"I AM the director of marketing and advertising. I AM the goddamn client. I AM taking responsibility for this. Now go ahead and get the blonde. End of discussion!"

"Okeydokey."

Both models were being handled by the Nina Blanchard Agency, and Warren Lollich had a direct line to Nina herself and did the dirty deed before we had gotten our coffee and key lime pies. I was feeling sick to my stomach and passed on the coffee and the pie. Whoever heard of a French restaurant serving key lime pie anyway?

We left dinner very sad indeed, knowing that a tsunami had been set in motion. Not only was the production of the commercial in jeopardy, but we anticipated the pain to come, which could not be overestimated.

I decided to call Albion Fenderson, Ernest's right-hand man, whom I referred to earlier as consigliere. I reached him first thing the next morning, and when I told him what had transpired, he screamed at me at the top of his lungs. I had to hold the phone away from my ear, but it still may be the cause of the tinnitus in my right ear. He blamed me for allowing this to happen, even if it was his new marketing director's directive. He ordered me to immediately get Erin Gray, the brunette, back and cancel the blonde. I called Warren Lollich to execute the new plan.

Warren was able to reach Nina herself again, but she advised that Erin had been booked already for another shoot. How this could have happened between 9:30 last night and 11 that morning I never quite understood. I always suspected that maybe, just maybe, Warren hadn't quite properly positioned the situation to Nina. I thought he may have told her the truth and she took advantage. You think?

Regardless, whatever was said, the only way Nina would even consider trying to get Erin back was if we were willing to pay her double the initial agreed-to rate AND that her husband be able to accompany her to Hawaii for the shoot because of changed circumstances. No doubt our agency was going to wind up having to pay for both of them, of course. Warren, without batting an eyelash, told her, "Done!" And we had Erin Gray back again. Warren was very proud of his accomplishment.

He was proud; I was relieved. I called Fenderson back and told him "the good news." He didn't bother saying thanks. He just grunted and hung up the phone. I had Warren call Terry and give him "the good news."

A few days later I was summoned to Modesto to report directly to Ernest on what had happened to cause this aforementioned situation. It was the only time in my years on the account that I was in Ernest's office. Standing next to him was, yep, you know who, Albion Fenderson. Ernest's son David was lurking around near the drapes by the window, or maybe he was in the drapes. He was a very strange dude. Ernest asked me to tell him exactly what happened and I did. Exactly!

Terry Laughren was very soon looking for another job. But it just shows to go you; everything turns out for the better. Last I knew, Terry ended up chairman of a merchant bank and his résumé lists, among other things, his extensive successful consumer packaged goods marketing and advertising experience including senior marketing positions at Procter & Gamble, Playtex, Mattel, and (drum roll here) E&J Gallo. I was told that when Gallo fired Terry, they had a limo waiting to take him to the San Francisco airport, and he was escorted out of the building by security and driven directly to the airport. Go to jail; do not pass go. What a full-service guy Ernest was.

Also included on Terry's résumé was that he was at one point president of Screenvision and as such got to go to the Cannes advertising film festival every year and schmooze and rub shoulders with lots of actors and actresses. Brunettes, redheads . . . and, yes, blondes.

About six months after this incident, fervor at the winery was heating up regarding the introduction of the Gallo upmarket Chardonnay and Cabernet. A huge investment had been committed to this endeavor years earlier. Now it was time to let the public know that Gallo finally made some truly fine wines, wines they hoped would significantly change the negative down-market image long associated with the Gallo name.

J. Walter Thompson had presented their recommendations on how to position these new varietal wines the day before, and October 16, 1978, was our opportunity. Not much was constant with this client except that just about every assignment was given to any number of advertising agencies in order to set up a continuously competitive situation and to provide Ernest and his merry band of men with that many more ideas to look at and compare. And also to be able to inflict more aggregate pain than would have been possible if only one advertising agency had been assigned to take the abuse.

Maybe the slyest thing about the way this all worked was that any advertising agency working for Gallo received no compensation whatsoever until they had an idea approved and actually on the air or in the magazines. However, when that did happen there was a handsome reward in receiving a full 15 percent commission on all the media that was placed. And Gallo was not shy about spending advertising dollars. This was at the heart of why any and all advertising agencies, large and small, wanted to play in this sandbox. It could be extremely lucrative. No matter how many bodies had to be sacrificed to the wine gods.

On that day, we were presenting our plan for the positioning and I was leading it. A fellow named Jim Hood, an account supervisor I had recruited from Y&R New York, had helped me put it together with some other folks and was there. We had a full-house audience, as everyone on the Committee was in attendance and several high-level executives from Y&R New York and

Los Angeles had flown out to acknowledge the importance of the occasion and to pay homage to Ernest.

Jim and I had built a completely objective and insightful interpretation and assessment, largely predicated on a huge market research study of the wine market that had been conducted by Mike Boyd, Gallo marketing research director. The presentation was extremely well thought-out, and I was quite proud of what we had developed and was happy and confident to be presenting it in front of my own management people. I was certain that we had nailed an appropriate strategic marketing and advertising direction for the new wines.

Gallo had invested tens of millions of dollars in bringing to market this attempt at a fine Cabernet and Chardonnay. Wines that would earn Gallo a place at the very top tier of the worldwide wine market because of their quality.

Over the years, through all sorts of marketing and advertising programs, Gallo had been unable to significantly elevate its image versus direct competitors like Paul Masson, Inglenook, Almaden, Taylor, and others. The investment in the new wine products was Gallo's strategic answer not just to equal these competitors but to leapfrog to another, higher level of perception. As such, it raised important questions on positioning the overall brand and the sub-brands carrying the Gallo name.

The fundamental issue was how to position these new wines within the Gallo family of wines. This was felt to be Gallo's last chance at elevating the name to the levels of other vintners. Gallo had tried many times, unsuccessfully, to do so in the past through products, publicity, and advertising, and this project's goal was to achieve that recognition within the industry and with consumers with the new products.

The task was immensely complicated by the fact that most of Gallo's volume and profits came from their well-known and best-selling Hearty Burgundy and Chablis Blanc, which were jug wines. These represented the primary face of Gallo that everyday consumers saw and purchased when they entered supermarket and liquor stores across the country. And that was what they were mostly buying and drinking from Gallo.

But beyond that, there was a dirty little secret that some knew and many suspected. Gallo also marketed tons of wines that had nothing to do with quality, but which many people knew came from Gallo. Night Train, Thunderbird, Boone's Farm, Carlo Rossi, to name a few. This association did not help elevate Gallo's standing as a fine winemaker to be taken seriously. They made a fortune selling gallons and gallons of this stuff, importantly to homeless street people, urban markets, and kids under the legal drinking age.

Each agency had been asked to present their completely unadulterated and objective points of view about all aspects of the marketing and advertising issues. As a side topic, no doubt included as a humorous exercise, each agency was asked to address how the agency/client relationship might be improved. I took both these challenges at face value and presented a brutally frank, objective, and unbiased assessment. Big mistake!

We had a long meeting where we presented these very well-thought-out recommendations on how to move forward with the new Gallo wines known as Wine Cellar Varietals. It is important to point out here that we were officially the agency of record for what Gallo referred to as the premium wines (Hearty Burgundy, Chablis Blanc). These were the generic red wines and white wines that accounted for the bulk of the Gallo brand business and were supported with by far the largest part of Gallo's overall advertising budget. J. Walter Thompson was the official agency for the mid-varietal products (high-end nonblended types) for which there was very little advertising or demand.

One part of our presentation recommended that Gallo not abandon support of the premium wines in favor of the introduction of the new high-end ones. This was concluded in a completely unbiased and impartial manner and was supported with many strong arguments and facts. After all, it was the meat and potatoes, generating most of the profit for the winery. If it had been my business, I would have been very concerned about jeopardizing this segment in any way.

However, Ernest and the Committee took umbrage with this recommendation and interpreted it to mean that we were simply trying to protect our billings and income on the account. JWT had recommended just the opposite of what we had and hadn't suffered the indignity of being called self-serving liars, as we were. Other recommendations we made having to do with each wine type positioning and overall Gallo corporate advertising were not well received either.

Toward the end of our presentation David Gallo, the eldest son, he of the drapes, who had been sitting directly across from me at the conference table, began to insert the end of a paper clip directly into his eyeball. This was something that he apparently did from time to time, although we never knew what the impetus was for such bizarre behavior. I think we found out during this presentation.

The last subject we addressed was the issue of the agency and client relationship and how it might be improved and made stronger and more valuable to Gallo. Big Mistake Number Two.

We took our seats after finishing our presentation, and as was not unusual in a Gallo meeting, there was not a sound. Nothing. Nada. Not even a nervous cough. There were at least 25 people in the room, along with this deafening silence. This continued for a full five minutes, which may have been a record. Some people stared at their pads with various notes they had scribbled during the presentation. Others just kind of looked around the room, up at the ceiling, out the windows.

And then Ernest, as he was prone to do when angry, started to slowly tap, tap, tap the tip of his pencil on the conference room table. This went on for a few more minutes with still no one saying anything. Then David Gallo burst up from his seat and started screaming . . . literally: "The agency doesn't listen! The agency doesn't listen! They don't get it! They don't get it! They don't understand what we're trying to do."

His hands were shaking as he held them up in the air like a preacher. Months later I found out that David was a desperate and depraved alcoholic or ex-alcoholic, whose mental balance had been dramatically affected. I wasn't surprised to hear that he was found unconscious in his bathtub years later. Dead at age 57.

So to make a long story a bit shorter, my presentation was an abject failure. The agency was viewed as making a case only to protect their own skin and not a case in the interests of Gallo. I was told to my face that I had no idea how to interpret the data that emerged from the marketing research study and that we needed to have Mike Boyd, their research director, re-present the study to all the Y&R people, because we didn't "get it" the first time. They ordered us back the next week. They did this even though they acknowledged that this was going to be an enormous waste of Mike Boyd's time, but out of the goodness of their hearts they would make this accommodation.

It didn't matter of course that I fully understood how to interpret the data, having been a marketing research director prior to joining Y&R, and that the other people at Y&R who helped me were smart and well grounded in doing this kind of thing on a regular basis. In fact they were far smarter and more experienced than Mike Boyd or any of the Committee members.

Nevertheless, the following week a group of us returned to Modesto to hear again the findings of the research. Some important executives from Y&R New York were there, including the creative director, Frazier Purdy. Mike Boyd was just about to begin when into the room walked Albion Fenderson. Then came David Gallo and a few minutes later Skip McLaughlin. I knew that I was in trouble and I was right.

Skip directed his remarks to me and had his one good eye intensely staring at both of mine. He demanded a full apology for what we had presented the week before. He told me what a moron I was and more, which was seconded by David Gallo, whose head was bucking up and down like a horse on a short bit in agreement.

Putting on an Oscar-winning performance, I took the fall. I said to the three of them, "It's obvious I didn't understand the material that was presented to us and I reached some spurious conclusions and I am very sorry I wasted all your time."

After I got up off my knees, Skip and Albion left the room without a word and Mike Boyd proceeded to re-present the research. David Gallo hung around crouched in a chair at the back of the room, emitting strange sounds every now and then like a chimpanzee.

I had learned that right or wrong did not matter whatsoever to these people. And the only thing that did to me at that point was making it to another meeting. And that is exactly how I ran the account from that day on, with Sid Marshall's strategy of making it to another meeting. It worked for another 30 months.

Turns out that when we next re-presented our recommendations, we still called for supporting the Gallo premium brands that Y&R represented. I had made some adjustments in the presentation language and the size of the budgets and recommended a new, considerably smaller budget to support an overall corporate advertising campaign. But most of the thinking was essentially the same, as were the recommendations from the initial presentation.

But this time Gallo and the Committee listened and offered no response when we were done. They must have needed to hear it all again to understand it, in the same way they thought I needed to hear the research again. I can only imagine that when we left the room the consensus was, "Gee, maybe they really do believe what they are telling us" and "Maybe they have a valid point of view."

In the end, Gallo never put any significant advertising money behind the new high-end varietals. They left it to wine reviews, PR and publicity, and word of mouth to get out the entire story. Just like we had recommended, the first time and the second time.

At the repeat meeting, I didn't revisit the subject of how the agency and client might work more effectively together. What was the point?

One day sometime later I was looking out my Y&R LA Wilshire Boulevard office windows, considering the situation in which I found myself. All of a sudden I got a stabbing pain in my left eye. It got worse over the next few hours and worse again after that. Someone suggested going to an eye doctor, which I then did. He advised that it was one of two things and we would know for sure the next day.

The next day I came down with herpes zoster (shingles) on the left side of my head from front to back and down into my left eye, including the pupil, iris, and cornea. I broke out in horrible boils and blisters over most of the left side of my face. It was extremely painful. I couldn't see out of either eye for a long time. I was on powerful painkillers for months. I was out of the office for almost six months and spent the first three months at home in bed on my back hardly able to move. I had contracted a particularly severe case of this disease, one I had never even heard of before.

I didn't have anything to do with Gallo during this period. And surprise, surprise, not a single person from the Gallo Committee called to ask how I might be doing. Several of the product managers, including Lynn Jordon and Rick Kurz, were in touch, and both remain lifelong friends.

I also heard a number of times from a man who may have been the greatest executive ever at Young & Rubicam. That would be Ed Ney, who was the chairman/CEO for a long period and whom I got to know a bit when I was in New York. He sent me a wonderful motivating note and some book audiotapes to help pass the time, as he knew I was unable to use my eyes.

During this time I never did hear from a guy named Alex Kroll, who was the president of Y&R and responsible for sending me out into the Gallo inferno in the first place. In my opinion, not a man known for his compassion or social skills. Others at the agency held a similar view of him.

However, I must say that Alex did once present me with a neat pair of Adidas running shoes in my earlier days in New York. He had someone sew bright red stars all over them. It was a gift for having won the Bristol-Myers new analgesic business, Datril 500. In those days I wouldn't have dreamed of spending $50 for a pair of sneakers and I admit that I cherished them and the thought behind them. So I guess Alex did have some social and motivational skills, but only for a winning perspective and not for a loser on Gallo like me.

Fred post herpes zoster shingles; note scars on forehead.

When I was finally well enough to return to work, I scheduled a meeting up at Gallo in Modesto almost the day I returned to the office. I was still pretty injured and fragile and I really shouldn't have been traveling, but I thought it was the thing to do in order to demonstrate a commitment and interest. I struggled getting there, and when I arrived it was to attend a creative meeting with the Committee.

These meetings always took place in the aforementioned main conference room, which had large windows on one side facing the seats where the agency personnel traditionally were told to sit and confront the Inquisitors. It was always hard to see the people on the other side of the table because the light behind them made them appear like dark silhouetted shapes. I could barely see their faces, which were masked by the backlight. It was harder still when the sun was bright, as it was that day.

I walked into the Gallo conference room uncertain with each step I took until I reached the chair I was to occupy. My head hurt quite a bit and every single hair follicle on the left side of my head was extremely sensitive to the touch, so much so that even the lightest wind made it very painful. I had a difficult time keeping my head in an upright position, and most discomforting, I couldn't see out of my left eye, which was extraordinarily sensitive to light.

I was one of the first in the room, and I got up and hobbled over to the windows and partially closed some of the blinds, as the sunlight was magnified and was reflecting intensely off the rows of huge white wine tanks situated a hundred yards or so from the conference room windows.

Moments later Albion Fenderson entered the room and grabbed the cords and raised all of the blinds so the sunlight came streaming in and directly into my face. He knew exactly what he was doing.

During the meeting, I could hardly hold my head up and had to keep my eyes mostly closed. I should have had my sunglasses on but didn't. It was not a pretty sight, as I truly looked like a wounded animal. When I returned to Los Angeles the next day, my boss, Sid Marshall, told me that Gallo had called and didn't want to see me in Modesto again. My immediate reaction was disbelief and anger, but then I felt, what else would you expect from these insensitive moronic people? I was only the latest in a very long list of victims who had suffered from their pinheaded way of conducting business.

As I write these words I still suffer from neuralgia in my scalp, sensitivity in the follicles of the hair on my head, reduced vision in my left eye, light sensitivity, and distorted skin in my left eyelid.

Strangely, the eyelashes in my injured left eye grow downward and into my eyeball so I have to remove them from time to time with blunt-edged tweezers. No one is sure what causes herpes zoster other than an activated dormant chicken pox virus that somehow comes alive again and travels up one of the spinal nerves. There are some who believe it might have something to do with stress. Duh!

So that's the way I got off the Gallo account. It was not very glorious and extremely painful in every way. It was my hanging by the Gallos.

Nevertheless, it allowed me to then go on and experience many more adventures in the crazy advertising business, none of which were as hateful and stupid as what this bunch of cretins in Modesto were able to dish up.

Remarkably, Gallo was an incredibly successful enterprise. They sold more wine than anyone for many years; they controlled the distribution in supermarkets with an iron hand; they were able to manage the unions that they dealt with. They treated many people like dog shit, but it didn't seem to matter.

I have been asked many times why these people acted the way they did, and to tell the truth I can't really say. If I had to guess, it was simply a lack of respect for advertising and for advertising people. And a large amount of hubris and a belief that they surely knew more about anything that had to do with business than anyone else. Even advertising.

It's ironic that with all their gymnastics and a fair amount of money invested in advertising, in my opinion Gallo has never truly built a premium brand in the wine category. I believe that Gallo to this day is still generally looked on as a brand far inferior to many others, including the most obscure and inexpensive ones. You just don't hear people dining at Le Cirque, the Four Seasons, or the French Laundry saying, "I'll have a bottle of the 2003 Gallo Cabernet Sauvignon" too often. If ever!

Several months later the end came for Gallo and Y&R as well. Ed Ney was able to engineer the acquisition of the United Vintners wine account in San Francisco, contingent on giving up Gallo. It was half the size in importance, but a no-brainer in terms of the decision at that point. And so this forms the last part of my story on Gallo, although I could write an entire book on many other escapades.

I was vacationing with my wife in Hawaii, when the decision to resign from Gallo was made. I received a call from Sid Marshall, still western regional director of Y&R, who had decided he was not going to advise Gallo right away, but wait until after we announced the United Vintners assignment in the press. I suggested strongly to him that this would not be a good thing to do, but he did it his way . . . anyway.

When Gallo finally learned what was going on, Albion Fenderson and company were fit to be tied. Ernest was out of the country but reportedly was livid. Not only did Y&R have the audacity to resign, but the agency did not tell them beforehand. They had to read it in the papers. Of course it was a wonderful way to slap them in the face and then rub some dirt in it, if one didn't think that they might retaliate. Which I did.

Gallo then insisted that we continue to work on the account for the contractual three-month termination period, and added more work than ever during that time. They even made up work for us to do, work that they had no intention of ever using. They were as mean as they could possibly be and made everything as difficult as they could. At the same time, we immediately had to begin servicing the United Vintners business because McCann Erickson, the predecessor agency, dropped everything on the account the minute they learned they had lost it.

Only two people believe the final piece to this story, Sid Marshall and me. Specifically what happened to Y&R six months later, on the same day, within 30 minutes. Without any prior warning, the agency was unexpectedly fired on Eastern Air Lines, Armour Foods, and Ralph's Grocery Stores. These were important clients, all with critical ties to important unions, we presumed the very same unions that worked with Gallo.

The relationships on all three accounts between the agency and each respective client were excellent at the time. Just one week before this happened Sid Marshall and I had lunch in a downtown LA restaurant with Ralph's Grocery Stores chairman Byron Allumbaugh and president Pat Collins. We had a terrific friendly lunch, they loved what we were doing for them, they liked all the people on the account, and they thought the advertising was right on and working. We were fired the next week.

Of course all this was just speculation, suspicion, and maybe coincidence, but there were at least two of us who believed that's how it went down. No one will ever know for sure . . . except maybe Ernest, but he's not going to tell.

Ernest Gallo: Salut!

CHAPTER 6

HOW I GOT INTO ADVERTISING

I was the general manager of the Young & Rubicam Los Angeles office, and I had worked for four years growing the office, an office that had had no identity whatsoever when I first arrived from New York City in 1978.

At the same time, I had helped manage the more important accounts then at the agency, including the difficult E&J Gallo Winery.

Critically, I had driven the effort to save the Security Pacific Bank account, a long-term essential business for the agency, which had been threatening to leave. Finally, I had been successful at winning some significant new accounts, including Sanyo Electronics, Suzuki motorcycles, Mattel's People Protection Products, and Ralph's Grocery Stores.

I was able to accomplish all of this while having to work for a very political and deceptive executive. It was always my feeling that this fellow had an uncanny way of not taking responsibility for any of the problems or things that went wrong but somehow managing to take all the credit for the good things that happened.

It all began just after a fateful meeting with an entrepreneur named Don Sawyer, who was a client. Don had successfully created several start-ups, among them Wimpy's and the Original Cookie Co.

When I first met Don he was heading up a start-up division for Mattel called People Protection Products. The idea was to provide kiosks in strategic locations like Sears, Roebuck; Kmart; and airports with products related to individual personal security protection of one kind or another. It was a clever idea that was too far ahead of its time.

We had just finished a key meeting with Don and were about to conduct the second in a series of focus group sessions that evening. It so happened that I had a long-planned dinner engagement with another client, Uri Harkham, and his wife. He was founder and CEO of Jonathan Martin Fashions. My wife Jeri and I were to meet them at a private club to which I belonged called Pips.

I joined this club at the urging of my boss, who was a member and who offered to have the agency pick up my dues. It was situated in Beverly Hills, on Robertson Drive, and was a place that many show-biz people frequented. Essentially it was a private eating club, but it also offered a small discotheque and backgammon and of course the celebrities. Underneath it all it was an upscale pickup joint in which Hugh Hefner owned a part.

I didn't disco and I didn't backgammon and I didn't pick up women, but the place sounded like fun and there was added prestige and exclusivity to having dinner there.

This membership gesture was offered to me after one of my successful new business conquests. It's funny how things work out, as it would end up being very much regretted by my boss that I was ever a member in good standing.

As the meeting with Don Sawyer wound down, my boss took me aside and asked me if I was attending the focus group session that night. I told him I'd been to the one the night before and had a previous engagement set up for that evening. It so happened I had already discussed the matter with Don and he was just fine with the arrangement, as others from the agency were going to be in attendance.

But my boss insisted. "I don't care what you've got planned. I want you at that research session tonight."

I replied, "I have a dinner engagement with another client that was set long ago. I went to the one last night. I know what's going on and Don has no problem with me not being there."

He raised his voice and ordered me to go. "You just be there."

I refused and said, "If it's so damn important to you, then you go."

Then he informed me, "I have something important to do."

"Oh . . . I see. Your important is more important than my important."

I was fuming and angry and very upset. I went to the bathroom and took some deep breaths and threw some water on my face to try to cool down. My heart was racing and I could feel the adrenaline shooting throughout my body. I had a headache.

I dried my face off and went down to the garage, got in my car, and drove off to Pips. The dinner reservation was for 7:30 and I arrived at the restaurant at 6:45. I went in, and as I entered the front door, coming in from the bright LA sunshine and the searing heat, it was cool and very dark. There was not a soul in the place.

I took a seat at the bar and ordered a straight-up vodka martini. With two olives. The drink arrived and I sat there mulling over the events of earlier, sipping slowly, nibbling on one of the olives, and letting the alcohol take its soothing calming effect. I remember thinking that my stonewalling and refusal was surely going to turn into a significant longer-term problem. I was right. I drained the glass, ate the second olive, and ordered another.

Now, the bar at Pips had a mirror that ran its length and from the back bar to the ceiling. And, if you were sitting at the bar, you could pretty much view about everything in the entire restaurant, which was behind the bar stools. I took another sip of my second "see thru" and noticed some movement in a dark corner of the restaurant, way in the back. I took another sip, and took another look. My eyes focused a little better through the dimness and I could not believe what I was now seeing and hearing. But could it be the second drink, I wondered?

No, it was not. Lo and behold there was my boss and my office manager. This gal was an attractive young lady, half the age of the guy she was with. I had heard when I first arrived at the agency that there may have been some kind of relationship between them. What kind I didn't know. It apparently dated back to long before I had arrived in California. Under his tutelage, she had risen up the ranks to administrative office manager, doing this and doing that.

Well, there they were, just the two of them, in this little corner booth. They each had cocktails in front of them and I could now hear the muffled sound of their conversation and then the distinctive laugh of a younger woman politely acknowledging some possibly witty comment from the older gentleman she was with. Or possibly not witty at all.

So this was the "important" engagement he had. This was the man charged with making responsible executive decisions for an entire region, which included five separate offices spread over three states. This was my boss.

If I was angry before back at the agency, now I was boiling over, foaming at the mouth. The calming effect of the martinis faded quickly. I could feel the adrenaline shooting again into my bloodstream and my heart started to beat rapidly. It was that fight or flight feeling that one gets when coming face-to-face with a big black bear. I emptied my glass in a swig, pulled up me pants, tightened me belt, and walked me straight back to where the two were sitting.

I never acknowledged that his lady friend was even sitting there but rather glared only at my boss and said, "You son of bitch, this is what you had to do? This is what you had to do that was so important? This is what was more important than what I had to do? I'm not going to forget this, my friend, ever." And neither would he.

Then I invited him to come over when my guests arrived and pay his respects to our mutual client. He didn't say a word. He looked up at me with a sheepish kind of grin. The lady friend sat there the whole time with an impassive and aloof, half-smirky smile. I turned and went back to the bar and ordered a third martini.

This guy was always pretty stoic, even under the most trying circumstances. He had this weird way of smiling, kind of sarcastically, during unexpected situations. And there was no doubt that this was one of those occasions. He stood his ground, although he was actually sitting, and just glared up at me. He kind of pulled his lips back across his teeth as if getting an injection in his buttock. You know, the way you think it's going to relieve some of the prick. But it doesn't.

My client Uri and his wife arrived, as did Jeri. We had a delightful and productive dinner. How could it not be after all the vodka I had consumed?

I happened to be seated facing that same mirror on the back bar when about midway through the dinner I noticed two people kind of creeping slowly along the bank of tables set against the far wall nearest to the exit. It seemed that they hoped their exit would go unnoticed.

But I saw them and they saw me seeing them. I realized right then that this was probably the end of my career working with this guy whom I had caught with his pants down, so to speak.

Not too long after this incident I made what was for me a very difficult decision. I had always thought that my career in "advertising" would be solely at Y&R. I had been there for 15 years. I had accomplished a lot. I had been rewarded for my efforts. It never occurred to me, in good or bad times, to consider leaving the company, although I had had several offers over the years. But now I made the decision to leave.

The thing that made me most nervous about this was protecting my family, since I had a wife and two teenage kids at the time. In addition, I had a mortgage on a small house in Bel Air. The house had cost me four times what I had sold my house back East for when I was first sent out to California. I do confess, however, that my aforementioned boss was kind enough to offer to help. He contributed $10,000 of company money to reduce my $300,000-plus mortgage. What a guy!

It seemed to me that not much good could possibly result in staying on. And I was aware too that, more often than not, when someone was sent out from the Y&R New York office it was usually with a one-way ticket. I figured I might have had one of those, because along with numerous successes at Y&R New York, I had left a somewhat scorched path among several executives. I had this nasty habit of being direct and telling things like they were. I thought that was being honest. In the corporate environment this was not a career helper, however, and was definitely counterculture.

For several months I wrestled with what exactly to do. I had a hard time sleeping and couldn't focus any longer on doing all the things I needed to do to run the office. My wife got me interested in building small plastic model cars. This activity took my mind off the problems at least for four or five hours at a time.

Then one day I had a vision or epiphany or whatever you want to call it.

I had a good track record in attracting new business. As it turned out one business in particular, Ralph's Grocery Stores, became the most important to me personally. It was the basis of executing my plan to leave Y&R.

Ralph's was a very visible business, being the most important supermarket in Southern California at the time. They also had a nice-size budget that was over $5 million.

But this had only indirectly to do with my decision. The greatest consequence was that when I pitched the business it was extremely competitive.

An ad agency called DJMC had had the account for many years, and when the review was started virtually every agency in Southern California and then some competed, including one called Chiat/Day.

Advertising agencies on the West Coast were doing very creative and edgy ads. But that's not what they believed on Madison Avenue. In their minds, New York was and would always be the center of the advertising business. The 1976 *New Yorker* magazine cover by Saul Steinberg of a map of the entire country said it all. Looking westward, three quarters of the picture was made up of Manhattan and the Hudson River, another 10 percent was the state of New Jersey, and the entire rest of the country plus Japan and China made up the remainder of the view.

The truth was, however, that the very best creative work was coming from West Coast agencies, large and small. And there I was at Young & Rubicam Los Angeles, sitting in the midst of it all but not participating.

As a student of advertising, or so I thought, I went home and, unlike most people, turned the television on at night to watch the commercials, not the shows. In doing this when I relocated to Los Angeles, I saw many neat, highly creative commercials. And more often than not, it turned out that this agency called Chiat/Day had been responsible for creating the commercials I liked. I very much admired the work they had done and were doing.

The review for the Ralph's account in the end came down to just two agencies: Y&R LA and Chiat/Day. This was a big deal for me. The fact that we beat Chiat and ended up with the account was an even bigger deal.

And it was this circumstance that gave me the chance to see what Chiat's losing presentation to Ralph's looked liked. It was terrific. It was so creative in every aspect, from the materials that they sent soliciting the business to the creative work itself. Every detail was well thought-out and clever and of the highest quality. I was impressed. Indeed it shaped my perspective for the rest of my career.

In my mind my presentation to Ralph's, while strategically sound, lacked most of the things that made for great creativity and great advertising. I had presented what you might call a brilliant strategy but the creative work was more like Cream Farina.

Reviewing the Chiat work was exhilarating and I was jealous. Very jealous. I had saved that presentation and referred to it from time to time after we went to work for Ralph's. At the same time, I increased my surveillance of their work as it appeared in the marketplace from that point forward.

So it was not really a coincidence that once I decided to leave Young & Rubicam, I woke up one day to conclude that I should turn lemon into lemonade. Use the difficult situation I was in to exploit a potential opportunity. What could I lose?

I spent a good amount of time crafting a thoughtful letter, which I finally sent off to Jay Chiat at Chiat/Day on April 23, 1982. It explained who I was, what my accomplishments had been, and why and how much I wanted to work at Chiat/Day. It was a damn good letter, much more than the typical résumé. It was something I had carefully constructed. It may have been my best new business letter ever, with me as the service being offered.

Weeks and weeks went by and I didn't hear anything. Then I got a call from Guy Day, the Day in Chiat/Day. He wanted to meet although he said they had nothing specific to talk to me about. "I'd like to get together but we really have nothing to offer you at this time."

That was OK with me and so we met at the Biltmore Hotel in downtown LA on the second floor, which was where the Chiat/Day offices were then housed. The minute I walked off the elevator, I knew that I wasn't in Kansas anymore. I had entered the real world of advertising. And it was definitely not what I had been doing for the past 15 years.

The reception lobby was simple but contemporary and stylish, as was the receptionist. She was also perky and friendly and enthusiastic. But what struck me more than anything else was the display of the ads that the agency had completed. Every single one was better than the next. They were exhibited with a certain reverence and pride. Every one was better than any one that we could have put up from my current agency.

Ultimately I came to learn that the Chiat ads were always referred to as the "work." Meaning the creative work. It was extraordinary that I had never once heard that expression in all my years at Young & Rubicam and yet at Chiat just about everything that was done was about the "work."

I admit the first few times I heard various Chiat people referring to the "work" I didn't really get what they were talking about. The concept of such intense focus on the company's product had initially escaped me. Just how ingrained it was in their culture was remarkable. And it eventually became ingrained in me as well.

A vitality and an incredible sense of energy surrounded me while I waited in that reception area for Guy Day. The people who worked there all tended to be, it seemed, bright, young, energetic, and enthusiastic. Of course I didn't know that they were generally smarter and more talented as well.

Everyone was dressed casually, mostly in jeans. There I was sitting in a Mies van der Rohe Barcelona chair, in a three-button double-breasted dark blue pinstripe suit, white collared shirt, and matching blue and dark blue striped tie. I was a stereotypical picture of a Madison Avenue man. There was not one person with a suit or a tie to be seen among those whizzing back and forth through the Chiat reception area.

Which led me to a first obvious but still relevant conclusion regarding the "work." The "work" has nothing to do with the way you look or the way you dress! This was a concept that clearly escaped most of the folks at my current employ.

From where I was seated I could see into the beginning of the innards of the agency. There were people sitting in areas defined only by a five-foot white partition wall and an entranceway in front. There were six-inch-thick pushpin boards hung on two thin wires from the ceiling at either end, which served both as a separation from the next office space and as a convenient place to hang the "work." That these separations looked really neat and swayed a bit when bumped was an exceptionally small but impressive design element of the office space.

Work in progress and work completed and anything else that could be attached to these makeshift walls were there. It was a jumble of creative output and input, and what a sight it was. This is what the agency did and everyone's office throughout the entire place reflected that understanding and passion. It reeked of creativity, inventiveness, and innovation.

This agency had in one year won more creative awards than most could hope to in a lifetime. I could see some of them, Belding Award silver bowls and Clios perched here and there on a desk or on top of one of the office partition walls. Some were just lying there on their sides. They weren't on display. They had just been put there as part of the gestalt. They belonged there, along with all of the great ads that were everywhere.

There was one office cubicle that had Belding Award bowls placed one after the other all around the top of the wall divides. There were at least 35. Some of the bowls were stacked one inside the other.

I thought to myself how just about every other agency I had ever visited had a special precious cabinet, usually located in the main lobby, wherein they carefully and reverently placed those few creative awards they had garnered over the years. They were often lit up with halogen lights to highlight them even more.

Here, there was no such cabinet, and while winning the awards was a very important part of the Chiat/Day culture, collecting them all in one place and displaying them was clearly not. It was much more about doing the next great ad and reaping the emotional rewards that came with it. More often than not, awards were simply an acknowledgment from colleagues at the agency and those creative folks who toiled at other creative agencies like Chiat/Day trying to do the same thing.

It occurred to me at that moment that this was indeed what the advertising business was supposed to be about. It was not about conducting a successful strategic review board with top management. It was not about holding a client's hand through thick and thin. It was not about coming to work from nine to five. It was not about scheduling the next golf game. It was not about being recognized with a pea green two-seat leather sofa that I was entitled to and was issued when I got promoted to account supervisor or getting a three-cushion version when I made management supervisor.

It was not about the very proper quiet hush-hush environment, elegant mahogany walls, and three-inch-deep carpet that graced the executive floors of the agency where I was presently employed. I thought back to my days at 285 Madison Avenue and the executive sixth floor, where there was a distinct absence of noise and oxygen. And ads for that matter.

It was definitely not about how many ceiling tiles you had in your office. In my past experience, both in New York and in Los Angeles, the number of tiles was directly correlated to the position you held and/or your seniority at the firm. This knotty problem was eliminated at Chiat/Day, since everyone essentially had the exact same space. No counting tiles necessary. And since the entire office was an open space environment, any discussion of this matter was completely irrelevant anyway.

It was not about being a vice president or a senior vice president or an executive vice president or even president. It really didn't matter much who you were or what station you held at the agency. It was about how smart you were. And it was about the "work."

When Chiat/Day did a self-promotion ad, it was also about the work. What a brilliant, simple way to explain the agency and totally focus on the work. Show their ads with a headline: "How to tell Chiat/Day from an ad agency." Brilliant!

Chiat/Day Advertising, Los Angeles, New York, San Francisco

⊘ ⊘ ⊘

Ten minutes went by and Guy Day finally strolled into the lobby and said, "Hi." He was a tall man, with a fuzzy gray beard and kind of unruly curly salt and pepper gray hair all over his head. He had a big friendly smile and a very casual manner.

Guy was a guy always trying to make a joke out of whatever. I had a sense that this may have been a bit of a defense mechanism since the contrast between him and Jay Chiat was so enormous, Jay being a slick, tough, no bullshit, get to the point kind of guy who was almost always sarcastic and trying to keep you on the edge and defensive. Guy would be wearing Rockports, and Jay, Bruno Maglis.

Without even shaking my hand Guy said, "Hey, let's go." I followed him to the elevators and was a bit disappointed that I wasn't going to get to see any more of the agency, at least not that day.

Instead of pushing down, he pushed up. The agency maintained a hotel suite on the eighth floor, which served a number of purposes, and interviewing people like me was one of them. I had expressed a concern that I might be seen and that the word would get back to my current employer with nasty ramifications since I was still gainfully employed.

This suite also served other, maybe more important functions, like providing a place for visiting executives and clients to stay; a "sick" room required by law, since there was none in the completely open environment on the lower floor where the agency was situated; and possibly a place for other extracurricular activities, although I can't be certain of that.

My meeting with Guy was fine and fun, but then I didn't hear anything for several more weeks until a fellow named Monty McKinney called. Monty was chairman emeritus or something. He said he'd like to get together for lunch although "we have nothing specific to talk to you about."

Monty was a considerably older fellow than Guy. He had a history of having been with other creative-oriented agencies, notably Doyle Dane

Guy Day, cofounder of Chiat/Day.

Bernbach. He was meant to be a symbol, I suspect, more than anything else.

We went to lunch at some private club in downtown LA. It was a pleasant lunch (I had a small house salad, scallops, and string beans) and I didn't hear anything from anyone for several more weeks.

Then I received a letter from Monty telling me how much he enjoyed our meeting and that while they "had nothing at the time," if something came up he would be in touch. Boy, how many of these very same letters had I written? It felt like a kiss of death, particularly since I had been on a cloud of excitement when I looked in the mailbox the day the first envelope had arrived with the Chiat/Day address in the upper left-hand corner. I had undertaken still more investigation and concluded that I really wanted to work at Chiat.

Two more weeks went by and I received a call from Monty asking if I could fly to New York to meet with Jay Chiat even though "they had nothing specific to talk to me about." I said absolutely. And I did.

I arrived in Manhattan around 8:30 p.m. and was to meet Jay that night at the then Chiat New York offices in the Tishman Building at 666 Fifth Avenue. The offices were kind of ominous, dark and quiet, and there was hardly anyone there. It was a stark contrast to what I had encountered at Chiat/Day Los Angeles. I learned later this was because they had very little business in the office at the time.

It was a weird meeting and Jay made it even weirder by including a gal named Jane Newman. Jane had recently been recruited to establish an account planning function at the agency. She was a Brit and had newly arrived from London. She was kind of aloof and strange. Big and tall too.

I had this odd feeling that the two of them wanted to get the meeting with me over as quickly as possible so they could get on with whatever other meetings they may have already planned for later that evening. What they had planned was only later confirmed by Chiat associates.

You probably couldn't find two people who were more different in many respects than Jay and me. But there was much common ground as well. He was smart, straight at you and to the point, critical, a perfectionist of sorts, driven, and competitive. He had Bronx blood in him, having grown up there, and he was Jewish, though I didn't know it at the time.

Jay Chiat

I shared all of these similarities with him but I wasn't quite as concerned about my appearance, physical or emotional, as Jay was. And while I was driven and had a reputation for being tough and tough on people who were less so, Jay carried this to an ultra-extreme. He had a strange way of motivating the people whom he most depended on and who were his most important assets.

He also, like Solomon of biblical fame, had many wives and concubines, although Solomon with 700 wives and 300 concubines had more. I had but one wife.

Jane Newman was another matter. As with most of the Chiat/Day people she was smart, competitive, and driven. She had a point of view and wasn't afraid to express it. But she was incredibly detached and haughty, and on first meeting she appeared to be a bit arrogant about herself and her station in life at Chiat/Day. She looked a bit like a lion to me for some reason, with a big mane of hair and large ominous teeth, which she bared when she attempted to smile. She used those teeth politically to further her position despite Jay's aversion to anyone who practiced politics around Chiat/Day.

At any rate, I got through the evening and flew back to LA in the morning and found a message waiting for me at home, asking if I could meet with Lee Clow, Chiat's creative director, the next day. Believe it or not, again the message reiterated that "they didn't have anything specific to talk about with me," but Lee was an important creative guy and it would be good to meet him anyway.

I kind of felt at this point that they very much had something specific to talk to me about, but they weren't ready to do it just yet. This was soon to be confirmed.

Even at that time Lee Clow was becoming a creative legend. He of course went on to become a full-fledged legend, and deservedly so. I met with him at a dark squirrelly bar of his choice, on the west side of LA somewhere on Pico Boulevard, no doubt because it was on his way home. We had a few drinks and talked about this and that for over two hours. It was very pleasant and enjoyable and I left really liking Lee. And I think he liked me. He was surely one of the very few great creative peo-
ple whose head was not completely infected with dancing sugarplums.

Things were clearly heating up. The next thing I knew, Jay called and asked if he and I could meet the coming Sunday morning. He suggested the Cheese & Olive in Marina del Ray. This turned out to be a few blocks from where he had a small but stylish oceanfront condo. He was quite gracious with me and it didn't go unnoticed that he had called me himself to make the invitation. This was the first real indication I had that they had some-thing quite specific to talk to me about after all.

We met. He wanted me to join the agency. I was ecstatic and excited although I kept a pretty good poker face. I had played

Lee Clow, creative director at Chiat/Day.

poker, gin, and hearts for almost four solid years in college, so I was pretty prepared for this.

But then he said, "We want you to come to Chiat/Day . . . "

I smiled and nodded my head some.

" . . . and run the Apple Computer account!"

I looked at him as I digested this information along with the rest of my egg white, mushroom, and onion omelet.

"Oh, and you will have to move to San Francisco."

It was not what I had in mind or expected. And it carried with it several complicating business and personal issues.

Not only had they never discussed what the job was, but it had never even been clear what accounts might be involved. I hadn't contemplated leaving Los Angeles.

In 1982 Apple was an important upcoming business and the agency had no one properly managing it. There had been a cry from somebody at Apple for a "packaged goods guy." That would turn out to be me: Jell-O, Minute Rice, Log Cabin, Old Grand Dad, Windsor Canadian, Ballantine Beer & Ale, Vat 69, and the list went on.

Although I had been general manager at Y&R LA, I didn't mind at all going back to being an account guy. I had a long track record of doing account management well and wasn't hung up with any ego issues. In fact I felt some relief at the possibility of just being responsible for running an account again.

But Apple was in Cupertino in Northern California. It was mostly serviced at the time out of the small Chiat/Day office in San Francisco with support from the Los Angeles office. I really didn't have it in my head to move to San Francisco.

Jeri and my daughters Robin and Susanne had only four years earlier been uprooted and disrupted from living in New York to move to Los Angeles. And we all liked it now that we were settled. Moving again, to San Francisco, was an issue.

I mentioned this to Jay and he said, "Commute. We'll get you an apartment in San Francisco and you'll fly up on Monday and come back on Friday. It's only an hour flight."

It was like everything else Jay did. He did it with gusto and irreverence. He always had an answer, regardless of the cost, as long as he could make an argument to sway you to his point of view.

It also immediately passed through my head that while I had worked on many various brands over the years, mostly packaged goods and a fair number of service companies as well, I had never worked on any product that had a wire even remotely connected to it.

More importantly, I knew absolutely nothing about the personal computer business. Didn't use one and hardly knew they existed. I was still using a dictation machine and a typewriter.

Jay and the others seemed not to care, but it definitely occurred to me that while I had successfully worked on lots of brands, Apple was different in many ways. And it turned out that I learned pretty quickly that technology clients and people like to talk with other technology-savvy people. And they talk about things that are quite foreign to a Jell-O Gelatin account guy.

The other thing that occurred to me was that I smelled the faint scent of doggie doo when it came to the agency's existing client relationship with Apple.

Nevertheless I was able to rationalize this situation in the same way that I ended up promoting my own agency years later to clients when told "but you don't have any sanitary pad experience." My answer: "We didn't have a computer before we had Apple; we didn't have an ice cream before we had Dreyer's; we didn't have a car before we had Kia"; and on and on. It was a persuasive argument and one that I eventually convinced myself of as well in accepting the Chiat/Day offer to run the Apple Computer account.

To top all this off, Jay made me an offer I that could have easily refused if my decision had been only about money. But it wasn't. It wasn't even about managing the Apple account. Anyone who knew anything about the personal computer category at that time would have jumped at it. I didn't know much so that really didn't motivate me.

What it was about for me was being able to join what I thought was the most exciting group of people, at the most exciting creative advertising agency, doing the most exciting and creative advertising anywhere in the world. Bar none!

It was about having been a very good champion for good ideas all of my career, but not having very many good ideas to champion. And it turned out that Chiat/Day was arguably the greatest and the best creative agency for the entire 1980s when I was there. I was getting on board just as the train started up to the crest.

I told Jay there was no way I was coming for $100,000. I was earning more than that in my current job at Y&R. I wanted at least what I was making. I had come prepared for a low bid and handed him a printout of my annual total compensation and benefit package. I pushed back my chair from the table and stood up and said, "Jay, I need to put some coins in the meter for my car. Look at my package and see what you think."

When I came back in, he stood up and said OK and extended his hand. I smiled and took his in mine and shook it once.

Now if I had known just how badly they needed someone to bring even a little bit of discipline to managing this client, and the entire agency for that matter, I might have asked for considerably more money. In hindsight, I am certain Jay would have provided it. But I didn't ask.

Most of all, my decision to join Chiat was about finally getting into the advertising business after having spent 15 years at Young & Rubicam.

And so I did!

The next most memorable thing about that morning I was hired came after we shook hands. He said, "Come with me." We walked across

Beverly Hills Billies off to San Francisco

Ocean Avenue to a place called the Baja Cantina, where about 20 of Jay's buddies and gal pals had gathered for brunch. It was only 11 a.m. and half of them were already drunk as skunks. The other half were high as kites. I thought to myself, what have I just done?

That no one in the Chiat/Day office in San Francisco was told of my arrival is the subject of another story.

Not long before I left Young & Rubicam Los Angeles, I took a trip to Chicago and New York and met respectively with my old Y&R boss's counterpart, then midwestern regional director and Y&R president to be, Peter Georgescu, and also with Alex Kroll, then Y&R president.

I am sure they both thought I was just trying to protect my job, but neither knew that I had already decided to take the situation at Chiat/Day and move on with my life. I simply wanted them to know some of the things that were going on with the West Coasters. Neither had a clue.

What a coincidence: A year later I read in *AdWeek* that my old boss had been relieved. That is, of his duties.

Lessons learned:

1. Good things often come from bad ones.

2. One door closes, and another opens.

3. Not all ads are alike, not all ad agencies are alike.

4. Don't shit where you eat.

CHAPTER 7

APPLE "1984" TV SPOT
(THE GREATEST COMMERCIAL THAT ALMOST WASN'T)

"IN THE THIRD QUARTER of the National Football League's Super Bowl game on January 22, 1984, Apple Computer introduced the Mac with a :60 commercial."

This is one of the few accurate statements reported by *Advertising Age* and the media regarding the commercial. The rest of all the other stuff is a wonderful example of revisionist history.

I was a part of the team that developed what became one of the most acclaimed television commercials ever produced. Maybe it has become the most famous commercial ever made, and it is arguably the most infamous.

The commercial was known as the "1984" spot and it introduced Apple Computer's Macintosh. Incredibly the myth and folklore around this commercial, which were continually perpetrated and expanded along the way, greatly exceeded the reality of what actually happened. I am sure this is part of the reason that the lore surrounding the ad continues to this day. Even more remarkable are the number of people who claim credit for this commercial. For example, there was a fellow named Chuck Phillips who was at Chiat/Day San Francisco for a time before spending many years reassigned to Vancouver, Canada. He had absolutely nothing to do with the Macintosh launch, but a Canadian magazine sent him off to retirement saying "he helped launch Apple Computers in 1984."

I was the senior account person responsible for the Apple Computer advertising account at the time of the development of this commercial. I oversaw the development of the first strategic marketing plan that Apple ever received from their advertising agency, Chiat/Day, and out of which the aforementioned commercial grew or fit in.

Apple founder Steve Jobs had never seen anything like a roadmap for the creation of Apple's ads or a way to assess their worth. Nor did he want to, when it was presented to him. Frankly he was of the "just show me the ads" school. That was the fun part after all, wasn't it? Previously he had always been shown a bunch of ads and would decide if one was "neat" or "cool" or not. If it was neat or cool, it ran. If it wasn't, it didn't.

This changed under my leadership of the account. A bit! I helped develop, refine, and sell an introductory communications strategy and the advertising, and I was present at the production for much of it as well. I also helped develop the strategy behind the media plan, which was highly unique at the time.

M. T. Rainey, the Apple account planner, actually identified the critical importance of adding one particular word to the Macintosh advertising promise, *radical*, as in radical ease of use. This certainly helped focus the development of a lot of the creative work.

But truth be told, most of the strategic thinking had Jobs barely keeping awake in his chair. Show me the ads already! M. T. Rainey, I'm told, believes her *radical* was the only reason for the success of everything. I wonder if that includes the development of the machine too.

You may have played the game telephone as a kid. You whisper something to a person, then he in turn whispers it to the person next to him, who whispers it to the next person, and so on. The last person to receive the whisper reports what he heard, and it is always something that bears little or no resemblance to what was first whispered. It gets distorted and perverted, with each person putting their own little twist and interpretation as they pass on the information. And that is what happened with the story of the "1984" commercial.

Who actually came up with the conceptual idea for the "1984" commercial in the first place? The coincidence of introducing the Macintosh the very same year that George Orwell wrote about in his 1949 premonitory view of what the world would be like in the future was incredibly fortuitous. But it took some considerable added brilliance to attach his idea to the introduction of Apple's Macintosh, as obvious as it may seem today. Actually the idea was not originally intended for the Macintosh but rather for a lesser computer, the Apple III.

John Sculley (ex–Apple Computer CEO) writes in his book *Odyssey* that he asked Chiat/Day, "See if there is a way to take advantage of the fact that 1984 was the year that George Orwell chose for his famous prophecy of a totalitarian regime in which Big Brother controls all of man's actions and thoughts."

Actually, the Orwellian idea had been bouncing around Chiat/Day before Sculley even arrived at Apple. I will give him credit, though, for recognizing a good idea when he heard one, since the idea had been discussed as part of the product launch. Steve Hayden, creative person extraordinaire and then copywriter on the Apple account, gets most of the credit for conceiving the idea. Brent Thomas, responsible for the brilliant art direction in the commercial, along with Lee Clow, a uniquely exceptional art director and creative director at Chiat/Day, gets some credit too. Ridley Scott, the director who actually shot the spot, brought much to the production as well.

The fact is that an art director and copywriter working in the Chiat/Day San Francisco office on the Apple account a year and a half earlier had come up with the idea, before Macintosh was even a reality. Art director Mike Moser and copywriter Gary Gussick created an ad in 1982 for the Apple III computer: "Why 1984 Won't Be Like 1984."

Steve Jobs saw the ad concept and rejected it. He didn't feel that the product it featured lived up to the revolutionary claim. Boy was he right, as the Apple III died a slow, excruciating death thereafter, not being a very elegant computing solution.

Ironically, when I first started working with Apple in 1982, I met with Mike Markkula, then CEO. He had a small brass replica of the Apple III on his desk, which he grabbed as I was leaving his office. Don't forget what the most important advertising job is here at Apple, he told me. "Put this on a chain and wear it around your neck so it hangs down below your belt." With that he handed me the thing that I still have today. I would have needed a real set of brass balls if I had listened to him literally.

Nonetheless, he was wrong. The most important job of advertising at the time was to introduce the Macintosh to the world, not to focus on the Apple III, which soon faded away. Compounding this lack of vision, he was highly skeptical of the 1984 commercial when he first saw it, and questioned whether it should air.

Gussick wrote the original copy on April 14, 1982. The headline was "Why 1984 Won't Be Like 1984." The copy began: "Somewhere along about our sophomore year in high school, most of the 'me' soon to be 'we' generation

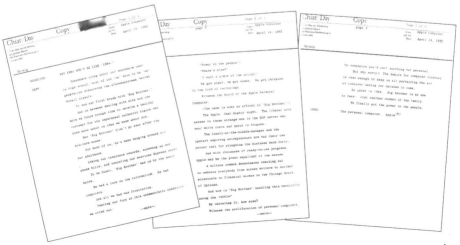

discovered the aforementioned George Orwell classic." And it went on from there. It wasn't very elegant copy writing but the message was pretty clear, just for the wrong product.

⊘ ⊘ ⊘

It was almost two years later during the development of the introductory Macintosh advertising, coincidental with the timing of the January 1984 launch, that the then creative team revisited the Orwellian concept, which made both strategic and creative sense. The Macintosh was such an innovation and truly gave individuals the ability to communicate far more easily and intuitively for the first time. It was a true revolution and put power in the hands of the people. And, it was out of this thinking that the "1984" TV commercial idea was born.

The "1984" commercial was one of 45 conceptual pieces presented to support the launch effort for the Mac. Also shown at the time was work designed for sustaining the other Apple products like the Apple II and III and Lisa, which were responsible for virtually all of the company revenue being generated and needed to be supported.

Our agency group met the night before this creative presentation at Ricky's Hyatt in Palo Alto. We were ensconced in a small, dingy, and dark conference room with four walls and no windows to review the work. The people assembled were creative director Lee Clow, associate creative director/writer Steve Hayden, art director Mike Moser, Brian O'Neill, a copywriter, and me.

Later, around 11:30 p.m., Jay Chiat joined us upon arriving from New York. We had already reviewed and agreed what and how we would be presenting the work. Jay entered the room and was irritable and surly. He was an unusually natty dresser but looked as if he had been through a washing machine and a dryer. His clothes were wrinkled and his shirt askew from his pants. His hair was all disheveled. He was tired and his body was telling him it was after 2:30 a.m. eastern time.

He wanted to see where we were at and upon looking at the very first ad threw a tantrum of disappointment and went on to crap on every single piece of advertising we had lined up around the conference room walls.

"Show me the work."

"This is all shit."

"What have you guys been thinking?"

"We're in trouble."

"This is shit."

All of this was expressed at the top of Jay's voice in an extremely irritated and condescending manner. Which was par for Jay's course.

Everyone was sufficiently demotivated and tired, when Lee Clow asked Jay to take a stroll with him, which they did. Lee used that walk to speak persuasively and in his usual calm manner. "OK, asshole, you go present whatever you want."

We all went to sleep and the next morning drove over to Apple and presented all of the work exactly as it was the night before. Of the 45 ads, 44 were approved for production.

This work was shown to a group of Apple executives consisting of Steve Jobs, Fred Hoar (public relations VP), Jean Richardson (advertising director), Henry Whitfield (advertising manager), and John Sculley (CEO), the newest member of Apple management. Everyone endorsed the work, including the "1984" commercial. Steve Jobs really liked it and thought it was neat and cool. However, Sculley, who had come from a bit more conservative environment at Pepsi-Cola, expressed some concerns about the idea.

"I wonder if people will relate to this imagery."

"It may be a poor reflection on the company."

"I'm not completely sure we should be doing this."

Usually when people include in their comments words like *wonder*, *may*, and *I'm not sure*, I am quite sure that they are sure. This was the case here. I'm sure! However, Sculley showed his marketing savvy and executive aptitude when he offered how at Pepsi sometimes they would take a chance and produce daring ideas but you don't have to run them. Clearly a man of conviction.

Some months later Sculley called to have a meeting in Cupertino. He didn't call me; he called Jay. He wanted to discuss some of the media planning. He wanted Jay there, and as it turned out Lee Clow, creative director, Steve Hayden, the copywriter, and I were part of the meeting, and Steve Jobs as well. We ended up having to meet late at night because of Jay having to fly from the East Coast and Sculley's availability. Most of what went on was general chitchat about some pretty nonspecific and unimportant media items but then Sculley turned to me as if he were going to raise a really big issue. He looked directly at me, and Jay, Steve, and Lee looked at him and then at me, and he asked, "What's the cost of a rating point in Houston?"

Say what?

I looked at him and thought he was joking. But he wasn't. I responded, "I haven't got a clue what the cost is but I will be happy to get back to you first thing tomorrow morning with that information." He just gave out a loud "hurumph."

This question was from the man who was hired by Steve Jobs to get out of the business of selling sugared water and to "change the world" at Apple. This was the man who succeeded in undermining and pushing out Steve Jobs, who hired him, the man who created the personal computer revolution and who more recently is being compared to Henry Ford and Thomas Edison, having changed the world as we know it now three times.

He may have succeeded in making me look unprepared in front of my boss. But there were four people who concluded he was just a schmuck. It was probably too soon for Steve to make that deduction. But he did eventually.

It continues to be reported that the "1984" introductory commercial cost a then staggering $1 million to produce. Actually the commercial was made for considerably less than that when you consider that four spots, not just the one, were included in the production package (two :60 and two :30 spots cut from the :60s).

At the time Ridley Scott had not nearly obtained the celebrity director status as he has subsequently. But even so, he was still an expensive part of the shooting costs, having already achieved considerable acclaim for the movie *Blade Runner*. And, he had made some monetary concessions to us because of his interest in doing the unusual spot. Being the director on this commercial, with all of the down the line publicity over the years, was, I am convinced, at least a partial factor in Ridley Scott's future enormous success.

Steve Jobs and John Sculley—during the honeymoon.

The commercial was shot at Shepperton Studios just outside London in Surrey, England. The production used about 300 extras as robotic proletarians. Three-quarters of these people were riffraff drawn from in and around London, most of them skinheads and/or Paki-bashers, as they were called (those folks who used to take pleasure in beating up Pakistanis with baseball bats in London). The entire group of lowlifes was paid $10,000 for what turned out to be three grueling days of marching and sitting having smoke blown in their faces. Amazingly, they only really got unruly on the last day, when they starting flinging rubble and rocks from the set at one another.

Thinking ahead and fortunately, the production company had retained police with police dogs who kept these dudes pretty much at bay. They didn't entirely succeed, as the actress Mamie Van Doren was also shooting a film at the studio, and anytime she was in her trailer, scores of these lads took the opportunity to climb up and peer into her windows, not to speak of their hyperactivity around the star actress of our commercial running around in tight little red shorts.

The police presence was a comfort, as Jeri and my younger daughter Susanne had accompanied me to this shoot and these skinhead boys were quite scary. A few of them were hitting on my daughter, who was only 14 at the time. Most of these skinheads were just that, shaven heads, completely bald, and with most of their bodies pierced and tattooed. They were setting trends way before their time.

All of this was recorded for posterity by Marc Chiat, Jay's son, who had been sent over to videotape the goings-on. But Brent Thomas and I were there to see it all in real time.

The other commercial that was part of the production package focused on the strength of Apple's technological and innovative prowess. It featured a business computer named Lisa (also a failure like the Apple III). The idea of

The lads just being themselves on the shoot.

that commercial, called "Alone Again," was not really to sell Lisa machines but rather to help sustain an important presence among computer users of Apple's technology leadership during the period of time preceding the introduction of the Macintosh. Both the "1984" and "Alone Again" spots were shot in :60 and :30 formats, thereby resulting in the four commercials.

In total, production costs were around $650,000. Considerably below the inflated million dollars for the "1984" spot alone, as reported.

The responsibility for approving the production costs somehow fell to a newly hired executive named Floyd Kvamme. Floyd was a technology person and knew nothing about advertising or commercial production estimates. He had never seen one before. I had the task of getting him to sign off

FG and Brent Thomas, CD art director extraordinaire, on the "1984" set.

on what even at $650,000 was a lot of money back then.

He asked a few questions. His face was a little pallid. Sort of whitish. But sign the estimate he did. And, off to merry old England we went to meet with Ridley Scott and to shoot.

When the commercial was finished, it was shown first to Steve Jobs and his Macintosh team at Apple, including Mike Murray, who headed that division. They loved it! Mike Murray, it seems, ended up being the single most important and the only assenting voice at Apple in favor of actually running the thing at the end of the day.

Sometime later it was screened for the Apple board of directors, who thought that Steve Jobs was completely out of his mind and that the advertising agency should be fired. I understood that John Sculley expressed his earlier "I wonder, maybe, and should we" concerns as well. Steve never lost his interest in the spot, and he and Steve Wozniak said they would pay to run it themselves.

A year later Sculley was able to get Steve Jobs fired and soon after was able to fire the agency too. But not before putting us through a horrendous competition with his old Pepsi agency BBDO. He also made them hire Steve Hayden, one of our finest creative people and an important part of the Apple work, as part of awarding them the business. What a guy.

Sculley took credit for developing the idea of the "1984" commercial and then had concerns; he fired the advertising agency that made the commercial and Apple the great brand that it was; and he got rid of the guy who hired him and who may be arguably one of the greatest marketers and executives this country or the world has ever seen.

It was fitting to see a few years later that Sculley had been forced out of Apple and had joined his two brothers at Sculley Brothers LLC, a venture capital firm. In an analysis of venture capital firm results in the business press, it was reported that just about every one of the investments that these guys had recommended to their clients, and had invested in for their clients, was underwater. Up to 80 percent under.

CNBC named Sculley one of the "Worst American CEOs of All Time," stating, "He proved to be disastrous as the top manager of a tech company and unsophisticated about the technology field" and that he was fired "when Apple was slipping toward bankruptcy."

But back to the Macintosh launch. The original media buy for the Super Bowl called for running a :60 spot and a :30 spot during the telecast. The media time had been purchased way in advance. As the Super Bowl approached, the Apple board of directors insisted that the media time be sold off. But it was late and we were only able to sell off one of the slots. Let me say, however, that if the agency had moved a mite faster, we probably could have sold off the other slot too. We didn't, and that's how it came to pass that the now famous spot aired. That, and since Apple decided they didn't want to air :60 of white space on national television.

During the "to air or not to air" debate, I put together a four-page written brief addressed to then new marketing director Bill Campbell as to why we should go ahead as planned and air the "1984" spot. It was a compelling piece, I thought. Eventually it found its way to Jobs and Sculley and others at Apple as well. I believe it helped convince some of the wisdom of going ahead and airing the commercial.

Additionally, I felt it would strengthen the arguments if we had some actual commercial testing data to support the worth of the commercial and our point of view. I commissioned Audience Surveys Inc., a well-known national copy testing company, to conduct their standard in-theater test of the commercial. I received the results of the test on December 13, 1983.

I forwarded my document with the recommendation to run the spot on the Super Bowl on December 14 while we were still in the process of trying to sell off the two Super Bowl time slots we owned.

In the document, I discussed the need for awareness generation and the affirmation and solidification of our launch "radical ease of use" strategy. I accurately predicted the significant amount of free publicity that would be generated from simply airing the commercial, without any regard for the messaging impact itself.

And I reminded them all that just a few weeks before at the Apple national sales meeting in Hawaii, Steve Jobs had shown the commercial to over a thousand employees and dealers with great fanfare and a promise to all.

"That ad will run one week before the introduction of Macintosh."

"I did not have sex with that woman" had the same authoritative and credible ring to it.

After the spot was shown, the lights came back on, and the applause in the room was deafening. It was all quite emotional since Apple was getting the crap kicked out of it by IBM at the time. They needed something to uplift their spirits and Jobs gave it to them in the form of this world-changing product Macintosh and incredible commercial and an unbelievably powerful pep talk.

The cheering and applause went on for many minutes with Jobs just standing in front of a multitude of Apple believers with a smirky shit-eating kind of grin on his face. Everyone was juiced up by the commercial and by Jobs's speech. (That speech lives on and is still available today on YouTube, where you can check it out.)

After this meeting and Jobs's episodic proclamation, we spent some time bathing in the warmth of the fantastic reception that we had just received to Macintosh and the advertising, in the Hawaiian sun.

I saved the photo of Steve Jobs and me relaxing poolside after his masterful performance.

The ultimate client handholding: yours truly and Steve Jobs.

When we returned to the mainland a few days later, Apple management was not convinced. They wanted the Super Bowl spots sold off, driven by a less than warm reception by the Apple board of directors. And, had it not been for Jay Chiat, the success of Macintosh might well never have happened. He gently reminded our media folk that they should take their time, if they cared to remain at Chiat/Day. They did, and the time was never sold, and the spot ultimately aired and history was made.

One year later, on December 31, 1984, *Advertising Age*'s editorial page highlighted Apple as the best example during the year of "boldness." They postulated what better way to end the year than with the selection of John Sculley as "Adman of the Year." It might have been more appropriate to select someone who had fully championed the TV commercial that created the Macintosh business in the first place. Like Jobs or Lee Clow or Jay Chiat. And a stretch might have been maybe even an account guy like me. But alas that's not the way it was to be.

Much has been written over the years since the Macintosh introduction as to how the spot ran only that one time on the 1984 Super Bowl. Wrong! Many attribute the product success to the media buy alone. To be sure, using the Super Bowl was a brilliant idea hatched by Camille Johnson, then in charge of media at Chiat/Day on the Apple account.

And while it's true the commercial ran only once on the Super Bowl, it also ran many times in the two weeks preceding the Super Bowl, in 13 spot markets around the country. That market list included Boca Raton, corporate headquarters for IBM where they built the PC. Why? For no other reason than Jobs's wanting to poke Big Blue in the eye in their own backyard.

Oddly, although a fair amount of money was expended on the spot TV market effort, there was little to no reaction. It was a nonevent until the commercial ran that one time on that infamous day during the Super Bowl. It took that venue to showcase the message. It took the captured audience, not yet trained to view commercials airing on the Super Bowl as much as "entertainment" as the game itself. The reaction was sensational, as was the succeeding down-line firestorm of publicity, not to speak of the sales phenomenon.

That single Super Bowl commercial generated massive awareness and conviction and went on to help sell vast numbers of Macintoshes. Sales over six hours the very next day were $3.5 million and $155 million over the next 100 days. Ultimately it made Apple the multi-multi-billion-dollar company that it is today.

Turns out I never showed anyone the results from an ASI copy test conducted on the "1984" commercial. The agency had paid for it, and if I didn't want to share, so what.

You see, according to ASI in their final report, the "key predicative" measure of commercial effectiveness was what they called the pre/post performance change. The norm for all :30 business commercials at the time was 29, with a range of results between 13 to 43, for all the commercials that they had ever tested.

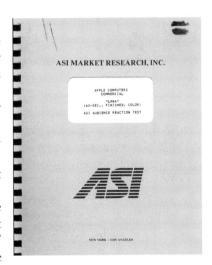

The Apple Macintosh "1984" commercial scored a 5.

And it was a :60 commercial to boot, not a :30, upon which the norms were built.

I am so sorry that Steve Jobs is not here any longer to read this chapter. I am almost certain that he never knew that the "1984" commercial was judged an unpersuasive research failure of the highest magnitude. I am also sure that it would have simply reinforced his personal belief in judging things from the gut and intuition, and not relying on "scientific" tools like creative research. He knew from the very first moment he saw the idea that it was "insanely great."

To this day, the commercial is one of a very few that keep on giving and giving, year after year. Every year, when Super Bowl Sunday rolls around, there is publicity on all the commercials that will air, and inevitably talk turns to the start of it all, the Apple "1984" Macintosh spot. The publicity value alone resulting for Apple as a technology leader has been inestimable, but surely it is in the billions of dollars.

Various advertising pundits have felt compelled to chime in ex post facto. For example, John O'Toole, ex-president of the American Association of Advertising Agencies and former president of Foote, Cone & Belding (parenthetical remarks are mine): "What '1984' as a commercial for Apple really signified was the first time somebody could put a great deal of production money [NOT!] into a single commercial [NOT!] and run it only once [NOT!] and get tremendous benefit from running it only once [NOT!]. It took great coordination with PR [NONE!]. It was really event marketing with sales promotion and PR built in [NOT!]. That was the beginning of the new era of integrated marketing communications [MAYBE, BUT WE SURE DIDN'T PLAN IT THAT WAY!]."

Ultimately the "experts" at *Advertising Age* selected the commercial as the commercial of the decade. Bob Garfield, *Ad Age* columnist, called it the greatest TV commercial ever made. Well, they got something right.

The commercial won many many advertising awards, including the most important creative award of all, the Grand Prix at the 31st annual International Advertising Film Festival in Cannes back in 1984.

Why? Because unknown to the client, and in the hopes that no one would see it, the commercial had been aired one time just before the end of 1983 in order to qualify for creative shows.

In Twin Falls, Idaho, in the middle of the night, at an obscure television station's sign-off time, so it could be entered the next year.

The agency got only one call from a traffic person at that TV station asking, "What was that?"

ONE MORE REASON
TO LOVE CALIFORNIA

I HAD A LOT OF REASONS TO LOVE CALIFORNIA and a few not to. But overall I came out to the Golden State and loved it and never looked back. Just one of the great experiences was winning the first significant nontech consumer advertising account in the Chiat/Day San Francisco office.

Two young fellows from California had started the company. Not to be confused with two other guys from California, who also started a company when they introduced a machine they called an Apple and which revolutionized the world. We happened to have had that business, started by the two Steves, Wozniak and Jobs.

But in 1981, around the same time Apple was beginning to heat up, two guys in Lodi, California, Mike Crete and Stu Bewley, had introduced a beverage, which they called California Cooler. It became a smash hit and at one point sold over 20 million cases in a year. It changed the beverage world dramatically. We had the good fortune to acquire this business and did two brilliant ad campaigns that really created the brand and drove its sales volume.

Picture this: sun, sand, surf, and a group of young people working up a giant, beach-party thirst. Michael Crete is acting as bartender. He decides he will become a hero by coming up with a drink that may be more thirst quenching and enjoyable than cold beer. Crete mixes citrus juice and Chablis in plastic tubs, with ice, on the beach and becomes a hero. Thirsty friends returning from a nearby volleyball game drain the tubs.

That early 1970s experience at a California beach made Crete more than a popular person at a party. It made him—eventually—a fabulously successful and wealthy entrepreneur.

It also led to the creation of the wine cooler industry, in which company after company introduced its own brand of low-alcohol (typically about 6 percent) mixtures of fruit juice and white wine. Sales of the sweet, refreshing, lightly carbonated coolers were expected to top $310 million.

The kings of coolers were not the big, diversified companies that entered the field, but were Crete and Stuart Bewley, who like Crete was 32 and hailed from the same small California farm town. Their California Cooler Inc. grew from a shoestring operation that produced 1,575 gallons of homemade cooler worth about $12,000 in 1981 to a high-powered company that sold 22 million gallons—worth more than $72 million wholesale in one year. California Cooler became the second largest "winery" in the world, behind Gallo.

Later on, Brown-Forman Corporation, the Kentucky distiller (Jack Daniel's, Early Times, Southern Comfort), bought the company for $146 million ($63 million cash plus payments tied to sales, which would add $83 million over the next three years). Crete and Bewley, who started it with $10,000, would remain in charge of what essentially was an autonomous operation.

California Cooler was one of the most important businesses that we ever won from a number of perspectives. In 1984 Chiat/Day San Francisco was primarily a technology-oriented agency with a bunch of the small accounts left over from the acquisition of Regis McKenna, which included Intel, Shugart, Calma, Fafco, and others whose names I can't pronounce much less spell. And, we were doing a lot of work for Apple Computer, which was our largest business and had come along as a part of the acquisition.

The California Cooler new business pitch was an extremely difficult and competitive one. Initially, we were competing with DFS/Los Angeles, Y&R San Francisco, J. Walter Thompson San Francisco, MSA, Ketchum San Francisco, and McCann Erickson San Francisco, the incumbent agency. We ended up facing off against J. Walter Thompson.

We worked around the clock in putting together our pitch for this account. We thought that we had identified a powerful strategic positioning, which came out of days and nights sitting in our little war room at 414 Jackson Street on the mezzanine level. At one point the spent paper and paper cups on the floor reached our knees. In addition we had identified a really great ad campaign that came right out of the strategy. We typically did not like to develop speculative creative work, but in this case we had no choice if we wanted to compete. And J. Walter Thompson was sparing no expense in producing their ideas.

In fact, they made their final presentation at a nightclub in downtown San Francisco, and I was told later by Mike Crete and Stu Bewley that it was impressive. It must have been, even though it was during the day. But it was dark inside and allowed for a great venue to present an alcoholic beverage campaign. Sound, lights, action, and a bar.

J. Walter Thompson recommended a "new beverage" strategy with an ad campaign: "I Want a New Drink." They had exciting videos of young people enjoying California Coolers and their effects. Underneath the visuals they had a soundtrack that used the Huey Lewis and the News smash hit recording of "I Want a New Drug." They had changed "Drug' to "Drink": "I Want a New Drink." This turned out to be very appealing to the clients. They were enamored with the idea and the glamour and the excitement of it all.

We followed the J. Walter Thompson presentation the next day.

Now, one of the most fascinating aspects of this story is the way the first advertising agency that Mike Crete and Stu Bewley hired, McCann Erickson, had positioned the product.

Funny how different people perceive the same thing. Irv Sonn, who was then the executive creative director for McCann Erickson in San Francisco, recalls how the agency saw it as an "upscale drink and tried to develop a mystique about it." He went on to say, "We took refreshment to a new level, whisked you away to an enchanted island. We gave them [California Cooler] their biggest success."

That's not the way Stu Bewley saw it. "Nobody noticed the ads and nobody even remembers them."

In fact it was all wrong. They tried to tell wine consumers that this new beverage was a wine substitute to be used as a replacement for white or red wine in those situations where wine was typically served. Cocktail parties, fancy food, upscale folks, and the like. The ads were essentially wine ads that substituted California Cooler for the wine, with good-looking people eating appetizers and nuts and crackers while parading around and smiling in the latest fashions.

It was remarkable how terribly wrong the strategic thinking behind this was, as much as the advertising execution itself. It was a classic example of a big monolithic ad agency telling an inexperienced client a bunch of crap. And yet, the clients, not knowing any better, bought it.

Wine was not a refreshing beverage that one chugged down to quench a thirst. Unlike beer, it was reserved for very different occasions. Beer on the other hand was a friendly, refreshing social lubricant as well as a personality statement or badge. When you think about it, the California Coolers were sold in single bottles and packs like beer; they were placed in coolers and on shelves next to beer; they had caps on the bottles just like beer; and they were often drunk right out of the bottle just like beer. For all intents they were far more similar to beer than to wine. And therefore it followed that the appeal would be much more to beer drinkers than to wine drinkers.

We argued that both the drinking experience and the taste that consumers had with wine were dramatically different than what California Coolers offered. And while the experience that consumers had with beer was more similar, the taste was not. We also pointed out that the incidence of beer usage and per capita consumption was vastly greater than for wine, offering far more volume potential if it could be tapped into.

So, we recommended targeting the light and medium and nonbeer drinkers who were seeking a beer drinking experience but did not really like the taste of beer. These were heavily women but also a significant chunk of men. Particularly young men. Very young men . . . like teens.

California Cooler was truly the best thing since beer, and lots of people simply didn't like the taste of beer and had to acquire one for it. Not so for

California Cooler, which tasted more like lemonade and fruit punch and had an additional benefit of a higher level of alcohol than most beers. California Cooler was a revolutionary new drink that delivered the beer drinking experience with a uniquely appealing taste.

Mike and Stu, I believe, genuinely liked us better than the JWT folks. And we had some powerful alcoholic beverage experience and knowledge. And we had a strategy in which they both saw great wisdom. However, the actual advertising campaign idea that we presented did not enamor them as much as the sexy Huey Lewis idea they had seen from JWT.

But, we were very persuasive in our strategic arguments. And while the client didn't know it, we had developed a brilliant campaign to execute the strategy. The idea was California Cooler: One More Reason to Hate California. We took all these iconic things that people believe are part of the California lifestyle and made fun of them and introduced California Cooler as yet another leading-edge lifestyle thing unique to the Golden State. We made fun of things that people outside California think make the place full of fruits and nuts.

We had a young East Coast man sitting down at a bar next to a pal and he was in a complaining mood. He grabbed the bottle that the guy next to him was drinking, which was a California Cooler, while the other guy looked on amused. He complained about California, saying, "I hate California, you know what I'm saying? It's like [sarcastic mimicry] 'Have a nice day' . . . 'Surf's Up' . . . uh-huh uh-huh. I mean, their idea of culture is yogurt . . . A formal dinner party means you wear socks. Blonds everywhere . . . pink tofu . . . excuse me? Soy burgers . . . I really hate it."

At this point he was looking at the California Cooler bottle and said, "I even hate what they drink."

The bartender asked, "What'll ya have, buddy?"

And our spokesperson pointed to the bottle as if he hadn't said all of the above . . . and said, "One of those."

Then the announcer said, "California Cooler. One more reason to hate California."

It was truly brilliant.

It was one of those ideas that I knew was spot-on and it was an idea I believed could win us the account. Dave Woodside (Woody) and Ross Van Dusen had put this campaign together. But as happens with most things that are really good and really different, several of the people working on the pitch at the time, John Yost, an account man, and M. T. Rainey and Betty Deepe, the account planners, had problems with it.

They missed how strategically correct against the beer drinker potential audience it was, and they missed the wonderful irony of the idea of putting down another great idea and innovation from those kooks out in California. We were working over the weekend before the pitch and they wanted to kill this idea. I remember that Saturday well, telling them all to get out of the agency and go home. They did, and Ross and Dave finished putting together what became the winning idea for the account and eventually made California Cooler something on everyone's mind across the country.

It turned out that some of the clients had problems with the "Hate" idea too. Stu Bewley in particular thought we were going to turn people off by raising all these things that people thought were weird about California. And that we would turn off the people in California too because we were making fun of their lifestyles. All of this was nonsense and I said so even after they ran some focus groups that confirmed their beliefs. People in focus groups just love to intellectualize, particularly about advertising when asked.

But Mike Crete was a staunch believer in the strategic approach we had recommended and he loved the advertising idea. It didn't hurt either when I told him that there was no way he was going to get Huey Lewis to perform the song for them, since the group didn't do endorsements at the time. And if they did, it would cost them a literal fortune. And, maybe more to the point was the fact that they would run a huge risk of associating their drink with the drug culture. I want a new drug; I want a new drink.

After considerable nail biting and significantly more dialogue, we prevailed and were awarded the account. I am certain that the work that we were doing for those two other guys down in Silicon Valley and their great success with Apple was beneficial to our selection.

As it turned out the California Cooler account allowed us to create two of the greatest campaigns that ever came out of all of Chiat/Day and were hugely important in establishing the San Francisco office as a real advertising agency. I knew for sure when the LA Chiat/Day office started taking credit for the campaigns.

Furthermore, this advertising helped in establishing Chiat/Day overall as the quintessential creative agency of the 1980s and helped win the Agency of the Decade proclamation along with its other great work. The campaigns won just about every conceivable advertising award that was given and resulted in an incredible sales success as well.

Mike and Stu had spent millions of dollars on the previous campaign from McCann with little to show for it. Awareness was low, as was trial of the product. We needed to raise awareness and stimulate trial as a primary objective. And we did just that, driving both dramatically and doubling sales in a very short period of time.

The initial work we produced was the campaign called "One More Reason to Hate California." It took a confident leadership stance and capitalized on mainstream beer imagery while delivering the relaxed, informal, social, and fun aspects of the beer drinking experience. It was trial oriented, and by using California as a branding device we preempted and defined the entire category as the California Cooler brand.

This campaign contrasted the East Coast urban ethic realism with California permissiveness. Just about everyone had some California envy and we tried to tap into it. It was a huge success with the distributors. And when it aired, it drove awareness of California Cooler through the roof and sales volume too.

A year or so later the marketing situation had become quite different. Now we had two formidable competitors, Seagram's Coolers and Gallo's Bartles & James, both of which had entered the market and were spending significant amounts of money on advertising and promotion. Far more than we had to spend. As such we needed to protect the California Cooler brand.

And so Mike Moser, Dave Woodside, and Dave O'Hare developed a campaign that came out of the California Cooler essence and unique attributes. The campaign capitalized on aspects that no one else could come close to claiming. California Cooler was the original and authentic cooler, among all coolers. We were able to develop another breakthrough advertising campaign that set the brand apart and added much value in terms of awareness and authenticity, and it too drove awareness and sales volume. It was called "The Real Stuff."

One of the reasons it was so real was because of Lee Clow, the creative director of Chiat/Day, who had suggested the direction and was quintessentially the kind of person that the re-creation of the California beach scene in the 1960s was about. He actually lived it. Lee was instrumental in refining and adding incredible subtleties to the work.

This campaign used the great surfing music like "Louie Louie," "Surfin' Bird," and "Pa Pa Oom Mau Mau." The intended target audience: young good-looking surfin' guys and gals on a beach, enjoying California Cooler with all this authentic West Coast surfing music.

Most people gave the Chiat/Day Los Angeles office the credit for creating this campaign not only because that's where the lifestyle depicted existed but because that's where Lee Clow resided. More importantly, he had been and remained a true California surfer dude in every respect. However, all the work was created and produced by the San Francisco creative people.

As with the first campaign, we had some trouble with the clients.

PA PA OOM MAU MAU

THE REAL STUFF

California Cooler had grown substantially from when we started and now they had marketing and advertising people on staff to offer their expertise. The marketing director, whose name escapes me, shit all over the campaign, mainly focusing on how unsanitary it was to show the coolers being prepared on the beach in a tub. He went on from there.

Fortunately Mike Crete was there and as usual spoke from his gut. "I've got to tell y'all this is the greatest thing I've ever seen. Go make it."

We ended up with a marvelous advertising campaign. In many ways it truly defined the brand and protected it through its authenticity. The agency won many accolades for this campaign and many more awards. In addition to Clios and One Shows, we swept the San Francisco Cable Car Award show. In that 1985 show we won 33 honors and 22 were for California Cooler, which netted us the top distinction, the Bell Ringer Award, for the overall winning agency. Ross Van Dusen, Dave Woodside, Mike Moser, and yours truly were there to accept the award with smiles.

We even won a boatload of Belding Awards, at the comparable award show in Los Angeles. And the "Real Stuff" campaign was selected by *Advertising Age* as one of the 10 best ad campaigns of the entire 1980s decade, as did the all-important One Club.

The campaign ran for several years

Ross Van Dusen CD, Dave Woodside CW, Mike Moser AD, and FG accepting Cable Car Best of Show "Bell Ringer" Award

with not enough spending behind it. Gallo's Bartles & James and Seagram's Coolers were spending ungodly amounts of marketing dollars. In order to compete, California Cooler required more marketing dollars and elected to sell the company to Brown-Forman for $146 million.

Mike Crete left soon after getting his share of the booty. Stuart Bewley hung on for a bit but then left too. As with most companies that have been built by entrepreneurs out of a great idea and with a special culture, California Cooler suffered painfully under the constriction of the Brown-Forman organization and eventually disappeared.

One of the great coincidences of this story is that 20 years before, in 1966, when I had been marketing research director at Ballantine Beer & Ale in Newark, New Jersey, I had initiated a project to develop "flavored beer," cola, root, and lemon-lime. At the time, I did some consumer research that suggested there might be an incremental market out there for a beer drinking experience (i.e., the bottle, the alcohol level, the casualness, the social aspects, etc.) if the beverage would only taste better than beer.

Here's the original report I sent to the president of P. Ballantine & Sons, Carl S. Badenhausen, and the other key executives.

P. BALLANTINE & SONS
NEWARK, NEW JERSEY

September 28, 1966

TO: Mr. C. S. Badenhausen

FROM: F. S. Goldberg

cc: Messrs. J. E. Farrell
F. E. Connery
J. H. Erikson
P. W. Whelehon

Flavored Beer – an Opportunity

Recently the Chicago Daily News reported that Falstaff has been developing a new flavored beer product with full alcoholic strength. It is understood that they have been experimenting with flavors such as black raspberry, orange, cola, lemon-lime, cherry, lime and punch. The addition of artificial flavoring in one of the beer processes is apparently the only difference between this new product concept and regular beer. Reportedly "the beer" has been in the developmental stage for two years and the market test is imminent (rumors have indicated that a test market has been Columbia, Missouri).

The purpose of the following memo is to discuss the opportunities for a flavored beer product and hopefully to initiate consumer research to determine what potential exists and in addition, to stimulate actual production development and testing of such products.

Total Beer Market

Industry surveys have consistently shown that a large percentage of adults do not drink malt beverages. The latest survey available was taken by the United States Brewers Association and indicates that nationally 48% of the adult population never drinks beer or ale. It is clear from this study the one specific major reason given for not drinking beer or ale was a dislike for its taste, more specifically because it tasted bitter. This was apparent for all non-drinking groups (19 to 25 years old; married; female; lower educational attainments; lower social and income classes). Of particular importance for this discussion was the non-drinking groups in the northeast region of the country where a higher incidence for not drinking beer for this reason occurred.

It was important too, that light drinkers (less than 7 glasses per week) cited taste as a main deterrent to their consumption of beer and ale.

Potential for the New Flavored Beer Product

For purposes of this paper, it is assumed that the new flavored beer potential would lie primarily with the current non-beer drinker. It also seems logical to assume that most of the sales for a new product of this type will come from

At the time almost half of all men didn't like the taste of beer, nor did almost 80 percent of women. The product we made at Ballantine didn't taste that much better than regular beer since it was beer with soda pop flavoring added to it. Actually it tasted pretty gross.

Needless to say, all but one of the top executives at Ballantine thought the idea was insane. I mean Ballantine was a beer company. What else mattered? Who would drink something that looked like beer, sold in a beer bottle, in a beer pack, in a bar or supermarket on the same shelf, with the same alcoholic content?

What I was proposing was heresy. The project was ultimately trampled to death but for good reason. The taste of that new flavored beer was worse than the taste of beer—that is, if you didn't like beer. And, the senior experienced executives who knew everything there was to know about beer didn't think it was a good idea. Ballantine shuttered its doors entirely in the early 1970s.

Ironically it took just about 20 years and two hillbillies from Lodi, California, and my ad agency to successfully introduce this concept to the world. A beverage that offered all of the beer drinking experience but with a taste that everyone could enjoy.

It was just one more reason I had to love California.

CHAPTER 9

HI! MY NAME IS TEDDY RUXPIN

WHAT'S YOURS?

That's what it said when it was first turned on and that's when another of our incredible roller-coaster rides began. It was the world's first talking teddy bear.

Two guys appeared in my San Francisco offices one day in 1985 carrying one of those big black 34-gallon plastic garbage bags along with their attachés. We all sat down in my main conference room and made the usual introductions and small chitchat that one does upon first meeting a prospect. It turned out that Don Kingsborough had been president of a division of Atari at one time and had relevant experience in the toy arena.

After all the platitudes and pleasantries, Don spoke as he started unfolding the bag and reached into it and pulled out a pair of eyes and a mouth that had been mounted in what looked like some kind of clear Lucite square box. There was some hair on the top and on the sides, bear hair sort of, and a slot the size of a tape cassette in the back.

Don Kingsborough was the founder of this new company that he had named Worlds of Wonder.

He said, "What I've got here is something that will change the world as we know it."

Gosh! I sat back in my chair and at once thought it sounded like he was talking about a new computer or something, because that is exactly what Steve Jobs at Apple had said when he first showed me a prototype of the Macintosh few years earlier. At the time the Macintosh was nothing more than a circuit board or two contained in a Lucite box. The case had not yet been completed.

Don placed his Lucite box on the table in front of us and reached around the back of this contraption and flipped a switch. The eyes started to move up and down and to the sides, and the mouth opened and closed as some sounds emerged, and this hairy tape recorder said, "Hi, my name is Teddy Ruxpin. What's yours?"

We looked at each other and we all smiled. It was actually quite wondrous. The idea was to create an entire world around this fellow. And he was positioned as a "friend," not a toy and not a bear. A friend.

I was sitting there with my two partners, Brian O'Neill and Mike Moser, along with Guy Day, who had flown up from Los Angeles to meet with these folks.

We stared at this thing and said almost in unison, "Wow." Wow meaning what a great idea and wow for Worlds of Wonder (WOW) as a potential client.

And it was a great idea. It wasn't quite the Apple Macintosh but it was an enormous step forward for mankind in the world of teddy bears. Up to then teddy bears had been the single largest selling toy in the world and they had never uttered a word. That was all to soon change.

We were looking at an honest to goodness real live talking teddy bear. It was cute and friendly and cuddly but it spoke. It was an animatronic talking teddy bear that they referred to as an iliop. No teddy bear that had ever been did this. And there were millions and millions of teddy bears sold around the world every year. I believe it was the most popular toy because it was a universal symbol for playfulness and friendliness. Every kid wanted to have a friend even if they never said anything.

Guy Day was there because he took the initial call from Don Kingsborough to explore whether or not the agency might have an interest in a new toy product. Since this new company was based in Northern California, in Fremont to be precise, it made sense to have them come into our offices in San Francisco.

At the time Guy was based in Los Angeles and his job was kind of to mess around with a little of this and a little of that. I was a big fan of Guy's but never quite knew what he was doing or why. In this case he decided it would be nice to come up to San Francisco for the day and have this meeting and offer some moral support and visit his son who lived there. The last was the far more important reason for the trek, I'm certain.

However, almost as soon as Kingsborough and the other fellow present named Paul Rago turned Teddy on, Guy suggested that maybe they should consider the Chiat/Day Los Angeles office since that was where most of the Chiat business was housed. This was Guy's special new business pitch. It was his way of trying to offer Kingsborough every option so that he would get the agency the account. Don and Paul nodded their heads appreciatively.

I was not appreciative, however. My head did a whiplash snap toward Guy when he made this offer and I wanted to jump over and strangle him right then and there. We first had to convince them that Chiat/Day would be the place to have the business but now it had become a much more difficult task to keep it in San Francisco. Chiat/Day Los Angeles was always perceived as the real Chiat/Day, and San Francisco and New York for that matter were looked upon as also-rans.

Guy left to visit with his son. And left me with one tough sale after he had told them that all the great work on Nike, Pizza Hut, and Apple was done in the Los Angeles office. This, despite the fact that some sensational work was being produced at the other offices. I spent the rest of the day, which turned out to be over six hours, trying to convince these guys that Chiat/Day San Francisco was the right place to house their business.

I gave them a detailed tour of the entire agency. I showed them more of our work. I introduced them to every one of our department managers. I showed them still more of our work. I let them play some pool, Ping-Pong, and foosball. I showed them more work. I took them up on the roof where some of our folks were hanging out. I previewed the guest rooms, living room, and meeting rooms in the penthouse. I showed them all the vibrant, young, dedicated talent we had running around the agency. And I showed them still more of our work.

Thanks Guy!

At the end of the day, literally, I prevailed. I was exhausted and spent and needed a shower. I had given it my all, as I felt this would be an extremely important addition to our clients and would make for the possibility of some great advertising history. I was so right!

Toward the end of this marathon meeting, Paul Rago mentioned that they needed a selling kit by the next Monday. It was Thursday. I told him "No problemo." I grabbed back Mike and Brian and we all sat for several more hours getting briefed on the specific requirements for what he wanted. Mike Moser drove this project over that subsequent weekend and we were able to present some wonderful material the next Monday which was enthusiastically received.

It was a pretty simple brochure, which explained all about Teddy Ruxpin and what Worlds of Wonder's expectations were for him. There were several related promotion pieces. None of it was advertising. This was another example of clients getting most excited about promotional materials for their product and also a belief that the agency really understood their business.

Don and Paul approved all of what we showed them and we went off immediately to produce it. And produce it we did by marching to the copying machines and making 100 color copies for them to take with them the very next day to the toy show in New York where they were previewing Teddy. I stood at one machine, Brian and Mike at two others, and we cranked out the copies.

We were now the Worlds of Wonder agency but had no written agreement of any kind. So I asked them for a check to cover our initial expenses for the brochure and some other incidentals. Paul reached into his case and pulled out a checkbook. Just like the kind I kept at home to write checks for the monthly electricity and water bills. He wrote out a check and handed it to me. It was a little spooky since they didn't have the company name on the check and as I found out later barely had enough money to cover the modest amount.

The check was dated March 20, 1985, and it was the number three check written by the company. Worlds of Wonder was printed by hand on the top of the check and the amount was for $2,298.48. The handwritten notation at the bottom left read "for ad company books." I had the check framed and hung in my office. Still have it.

Accounting turned out to be a bit of a short suit for this company. I was not at all comforted on my first trip down to the client's offices, which were in a rented trailer with three desks inside and a phone on each.

Nevertheless, it wasn't too long after that Worlds of Wonder moved into a newly constructed office building in Fremont right next to the parking

lot where the trailer had stood. And for the next two and a half years they didn't look back as they exponentially increased the number of their employees and the office space required to house them.

The "ad books" turned out to be a key selling tool at the New York show. They were used to promote the very first Teddy Ruxpins to retailers and others. We had included a number of ideas, one of which was to buy a huge outdoor space or side of a building in Times Square the week or so before the launch of Teddy in Manhattan. This was a super idea that the retailers all got excited about, and Don positioned it as part of the launch plan. We never did it.

Also contained in this "ad book" was a product positioning line or a tagline that first expressed and then became the underpinning for everything else that we did with Teddy: "A friend for life has come to life."

Teddy Ruxpin was so successful that the company couldn't produce the toys fast enough to fill the orders. It received the Toy of the Year award and over a million bears were sold in the first year alone. Rain checks were issued for delivery four and five months away. The black and gray markets drove the price of these bears through the roof and you could find them in the classified ads at one point selling for over $500.

We did an ad directed to the trade promoting the incredible success of Teddy and assuring that more product was on the way. Turns out that the scarcity of the Teddys resulted in an even more pent-up demand as a feeding frenzy of desire for the product occurred. It was not unlike Hula Hoops, Cabbage Patch Dolls, and tulipmania.

Another ad expressed well the philosophy that Don Kingsborough had brought with the creation of the Worlds of Wonder Company: "Give people more than they can imagine."

Just about every one of the many toys created by this company made you say "WOW!" I think it was just a coincidence that the acronym for the Worlds of Wonder Company was WOW. But what a great coincidence it was. WOW!

Both Don Kingsborough and Paul Rago were ideal clients when it came to the advertising. They wanted what Chiat/Day did best. Breakthrough work. There were times when they would push us beyond to make it even more edgy and unique.

And Don was no slouch when it came to underwriting the work if he saw the potential in it. Production expense was never a problem and this was even truer once we had our first success. Of course this became a part of a pesky accounting problem.

We did two commercials for Teddy Ruxpin initially, one directed at children and one at adults. The one for the kids demonstrated the wonder of the toy and the wonder it created in other kids who saw it. The commercial was called "Show and Tell" and was a dramatization for kids of what happened when we first saw Teddy Ruxpin. The reaction of the kids in the spot was precious and timeless. It was filled with fun, wonder, and envy. It was a very effective commercial and succeeded in driving kids in droves to ask their parents for a Teddy. Or rather harass them.

The second commercial was directed at both parents and kids and ran in much broader media. It was a parody of the old Frankenstein movie where the laboratory assistants help bring Teddy Ruxpin, who is strapped down on an operating table, to life. At one point in the commercial after they administer a bolt or two of electricity, Dr. Frankenstein is seen shouting "It's alive. It's alive!" and Teddy starts to move his eyes, opens them wide, and says, "Hi, my name is Teddy Ruxpin."

It was an edgy commercial and was produced with extraordinary attention to detail. It was a 30 second mini-movie in every sense. When we showed the finished spot to Don and Paul and others at Worlds of Wonder, they loved it.

The next morning Don called my office with buyer's remorse. "Fred, we're not going to run the Frankenstein spot."

"For God's sake, why not?"

"I showed it to my wife who had some of her friends over last night and they all think that kids are going to be scared."

"No Don! No Don! I'm coming down to see you."

I had a bright account planner named Betty Deepe and I corralled her to hold some quick and dirty interviews where she would show the commercial and get some reactions from parents. They all turned out to be positive.

With Betty's results in hand and a brief of arguments, I set off the next day to meet with Don. As is common to groups of ladies getting together and

being asked about commercials, they were all advertising experts.

"It's too scary."

"It's not funny."

"I don't get it."

"My son won't understand it."

"It's silly."

And so on.

The spot was so well produced and it was a gas. In the real world everyone got the joke and the parody. Viewers were riveted for the entire spot and loved when the thing came alive. I knew people would respond well to it and moreover it was so attention getting that it would easily drive awareness to levels that the budget would never achieve otherwise. The publicity that ensued from running such visible advertising was an added extra bonus. And guess what, kids absolutely loved it and I never heard of one getting scared.

After hours of discussion and argument, I was able to convince Don that the Frankenstein spot should run.

It did! And Teddy became one of the greatest new product success stories throughout the land. It was the number one selling toy during the 1985 holiday season. Don handed out 14K gold necklaces with Teddy as the charm to everyone who was a part of the grand success.

We were able to generate a share of voice in the plush toy category of 10 percent and garnished a 40 percent share of the market. Worlds of Wonder became only the second company at that point in American history to book over $100 million in sales in its first year. Actually they did $110 million in the first 12 months. Prior to this only Compaq Computer had succeeded in achieving this milestone, generating $105 million in its first year.

Don had a vision from the beginning of developing and bringing innovative and wondrous toys to the market and that the advertising had to reflect that attitude. A very high percentage of the people who purchased Teddy Ruxpin credited having seen the various commercials and said that was their motivation to purchase.

The toy category has traditionally had some of the worst, most boring, and most repetitive advertising, and that is at least partially because of all the restrictions placed on running advertising to kids in kids network TV.

The other part is that advertising people traditionally just accepted the guidelines established by the networks and ended up doing all this crappy kids advertising for Saturday morning television. We challenged those rules and regulations and more often than not were able to break down the barriers and have meaningful and effective advertising on air directed at children.

The creative work for Worlds of Wonder was always different and engaging and it was mostly breakthrough. And it all started with a commercial that almost didn't make it to the air.

The single biggest issue for the agency with Worlds of Wonder was the fact that Don Kingsborough, its founder, was himself a world of wonder in the way he positioned and promoted anything and everything. I really liked Don but over the years we worked together I never figured out whether he actually believed his own shit or he was just an incredibly driven salesperson.

There are people who are unimaginable storytellers and yet come off as the most sincere and honest folk you'd ever meet. You can't help but believe them and believe in them. Bernie Madoff and other grifters come to mind.

Don liked to talk about his family a lot. How he went to church every Sunday. The things he did for his community. How much he cared about kids. And he did a lot of these things to be sure.

But Don was the ultimate promoter. He could have a single exploratory conversation with someone and would turn it into becoming "a deal."

"The Abercrombie estate and trust is underwriting 49 percent of the company."

"Their controller is sitting in our key meetings."

"We have been given unlimited use of the Abercrombie corporate jet."

If Don met someone, even just once, all of a sudden he was "tight" with him or her and the best of friends.

"I met with Peter Magowan [then CEO of Safeway] and we should set up a dinner with you and him."

"Jack Tramiel [then CEO of Atari] is going to sell us his video game

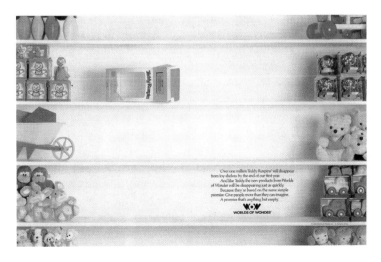

Over one million Teddy Ruxpins' will disappear
from toy shelves by the end of our first year.
And like Teddy the new products from Worlds
of Wonder will be disappearing just as quickly.
Because they're based on the same simple
premise: Give people more than they can imagine.
A promise that's anything but empty.

W•W
WORLDS OF WONDER

operation and we will fold Teddy Ruxpin into it."

Never had dinner with Magowan; Teddy Ruxpin never became an Atari product. It was true that a Texas heiress put up the first $15 million at the start of 1985 to get Worlds of Wonder off the ground. And Don may well have gotten airborne in the Abercrombie corporate jet.

From the start, with that very first check that was handed to me, until the end of our relationship, managing the money and credit on Worlds of Wonder was a huge issue and a top priority for me. After all is said and done I believe we did it extremely well and we made a ton of money along the way because we were willing to put in the effort, take the managed risk, and reap the rewards.

At the beginning I predicted that they were going to be a $50 million a year account. I was wrong—they grossly exceeded that number.

It was about this time, maybe a little premature, that Don undertook another project. He was living in Danville, California, an upscale community not too far from WOW headquarters. He had a very large house by most standards. However, he decided to build a bigger one. A 30,000-square-foot one. This one would have everything you can imagine including a bowling alley. And so construction began.

Soon after we were awarded the account we had to make our first media buy. This was for a children's network in the amount of $1.4 million. We had to make a commitment in a matter of only a few days and we had clearly explained to Don right from the start that we needed to have the money up front or guaranteed somehow.

And so began what became a major part of running this account. It was a constant cat and mouse game with WOW always trying to have us make commitments without any guarantees and us always trying to have some insurance that we were going to be paid for those commitments we would be making on their behalf.

With the children's network buy, for example, we had them sign an agreement, which put a lien on their accounts receivable in the event of a default. But as it turned out there were limited amounts of product being sold at that point and there were very few receivables.

We were told that the company had $15 million in funding but was fully committed. They didn't want to give us a letter of credit or a legal guarantee from their big investor Abercrombie because "it would dilute Don's ownership." And so on. There was always shucking going on when it came to the money.

Don proposed at one point that another agency make the media buy. Doyle Dane Bernbach, who he said "owed me a favor." He also suggested that Toys "R" Us, the big retailer, could make the buy for them and that they had already agreed if we wanted to go that route.

At the end of the day we gave up part of our commission and let Toys "R"

Us and a media-buying service make the buy. And for future buys we were able to get a letter of credit put in place. However, managing that letter of credit was a full-time job, with Worlds of Wonder regularly changing banks and locations without bothering to tell us.

Part of the problem was that Don had a knack for hiring financial executives who were sleazeballs. The financial people would keep things really close to the vest and went out of their way to mislead us.

We had a letter of credit in place for several million dollars but the then financial man had it set up so that it would be "rolled over" every 30 days and then extended. We were supposed to be notified each time this took place. Of course this meant that if the LC expired at any point, we could be left holding the bag for the outstanding commitments at that moment. It would have been proper and so much easier to leave the thing in place as long as it was needed but they always elected to keep up a veil.

Don Kingsborough—DK

The financial guys would give us the names of contacts where for example they had established a new line of credit with a new institution like First Chicago. We would call and find the guy was not there any longer or that he knew nothing about the situation or more likely that nothing had yet been resolved.

We would be given the names of the company's outside auditors like the accounting firm DH&S and an individual's name to get the WOW financial statements. We were always assured they were on the way, "in the mail," but they rarely arrived. We could never get the firm to fax, e-mail, or electronically transfer funds for some reason. Duh!

At the same time Don was an absolute master at the good cop/bad cop game and he always played the good cop. We were onto the game early on and kept at it with an intensity that allowed us to mostly protect ourselves during the course of our relationship.

At the end of the first year, having placed print ads, a children's network buy, a prime-time buy, and a big spot market buy, we were only owed $2,500 for a research study we had completed, the invoice for which apparently had been lost in their system.

After the enormous success of Teddy Ruxpin, it was hard to believe that Worlds of Wonder could do anything as sensational but continue to drive more Teddy and related product sales in the second year. They did that but also came back with blockbuster number two. An electronic laser toy game of tag called Lazer Tag.

The idea of Lazer Tag was to fire a laser beam from a toy gun at the opponent's target shield, which each player wore. If you hit the target with the beam, you heard a noise as you scored. This product was so well made and so well advertised that it too became a giant success.

Don wanted an even bigger idea for the commercial to launch the Lazer Tag product and we did not disappoint. It was a huge production and incredibly expensive but he approved it. Our creative director Ross Van Dusen developed the idea and oversaw the intricacies of the production. The commercial was exciting and engaging, more like a short movie. It had futuristic combatants engaged in a mock battle using the Lazer Tag guns and related equipment.

Stadium not included.

The commercial drove awareness of the product through the roof. It too received much added related publicity because it was so unusual. It helped sell another $100-plus million of this product alone in Worlds of Wonder's second year.

The publicity that the commercial spawned was fantastic. Lazer Tag was talked about on the late night television shows and elsewhere. *The San Francisco Chronicle* reported that Elton John saw the commercial and "immediately ordered sets for everybody he knows."

Herb Caen, columnist for *The San Francisco Chronicle*, had some fun and gave us some free publicity on September 25, 1986. He wrote in "Tales of the Town": "Goldberg variation: Whoopi Goldberg was so desperate for a Lazer Tag that she phoned Fred Goldberg (no relation), gen. mgr. of Chiat/Day, the ad agency handling the product, who told her to call Bob Goldberg (no relation to either), exec veep for marketing at Worlds of Wonder. Goldberg came through, but I forget which one."

Even President Reagan was a part of the fun and action in a cartoon that ran nationally. It pictured him playing with the toy and an aide standing by on the phone saying, "Hold all calls. He's playing Lazer Tag."

Don later received an Outstanding Contribution Award for the Private Sector from Ronald Reagan. Probably not related to the cartoon.

All this favorable publicity was helped immensely by Steve Smith, who along with his firm was able to generate oodles of positive "ink" and heighten the awareness of WOW and all of its doings still more.

Everything was going absolutely marvelously until some cops in Los Angeles spotted some kids in a parking lot at night firing what they thought were pistols at one another. Somehow one of the policemen shot one of the kids and he died.

And so did Lazer Tag.

There were other wonderful and unique products that came out of Worlds of Wonder, including Jaminator; a talking Donald Duck, Mother Goose, and Mickey Mouse; Action Max; and Julie, a talking doll. None of these ever reached the proportions that Teddy Ruxpin or Lazer Tag had achieved.

The company had an incredible run and we ran with it. It was on a track to being the greatest toy company that ever was. They had great products, great promotions, great advertising, and lousy financial management. In year two they were able to do $320 million in sales, which was remarkable and unmanageable.

In the end it was the mismanagement of the money that took down the company. They had created what looked to my inexperienced eyes like a Ponzi scheme of sorts by extending themselves and spreading around what receivables they had and making far too many future commitments that they ultimately couldn't cover. But what do I know—I'm only guessing at what actually happened.

One day it was disclosed that many of the top company executives were selling their Worlds of Wonder stock. It also didn't help that the stock market had crashed in 1987. Worlds of Wonder filed for Chapter 11 bankruptcy in 1988 and defaulted on $80 million of new debt they had acquired. And unfortunately, so ended Worlds of Wonder.

We were able to claim a unique partnership in building yet another wondrous entrepreneurial start-up company to a phenomenal, if relatively short-lived, success. Our association and work for Worlds of Wonder allowed us to attract many other new businesses to the agency.

Most importantly we did some absolutely fantastic advertising. Oh and I still have the solid 14K gold pendant that Don Kingsborough had a jeweler friend of his make up and which he handed out to all of us involved in getting Teddy Ruxpin and Worlds of Wonder off the ground that first year.

On the front, signed by Teddy Ruxpin, it has engraved, "And if our dream's a good one . . . someday it might come true."

On the back, signed by Don, it has engraved, "Many people dream. But

few can make them come true. And you have. Thanks. Don."

If only Don had dreamed of cost control. What might have been.

Don formed another company a year or so after Worlds of Wonder blew up called Yes! Entertainment, for which we did some work. It had some good ideas behind it but never achieved close to the success of WOW and soon faded away.

Work stopped on the 30,000-square-foot house soon after that kid in the parking lot with the Lazer Tag pistol got gunned down by the LAPD.

Last I heard, Don landed in the promotion department at Safeway and more recently operated as head of the Blackhawk Network, which markets prepaid card products and was a part of Safeway.

And I am a happy camper. I'm retired and the price of gold is currently at around $1,800 an ounce. My Teddy Ruxpin pendant is worth a small fortune.

CHAPTER 10

CHRISTMAS BALLS

WE HAD LOTS OF EXPERIENCE with software companies over the years, first at Chiat/Day and then at Goldberg Moser O'Neill. Small ones and not so small ones, start-ups and established companies. A lot of our attraction had to do with having been in at the start with Apple Computer and helping put them on the map. Every one of these companies had similar aspirations. Most never came close to realizing them.

Over the years we worked with such companies as Epyx, Menlo, Hesware, Breakthrough, Ask, Software Toolworks, Santa Cruz Operation, Lucas Learning, Sybase, Timeline, Paladin, Lightyear, Ansa, Symantec, Ashton-Tate, and others. Some got bought early on or went out of business. A few went on to become industry leaders and giants. All of them had one thing in common: they were incredibly dysfunctional organizations.

Ben Rosen was a giant in technology and Silicon Valley. He started Compaq Computer and went on from there. At one point he formed a start-up software company called Ansa. They had a database management software product. Ben and his Ansa president, a fellow named Steve Dow, came into the agency one day in April 1985 and gave us their business.

In turn we created a truly fantastic advertising campaign for Ansa that could be implemented for not very much money and would have an added benefit of generating enormous buzz. The Ansa product had the capability to take data and forecast powerfully. We developed an idea to be implemented the next fall when they were launching the product at the start of the NFL Monday Night Football season. The idea was that we would utilize the Ansa software to predict who would win each Monday night game, and ultimately, if you followed along, who would win the Super Bowl. We planned to run a powerful, attention-getting ad in the *Wall Street Journal* each Monday morning. It was a very strong product demonstration with huge potential for publicity. The ads were terrific; the media idea was inspired.

Well, we presented the idea to Ben. He hated it and rejected it outright. Steve Dow never had a chance to say no. We did several other campaigns after trying a number of times to convince him of the appropriateness of the football idea. But he never agreed. As these things go we soon resigned the business.

It so happens that Ron Posner, a good friend of the agency, arrived at another database company and he hired us just a few weeks after we parted with Ansa. The company was Ashton-Tate and they were a leader in this field at the time.

Ben Rosen wasn't happy at all. He was angry that we were going to work for a competitor of his. And I am certain that mostly his ego was bruised after we had resigned the Ansa business.

Not only did he threaten to sue us. He did sue us. I'm not quite sure for what, but he did. It turned out that he was most concerned that we would share the football idea with a direct competitor. Clients are funny, aren't they? He hated the idea but he didn't want anyone else to have it. Unfortunately he succeeded in tying us up long enough for the football season to pass. Literally.

When we won the Ashton-Tate account, they had some very important business software, including database management software called dBase. After a successful almost four-year relationship, and some highly effective and award-winning advertising, we were summarily fired by them. Management had changed and we were eventually sacked by a woman some referred to as the Dragon Lady. First, however, she hired away one of our most experienced executives who had been assigned to the account. A very bright, highly motivated, and knowledgeable fellow named Floyd Miller.

Floyd would have become one of our key senior management executives had he stayed. He only lasted a short time with the Dragon Lady but went on to found his own extremely successful company, Miller/Kadanoff Direct. Parenthetically he later had a falling out with his partner, who some said was also a Dragon Lady. Eventually Floyd sold his company to the very same Interpublic folks who purchased Goldberg Moser O'Neill. (They did not have a long term success with his company nor with ours.) Fortunately Floyd got most of his money before that happened.

But back to Ashton-Tate. In addition to taking the key guy on the business, the Dragon Lady called another advertising agency, Doyle Dane Bernbach, where she had some friends. I found out about this by accident and was able to fend off her efforts the first time with the then CEO, Ed Esber, but alas as advertising agency history has shown in most cases like this, if you're going to shoot the queen, make sure she's dead. She wasn't. And so ended our relationship with Ashton-Tate.

Not very long afterward the Dragon Lady surfaced at another company where we had some friends and acquaintances. We were able to honestly answer some candid queries that were directed to us about this lovely lady. (Actually she reminded many of a sour prune, always puckered.) She was history in a matter of months. Lesson learned: an asshole generally ends up getting stuck in the rear end. And she did!

I was pretty upset with the loss of Ashton-Tate and came to the conclusion that maybe the best revenge would be to go out and get a direct competitor as quickly as possible. The management at many software companies had two consistent qualities I observed: one, they really hated their competitors' guts; two, they really had a confidentiality problem with sharing any knowledge, particularly if it came from people who were no longer associated with them. Like us.

It didn't take us long to make a score again. I had read a lot about Larry Ellison, founder and CEO of Oracle, and it seemed he was the single most aggressive software competitor out there to Ashton-Tate's database management business.

He appeared to be a real hot dog. So I targeted Larry Ellison and his company Oracle. A company and an individual known to have a huge level of dislike for Ashton-Tate. And, known to be maybe the fiercest competitor with a take no prisoners approach.

⊘ ⊘ ⊘

I prepared various communications and sent them from time to time to Larry, each with some relevant points concerning Oracle's marketing and advertising efforts. And then I sent him a poster, which was very simple. It had Ashton-Tate's logo in the middle with a big red circle around it and line through it. The international symbol for no, or don't, or eliminate. It had one line of copy, which spoke to a mutual ambition.

Larry's ears, eyes, and ego lit up. It came to pass that we went to work for Oracle in February of 1989 not too long after Ashton-Tate had summarily dismissed us. We immediately did some very competitive, directly comparative advertising against them. How sweet it was!

Now Larry was a pretty wealthy guy even back then, although nowhere near what he's worth today. He had been enormously successful to that point and he terrified most people just saying hello. He was extremely smart. He really knew his business. He didn't suffer fools. He was incredibly opinionated. And as it turned out he fancied he knew how to develop advertising as well. That is, he knew what he wanted in his advertising for Oracle. He was particularly enamored with

military tactics, analogies, and competitive comparative claims. He loved setting up this is them and this is us.

Our relationship with Larry and Oracle lasted over three years. But it was a tough road. Two of my partners, Mike Moser and Mike Massaro,

Here's Larry!

and occasionally I, would find ourselves on a Friday afternoon sitting in Ellison's office at Oracle down Highway 101 in Redwood City. We would huddle in his Zen-like office. Hummmmmm! In this serene atmosphere Larry sat with his Macintosh at the ready, banging out his ad ideas as quickly as Mike Moser would present one.

Larry had a penchant for things Japanese. His office was done in Japanese minimal. Not much there but a spacious room and a long conference table with a few little rocks in water placed strategically in a small plate-like thing in the center of the table. Hummmmmm! The two Mikes and I would stare at the rocks and watch the slight ripples in the water while Larry tapped out his next "ad" idea. Most of what we were thinking about was the ride back up Highway 101 to San Francisco at 4:30 on Friday afternoon. Contemplating the rocks and water didn't seem to help much. Hummmmmm!

Larry basically had one ad. He would list all the product features or attributes for an Oracle product down the left side of a page and then all the product features or attributes for, say, the comparable Ashton-Tate or Sybase product. Oracle always was one better on most every feature. He could have been the creator of the FASTER! BETTER! CHEAPER! school of advertising. It didn't matter to Larry whether or not they were meaningless differences to the customer. He ended up with essentially the same headline and layout for every ad.

ORACLE BEATS SYBASE

Runs faster —	*Runs slower —*
1,000 miles per hour	*500 miles per hour*
Used by 5,000 companies	*Used by 2,500 companies*
Costs less $/cpu	*Costs more $/cpu*

Well, you get the idea. He really didn't need an advertising agency to do this kind of work. And he certainly didn't need a creative-oriented one like us. And most definitely he didn't need a creative person with the talent of Mike Moser. Even today Oracle is running essentially the same comparative boring ugly ads. "Runs Oracle 10x Faster."

Over 36 or so months we were able to get Larry to run only one decent ad and that was our very first one. It was a great one, however. After that they all deteriorated into product feature and specification ads like Oracle Beats Sybase. And, they were just like every other software ad running in *PC Magazine*, which lacked attention-getting value and credibility. At the end Mike Moser was ready to hang himself and Mike Massaro needed a sabbatical. I had attended enough of the Friday afternoon sessions to identify and sympathize with them.

And over this period of time other Oracle executives, or should I say knaves, became involved in the ad development process, which complicated everything by a factor of five. We were continually threatened with being fired and were doing lousy work. So despite the fact that the business represented a sizable income I decided to part with Oracle. We gave them an ultimatum. Shape up or we ship out.

As you might expect, Larry didn't take to this kindly. Larry liked to be the firer . . . not the firee. Who would have guessed? But sometimes, strange things happen when you least expect them to.

For example, I was in the habit of throwing fairly elaborate year-end holiday parties for our employees and select clients and friends. I started a tradition of creating each with a unique theme with which we were able to build the event around and then tried to put all the appropriate details together to make it a very special and festive get-together.

One of the most eventful parties was set at the old Christian Brothers winery in the Napa Valley (now the Culinary Institute of America). It was a Renaissance theme and it was carried out to the nines, including the roast suckling pigs. We arranged to have everyone stay at the Napa Valley Inn that evening. That was my swan song party before retiring from the business.

In 1995 another memorable party took place at the Galleria Design Center in San Francisco for a GMOasis

Party invitation.

where we imported real camels (from LA), which, if you were so inclined, you were able to ride, in keeping with the Moroccan theme. And in 1998 Una Fiesta Espanola at the Golden Gate Club in the Presidio included the hot band at the time, Los Lobos.

Le Petit Trianon party.

For the holiday season of 1994 I had the good fortune of finding a location in San Francisco, in the Presidio area, that was incredibly unique. Real estate developer Charles Pankow owned a small but perfect replica of Le Petit Trianon as it exists in Versailles. That's the one where Louis XVI and Marie Antoinette spent their weekends.

Pankow kept an impressive art collection, with different themes in each of the rooms: Chinese, French impressionists, Russian icons. There was a full-scale ballroom. It all looked out on San Francisco Bay, Alcatraz, and the Golden Gate Bridge. It was beautiful and spectacular.

That evening, as was my habit, I generally was the first to arrive at the party scene to check on all the details. I met with Kristen McCormack, the event planner who did most all of my parties over the years. She and her company were simply the best. They understood the importance of attention to details and quality.

As I walked into the "house," it was evident she had once again done a superb job. The place was prepared extraordinarily and magnificently and I was pleased. I grabbed a vodka martini and sat down next to a large beautifully dressed Christmas tree. The tree was exceptional with silver trimmings, hundreds of little white lights, and many glorious gold balls glittering and shining. I watched as the guests began to arrive, each dressed up and looking as special as the party venue itself. Many came in period costumes to fit the occasion.

I had earlier learned that the *San Francisco Examiner* was doing a story on parties in the city. I happened to have known the reporter, Julian Guthrie, who was assigned to the story. I thought it would be good publicity for the agency to have her attend the party and let her see firsthand just how spectacular a really well-planned event could be, and that it would reflect well on the quality of the agency. She was more than happy to come and did.

As I was sitting watching each of the guests arrive, I saw her come in and I blinked, rubbed my eyes, to be sure that I was seeing straight. I hadn't even finished my first martini. But yes, there was Julian Guthrie, the *Examiner* reporter, and hanging on her left arm was none other than . . . Larry Ellison. Julian was celebrity enough, having dated Mayor Willie Brown. But having her and Larry was double the fun.

I walked across the room to welcome them. Now here's this guy who was a multi-zillionaire, and the first thing he did was to ask whether it was "OK if I'm here." And then he said, "I mean you fired me." He knew he had put us through hell for four years but I believe he was still pissed when we told him we were leaving. I was uncharacteristically gracious and told him that I was honored that he was there. And anyway what was I going to say? He was there with the ticket to some free publicity. Which by the way turned out to be spectacular publicity worth far more than the cost of an extra guest. The article in the *San Francisco Examiner* was entitled "The Best Christmas Parties in San Francisco" and we were featured in it.

I really have to thank the Dragon Lady because without her this story could not be told. And Larry, who made this Christmas party a bigger success than it would have been otherwise. So thanks to him for that and also for helping to put Ashton-Tate out of business along the way. Another salute because he let the next advertising agency he hired do some decent advertising. But not for long.

A final, even bigger salute to Larry Ellison for having the guts and gall to show up at our company Christmas party after we told him we didn't love him.

And that is why this chapter is called Christmas "balls."

CHAPTER 11

THE EMPEROR HAD NO CLOTHES

"Jay, you should use the restroom before we begin."

I was sitting next to Jay as he was about to call the meeting to order. I looked up, leaned over, and whispered to him.

He glared at me quizzically with a "What the fuck are you talking about?" look. I slowly rolled my eyes up toward his forehead and beyond. He seemed to immediately understand, got up, and left the room. He returned a few minutes later, took his seat, and started the meeting.

It was a cold and windy day. We were having a regular quarterly board of directors meeting. It rotated from Los Angeles to San Francisco, and this time it was being held in New York.

Jay Chiat, chairman and CEO of Chiat/Day, had strolled into the room. After getting coffee and a sweet roll, making a few smart-ass off-the-cuff remarks, and partaking in the usual small talk and banter that preceded these meetings, Jay headed to his chair. He seated himself at his customary place at the head of the table, where

Jay

the King, I mean Emperor, felt most comfortable. This day I happened to be sitting just to Jay's left.

What had occurred was classic. There were 10 people chatting with Jay for 10 minutes before the meeting started, and no one cared to tell Jay he had a problem. The problem was with his plugs. His hair plugs.

The wind had blown his hair across to the right side of his head, exposing several rows of what appeared to be a series of small buttonholes in his scalp. It looked kind of like an old ladies shoe from the turn of the last century. In order to camouflage this situation, he customarily combed his hair in the opposite direction. And that's the way it generally appeared, but not on this breezy day.

We had the Intel account for most of the 1980s. Back then Intel spent only about $4 million across 20 separate divisions, and it required a lot of effort for not much revenue. But it was an important brand name in technology even then.

One time, Jay and I had a meeting at Intel in Santa Clara. We drove down together from San Francisco. I was the designated driver, as I can never remember Jay ever sitting behind the wheel of a car. Rumor had it that he lost his license at some point, for some reason, but I never knew for sure. Maybe he just liked being driven around.

We were heading down Highway 101, and as we approached the exit for Intel, Jay turned to me and said, "You know you should get some plugs. I have a great guy in Pasadena." I didn't know what the hell he was talking about. Was he suggesting some special electric outlets for my house? Or at the office? Or, was he advising me that I needed a publicist?

Then it struck me. He was looking at my head and at my hair.

Now I had had a receding hairline for as long as I could remember, combined with an expanding bald spot in the back of my head for at least the previous 15 years. I'm not sure what plugs would have done for me, except hurt like heck on the way in. But Jay offered this advice, and then to my surprise he even offered to pay for them. I thanked him and told him I'd give it some thought.

I have reflected on this discussion numerous times over the years and wondered what Jay's real motivation was. Did he really think I needed more hair? Was it something he felt would improve my perception at Chiat/Day? Had he spoken with my wife? Was he simply a kind and generous man? All of the above? None of the above?

My conclusion is that in his own Machiavellian way he was thanking me for letting him know that his plugs were uncovered that day at the New York board meeting. Those who know Jay may agree. Those who do not, read on to learn just how Machiavellian this man could be.

People admired and feared Jay, and the fear part often worked to his personal disadvantage and against his dignity. I think it also caused some serious negative effects on the way the agency was managed.

Few people wanted to tell it like it was to Jay. Like in New York when Jay stood sipping his coffee and chatting with some of the Chiat executives, who tried to look away from the disheveled nest on Jay's head.

I remember another time, when Jay walked into a client meeting with something gray and shiny drooping out of his nose. I mean everyone has this problem now and then. But who do you think told him it was there? Yep, that's right, it was me. Nobody else stepped up to the plate, or the nose if you will.

While Jay always seemingly exhibited annoyance when this happened, I do believe he appreciated the directness and honesty. Though he never said it, I felt it. And hey, he did offer to give me my own set of plugs once before. Who knew what a "booger" might be worth down the road.

Truth was that Jay had a soft underskin. I truly saw this only once in my nine years of working with him. He was visiting San Francisco and was in our offices at 77 Maiden Lane. He got sick in my office and became very weak and disoriented. I took him downstairs and got us into a taxi and to St. Francis Memorial Hospital. On the way he was throwing up: on the street, in the cab, on himself and me.

When we arrived at the hospital, I cleaned him up as best I could and got him checked in. He stayed overnight and left for Los Angeles the next day seemingly having recovered. During this incident, I saw a different side of Jay, one that was kinder, gentler, and grateful. It was the only time I experienced this with him, as it was back to "normal" the next day. It may well have simply been how helpless this macho strong-willed guy was in the situation. Or maybe not.

The single most important time I can recall when Jay didn't get a straight answer was during the preparation for the new business pitch to Nissan automobiles. The situation could have worked to his enormous disadvantage as well as the agency's. As it turned out, it became maybe one of his greatest triumphs personally and for the agency.

$$\oslash \; \oslash \; \oslash$$

Some 40 souls were huddled at a media presentation company, somewhere in or around Culver City, which is west of Los Angeles. It was already dark and the Nissan presentation was the next day. This was to be the final pitch for the business and we were competing with two other agencies for what would be our largest single account.

At the time, I was the chief operating officer for Chiat/Day. I had been asked by Jay to attend the rehearsal meeting that evening and to be present at the final presentation as a member of Chiat/Day management. I had no speaking role, as it was just a respect thing in Jay's mind for the Japanese management.

The rehearsal dragged on and on as these things do, for about five hours. There were nine presenters and lots and lots of charts and ads. It got late, maybe 10 or 11 when they finished the run-through. Everyone was tired, nervous, and a bit depressed.

Jay announced, "Well that's it."

Forty-plus people were completely silent. A few looked at one another, shuffled their feet a bit, but no one said a word. The Emperor had spoken. "Well that's it."

Then he said, "See you tomorrow."

And, like lemmings the group started to slowly file out toward the exit, dragging their feet a bit as they went.

I stood up and declared, "Wait a minute."

Jay spun around and glared at me and said, "What is it?"

I said, "This is terrible and we're not going to win the business if we go forward with the presentation as it is."

Jay didn't hesitate a nanosecond before he launched into a tirade directed broadside at me.

He yelled, he cursed, he belittled my judgment, and he criticized me for demoralizing everyone in the room, the agency, and the world with my remarks. Then he ordered me outside into the parking lot, where I thought he was going to throw a punch at me. He didn't, but he continued ranting and raving to the point where I finally said, "Jay, you do whatever the fuck you want."

I walked to my car, got in, and left.

I had told him that there were too many presenters. At times they were jumping up and down every minute or so to make only one point. Some of them were awful in their delivery and some were saying things that were incredibly spurious. It wasn't focused. It was way too long. Other than that it was great.

I found out afterward that Jay had gone back into the room and cut four of the presenters out of the nine. He knew exactly who the worst four were. Some other significant changes were made in the flow of the presentation and in the dialogue. I don't know when they left, but it must have been very late.

The next day we all assembled at Nissan headquarters in Gardena. When I arrived, I went to the company cafeteria and spotted Tom Patty and Gene Cameron, two of the Chiat/Day executives, sipping coffee out of Styrofoam cups. Tom was designated to be the key account guy on the business and was an important and good presenter. Gene was a great speaker and was also presenting some important material, but his main role had been to oversee and coordinate the preparation of the presentation these past many months.

Gene saw me enter the room and came running toward me. Although he was one of the most affable people I have ever met, it crossed my mind as he approached that maybe he was going to throw a punch at me for my performance the night before. But no, instead he came up to me and delivered an even bigger punch than he could have with his fist. He told me that Jay wanted me to close the presentation.

I have had some pretty intense situations throughout my career, but never had I felt like I did at that moment. The adrenaline shot through my body, my hands started to shake a bit, and my heart started pumping real fast. I thought I was going to lose what little I had in my stomach. I was used to writing out just about every word of my presentations.

As I mentioned earlier, I was only supposed to sit through the meeting as a show of importance and respect for the Japanese management. I had not been given any speaking role.

But now, I was being thrust into what typically can be a highly critical part of a new business presentation. Sort of like the final summary made by a prosecuting attorney at trial. It required providing a smart, passionate, and credible closing argument as to why our company should be hired for the account.

To say the least I was in a panic. I was shaking and had a headache.

I went to the restroom to try to calm down. Threw some cold water on my face. When I came out, the meeting was about to begin and everyone started to take their seats and the presentation room began to fill up. By this time I was settled enough to walk straight to my seat, but not do much more. I was still a bit dizzy.

The room had been set up with a big U-shaped table with the bottom of the U as long as each of the sides. The open end of the U was facing a huge projection screen below which, on either side, were two speaking podiums where each of the agency presenters was to stand. The clients all sat mostly along the base of the U, and the attending Chiat/Day folks took seats on both tips of the U.

I took a seat at the very top of the left part of the top of the U. In this chair no one could look over my shoulder except the presenter behind me and presumably he would be busy.

The presentation began with Gene Cameron opening the meeting and I began to try to concentrate and think of what I might possibly say and do to provide value at the end of the presentation. Exactly three hours was allotted by the client for the presentation and they had made it clear that it was not to exceed that allotment.

I spent the first hour or so staring at a blank three by five card, drawing an empty white cloud as my hands continued to shake a bit.

Then, during the second hour I had an inspiration. I started jotting down a few thoughts and concepts. Soon I had two cards full of things, not all of which made sense, but which I felt were the start of something that might not embarrass us and more importantly me. I spent the next hour cutting and pasting my thoughts, and finally got what I wanted to say down onto the front of three cards.

I hadn't heard a word spoken by the presenters, but I sensed everything seemed to be unfolding quite well. The next 30 minutes, I considered how I was going to actually deliver what I had crafted. It was now about 2 hours and 30 minutes into the presentation and I sat back, breathed a sigh of relief, and relaxed a bit. I turned my head to Lee Clow, the creative director of the agency, who was presenting the second of our campaign recommendations. Lee did a great job, I thought, and finished with about 15 minutes left and then glanced over at me.

I stood up, grabbed my cards, put one of the several client presentation leave behinds under my arm, and walked to the center of the U directly facing the Nissan clients. I felt that I spoke clearly and confidently and credibly for just under 10 minutes. I addressed our competitive uniqueness versus the competition in the review; our advertising and sales track record; and our creative prowess in the sea of sameness of advertising. And I spoke to our commitment to the Nissan business.

I felt I was making a connection with a number of the clients. I had spent several years at Young & Rubicam working with the Japanese ad agency Dentsu and with many Japanese clients, and I knew it was a bit hard to tell much with the Japanese.

For example, an up and down movement of the head most often means I am receiving your signal. Rarely does it mean I hear what you're saying and agree with you. Then, too, some Japanese are given to closing their eyes while you're talking directly to them. It was my understanding that the senior Japanese client has the right to do this, as it is in keeping with his level of responsibility. Personally, I think it is really deep, deep concentration or that they were out late the night before and had too much sake.

I ended with an argument that I had used successfully before in winning new business. I professed, in my most humble and believable way, "If Chiat/Day were fortunate enough to be awarded the Nissan business, everyone in our top management would be forever at their disposal and fully committed to the Nissan business."

Furthermore, that Nissan was not A but THE defining account for the agency. It would be a springboard that launched the agency to a critical mass. For this we would be forever in their debt and gratitude. For the other agencies in the review the Nissan business was just another big account.

The bottom line was that Nissan would "own" what was arguably at the time the most creative and exciting advertising agency in the country. An agency that was developing the most creative work, which was impacting our existing clients' business dramatically.

I ended by mentioning what was contained in the four binders we had prepared as a leave behind, one of which I held up in the air. I then thanked them all for inviting us into the review and sat down.

Gene Cameron was a big-time sweater. He would sweat just having a cup of coffee. You could shake his hand and you would have to dry your hand off. Gene was seated near me and I saw the sweat dripping off his brow and he had his characteristic armpits with circles of perspiration. On the other hand I wasn't a sweater, but when I sat down I discovered my shirt was completely drenched and I had parts of my underwear stuck in places they had never gone before.

There were just about five minutes of allotted time left, and like Lazarus, Jay rose up! He was inspired by what had transpired over the past 2 hours and

55 minutes. He looked engaged, enthusiastic, and energized. He had decided that he was going to close the meeting after all. Or should I say after me. Maybe he had decided to do this all along, but I never knew.

Jay was brilliant and eloquent. He repeated all of what I had said in his own words, and then more. It was very, very good. And I felt we had scored a direct empathetic hit . . . back to back. Jay had an incredible talent for speaking spontaneously and off-the-cuff, and most of the time he was superb at it. In this case, he was able to key in on all the critical points and issues in a credible and persuasive way.

It was masterful. It was perfect, even if a good chunk of it was bullshit.

The meeting ended right on time. The clients filed out of the room. Several came up to various Chiat/Day people and congratulated them on a good presentation. We packed up our wares and everyone gathered at a nearby watering hole for drinks. Just about every one of the folks that had worked on the presentation over many months was there when the pitch team arrived. Everyone was feeling pretty good about what had just happened.

And they should have. Chiat/Day won the account. This was back in 1987, and as I write this story 20-plus years later they still have it and I believe it is their largest. Over the years, the account has been worth billions of dollars in advertising billings and millions and millions in profits.

In the earlier years the account allowed for some remarkable automobile advertising. It won many accolades and awards for creative excellence. The scope and size of the business brought a needed discipline to the agency. Nissan clearly put the agency at a new important plateau and was responsible for attracting much additional business over the years.

But that's not the end of this story. The end of this story has to do with Jay yelling at me back in the parking lot of that multimedia place after the almost fatal "final" rehearsal of the presentation the night before. It's about no one else standing up there and telling Jay the presentation sucked. It's about Jay throwing me one of the biggest curveballs I ever had to catch in my whole career. And it's about why he did what he did.

It's pretty clear to me. Jay was a Machiavellian guy and he knew exactly what he was doing by making me close the meeting on a last second's notice. It was the most important new business presentation in the history of the agency.

He put himself in a win/win position. He put me in a lose/lose position.

If I had screwed up and/or we had not won the account, he could have blamed me, big time. If I did well, and made some kind of positive contribution and we got the account, he looked real smart putting me up there. It was not the first time that Jay had taken my far more structured words and arguments and turned them into more eloquent and engaging spoken words.

At the same time, he knew he was going to inflict a huge amount of pain on me by making me do something like this at the very last moment. I was a guy who prepared, maybe overprepared, everything and Jay knew it. He had criticized me for that numerous times over the years. He was much more enamored with people who spoke spontaneously and off-the-cuff, although he sure didn't like it when those kinds of comments backfired. It was amazing, too, how often Jay was the one who often stepped in shit with his unplanned off-the-cuff remarks.

But Jay was a guy who liked to bet all the chips he had in his hand. I saw him do it one day at the Hyatt at Lake Tahoe when he couldn't really afford to lay a thousand dollars down on black or red. But he did and he won that day! He took big risks and didn't often think or concern himself about the consequences. He very often acted on impulse.

Fred Goldberg
Executive Vice President
Chief Operating Officer

I think that's what happened at Nissan. Jay didn't think about the consequences. Or perhaps it was simply that he had confidence in my abilities. Do you think? Naah!

He never said a word one way or the other. Not "Good job," not "Thank you," not anything.

On the other hand, I was subsequently rewarded regularly with large raises and a big equity stake in Chiat/Day. The job of chief operating officer of all Chiat/Day, however, turned out to be unrewarding and thankless.

A lot of people didn't know that Jay was Jewish. Or, that his name was pronounced with a hard C (Hch-eye-it) in the old country. Or, that someone told me once that *Chiat* meant "tailor" in Yiddish. But I did.

Jay proudly rode through the streets of the advertising industry but this Emperor was very often not told when he was naked. He should have called a relative from the old country to help him out with some clothes.

Well, maybe he did. Me!

Letter to the Editor
Advertising Age
May 1, 2002

I worked for Jay Chiat from 1982 to 1990. These were argu-
ably the most creatively prolific years for Chiat/Day and I was
fortunate to have been a part of it.

Jay was a difficult and demanding person. Intellectually and
emotionally. It is incredible how most all of the talented people
that he attracted to his agency have gone on to become successes in
their own right. It was not a coincidence, but rather because of
their interaction with Jay and the impact that he had on them.

In my own case, I learned and benefited enormously from having been touched by him. Sometimes with pleasure; sometimes with pain. Others who will not now have that opportunity will have missed something of notable importance.

I spent 17 years thinking I was in the advertising business before meeting Jay Chiat. I was wrong. Thank you Jay for enlightening so many others and me.

Fred Goldberg
Retired Chairman/CEO & Founder
Goldberg Moser O'Neill (Formerly Chiat/Day)

Written on Jay's death at only 70 years of age. One of only two letters that appeared in *Ad Age* regarding his passing from the ad business. Of course much much more was written about him editorially in the days that followed.

It is not so surprising that Jay's obituary appeared in the *New York Times,* April 24, 2002, right next to another for Linda Boreman. They both plowed territories that had heretofore been unexplored. He in advertising, art, architecture, and relationships; she in somewhat darker, maybe more subtle places. Linda was best known for her role in *Deep Throat* in which she starred as Linda Lovelace.

Jay would probably have been the great success he was regardless of the fact that he was able to acquire the Apple Computer account. No one could have predicted at the time the enormous success that Apple would become and the importance of the advertising in making that success come to pass. And the enormous role that played in Chiat/Day's success.

Jay was consistently inconsistent. He would hire someone on a whim, and if that person was loyal he could reward him handsomely even if he was inept.

I remember hearing the story of how Jay came into the San Francisco office one day and threw a set of car keys to the then GM of the office. This person would lie down on the road for Jay with a caravan of trucks only a few feet away. All Jay had to do was ask or bark as he usually did. So Jay gave him a brand-new Jaguar.

The guy who was GM at Chiat/Day San Francisco when I was first hired to run Apple out of that office thought it might be a good idea to "interview" me when he heard I was hired and he flew down to Los Angeles to do so. We had dinner at the Hotel Bel-Air on Stone Canyon Road, just a few houses away from where I was living. It was a very uncomfortable meal, with the GM pretending that he knew all about my being hired and playing at being my boss to be.

Turns out, Jay never said a word to him about me until after I was hired. In fact, I was on board only a few weeks and Jay started calling me from

New York and ranting about various things that had gone askew in the San Francisco office. It didn't matter to him that I was unaware of most of them.

I remember one conversation.

"Jay, I'm not the manager. There is somebody here who is the manager. You hired me to run Apple."

"Just fix it."

Click.

Three months later he called me and advised that I was now the general manager of the San Francisco office. I asked him if he told anyone else and he didn't answer me. He hadn't but did finally get around to it a few days later and sent out an memo.

Just after I was hired Jay told me to report to the San Francisco office in two weeks. I did and I walked into the office at 414 Jackson Street, and no one knew who I was or even that I was coming. When I explained the situation to the office manager, Rosalinde Estes, she showed me to an office with a completely barren desk, laid down a yellow lined pad in the center, placed a No. 3 pencil next to it, and said, "Here you go."

That's the way it was under Jay's leadership. You either rose to the occasion or you sank very quickly. He often provided the most unexpected opportunities and forced an individual to confront his own abilities or inabilities head on. Bless him.

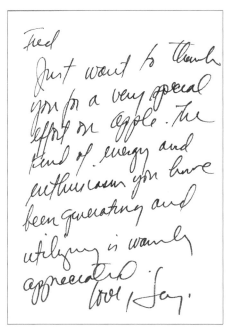

For me, it was incredibly refreshing to be handed such real responsibility and authority after having been in a bureaucratic environment for so long where everyone looked over their shoulder and where absolutely no one had real decision-making authority. At Chiat/Day it was way different. You had the authority and you had better use it. Oh and you had better make the right decisions too because you had to live with them. And with Jay.

Jay could be Dr. Jekyll and Jay could be Mr. Hyde. It wasn't very motivating when he was attacking your work and efforts and you personally. On the other hand, when he wanted to, he would turn around and offer the most gracious compliments and rewards, monetary and otherwise.

I received this little note at the end of my first year, which made me double down and work twice as hard.

When I was executive VP and general manger of Y&R Los Angeles, I couldn't get the pencils changed from a No. 2 to a No. 3 without approval from the New York purchasing department. At Chiat/Day, the lowest level people had vastly more authority and power. I mean the mailroom guy actually did order the pencils when needed in each office.

And I found that most people were far more careful in using their given authority, simply because they had it. It was very egalitarian, and intellect was praised far more than a person's job title.

⊘ ⊘ ⊘

I learned so much from working for Jay, who never failed to surprise. The only thing that was predictable about Jay was that he was always unpredictable. One day Jay received a letter from David Ogilvy from his Chateau de Touffou in France. Ogilvy was bothered greatly by an ad that we had done for a new product called Savory Classics from Rice-A-Roni. It was an upscale rice mix.

He was upset that the visual idea in our ad had been "borrowed" from one he had done 50 years earlier and felt it was as irrelevant in our use of it now as it was when he had used it years before.

Ever the statesman, Jay wrote him back and thanked him for the letter and agreed with him about the irrelevance. He also said he was sending a copy of David Ogilvy's book, *Ogilvy on Advertising*, to the then creative director in San Francisco, Ross Van Dusen, since that's where the original ad was developed.

I'm not sure, but I don't think Jay knew that Ogilvy had also written a letter to *AdWeek* criticizing their critique of our ad, which they considered both new and noteworthy enough to feature one week.

I thought it was kind of cheeky to write Jay and *AdWeek* at the same time. I mean David Ogilvy was a legend in his own right. Would've thunk he'd have something better to do that afternoon in the French countryside.

Here's this famous ad industry personality, sitting in his castle in Bonnes, France, with a copy of *AdWeek* and a chance for some publicity, it seemed.

The ad that Ogilvy had written so many years earlier had been his first and he was clearly not proud of it. He even stated in his book that he was embarrassed by it. It used as a visual the famous Edouard Manet painting of a picnic attended by two men and a naked woman. And that's the one that we used in our Savory Classics ad.

But here's the thing. I agree that the painting as used in his ad was totally irrelevant. But our use of it was not at all. Sexist? Yes! But irrelevant? No! We were dramatizing the impact that this new product might just have on a half-baked run-of-the-mill picnic.

Our mistake may have been in using a naked woman to draw attention, as it was a bit politically impolite at the time. It was meant to be a joke, however, and the headline made sure of that: "Before Savory Classics, people went to extremes to make meals interesting."

Ogilvy's ad was for a thing called the Aga Cooker. It had no headline, so unless people read the entire body copy, they weren't going to get the connection with the famous Edouard Manet painting even if there was one. Which there wasn't.

I'm no David Ogilvy, but I think our ad was actually pretty good, particularly for packaged goods, which are not known for doing very inventive advertising. So what if it was a bit sexist. We could have used two naked men just as easily, had Manet painted the work that way.

So there!

⊘ ⊘ ⊘

In my opinion one of the absolute worst decisions Jay Chiat ever made was when he decided to purchase and merge with an Australian ad agency named Mojo. He paid some $55 million and had to eat most of it when he later sold Chiat/Day to Omnicom.

At the time of the purchase, Chiat/Day was arguably the greatest creative agency in the country. Maybe in the world. But out of his frustrated quest to become more global he tried to transplant a totally foreign, not "creatively well" body into the healthiest one in the entire ad agency world. And then announce it by changing the name of the agency to include the lesser entity and become Chiat/Day/Mojo.

The front page of the January 16, 1989, *AdWeek* reported on the merger and the impact of it in San Francisco in a lengthy article with the following headline:

Chiat/Day Golden Gate Headache?
S.F. Merger Could Be Tough

Not very long after, we were on a 14-hour Qantas flight to Sydney, Australia, to meet with our new Mojo partners. I had the unfortunate luck of sitting between Jay and my wife Jeri.

We were about an hour out of San Francisco and Jay leaned back and opened up that morning's *Wall Street Journal*. He turned immediately to the advertising column, where it so happened I was quoted in an article regarding the aforementioned merger. The office in San Francisco had been Mojo's largest in the US (they had previously bought an independent agency called Allen & Dorward), which was now going to be brought together with the San Francisco Chiat/Day office.

When asked by the reporter whether there were any culture issues, I said, among several other things, "We don't give good golf."

Upon reading this, Jay let out a sudden piercing loud screech at me, "What the fuck were you thinking?"

"What are you, an asshole?"

"Why would you make a remark like this for attribution?"

"Schmuck!"

At first I didn't know what had set Jay off. But I opened up my paper and glanced quickly at the ad column. There it was: "We don't give good golf."

I sat there stoically, looking straight ahead at the back of the seat in front of me. I had learned over the years in this kind of situation to react to Jay by hunkering down, silently gritting my teeth, while letting his anger roll over me, wave after wave, shriek after shriek.

Jeri sat there but was horrified. This was the man to whom I had entrusted my current career and livelihood. He belittled me, he criticized me, he defamed me, and he disparaged me. All of this in front of not just my wife, but also the rest of Chiat/Day top management and 343 other people on that 747. I was kind of mortified, but I sat my ground.

The thing is that Jay was often quoted on various matters not dissimilar to this one. He usually had a hard edge to whatever he said, a New York attitude if you will. Read Larry David in *Curb Your Enthusiasm*. His comments were almost always off-the-cuff and I thought it strange that he didn't cotton to mine.

Even stranger was that I had been privy, as had been Jay, to a confidential memo written by a top Mojo executive, Richard Whitington, who was responsible for the Mojo San Francisco operation. In it, he noted that he had a conversation with the fellow who was running the agency, Don Dorward, and that Don had accepted "that he should spend more time at the office, less time on vacation, especially 'work' vacations (golfing and fishing trips with business contacts) and less money on entertainment and hospitality." End of quote.

FG, Jeri, and Jay: a calm before a storm.

In the second season of the television series *Mad Men*, a British senior account guy loses a foot to a John Deere tractor. His boss is extremely upset and remarks what a wonderful account man he was and that he won't be able to perform any longer. Someone then said that wasn't true, but the boss continued, "He was such a good golfer."

Maybe "We don't give good golf" was not quite as pithy as this sequence, but I still think and thought then that it was quite funny and very relevant to the situation. It also did a great job in positioning the newly merged agency, although I admit possibly to the fear of some of the old Mojo San Francisco clients who would be losing frequent golf invites.

OK, so I received my dressing down for something that Jay himself might very well have said. I just happened to beat him to the punch. I still think it was humorous and relevant.

A few weeks after the incident on the plane, Jay and I were having dinner with Don Dorward and his acting general manager Bob Riddell in San Francisco at Rosalie's on Van Ness. We all had ordered drinks.

The drinks came, and out of the blue Jay began to viciously attack Don, and it wasn't just about playing golf. He didn't like the way he dressed, he didn't like the provincial attitude of the agency, he didn't like a lot of their work, and so on. I couldn't believe his outburst. It was extremely uncomfortable. I got up and went to the restroom.

I was embarrassed not for myself but for Don. After all Don was a successful agency guy who had built a substantial ad shop in San Francisco. He had done some very good work. He had sold his agency for a good price to Mojo and had been asked to stay on. And now, they had sold and he was in this precarious position.

But he really shouldn't have had to suffer this kind of indignity, which was no different than the one that I suffered on the way to Sydney. If Don had any visions of staying on at the newly merged agency, I think they went out the window before we had even ordered the appetizers.

Jay always had a genuine distaste for San Francisco and all things San Francisco. He didn't like the people or their thinking. He thought the town was precious and provincial. He always bitched about the place and avoided coming to it as much as he could. Maybe he was taking out this frustration on Dorward this evening or maybe it was his way of ensuring that Don had no thoughts whatsoever of remaining.

Years later the *Wall Street Journal* ran a very unflattering piece on Jay. In response Lee Clow, Chiat/Day chief creative director, turned around and ran a full-page ad in the *New York Times* defending him to everyone. The ad was essentially an open letter to the *Wall Street Journal* and in it Lee told how Jay had changed the advertising business like no one else. All of which was completely true.

He even said, "He changed the process. Understanding the consumer and hitting him right between the eyes having replaced golf and three-martini lunches as the product of advertising agencies."

Yes indeed. He replaced golf and three-martini lunches in the ad business. Chiat didn't give good golf.

I think it is referred to as schizophrenia or characterized by a loss of contact with the environment, probably more paranoid schizophrenia with contradictory or antagonistic qualities.

Not long after that, all of the Mojo people in San Francisco were moved into our 77 Maiden Lane Chiat/Day offices. Everyone, that is, except Don, who decided to retire.

This chapter was originally titled "Jay. Oy Vey!" For good reason.

CHAPTER 12

IMAGE IS EVERYTHING

After hounding Doug Tompkins, founder and head of Esprit, the clothing company, for years, I finally got a chance to work with him.

Esprit's headquarters in San Francisco was a really hip and cool place, although it was located in an area in San Francisco that was not so hip and cool. A place in the southern part of the city mostly populated with warehouses and an occasional antique store.

Esprit was in an old warehouse or a sometime factory, converted into spectacular office space. It had lots of open and airy areas, a great deal of light streaming in everywhere through skylights and huge windows, beautiful wooden floors throughout, and Doug Tompkins's personal tapestry collection hanging all around the place. It was very impressive.

In addition there were hundreds of fashionably dressed hip and cool young people scurrying here and scurrying there throughout the place. They were a bit like a bunch of crazed hamsters, running all over, energized and hyper-excited but not knowing what they were doing or where they were going.

Nevertheless, the atmosphere definitely gave the place a sense of spirited vigor and lots of energy. Along with all this, however, came a potentially ear-damaging, very high-decibel noise level, as every single word and sound reverberated off the wooden floors, up to the high ceilings, bouncing off the windows and then back and around again. And again.

It didn't occur to me at the time, but looking back I think that is probably why Doug agreed or possibly suggested putting up all those precious tapestries, beyond their obvious added aesthetic value. I can't imagine what the sound would have been like without them.

To further help with the noise problem and in adding to the Zen-like vibe, visitors were asked at the reception desk to remove their shoes and leave them there in the lobby area. Soft slippers were provided for guests. Oh my, it was so quaint and Japanese-like.

At the time our agency was hired, Esprit was in search of marketing consultation. They wanted us to do some overall marketing thinking, some media, and some research. But Doug wouldn't even begin to entertain the idea of our doing any of the ads. That was his area of supreme jurisdiction and he had his chosen suppliers. Here we were, Chiat/Day, the most creative advertising agency in the country at the time, and he never let us do a single ad.

When it came to advertising, most of the fashion industry believed that only the people in it knew how to do it. Or so they thought. I think they still do. And at Esprit, Doug had hired a fellow, a photographer, who reinvented himself as an advertising person.

His name was Oliviero Toscani and he was most famous for developing a series of photographs for the clothing manufacturer Benetton. Most of these ads attempted to be outrageous. And not much more. Some were disgusting, and all were almost totally irrelevant to the products being advertised, those

being sweaters, hats, shirts, and dresses.

To be sure the photos created a stir and generated publicity because many were so bizarre. Toscani did not believe in developing any underlying strategic thinking other than to shock people into looking at the page.

His Benetton ad with a black horse humping a white horse was but one example. As a social statement it was one thing, but if anyone ever wanted to question the validity of advertising or for that matter the advertising business in general, this could very well have been a prized exhibit for the prosecution. In my experience over the years, trying to sell products by association with social justice is a big leap.

Toscani had been doing the Esprit ads for a while when we received our marketing assignment. The photos he was shooting for Esprit were far different from those that he had been doing for Benetton.

Actually they were quite unremarkable in their sameness and their similarity to the photos from so many other fashion advertisers. But Toscani did seem to have a penchant for shooting mammals mounting one another whether horse on horse, woman on man, boy on girl, girl on boy, or man on woman. He did this in a few of the Esprit ads.

One day we were at Esprit for a meeting on media. Mike Moser, creative person par excellence; Gaynor Strachan, account planner; a few other people from the agency; and I were gathered in a fashionably and dimly lit conference room, along with Susie Tompkins (Doug's then wife and business partner) and a few of her young and enthusiastic but entirely inexperienced staff (they were more like groupies).

Most of the people at Esprit had similar credentials of inexperience, but they were young, looked good, and dressed hip, and all harbored a fascinating level of enthusiasm and zeal. They giggled a lot but didn't know much about marketing or advertising. In fact they knew nothing.

At a point in the midst of our media meeting we were interrupted. One of these fevered staff folks knocked on the conference room door, poked her head in the room, and then pulled in the rest of her body. She went over to where Susie Tompkins was seated and leaned over and whispered in her ear. Susie responded immediately by breaking into a huge animated and excited smile and kind of clapped her hands together softly.

For a moment I thought perhaps she had been so bored with the media discussion we were having that no matter what the interruption was, she would have been happy. But it wasn't that.

Susie stood up and clapped her hands again twice and then clasped her hands together in front of her and announced to all of us enthusiastically, "The images are here."

I thought to myself, Oh, of course, the images are here. What the hell is she talking about?

All of the Esprit people knew exactly what she was talking about and they went into a twitter of excitement. No one else from the agency had a clue what the "images" were that caused such an arousing exhilaration.

Then Susie continued, "Let's look at the images."

Again, the Esprit groupies went into a scary level of animated twittering, chittering, and chattering. They could hardly contain themselves.

Someone soon arrived with a Kodak Carousel projector and set it up on the conference table, and into it went a carousel rack. It was only then that everyone finally settled down from their excitement, and some took seats while others remained standing. They dimmed the lights and we were off to the slide show.

Turns out that what we were about to preview was the coming season's "advertising campaign." Photos taken by Toscani, on location, at some exotic sites, at great expense.

The expense came because the locations were about as far away from San Francisco as you could get. Tahiti, Bali, Australia. And the irony was that you couldn't tell from a single one of the photographs where you were, as most of them were body or head shots.

So there we sat and we viewed one slide after the other for a full 90 minutes. And as each photo lit up on the screen, there was an emotive positive sound from all of the Esprit people along with bursts of hand clapping. All in unison.

"Ohh!"

"Ahhhhhh!"

"OOOOOhhhh!"

I thought what we might have had here was some of the offspring of Grateful Dead admirers. A gathering of a group of individuals, involved in obsessive adoration. Such behavior is juvenile and influenced oftentimes by crushlike emotions or lustful sentiments, and frequently infringes on the rights of the figure experiencing the attentions of the frenzied fanatics. The latter was not the case here at Esprit. Susie and Doug ate it all up like bears with honey.

The pictures were of young men and women and a few children, all dressed in Esprit clothes, looking directly into the camera lens. Every now and again there would be a picture where the model would appear in a colorful or scenic setting like a nondescript beach or with a colorful oversized beach ball. But mostly the photographs were just head shots or full body shots. Sometimes the head might have a cap on it but most were just of pretty faces.

When these photos actually became ads, the only copy that accompanied them would be the Esprit logo tucked in discreetly at the lower right or left corner of the page, barely noticeable. Rarely did the ads break from this design format, but when they did they might have the Esprit logo on the top left or right part of the page instead of the lower left or right.

So I learned several things from this experience. First, that "images" are in the fashion world what are commonly known in the rest of the world as the photography. Second, that media was incredibly less important than reviewing the "images."

We were awestruck with the level of enthusiasm that these photos—excuse me, images—engendered. I mean they were nice. They were lit well and the models were attractive. The Esprit clothes they were wearing looked pretty, when they had any of the clothes on, and the shots that had the models doing something, anything, were inherently somewhat more interesting to look at than the ones where the models just stared blankly into the camera lens and out at you.

But the way the group from Esprit reacted, you would have thought that this was the first time they had seen a real color photograph or Kodachrome as the case may be.

It was very much like those African natives in the movie *The Gods Must Be Crazy*. The bit when they first discovered a Coca-Cola bottle, at their feet, apparently having fallen from a plane passing overhead. Wonderment. Excitement. Awe. Wow, a real Coca-Cola bottle.

Fashion advertising is indeed different from the other kind. And there is no doubt in my mind that only people in the fashion business believe they know how to do this kind of advertising. And only they can truly appreciate and respond to it as the most effective, legitimate, and persuasive sales tool for the industry.

The shots we looked at that day were completely lacking in any conceptual idea. And even though the fashion folks spent so much time self-indulging in regard to the "attitude" of the models in the "images," as far as I could see, you could have put any number of other clothing manufacturers' products on the very same models, with the very same expressions, and have had the exact same outcome in the photos, er, I mean the images.

The Esprit folks had convinced themselves that they had captured some magical moments and necromantic attitudes and that the photos were perfect. And importantly they were committed to spending upward of $10 million behind them. So you know in their heart they must have truly believed.

For sure when the Esprit ads were first introduced years before, they were a bit of a breakthrough. They were among the first to use real-life models exhibiting a certain happy playful attitude always with an uplifted gusto. It worked with the brand named Esprit. But over the years, many clothing manufacturers had copied them. Now they were just another pretty face in the crowd and the ads were tired.

The fashion industry is a very inbred one, like the movie business. Those in it think that they are the only ones who know exactly how to market and advertise to their targets. They think that anyone who hasn't had direct experience in the industry couldn't possibly have a relevant or meaningful perspective or idea.

And the thing about it is that most of the people in the fashion business think exactly in the same way. This is particularly true when it comes to the advertising. It is a rare occasion when you could pick up *Vogue* or *Vanity Fair* and discover a fashion ad and think, "Wow, that's really unique and good and motivating." There is rarely any strategic thinking underlying the "images."

"Let's get Cindy Crawford or Linda Evangelista and fly to Bora-Bora and photograph them with the natives."

"Do you think we need to have them in our clothes?"

"Naw!"

Most of the fashion ads you look at have little more to show than a model dressed in or holding the product. This is true for Gucci, Louis Vuitton, and Prada and the list goes on.

A few years after our Esprit experience, I came across a creative critique by *AdWeek* columnist Barbara Lippert. She was reviewing a Polo Ralph Lauren ad for their Surplus Collection. She gave the ad a glowing review.

The ad had a photo of a good-looking male model stretched out on an army cot. He was on his stomach and propped up in an unnatural manner, holding on to a blanket under him. He had a big tattoo on his left arm of two girls with the words *Lonesome 'n Heartbroken* superimposed over their images. Oh and he was naked with a blanket discreetly covering the lower part of his butt so that only a tiny bit of crack showed. The ad had the proverbial Polo Ralph Lauren in the upper right-hand corner of the page.

Barbara Lippert looked at this ad and endorsed it with all of the enthusiasm that the Esprit groupies might have. She was, she said, "stopped in my tracks" by the image. Her words. Give me a break.

Lippert quotes a friend of hers saying, "All these campaigns for Tommy, Ralph, Calvin, Abercrombie & Fitch seem to be shot at the same boys' camp, with the photographer acting as head counselor." Bruce Weber, another well-known fashion photographer like Toscani, took this particular photo. He did a lot of work for Calvin Klein as well.

In my mind this work suffered from the same insider perspective as that which caused the commotion at Esprit. The photo is a typical fashion shot without any strategic concept underneath it. It would have been a lot more effective if they could have figured out a way for the ad to show the product or at least have it appear somewhere in the ad in some conceptual context.

"Image Is Everything" was a great campaign for Canon cameras. I understand that it was very successful and that was why it ran for so many years. The ads brought together an innovative product and an exceptional athlete, both of which had common attributes and values. The two were inextricably linked by their exquisite performance and technical know-how. And, as importantly, they were connected by the fact that their images were as meaningful as everything else.

These Canon camera ads using Andre Agassi were a great example of a relevant strategic position that had been identified and a creative execution that had been developed to drive home the connection. To get attention they used Agassi with his long bleached blond hair, wearing no shirt, revealing his hairy chest. It worked because he was an icon with an attribute relevant to the product being advertised. The Polo guy was naked for no explicable reason other than the obvious.

The ironic thing about the situation at Esprit was that while our agency never had the chance to create an ad for them, they turned around and hired one of our smartest people to manage their marketing and, yup, their advertising department. Gaynor Strachan, our account planner, was a very fashion-forward gal who had a great sense of taste and style, but also was intellectually a very smart strategic thinker.

In her job at Esprit she never got to run any ads that were any different from any of the ones we looked at that infamous day.

But we had made an impression on them regardless, it seemed. They hired a talented and skilled real advertising professional. It was still about the image, as it always was.

Their image.

CHAPTER 13

CHIAT/DAY/NO/MO

RING! RING!

"Be down here in my office first thing tomorrow morning."

That was it. He didn't ask if it was me and I didn't ask if it was him.

I just answered, "OK."

Click!

It was Jay Chiat calling. No hello, how are you. Just be down in my office tomorrow morning. I slowly put the phone back into its cradle thinking, Well he is going to fire me.

After gazing out my window at the side wall of the Neiman Marcus store down the block for a minute or two, I decided to call him back. I hit the speed call.

"This is Jay."

"Jay, what's up? Do I need to bring anything along?"

He responded, "Just be here!" And hung up.

Click.

Now I was almost certain he was going to tell me I was canned. I thought about my wife, my kids, my bank account, my age, among other things. And I booked the first flight down to Los Angeles for the next morning.

I arrived at Chiat/Day headquarters, which at the time was in Venice in what was called the Warehouse. A huge sprawling open space designed by Frank Gehry. It was unique and quite spectacular. This was the temporary office until the famous Binocular building would be completed.

Chiat/Day's Frank Gehry–designed building in Venice.

I walked slowly down to Jay's office and stuck my head into his cubicle so he would know that I had arrived. He brusquely told me to take a seat in the conference room next to his office, which I did. His actions reaffirmed my thinking that I was going to be canned.

I waited for over an hour sitting and thinking about what was to come. Clearly Jay had me on slow cook to tenderize me for the blow to come.

And then the door slammed open and Jay burst into the room. Wasting no time, he didn't even sit down and got right to the point.

"I want you to buy the San Francisco office!"

My reflexive response was the same as it had been in the past. "I don't want to buy the office!"

"If you don't buy the office I'm going to close it up."

"I don't want to buy the office!"

"God damn it I want you to buy the office!"

"I'm not interested in building another agency. I don't want to start again."

"What's it going to take?"

"What do you mean, what's it going to take?"

"What do you want? Tell me. I want you to do this."

At this point he became angry and obviously frustrated. Jay had made promises to me all along my nine-year stint with him and most of them he kept, albeit many belatedly. As far as shuttering the office, I believe that he did have moral trepidations about doing something like this to all the people that had committed themselves to the San Francisco operation.

He also didn't wholeheartedly buy into the arguments of Bob Wolf (the newly minted C/D president) to close San Francisco, something that Wolf had long pursued whenever he had the opportunity. But Jay had put Wolf in charge and this was one of the items on his agenda. Jay easily could have had Wolf do the dirty deed, and he would have with absolutely no hesitations or compromises.

Advertising Age editor Rance Crain wrote an article titled, "How one agency lost its way." It was about Chiat/Day and the root cause for its implosion at the time.

> *Jay Chiat gave the job of running the North American part of the agency to Bob Wolf, a man who succeeded at the agency despite himself, since he embodied everything the Chiat/Day lifer was taught to be skeptical of.*

> *Jay joked that Wolf always needed an extra minute to translate his ideas into Chiat/Day dialect, while Lee Clow instinctively understood what the agency should and shouldn't do.*

Deep down Jay knew he owed me, and the folks in San Francisco, for many contributions in bringing Chiat/Day to its current level of greatness. And that was why he felt obligated to deal with me directly and personally. I am glad and fortunate that he did.

But right now all he wanted to do was get this distasteful discussion behind him. This conversation had been going on for a year and half. But now it seemed to have finally come to a head.

It didn't look like I was getting fired, but if they closed the San Francisco office, what then? Where was I going to end up?

I honestly wasn't interested in building another agency. I had made Young & Rubicam in Los Angeles into a significant agency; had built Chiat/Day San Francisco from almost nothing into a significant entity and a creative force; and during my five years in the corporate role as chief operating officer of Chiat/Day, I had made many critical contributions to its growth and stature as well. I was now 50 years old and not really wanting to have another level of pressure that owning, building, and running an agency would carry with it. I had already made a fair amount of money from the earlier Chiat/Day ESOP and LBO transactions. Besides I didn't want to pay for the fun of taking a new company forward.

For the past 18 months I had resisted all of Jay's attempts to get me to take the Chiat/Day San Francisco office off his hands. From the start, Wolf's idea was to close the office and move the "good" accounts that he liked to LA and service them from there. Jay had been resolute with Wolf and had held him at bay, despite his growling, until now. At the same time Jay had kept trying to persuade me to purchase the San Francisco operation.

I never bought into it. I had a lot at stake in Chiat/Day. I believed I contributed mightily to its success. I owned a lot of Chiat/Day equity shares and bonds that were worth a considerable amount of money and would be worth even more when Jay finally decided to sell the agency. And, I resisted just because Wolf was the instigator behind the whole thing.

When I had first told Jay I wasn't interested, he said he was going to move the accounts and people down to LA and shutter the office. I told him all along that he wouldn't be able to keep any of the accounts because they would never accept the Chiat/Day Los Angeles way of doing business and that he wouldn't be able to move most of the people because they hated Los Angeles. All of this was true.

I reminded him on several occasions that he was the one that hired me and along the way kept motivating me to build the San Francisco operation into something important, which I did. He rewarded me significantly over the years financially and had made me chief operating officer of all of Chiat/Day, a position I held for five years. We had built a significant $140 million billing operation in San Francisco with some great clients and hundreds of

Memo from Jay announcing Fred's promotion to COO of Chiat/Day.

employees and were doing really good creative work on many accounts. And now he wanted to shut it down.

He and I had come a long way from his 1985 announcement crowning me chief operating officer.

I said to Jay, "What bullshit this all is. You're the guy that hired me to run Apple and then to build San Francisco and then you made me COO of Chiat/Day. Yeah you rewarded me well financially, but don't you have some sense of obligation after all that has been accomplished?"

He repeated, "Just tell me what you want."

It sounded and felt like he was ready to sell me the office for whatever, just to be rid of the problem. Now this was a man who had lots and lots of experience buying and selling agencies. However, he seemed never to have done it very well. He ended up off-loading most of them at considerable losses and several times had sold them back to the people from whom he had bought them in the first place. Usually at a massive discount. I am certain this helped absolve any moral issues he may have had.

In order to get a foothold in San Francisco he had purchased the old-line Hoefer Dieterich & Brown agency in the early 1980s, and with it came some wonderful blue chip accounts like Transamerica, Wilsey Foods (which made Saffola margarine), Harrah's Casino, Genstar, the California Brandy Advisory Board, the California Prune Advisory Board, and a few other fruity California boards.

Almost at the same time he was handed the opportunity to purchase the advertising part of Regis McKenna, which was primarily a technology public relations firm based in Palo Alto. This brought with it such clients as Shugart, a disc drive manufacturer; Fafco, a solar heating firm; GE Calma, a CAD/CAM company; Intel, a microchip producer; and an even more obscure and unknown company called Apple, which was trying to sell a personal computer.

Later on Jay had bought Mojo, a large Australian agency with 15 offices down under and around the world, including a few in the United States and one in San Francisco. The predecessor of Mojo San Francisco was Allen & Dorward. This agency brought along such clients as Rainier Beer, Qantas airlines, the Australian Tourist Commission, Koala Springs Beverages, Lone Star Beer, and the Schlage Lock Company.

All three of these acquisitions, along with significant organic growth, contributed to what became Chiat/Day San Francisco. But now after all of it he wanted to just unload San Francisco.

Truth be told, Jay had mentioned to me on many occasions how much he personally hated San Francisco and what he considered its parochial views and practices. I never really understood his reasoning, as San Francisco was pretty cutting-edge liberal and left in terms of social and moral behavior, not to speak of the vast number of technology companies that were forging truly new frontiers virtually every day. But he viewed Los Angeles as the more perfect environment with its fluidity, its glamour, and its free-for-all anything-goes atmosphere. Anything else for him was stifling.

In the nine years that we worked together I can count on one hand, and maybe two fingers, the number of times that Jay came to pay us a visit up north. So with Bob Wolf whispering in his ear to consolidate San Francisco and have one bigger Los Angeles operation, it didn't take too much more to bring him to this point, despite all his promises and trepidations.

With these thoughts and remembrances rushing through my mind and Jay sitting next to me with his legs crossed, doodling on a paper napkin, I decided to test his level of desperation. Not knowing where I might end up if he really did shutter the San Francisco operation weighed heavily on me at this moment as well.

"OK, I'll do it but here's what I want."

I outlined a number of things that I felt were essential if I was going to do it. Jay listened, kept doodling, and finally looked up at me when I had paused, and he said, "OK, is that it?"

He stood up and put out his hand to shake to confirm the deal.

"No!"

"No what?"

"Not that I don't trust you and your commitments, but I want this in writing."

He looked around the room and there was nothing to write on, so he grabbed a discarded paper cocktail napkin sitting on a credenza. He asked for the points again and he proceeded to write each item down on the napkin.

- Fred to forfeit 600,000 shares of Chiat/Day Class B Common Stock, but retain payouts from existing stock.

- Fred to retain all C/D bonds issued to him.

- If the new San Francisco company couldn't meet its payroll obligations there was a salary guarantee.

- Chiat/Day would provide a low interest loan to the new company to pay for the assets.

- If the new agency couldn't meet the interest and/or principal payments to Chiat/Day, payments would be extended indefinitely.

- Receive funds from C/D building sale.

He looked up at me and asked, "OK, is that it?"

"No."

"What else?"

"Sign it and date it."

He did and stood up, we shook hands, and he muttered something under his breath and left me sitting alone in the conference room. He had flushed the San Francisco office and me down his personal toilet. We were history and he finally didn't have to concern himself with any of it anymore. I never saw Jay in person again.

I sat and reflected back on the days when I first joined Chiat/Day and how important and respected I had been, being promoted quickly by Jay several times. He made me an executive vice president not too long after I joined the firm. I still remember his comments in his announcement to the agency: "Although the way he has responded to the demands of Apple without cracking has been admirable, his most important contribution has been his ability to quickly understand and implement Chiat/Day values." Jay had drifted a long way from the importance of those values to him or the agency. Nevertheless I was able to incorporate many of them as I began my new adventure of owning an advertising agency.

I stayed in the conference room for a few minutes. I called Jeri and told her that I hadn't been fired and that I was going to buy the Chiat/Day office in San Francisco, to which she said "Really!" the way women do, like "Oh right!" I finished my cup of coffee and got up and strolled through the conference room door, down a corridor referred to in the office as "Main Street," and out the front door of the Chiat offices for the last time.

So now I was about to acquire a company that I hadn't planned on nor particularly wanted. The truth was that I wasn't being required to pay a huge amount of money, if only I were able to have a little bit of luck. The preliminary term sheet called for an initial payment of $500,000 at the closing and another estimated $2.5 million over the next five years. I personally put up the $500,000.

The luck came along with a lot of hard work. Turned out it was a good bet for me and another wildly wrong one for Jay financially. Not only did the agency become a significant creative force but the San Francisco market became a hotbed of creativity, spawning a bunch of highly creative and successful agencies like Goodby, Silverstein & Partners.

The *Wall Street Journal* ran a wonderful "Pepper . . . and Salt" cartoon with an executive standing behind the boss, who is facing a conference table full of other executives and saying, "This gentleman is willing to purchase our company providing we're willing to lend him the money." Someone sent me that cartoon with my name written on the "gentleman." And that's exactly what went down.

The Bay Area market also continued to provide some very significant clients who became huge advertising spenders. Silicon Valley became an even more important place than it had already been. We were fortunate to acquire several key businesses, among them Cisco Systems. It didn't hurt that Chiat/Day San Francisco was the original home of such technology clients as

General Electric Calma, Shugart, Intel, and Apple Computer.

Oh and our agency went on to generate $215 million in income over the next nine years. Not a bad return from our $3 million investment.

But I didn't know that was to be, and my most critical task, it seemed to me, was securing the people, particularly the right people. Without them, I would be buying nothing. Much has always been made in the advertising industry about how your assets go down the elevator at the end of the day. It was only now that the realization of this concept truly dawned on me. This was clearly the biggest issue I had before me and I needed to convince my key management people that this was a good idea and that they should stay on with me.

I knew that this was not going to be a cakewalk. Chiat/Day was the quintessential creative agency in the country, and working for it carried a cachet that any new unknown agency would not. Nor would just about any other agency for that matter.

There was also the issue of security. In situations like this people get scared and concerned, and rightfully so. They want to bail.

Of one thing I was certain and that was that if I couldn't keep most of my management team together I would not succeed in taking the agency forward. And if I couldn't do that I was prepared to renege on the agreement even though Jay thought we had a deal. Hell, he was the one who signed the napkin. Not me. And he was the one who reneged on San Francisco.

As far as I was concerned I felt that Jay had bailed out on San Francisco and me after making many demands and promises over the years. We delivered for him but he pulled the rug out on us.

I had no moral issue if I had to jettison the agreement. I figured it was only fair; after all, I didn't really want to do it in the first place.

As Jay was leaving the conference room, what he had mumbled under his breath to me was that he didn't want me to discuss this with anyone until he was ready to make an announcement.

This was the first thing I ignored since I didn't quite hear him. And I figured I didn't have anything if I didn't have my group of people, and I needed to talk with each one in due haste. I didn't think I was going to be a hundred percent successful, but felt if I could retain enough of the group I'd be OK. I was a pretty good salesman but this could no doubt tax my selling abilities.

I decided to go down several paths at the same time with these personnel explorations so that I would have some options if somebody dropped out along the way.

Of course the creative people were by far the most critical and essential to the success of the new venture. I immediately identified several avenues I thought could make sense.

I started with the most obvious, the current creative director, Ross Van Dusen. Ross was a talented, likable, well-intentioned fellow whom I had hired shortly after I came on board at Chiat/Day in 1983. It was Jay who had actually put me in touch with Ross to begin with. We had a first lunch meeting in Santa Monica alfresco, overlooking the Pacific Ocean. It went well, and Ross had been a great addition even though it turned out he had some serious limitations, creative and otherwise.

Ross was as dedicated and hardworking as I could have asked for in a creative director. He was quite creative as well, although sometimes his work tended to be a bit hokey. He was excellent with clients although maybe a little too accommodating at times. And it seemed to me that Ross was slightly unpredictable in certain situations, particularly so when the pressure rose. I could expect to on occasion get a frantic, angry e-mail during the years we worked together. These would express his extreme frustrations and umbrage with this or that. A dumb account executive, a badass client, too short a timetable, want a vacation, going home early out of frustration, whatever.

I went to meet with Ross at Winship Restaurant in Sausalito first thing the next morning, the day after I had met with Jay. I went over the whole enchilada with him. The opportunity to have our own agency, to run it any way we liked, the potential benefits that would come of that both emotionally and financially, the risks and the rewards.

Importantly I included that I was not expecting him to contribute anything financially to the start-up situation. I presumed that if I had, this would add to the difficulty of persuading anyone to join the effort. I planned to front what was initially required with my own capital and not take the chance that asking anyone for skin in the game would sully his or her interest. I ended my presentation to Ross with an emotional plea as to how much I wanted, indeed needed, his involvement going forward.

Without exaggerating, we began with bacon and eggs at 8 a.m. and Ross finally left for home at 4 p.m. We moved from the eggs and the coffee to the dock of the bay adjacent to the restaurant and sat there and talked and talked and talked and talked. Ross was nervous and scared and concerned and didn't know what to do. But finally he agreed to join me and we shook hands, although it felt like the same kind of handshake that I had given Jay a day earlier, without the comfort of a signed napkin.

As we parted for the evening I said, and not under my breath, "Oh and Ross, please don't mention any of this to anyone just yet."

At the time I lived in Sausalito so my commute home was only three minutes up the hill. I was drained and exhausted both mentally and physically. To think that when I had arguments with Ross over the years, it was tiring. This day's discussion with him was worse than a root canal without anesthetic.

I got home, mentioned to Jeri what a great day it had been, marched upstairs, and went to sleep.

I didn't sleep too well that night. The next morning I was nervous thinking about how much I had to do, so I went into the office earlier than my normal early. I arrived at my desk at 5:45 and surprisingly a few minutes later the phone rang. Not good I thought.

Sure enough it was Jay and he was howling. I had to hold the phone a foot from my ear.

Jay screamed, "Why the fuck did you say anything to Ross? I told you not to say a word to anyone. What the fuck are you doing?"

"I told Ross because without a creative director there is no deal because there is no agency. And now that you brought it up I plan to talk to the other people I feel are key as well."

Click!

He hung up on me and I didn't hear from Jay for six years when he sent me a note asking for a reel of some Goldberg Moser O'Neill TV commercials he admired for a speech he was giving. What a guy.

Well, I had learned something about howling from Jay and a few minutes later I went down to see Ross, also an early arriver, in his office and I started howling at him.

I yelled, "Ross, why in the world did you call Jay after I specifically asked you not to discuss our conversation with anyone?"

Ross ran his fingers back through his hair and kept his head down like a shaggy dog and then looked up at me in an odd kind of way. It turned out he had gone home and talked the day over with his wife, who encouraged him, because of his long-term relationship with Jay, to call and discuss the matter directly with him. I can't blame her in hindsight but I was still angry.

My thinking was that Jay was probably more upset that he had his evening interrupted than that I had discussed the matter with someone else. Ross had an inability to bring closure to a discussion, any discussion, so it must have been a really, really long conversation, with Ross not wanting to get off the phone.

I can't remember a time that I was angrier than at that moment with Ross. I just couldn't believe that he would turn around and do something so stupid and violate our understanding. It truly shook my confidence in him.

I screamed, "Well that's it for you and me. We're finished. You're out of this deal. I have no faith in you as a partner. I can't trust you."

Ross just looked at me with a dumb sheepish hurt sorry look. As far as I was concerned, he was now toast and history. He was out of the new agency regardless of what happened. I had lost complete confidence in him and didn't want him as the critical partner and creative director in the new venture. He couldn't be trusted.

Ross ended up retiring from the business, moving to Arizona, and becoming the sculptor and painter maybe he should have been all along. He was very talented and I still have a very nice contemporary wooden animal sculpture that he gave me during more affable times. Last I heard he was a very happy guy still in Arizona and still painting and sculpting away.

The next day I went on to have discussions with John Coll, who was an associate creative director. He too was a talented affable guy whom just about everybody liked. He had one Achilles' heel, however, an inability to make a decision. Ever! I told him just about everything I had gone over with Ross the day before and he was excited and interested but nervous and wanted to think about it.

Think about it he did, and over the next several weeks after much consternation, and back and forth, he finally agreed to become a part of the new agency. But then the next day he had a change of heart. Then the day after that he reconsidered again. Then the next he was concerned. I finally sat down and presented a pro/con analysis I had prepared for him. It outlined simply all the benefits that would accrue if he came on board and the potential negatives as well. On balance it looked like a quite positive decision. I left the analysis with him to review and think about with a request to get back to me with his final decision as soon as possible. I had determined beforehand that there was no way John was to be the creative director but instead he would still be an important creative resource at the new agency.

I invited John and his wife to join me for dinner at the Lark Creek Inn in Larkspur the next night. Unfortunately my wife and I had an argument on the way to dinner and it boiled up at the table soon after the Colls arrived. John had a glassy-eyed look, as it seemed he thought our heated squabbling had to do with the formation of the new venture. It didn't, but he and his wife left the dinner less enthusiastic about the whole thing than they might have been otherwise.

John came into my office the next morning and asked how much he could expect to be making if he agreed to be a part of going forward. I told him, and it was a significant increase and had an equity stake as well. He was happy.

The next morning he again came into my office and he had changed his mind despite the salary increase and ownership. I said why don't we forget about it and that I would go down another path.

I had several conversations with a number of creative people with whom I had worked at Young & Rubicam and a few at Chiat/Day as well. I was hopeful that one of these avenues might yield a solution to provide the essential creative direction for the new agency. Without an incredible creative talent to lead the new agency, there was no way that I could or would go forward with the venture.

Mike Moser had worked with me on Apple from my very first day at Chiat/Day. He was a brilliant strategic thinker as well as a highly talented art director. He had partnered with copywriter Brian O'Neill for most of the past decade and they had together assembled a remarkable body of work for just about every client they ever worked on. Brian had left 18 months or so earlier to return to Chicago, which he and his wife Shelly thought was a more appropriate environment than California to raise their kids.

Unknown to me, Mike had recently decided it was time to do something different and he had been shopping his "book" around and had landed a job at Hal Riney & Partners across town. Truth be told, he had never been the same since Brian had taken off for the Midwest. And neither was his work. Brian had been a real catalyst for Mike when they worked together, allowing them to do great things.

I was caught by surprise by this development. Mike was an exceptional creative resource and an important asset. I really wanted Mike as a part of the new agency and didn't want him to leave. I was upset by this turn of events. I had written off Ross, and while it seemed John Coll would probably stay on, the loss of Mike would be very debilitating. I wasn't sure I would be able to move forward.

And so I began another exhausting round of discussions trying to persuade Mike to stay on and not go over to Riney. I posited many of the same arguments that I had to Ross and John and then some. All of this fell on Mike's deaf ears. He just looked at me throughout it all and never changed his expression; he never even asked a question.

Mike was always a pretty stoic fellow. But in this situation he was even more so than I was used to. He had a way of appearing totally unmoved by absolutely anything that you could say to him. In this case his mind was made up and he was ready to ply his trade at a new place, which happened to have a pretty good creative reputation as well. He had nothing to lose except by staying on at the soon to be new agency.

It seemed there was nothing I could say. Mike was not convinced. Mike was not going to be convinced.

That is until the subject of Brian surfaced.

"What if we could get Brian to come back here? What if you and Brian were co-creative directors for the new agency?"

Mike was usually a marble statue with an introverted personality. He kept his emotions very close to the vest. And yet this thought sparked a fire I rarely saw in him. His eyes lit up and he actually smiled.

"Well, that would be something to talk about."

He and I agreed to explore the idea with Brian. He actually called Brian before I had the chance, a demonstration of his interest level in the concept.

We made a decision to get together. The next day Mike and I flew to Chicago and met Brian for dinner at a seedy steakhouse in the O'Hare airport. It was at that meal, as we huddled in a booth in this dark and dingy restaurant, that we agreed to move forward together. There was, it seemed, only one obstacle remaining. That was Shelly, Brian's wife.

I spent that night preparing an oral presentation. That is, the most appropriate remarks and reasoning with which to make a convincing case to Mrs. O'Neill. After having all the discussions with Ross, John, and Mike, I was pretty familiar with the thrust that the arguments would take. However, I had not succeeded with either Ross or John, or Mike for that matter. I needed something more.

Mike and I were to meet at Brian's house the next morning in the Chicago suburb where he lived. We headed out of town in a rented car. On the way I stopped and bought a Steiff teddy bear for Brian's little girl, hoping to grease that skid a morsel.

Shelley greeted us at the front door enthusiastically. She was her usual effervescent self. She had worked for me at the agency and was a terrific resource. I knew her well. She had coffee and some pastries waiting for us. After all the "good to see yous" were done with, I said, "Well, I guess you know why we're here."

I started to outline the proposition and opportunity. To my surprise the more I spoke, the more excited she got about the prospects of California. When I finished with the potential financial upside part, Shelly gave us her blessings.

"We'll come back to California. It all sounds great. How much is Brian going to be making again?"

What we had achieved here was beyond my expectations. Way beyond the earlier paths that I had gone down. It looked to me like Brian, Mike, and I could in fact make a realistic go of this venture.

The potential money that Brian and Mike could expect was enticing. The freedom and opportunity for them to create some great advertising again, together, was heady. And the teddy added the final touch when their daughter Molly said, "I am going to really like California and so is my new teddy bear."

Years later I heard Molly still had the bear when she was 17 and going off to her first year at college.

Yes!

I was ecstatic. I was elated. Things do seem to turn out for the better no matter how dark they may at times appear. Sometimes anyway, and this was one of those times.

The *San Francisco Examiner* reported on June 11, 1990, that a special meeting was held at the agency to announce the formation. "The reaction was unbelievable. There was a state of euphoria. The reaction was so positive because there was an acknowledged chemistry that existed between the three principals. There was an overwhelming feeling there's a great team in place, from the key executives to the creatives. Their creative history really speaks for itself." It didn't hurt that Brian and Mike had won over 500 creative awards together.

The walls of resistance and the disasters that I had encountered first with Ross, then with John and Mike, had turned around into something more than I could have hoped for. It was a far better solution, as Brian and Mike as a team were without exaggeration among the absolute best creative minds in the country. Together they had done some of the very best work that had been accomplished at Chiat/Day. Brian, Mike, and I were three of only 19 people at Chiat/Day to whom Jay had awarded ownership stock and designated part of the critical management group for leading the agency forward. I guess not that critical at the end of the day. Nevertheless, our joining together gave me an enormous amount of confidence and a much stronger case to present for the new agency to anyone, employees and clients alike.

In addition I very much liked the way this had turned out because it would be an incredible surprise. It would be something that no one had contemplated or expected. It immediately raised the probability of our success as a creative shop. It resolved all of my issues with Ross, John, Mike, and the other creative resources that I had been talking to. It would improve our work, motivate my people, and attract clients. The wisdom of this plan would, I was sure, even impress Jay although he would be the last to admit it.

Of course there were still many issues to work out. The first one came up before I even left Chicago to return home.

Mike raised the issue. "What are we going to call the agency?"

"Moser O'Neill Goldberg?"

"O'Neill Moser Goldberg?"

He suggested Moser O'Neill Goldberg or O'Neill Moser Goldberg because we were a creative agency and the creative people should be featured. Therefore he or Brian should be identified first in the name.

I first argued that it didn't sound particularly lyrical to me, and when the names were abbreviated, as people in the ad business are prone to do for advertising agencies, they would come out as OMG or MOG. Oh My God or Mog, neither of which felt good. Like we're meeting at MOG today!

I didn't argue with the importance of the creative focus but postulated that I wanted to remove any suggestion of hierarchy and/or egalitarianism and thought we should simply do the naming alphabetically. Goldberg Moser O'Neill or GMO. Brian was OK with this but Mike persisted in wanting to communicate that creative was king.

I argued further that Scali, McCabe, Sloves had the creative guy in the middle and that Bernbach was at the end of Doyle Dane, and the latter may have been the most renowned creative agency ever. Mike was unwavering.

Then I offered that since I was putting up all of the front money and I would own the majority of the to-be-issued stock, the name should be Goldberg Moser O'Neill. Turns out I needed to contribute more than the initial $500,000 of my own money to get us through some initial cash flow problems.

I hadn't asked Brian or Mike for any money, and neither offered any. But true to their creative mentality I doubt that they even thought about it. In the end this turned out for the best since it might have created an issue and jeopardized their coming on board. Additionally, it worked importantly in my favor regarding the naming of the agency.

And so it was that we became Goldberg Moser O'Neill.

Goldberg Moser AND O'Neill.

Before I went to Chicago, I set up a meeting with Mike Massaro. Mike

was the first hire I had made when I joined Chiat/Day San Francisco back in 1982. It was one of my best decisions, bar none. Mike was an extremely bright and thoughtful person and had an unusual understanding of what was great creative work. He was hardworking, dedicated, trustworthy, and reliable and he knew the technology landscape better than most. He had been a critical counselor to me over the years and an essential ingredient in the agency's success. I very much wanted Mike as a part of the going-forward venture. As it turned out the ultimate success of Goldberg Moser O'Neill was very much because Mike Massaro was a part of the team.

But Mike, being a scrupulously contemplative guy and a person who just loved to play devil's advocate, could make winning an argument difficult, even painful. We met on a Sunday morning, on Mother's Day as it happened, in a park next to the Sausalito library and spent a good three or four hours going over the situation.

I knew Mike was interested, but I hadn't yet secured the deal with Mike Moser and Brian and I thought that not having Ross might be an issue for him. He was his usual self and asked just about every conceivable question that could be asked. Even when we finished up our talk, he was noncommittal and wanted to think further about the situation.

I had learned not to push Mike but to let him reach his own conclusions on most things. And so I went back up the hill to my house somewhat less elated than I could have been. Deep down I felt that Mike was as critical to the success of the new organization as was anyone, and I would be reluctant to go forward without him as a part of the team. Mike made it easy when he came into my office early the next morning and announced he was on board.

I went through the same process with each of those I considered the other essential executives: Camille Johnson, media director; Catrina McAuliffe, planning director; Tanya Stringham, art production manager; MJ Rockers, print production manager; and Rosalinde Estes, human resources and office manager.

All of these people were among the best in the business and I was fortunate to have them as a part of my management to this point. That they all decided to join the new venture was importantly why we were such a stunning success. I always believed that we had the very best group of people in our management and that was the reason we were ultimately so successful.

My first and best hire at Chiat/Day

And all of these people said yes to the proposition even before I was able to tell them that Mike Moser was going to stay and not go to Riney and Brian O'Neill was going to return to the new agency from Chicago. What a vote of confidence this was for me, and it was something I tried never to forget.

To her everlasting credit and my extreme appreciation, when I discussed the deal with Rosalinde Estes she did not hesitate for a nanosecond in committing to be a part. She did so without any reservations whatsoever. Rosalinde was a calm and comforting part of our management group and she brought a perspective that dramatically helped the agency over the years. We would never have succeeded as we did without her wisdom, involvement, and commitment. My meeting with her was by far the shortest, for which I was grateful.

In addition to Rosalinde, I ended up with Camille Johnson, Catrina McAuliffe, Tanya Stringham, and MJ Rockers.

There was one person in my management with whom I did not need to have a conversation about joining the new agency. A fellow who had worked for me years before and whom I had hired at Chiat/Day as director of account management. He was a bright enough guy and hardworking. He did well with most clients. He had a great sense of marketing and a good sense of creative, but . . . what he didn't always have was common sense. He would do things seemingly without at all realizing the impact that they might have on the people around him. He thought nothing of making chauvinistic remarks about women when we went out of our way to make the agency one of real equality; he would make sexist comments in the most inappropriate situations.

It was reported to me firsthand that he once had a breakfast meeting with two women executives from a software client of ours. The women had arrived first and were already seated. He approached the table and greeted them by saying, "You babes are really something."

This fellow was once at a client meeting and for whatever reason decided to bring some levity to the situation by placing on his forehead a rubber suction dart from a toy gun that happened to be nearby. Well, after he put it there and everyone looked at him and smiled embarrassingly not knowing how to react, he couldn't get the dart off. When he finally was able to get the thing off, it left a bright blood red spot the size of a quarter dead center above and between his eyebrows. He wore that badge like a scarlet letter for weeks before it finally began to fade. The incident lived on long after, however, as Camille Johnson, my long-time media director, relished retelling the story, as she had been witness to the entire episode. But even this incident didn't stop him from continuing to inexplicably do stuff like that.

I failed miserably over the years, and I am not quite sure why, in hiring directors of account management and a few GMs too. It may simply have been that I thought I did that job pretty well and believed I knew how it should be done and was intolerant of anyone who didn't quite see it my way. On the other hand, it may be that I simply hired one person after the other who just wasn't able to fit into the organization and culture we had created. No, more likely that I couldn't tolerate that someone might do it a different way. Guilty!

Along the way, I made a gentleman named Matt Crisci the general manager. I had been promoted to chief operating officer of all of Chiat/Day, and it was expeditious to anoint Matt in San Francisco. Big mistake. I ended up having to demote him under considerable pressure from Jay Chiat.

Jay in particular did not like anything about him, as he always felt Matt was manipulating and conniving one thing or another. He may have been right. When I finally demoted Matt from general manager, I received a handwritten note from Jay saying, "Tough job, but well done." He really didn't like him.

When Matt first arrived at the agency, he created a firestorm of complaints in the agency and with many clients too in the way he presented the agency and handled himself. And, it was no different when Matt got wind of the sale of the San Francisco office to me. He immediately scheduled a meeting with me. We met in a small conference room on the sixth floor at Maiden Lane and he reviewed for me all the accounts that he "controlled." He laid out what he expected in return for joining the new venture. Among the demands was a 50 percent ownership stake.

I told Matt that he must be smoking something. I suggested that he was kidding but then realized he was completely serious, and I advised him that he might benefit from beginning an immediate search for new employment. Our meeting lasted about four minutes. I stood up and left him in the room to contemplate his next move, which turned out to be an attempt to join forces with Ross Van Dusen and try to steal our accounts. He didn't realize Ross was already dead meat with me and I had written him off.

Matt's scheme was to form a new agency with Ross and take whatever of our clients he could with him. I learned later that he was actually trying to recruit some of my other management folks for his venture as well. Matt's timing was always a little off.

One of my daughters was getting married and we had a very nice party to celebrate the occasion. It was at this time that Matt chose to canvass others in my management group. We had sent the invitations out months before and Matt was one of the recipients. It would have been inappropriate to take back the invitation regardless of what he was attempting to do. And what he did do was move around from table to table at the reception on his recruiting mission. A number of my department heads informed me of his activities the next day in the office.

None of my clients and none of the management group ever seriously considered joining Matt's mutiny. As was often the case, he misjudged the people he was trying to persuade and in this case never read just how disturbed by him these folks actually were.

He never ever saw it.

Maybe it was to be expected. There are some people who actually don't see the world around them. It's not rose-colored glasses but rather blinders. I'm not sure if it's a personality quirk, a defense mechanism, hubris, or just bad insight or maybe eyesight. It was really quite remarkable how Matt could seemingly appear a key player in the midst of some bizarre episode like the one described in the *Delaney Report*, on the next page. Whether this one was true or not, I'll never know.

One time Matt needed a new shirt and went across the street to a department store and bought a very nice one. He came back to the agency and put it on. Half an hour later he came into my office for something and I said to him, "Matt, what the hell is that on your shirt?"

THE INTERNATIONAL NEWSLETTER FOR MARKETING, ADVERTISING AND MEDIA EXECUTIVES

Vol. 2 No. 16   April 22, 1991

Call Security

They're fighting over at ad agency **Backer Spielvogel Bates Worldwide**. Latest outbreak involves firing/hiring of executive vp **Matt Crisci**, who had been the shop's key account man on the $100-million-in billings Miller Lite beer account, which the agency recently lost.

E.g., Crisci originally fired by BSB Inc. president **Dean Scaros** two weeks ago. Scaros hires security guards to keep Crisci out of agency headquarters building. Executive vp/creative director **Jim White** then convinced agency co-founder and worldwide creative director **Bill Backer** to rehire Crisci in creative department despite fact Crisci has no creative experience. Situation leads to battle of wills between Backer, Scaros as well as continued sense of unrest now prevalent among agency's middle management. "There's no way Scaros is going to win by taking on Backer," said one senior BSB executive.

Mars intervenes personally to have BSB-developed Snickers campaign pulled from TV (spot featured music from rock band **Rolling Stones**). "(BSB) spent more than $1 million producing the commercial, and Forest Mars hated it," said one BSB executive.

Move by Mars chairman forces BSB to tap parent **Saatchi & Saatchi**'s London office for creative help. Mars dissatisfaction remains. Look for Mars to pull either M&Ms or Snickers from BSB as slap on hand to shop. "Mars won't fire (BSB), but there could easily be a reassignment of brands," the BSB source remarked.

Meanwhile, recent recruitment of creative talent **Don Easdon** as new executive creative director at BSB and anticipated appointment of new client services head (candidate talk now centering on Saatchi's **Dorland** agency operation in U.K) fails to address key issue facing BSB: lack of culture/vision for future. Shop now led by **Carl Spielvogel**, Backer (both in 60s). Contracts

He looked down and saw a blue ink spot the size of a silver dollar as it grew larger just below the lower part of the pocket on his brand-new shirt. He laughed, "Oh geez!"

The blue ink from a pen sticking out of the top of the pocket had oozed out the bottom of the pocket. He never knew it was there.

⊘ ⊘ ⊘

One very critical part of the new agency was, of course, media, specifically media buying. I was fortunate to have been able to secure a partnership with Dennis Holt, the founder and head of Western International Media. Dennis was incredibly bright, and his company became not only an asset but a weapon for GMO.

We officially started the new agency on June 1, 1990. We retained all of our clients. We kept every single person I wanted. We gave everyone a sweatshirt that said, "Good Is the Enemy of Great." This was a slightly different, maybe more strategic take on what we had philosophically embraced at Chiat/Day, "Good Enough Is Not Enough." Both were about not settling.

And of course we had to change the phone number. We sent out a clever card announcing this fact.

Finally we wanted to change the name on the door and awning outside the entrance. I was returning from Greene Radovsky Maloney & Share, our law firm, with our attorney Dick Greene, where we had just inked the final papers on the deal. One of the stipulations written into the agreement was that we would not change the name on the awning of the building at 77

Maiden Lane for three months. This was supposedly to "protect" the limited staff that Chiat was keeping in the office there and who worked on the regional Nissan account. We also were under a strict agreement not to defame Chiat/Day/Mojo in any way or we would be subject to various penalties.

As the taxi pulled up in front of 77 Maiden Lane, I saw someone on a ladder working on the signage. My eager staff had already done the dirty deed.

Dick Greene said, "Uh, oh, that's gonna be a problem."

He soon received a call from David Weiner, who was representing Chiat/Day/Mojo in selling the company to us. "What the fuck are you guys doing?"

Someone from the Chiat/Day/Mojo Nissan group had seen the awning name being changed and called someone in Los Angeles who told someone in management who called David Weiner who called Dick Greene who told me, "Uh, oh, this is gonna be a problem."

What actually happened was that the name on the awning was being changed from Chiat/Day/Mojo to Chiat/Day/No/Mo. Which was pretty clever and funny. It was simply a matter of fact, a joke, but they got real defensive about it and wanted it taken off.

To add further insult to the situation, every one of the employees was being handed a high-quality sweatshirt that had Goldberg Moser O'Neill on the front and Chiat/Day/No/Mo on the back. Double uh-oh! We had to collect the sweatshirts and hold them for 90 days until we were officially allowed to give them out again.

The folks at Chiat/Day were angry, but we argued that we now had 80 percent of the building and we were a new entity that needed the proper signage and recognition. We soon changed the signage from Chiat/Day/No/Mo to Goldberg Moser O'Neill.

We were able to keep our name up from the get-go, although we took down the Chiat/Day/No/Mo signage and put up Goldberg Moser O'Neill. But the Chiat people went on to punish us for our naughty actions, which is the stuff of another chapter under covenant violations and punitive actions.

And so our adventure as an independent ad agency started with a good base of clients and grew into a great base of clients over the ensuing years. Celestial Seasonings tea, Oracle, Qantas airlines, Atari, Worlds of Wonder, and Dell computers were some of the originals.

We also had Golden Grain Rice-A-Roni, which offered to help us by paying a full year of fees up front. This amounted to well over a million dollars and subsidized the money that I had contributed. Their gesture was a major help in getting us through some rough cash flow problems and was enormously appreciated. Despite doing an above-average amount of mediocre work, we had a special bond with this client and remained together for eight years until their top management changed.

I personally felt we owed the president Verinder Syal and the marketing VP Steve Odland a huge debt of gratitude. They were truly good clients and great friends. Unfortunately a few years went by and they left to pursue other things. I lost track of Verinder but caught up with Steve when I found he had become CEO of Office Depot.

The new president, Chuck Marcy, I felt was a terrible judge of advertising and an intellectually dishonest person. This is a deadly combination when it comes to doing decent advertising and is the bane of every creative-oriented advertising agency. It became way too difficult to do any good work and Marcy was always a source of creative friction, so we finally parted ways. It didn't help that I discovered he was interviewing my old agency and, more to the point, his old agency Young & Rubicam.

When we were still part of Chiat/Day we were prevented from going after many accounts because the New York and Los Angeles offices wanted to keep the agency conflict free for the much bigger accounts. This was always a point of contention and frustration. On August 1, 1990, I told Tom King at the *Wall Street Journal*, "I'm in areas that I was never allowed to go in before. I've got 10 new business things cooking right now and I think I'm going to hit a few."

⊘ ⊘ ⊘

We were fortunate in that we were able to win new business almost immediately on starting out. The first came just three weeks after we incorporated when Intelligy Corporation gave us their account. This was a personal learning system for children, and some of the people who were at our old client Worlds of Wonder were behind it.

The bigger deal was when we won Dreyer's ice cream on our 47th day of existence, an account that we retained for the next 10 years. A big account that allowed us to do remarkable creative work. We won every major advertising award and made a lot of money along the way. And Dreyer's market share grew and grew and grew through it all.

Nicer still was that we won both of these initial accounts from creative agencies: Intelligy had been with Wieden & Kennedy in Portland and Dreyer's had been with Hal Riney & Partners in San Francisco. How sweet and delicious it was! Particularly the ice cream business.

We were on a new business tear that would catapult us to a significantly sized agency. Before the end of our first six months we had won, in addition to those clients, Wordstar International, a software company, and TakeCare Corporation, an HMO. We had successfully retained both Koala Springs Beverages and Qantas airlines, accounts Chiat/Day had hoped to move to the Los Angeles office. We ended the year winning the Round Table Pizza business.

Brian and Mike had more work then they had ever thought possible. But I was happy. We sent out another of our famous GMO postcards which had three smiley faces. Well actually only one was smiling. The other two had their mouths open in frustration. The first represented me and the last two represented Mike and Brian. The headline read, "The first year is over and it's been a real scream."

What started as Chiat/Day San Francisco had become Chiat/Day/Mojo. Now we were Chiat/Day/No/Mo or Goldberg Moser O'Neill.

Three months later, in September of 1990, the *Wall Street Journal* reported that Chiat/Day/Mojo had been hurt by a rash of account losses and was replacing the management in the New York office. It was more like a crippling disease, as the company lost more accounts than most advertising agencies ever even acquire: Reebok ($40M), Sara Lee ($12M), Gaines

The first year is over and it's been a real scream.

Our first year in business
gave us lots to shout about.
Join us today
on the 5th floor for cake
and champagne,
but not until 4:30.
That should keep Fred happy.

Dog Food ($16M), Ricoh ($8M), VeryFine juices ($8M), Rockport Shoes ($4M), Bissell ($10M), Mr. Goodbuys ($2M), Grandy's Country Cookin'

($2M), and Royal Caribbean ($35M). American Express and Arrow Shirts had cut their budgets and would soon be lost too.

The manager, Jane Newman, was removed from that job; people were laid off in droves; pay cuts for senior executives were put in place; bonuses were eliminated across the board.

They say timing is everything. Amen.

I never did get paid a nickel for my share of the famous Chiat/Day Binocular building in Venice, California, that was part of my signed "napkin" agreement with Jay. But it didn't matter.

CHAPTER 14

FOR WHOM THE DELL TOLLS

ONE OF THE MOST REMARKABLE and challenging situations in which I was involved was with Michael Dell and his Dell Computer Company. It is a long and wonderful story since we represented Dell for 11 years, during which time they grew from being number 20 in personal computers, a $200 million company, to a $25 billion behemoth and number 1.

They were actually the fastest-growing company in the world during the time of our working together. That is among all kinds of companies, bar none.

We were a part of making them the biggest and the best. Here was a 19-year-old kid who started selling PCs in 1984 out of his dorm room direct to the consumer. Then he became even smarter, got out of the dorm, and concentrated on selling PCs direct to the consumer. No BA, no MBA . . . no BS.

Ironically that was the same year that I was working at Chiat/Day and helped launch the Macintosh with the "1984" television spot for Steve Jobs and his Apple Computer. We started working for Dell a few years later, after John Sculley at Apple fired us.

So over two decades we participated in two enormous revolutions, both of which changed the world considerably, and our advertising efforts were instrumental in each.

We had many great successes with various clients over the years, but Dell may have been our greatest. It wasn't simply the challenges of this business category or that Michael Dell was only 23 years old when we first began working with him. It wasn't just that we had told Dell to find someone else a few years earlier when they first rang at our door. And it wasn't just the fact of their phenomenal sales growth during our partnership.

The single most important reason why Dell was so significant for us was that the advertising really mattered. Many clients think that advertising is a necessary evil and they do it because their competitors are doing it. But Dell was a direct seller of personal computers, and when they didn't advertise they didn't sell computers.

It was very simple: no advertising, no sales, no profits. So they had to advertise in good times, in bad times, in all times, and they knew that. Or should I say Michael Dell knew that. Michael said it very well right at the start: "When the ads aren't running, the store isn't open."

Another reason Dell was key to our agency was that not only did they know that powerful and emotional advertising worked but they believed it passionately, at least in the early days of our relationship.

When you work with most clients, they say all the right things about why more creative advertising is important, but at the end of the day few

THE LAP OF LUXURY.   THE LAP OF LUNACY.

$3,899 $6,799

The New Dell System 320LT 20MHz 386SX Laser $141/mo   *The Compaq SLT 386s/20 20MHz 386SX*

truly really believe and are able to step up to the plate and approve it and support it. I mean really believe. When things get tight, the first thing they do is become more conservative in their messaging; the second thing they do is cut the advertising budget to save money.

Dell believed because they had to believe and they had the experience in tracking the impact on their business. They also believed, before they got big enough to worry about losing what they had built, that the more aggressive, the more in your face, the more balls an ad had, the more impact it would have and the more PCs they would sell.

This thinking allowed us to create some truly outstanding advertising over the years. Advertising that was creatively brilliant, advertising that generated far greater awareness than it would have otherwise, along with much free publicity. Advertising that made their phones ring off the hook. Advertising that sold computers and advertising that won accolades and awards.

Ads like those that helped put Compaq, their most direct competitor at the time, back on its heels and become a banished and then a vanished brand.

Competitive and comparative ads of Dell and Compaq like these:

- *"The Lap of Luxury … The Lap of Lunacy," showing the $3,000 price difference between the two laptops*

- *"To Market, to Market, to Market We Go… To the Cleaners, to the Cleaners, to the Cleaners You Go"*

- *"Top of the Mark… Top of the Mark Ups"*

And so on.

According to Chilton Research, which reviewed 3,533 ads in 23 different publications in 1990, the "Top of the Mark . . . " advertisement outscored all 3,532 others with a 97 percent noticed score.

And then there was an ad that was pure genius. It showed Dell compared with IBM and Compaq and rated number one in eight separate categories. The headline was "After years of losing market share to Dell, it seems IBM and Compaq want to play hardball. So far, we're ahead eight to nothing."

With this effort we were able to seriously hurt Compaq, and Dell emerged as the most viable brand alternative. Compaq floundered and they sued Dell and our agency, but it was too late, as we had inflicted a mortal wound.

And so much for all the critiques at the time of how ineffective comparative advertising was, and there were many. Not only did our advertising drive sales but it created a strong brand image that Dell sorely needed, as they had been previously positioned as, and had become, just another cheap price brand in a sea of sameness. That was hardly an avenue by which they could become the number one personal computer in the world.

It is interesting how many negative critics came out of the woodwork against this advertising and the use of the comparative per se.

Ad Age editor Fred Danzig wrote of the dangers and ineffectiveness in an editorial on April 15, 1993. In his piece he cited famous adman David Ogilvy who said that "customers don't buy products from bad-mannered people" and that advertisers should use the "handshake" in ads rather than the "hammer."

I wrote Danzig a letter challenging his view . . . and Ogilvy's as well. In my opinion if a comparative ad didn't work, it was because it hadn't been developed properly and wasn't relevant. The product wasn't positioned properly. I argued that the loyalty customers have is to a product that's better than the one they are using, and comparative advertising helps dramatically to demonstrate those differences.

We had been using comparative ads that delivered on the demonstrably superior computer ownership experience provided by Dell as well as their technical superiority in some aspects. We leveraged it not just against Compaq but IBM and others as well.

Danzig made a comparison between Hulk Hogan and Michael Jordan and asked which kind of advertiser the reader wanted to be more like or identify with. I observed that marketing is about winning in the marketplace, and anyway, in that year of 1993, a lot of people thought that Charles Barkley was going to get the MVP award. And he did. He was the Hulk Hogan of basketball.

During the time we used this comparative competitive approach, Dell grew over five years to become a $2 billion company with the highest growth in profits of any Fortune 500 organization. They ultimately became the most valuable personal computer company, at number one in the world.

Ad Age never ran my letter but a cartoon said it all when it showed an executive at his desk at Compaq with a huge rocket emerging from the side of his desk, which had on it Dell Computer price comparison ads. And the balloon above the executive said, "Suddenly one day it came to me . . . why not try cutting our prices?"

⊘ ⊘ ⊘

But I want to go way back to the beginning, during the mid-1980s, when a fellow named John Leonardo was consulting for Dell and he rang our bell and inquired if we would be interested in the advertising account.

"How large are the billings on the business?"

"A million dollars in media billings. Plus production."

"Thanks, but no thanks."

They were small, they were a direct marketer, they were doing terrible ads, and we had a conflicting client for whom we were doing great ads. Businessland, the premier computer retailer at the time, with what we thought was a good upside.

Dell's being based in Austin, Texas, didn't help our decision either. It gets hot as Haiti and they have really big black bugs there (but I later found out only for about six or seven weeks every year, when they are everywhere). Imagine arriving late at night, opening your hotel room door, flicking on the light switch, and seeing 50 of these things crawling all over the place: on the floor, walls, desk, and bathtub. It brought with it visions of Papillon in his prison cell in French Guyana. But he ended up eating them.

Furthermore, how rested would one be for a meeting the next day after turning the light on and off all night to see how many of these critters were still in the room with you? On several occasions I called the front desk to have them come up and fumigate the room in the middle of the night. This raised a secondary problem: breathing.

At the time just about every one of the product ads that Dell was doing was god-awful. Bits and bytes. Specs and techs. Boring. Boring. Boring.

So we had lots of reasons to pass on the account the first time they rang our bell. And we did.

Fast-forward a few years later to 1988 when Dell decided to hold another agency review for their account. Dell had been using the Riney agency in San Francisco for a few years, just across town from us.

⊘ ⊘ ⊘

Hal Riney & Partners had convinced them they should take advantage of a Texas cowboy heritage and was running some incredibly superficial branding ads using cowboy hats, spurs, and, yep, branding irons. Folksy, downhome Americana was the kind of advertising Riney was famous for, but it was incredibly wrong for the leading-edge high-technology Dell business in so many ways. Moreover, it wasn't working, that is, selling computers.

Dell didn't think they were getting the respect from the agency they deserved either. The feeling was different on the agency side. They simply had a pure dislike for the business. This was later borne out in interviews we had with various employees from Riney who had been assigned to the Dell business.

They hated everything about Dell: the products, the people, Austin, and the black bugs. It was an unusually bad case of disdain for their client and their products and they should have resigned the account before getting fired. We ended up hiring none of these people, as they were all in need of major attitude adjustments.

The Riney gang disliked Dell so much that when they traveled to client meetings in Austin they stayed at a hotel far from Dell, way downtown. This was an inconvenient half-hour or so ride from Dell's headquarters. But they detested the account, so much so that they never wanted to accidentally bump into a client lest they would have to spend any additional time with them.

There was this really nice Stouffer's Hotel conveniently located not 30 steps from the Dell building. The Riney folks never, never stayed there, preferring instead the Four Seasons in downtown Austin as their beds of choice.

Talk about ego, hubris, and insensitivity in the advertising business. Michael Dell at the time was known to fly coach wherever he went and surely would have frowned at the up charges that these hotel stays added to the agency costs, for which he was paying. If he knew! Actually he probably did know and that may have been a part of the decision to get rid of Riney.

We decided to pitch for the account this second time around. It had grown to around $8 million in billings. However, we insisted that any meetings had to be kept completely quiet because we still had the Businessland account, which could be considered competitive, and didn't want to upset that situation needlessly if we didn't get Dell.

We had a good relationship with Businessland and had grown with their growth over the previous four or five years. Importantly we had done some really great branding and retail advertising for them. It had gotten to be about a $5 million account for us from only $1.5 million when we started.

But Businessland was hitting a wall and was having some financial problems. The two founders, David Norman and Enzo Torresi, were both smart and motivated people but were at odds on several critical business issues, not the least of which was the importance of advertising. We felt that these problems would eventually catch up with us.

Not very long afterward Businessland indeed was on the brink of bankruptcy and agreed to sell itself to a Purchase, New York, company known as JWP Inc. JWP was a company that installed heating, ventilation, and electrical systems. What were they thinking?

We put together an insightful strategic presentation for Dell. It basically showed Dell how the Riney agency had them terribly and incorrectly positioned in the personal computer marketplace. It also postulated that they had an enormous opportunity to target computer retailers like Businessland and Computerland directly and build share from that part of the market. These insights came largely from Mike Massaro, who was quite brilliant in his understanding of technology and his strategic sense of marketing and advertising, particularly for Dell.

Riney had been running those trademark down-home, western, soft, and mushy ads with cowboys and branding irons to try and sell fast and cheap high-technology computers to the entire PC target. This was so wrong that it was incredible that Dell had allowed itself to be convinced to do it in the first place. But the Riney folks were the "ad experts." Right!

There was, however, one issue with our recommended strategy and that was that another of our clients would be sitting like a duck directly in the gun sight for the approach. That, of course, was Businessland. Since Dell was a seller of personal computers direct to consumers, consumers would never have to visit a retail computer store again if they believed what we were going to say about Dell.

Nevertheless, we flew down to Austin and assembled our presentation group outside the Dell headquarters building while we waited to go up to make our pitch. It was 105 degrees that day. In the shade. I had some sympathy for the people from Riney who had worked on the account.

We had a terrific meeting with Michael Dell, Joel Kocher, and the rest of Dell management, and before we left to catch our plane back to San Francisco they had halted the agency review process and were ready to give the entire Dell account to us.

At this point in his company, Michael had surrounded himself with some very good and experienced people, one of whom was a senior executive named Lee Walker. Lee was president of Dell for a time and he was referred to as a "serial entrepreneur." He was someone we could all relate to and he was in our pitch meeting and he was inspiring.

He said later on, "We hired your agency because we thought we would learn from our mistakes."

How true this turned out to be.

And we viewed his observation as giving us permission to make mistakes, and this also turned out to be true. It was incredibly empowering and motivating. In turn Dell got the very best thinking and work from us. Lee Walker was one smart guy. We were very sorry when he left the company a few years later.

We were treated as if we were actually a part of the Dell organization. Michael Dell, Joel Kocher, and a wonderful woman, the advertising director M. J. Lawhon, all made this happen and in return they received our complete and utter commitment. We ended up doing cartwheels for these people because of the respect and trust they had for us.

On my return trip to San Francisco, I called Businessland from the Austin airport and told them that a competitive opportunity had come for us that was too good for us to pass up and that we were unfortunately going to have to part ways with them. They were very disappointed but gracious.

It wasn't very long after that Businessland folded up their tent but not because of what we were doing for Dell. Rather they had too many systemic problems and high costs in managing their network of computer retail stores. And the personal computer business model was changing dramatically.

And so we now had the Dell Computer business. All that had to be done before we officially announced the account was for me to negotiate a contract with them. Back then, the "them" at Dell was Michael Dell.

Once we were awarded the account I sat with Michael for about 30 minutes in his office, and like two Turkish rug merchants we met in the middle somewhere and we agreed to what we both considered a fair compensation deal. I gave a little, he gave a little, I gave a little, and he gave a little more. However, unlike the Turks, neither of us felt unfulfilled when we reached our agreement and finally shook hands. Our agency ended up with a hell of a deal that stayed in place without a single change for our entire 11-year relationship.

In our negotiation the two things that Michael held fast on were kind of funny. He didn't think any "supplier" should be compensated relatively more from the size of a cost estimate. In other words the supplier (us) should not benefit from providing, for example, a larger size production estimate since we were getting a percentage commission. Good point!

Michael never trusted the Riney production estimates and he always thought that they were ripping him off, which was probably true because advertising agencies in general didn't carefully control the costs of production. It's an "it's their money, not our money" mentality. And the higher the production estimate, the greater the income yield from the commission rate.

So Michael had insisted that no commission be paid to the agency on any production estimate. I agreed, not realizing at that point we would end up doing some 500 ads a year and not get a nickel of traditional compensation in this manner. So you shouldn't worry, we more than made up for this shortfall by billing out time and materials on every single ad, which Dell happily paid. Just one reason happened to be that we were ultimately able to drive down our error factor to zero.

It has struck me many times over the years just how much clients are so hung up on production budgets. They review them with a fine-tooth comb trying to identify and squeeze out a dollar here and a dollar there. I think they are simply comfortable dealing with the more tangible aspects of a production estimate, which is right there in black and white: cost of talent, cost of props, and cost of travel.

The irony is that most clients do not pay nearly as much attention, if any, to the millions and millions of dollars that they are spending in media, and that is where the real accountability and forensic study should be focused. But most clients don't really understand exactly how the media-buying process works and therefore leave it to the agency "experts." Big mistake!

I had a client at Sutter Home Winery who attended a print shooting in Manhattan one time. His name was Alex Morgan and he was a large man, well over 300 pounds. At the shoot he thoroughly enjoyed two or three corned beef sandwiches that the production company had catered for lunch. He enjoyed less discovering that the sandwiches reappeared on his final production billing and were $13.50 per.

In the six-year relationship we had with this client, Alex never let me personally forget how we ripped him off. He could get a corned beef sandwich in St. Helena, California, for $1.50. He failed to accept that the deli in St. Helena just might not be the Stage Delicatessen in New York City. I guess he didn't appreciate or taste the $12 difference or that things in Manhattan might be a tad pricier than in rural Northern California.

I had another fellow who was head of Class Act, a division of our client Worlds of Wonder, the inventors of Teddy Ruxpin and Lazer Tag. He suffered from agency production cost issues too.

I was at dinner with him one evening at a Chinese restaurant near Fremont, California, where the company was based, and the check came. As was usual, my hand reached robotically for the bill, as it is a rare occurrence when a client moves their hand toward the tray the check is sitting in.

I took a few moments to peruse the check and, seeing that everything looked correct, placed my credit card down in the tray. The client looked at me and said, "Fred, I have never ever seen an ad agency guy look at a lunch or dinner check."

In his experience ad agency folks just threw down their credit card and let the server take it away and run it through. He appreciated that I took the time and concern to check the bill. As a result I never again had an approval problem on any production estimate or bill with this client after that dinner.

After that conversation I made sure that I looked at every dinner check. Not only have I gained confidence with clients and friends, but it's surprising how often I save a few bucks.

But getting back to Michael Dell and our negotiation. The other thing that he insisted was to keep the 15 percent agency commission on media that they had paid to Riney in place but only up to the first $10 million in billings, where it would then be capped. Thereafter we agreed to let it drop to 10 percent.

This sounded pretty good to me. Now this was about the time that clients were just beginning to throw out the commission system by which agencies got paid. Moreover, Dell's budget was around $8 million so we had some upside cushion before the commission percentage would begin to decline. Mostly, I felt that Dell was going to be a very successful company, and knowing that their success was so importantly tied to advertising spending, I figured this would work to our longer-term benefit when they became a $15 million or $20 million advertiser. I miscalculated terribly, as they would ultimately spend close to $100 million through our agency in just a single year. So that last $90 million yielded $9 million in income. Sweet!

Our agreement turned out to be a very good thing for the agency but also a very good thing for Dell. We put our commitment, energy, heart, and best talent into this business, particularly in the early formative years. We may have invested more in this client than in any other because they were reliant and believed in us. We did great work, we crafted a unique brand in a commodity industry, we helped sell many computers for Dell, and in turn we made a hell of a lot of money along the way. But then so did Dell make a hell of a lot of money selling PCs direct, and a significant part of that came directly from our efforts.

Mike Massaro was a critical ingredient in our agency for over 17 years, first at Chiat/Day and then when we became Goldberg Moser O'Neill. He was essential to our management of the Dell account for its entire run at the agency. He made it possible to have an unusually close and strategic relationship with Michael Dell himself. He often was responsible for establishing Dell's marketing direction for them.

I remember traveling with Mike down to Palo Alto where Michael Dell was taking some executive management courses at Stanford University. We picked him up at the dorm where he was bunking and went to a local Chinese place for dinner. These were very pleasant times, and much was accomplished that moved the strategy for Dell forward as well as its advertising. Talk about hands-on entrepreneurial management, this was it in spades. The egg foo young was very good too.

One day I received an unusual request from Michael Dell's assistant, Kaye Banda. Michael was going to be in San Francisco in our Maiden Lane offices and she wondered whether I would be kind enough to do him a favor. Well, I wasn't going to say no, was I?

She asked me to personally take delivery of a special package that he was hoping to send to my attention. I was instructed to hand it directly to Michael and to him alone. The package arrived. Michael arrived. I successfully carried out my mission and transferred the secret package to him.

Turns out it was the engagement ring he was presenting that evening to Susan, his soon wife to be. Now that's a full service account guy at work.

Dell kept on getting bigger and bigger. When they started having multi-billion-dollar sales years, instead of multi-hundred-million-dollar sales years, it became harder and harder to get them to approve the more effective but creative and aggressive, hard-hitting advertising we had used that put them on the map during the first half-dozen years of our relationship. That initial advertising was what had very importantly shaped the perception and image of Dell in the personal computer market. It created a brand where there had really been none before.

Michael and Susan Dell

But things were changing at Dell. More people begat more bureaucracy, which begat more turf building and defense. Most of all it brought fear and constipation. And it brought the safety of falling backward on the tried and true and doing only what had been done before.

Dell's size and the fact that Joel Kocher, who had been president of worldwide marketing, sales, and service, and who had been instrumental in originally hiring us, had been pushed out. Joel was a man to whom you could show the most clever, ballsy, and/or controversial work and he would respond with an instant approval to run it or he would insist on making it even more aggressive and in your face.

I would venture that Joel's leadership was responsible more than anyone else's for Dell's growth in those early years when our agency was first involved. Joel was an important part of the brand itself. Once Joel was gone and Dell had grown to a certain scale, they became more worried about offending their competition than about beating them. They started running scared. We had always argued that you couldn't make history by looking back over your shoulder. But that is in fact what Dell now did.

Along too came new members joining the Dell board of directors. One in particular started what was to be the beginning of the end of our involvement with Dell.

I knew we were going to have problems when I learned that Michael Dell had met with Charlotte Beers, the ex-head of Ogilvy & Mather, about possibly joining the Dell board. She being of the self-professed experts on branding strategy. It was later decided that since O&M had IBM, and Charlotte still had relationships with both of those companies, maybe her being on the inside of Dell wasn't such a cool idea after all.

Instead they ended up going down a different path with an ex–packaged goods guy and CEO of Kentucky Fried Chicken and Kraft, Mike Miles. One of his most well-known accomplishments was that he started a price war in the tobacco industry by dropping prices on established brands like Marlboro. He didn't last long after that at Philip Morris as chairman/CEO.

It was rumored that it was Miles who, as a director at Dell, suggested they needed a corporate "branding" campaign and then an international "branding" campaign. As if what we had done for the prior decade wasn't branding.

The funny part of this, the ultimate irony actually, was that I had been meeting with Michael Dell regularly over the years. As a part of every get-together I strongly recommended that he seriously consider setting aside some funding for an incremental branding campaign. An important component of my argument was always to include television as a powerful addition to Dell's media arsenal. Dell had never used TV.

Every time this discussion came up, Michael would argue that the advertising had to pay back itself in sales. A dollar of advertising had to return a dollar of sales. Every print ad we ran for Dell had to deliver back its investment.

Well, that ain't the way most television ads work in building and

Michael Dell and Joel Kocher: advertising leadership par excellence.

solidifying brands. There is an investment mentality required along the way but Michael never bought into that idea—that is, until Mike Miles got in his ear.

Michael's other argument against investing in "branding" had always been that they were doing so well they really didn't need this type of advertising. The very last time I brought this subject up, Michael actually got a little testy and told me to please not bring up the subject any longer whenever we met. He wasn't interested. Dell didn't need it and Dell didn't want it. That was until it was suggested by Mr. Miles, author of the brilliant tobacco price reduction strategy that damn near wrecked the cigarette industry profitability.

Long story short is that when Mike Miles said the same thing, it carried more weight. His credibility was surely enhanced by having worked at Philip Morris, a company that could hardly live without imaging advertising. I always found it extremely amusing, however, that Miles advocated cutting prices to generate volume at Philip Morris but now was advocating just the opposite. I mean Marlboro had to be one of the greatest brands ever built with brand advertising. Cigarettes were essentially all the same. But by cutting the price of your brand leader, you also destroy the imaging over time.

At Dell we had a price brand that had already become a real value brand in a commodity market. If Dell had invested sooner in establishing a broader brand image, they would have been that much more ahead of the game. As it was, they ended up being late in doing this, and in my opinion they never got it right from a positioning standpoint. What they did was try a lot of unsuccessful jabs but never scored any points.

At the same time as Mike Miles was advocating for "branding," he apparently also lobbied that they needed a "real international advertising agency" on board to implement a global corporate branding assignment. This cry now fell on eager ears and that was the start of their search for a large monolithic international advertising and communications company.

As is often the case in the ad business, it is fraught with irony. The people at Dell had insisted over our protestations that we manage their business in the UK and Canada. They wanted it run out of our San Francisco office as well for better control and continuity. For some of the other European countries like France and Spain, they asked that Mike Massaro be personally involved in the selection of the ad agency in those respective countries. And that we would be the central coordinating point for all of the agencies. Oh my how things change.

We were led to believe that Miles recommended talking to three agencies: Leo Burnett in Chicago, J. Walter Thompson in New York and Chicago, and Young & Rubicam in New York. By the strangest coincidence these were three agencies that he had used at Philip Morris and at Kraft before that. Oh and all this "talking" was to be done secretly. I guess they didn't want us to know so they never told us that this review was taking place. Kind of shitty when you consider what we had helped Dell achieve over the previous years and the commitments to the business we had made. Not to speak of the relationships that we had built up over the years.

I would have thought that Michael would have been a mensch in this regard and feel obligated to tell us what was going on. But he didn't. Heck, no one ever said advertising was an ethical business, so why should this client be burdened with any of those pesky morality issues? But less cynically, he probably was preoccupied in Taiwan making sure he had the best and lowest cost supplier for motherboards, or in Ireland making sure the IRA didn't blow up his factory there.

Actually Gallup and other researchers who care about these things have ranked advertising close to the lowest of all professions in terms of trust and honesty. Only used car salesmen and more recently politicians and lawyers are at the same low levels. But what of clients who do this kind of thing? Gallup didn't measure it that way.

Well, a funny thing happened on the way to this secret review. I found out about it! Someone at Leo Burnett had leaked the fact to *Advertising Age* that they were talking to Dell. Before it hit the newsstands I was on the phone with some Dell folks, several of whom were denying that anything was going on. Some knew and some didn't. Our friends confided in us and told us the truth of the situation.

Burnett was quickly dropped from the review when the item appeared in the trades. When asked by the press about the review, Michael Dell was quoted as saying, "I wouldn't want to speculate on that."

After this happened, Dell then, and only then, invited us to participate in the review if we wanted. We agreed, angry as we were. After all they were still our largest account, and gaining this additional branding assignment would have provided lots of insurance. At least that's the way our flawed thinking went. That and that advertising people are incredible optimists even when the engines on the plane they're traveling aboard are failing one by one.

This turned out to be a costly and time-consuming exercise over a nine-month time frame. When I look back, the smart thing would have been to forget about competing for this new assignment and immediately start trolling for a new personal computer client.

We knew from conversations that our planning director Catrina McAuliffe had had with some people who worked on the Compaq account that those clients were in awe of the advertising that we were doing for Dell. They thought it was wonderful, and they loved the personality and branding that we had developed and the aggressive nature of it. They wanted to emulate it, we were told, for Compaq. We should have called and done it for them but we didn't.

In June of 1997 Mike Massaro had a face to face with Michael Dell and asked him point blank about a number of the issues that were swirling around regarding the agency.

"Michael, why didn't you tell us that you were considering other agencies for a global branding assignment?"

"Mike, we didn't think you could help us on a global basis with a megabrand."

And furthermore, "Somebody told us that your agency had a policy that you would stop work if this happened."

Our Mike reported to me that he offered this explanation "weakly."

Despite the cry for the branding campaign, it was our work over 10-plus years that had shaped and built the brand then known as Dell. Who better understood the brand? Heck, we had helped form it without any specific advertising devoted to branding alone. I can only imagine if we could have gotten some of our general branding work to run. What would have been?

We had even created and published a comprehensive booklet on the essential elements of the Dell brand to be applied across all elements of the marketing mix. This had become somewhat of a bible at Dell in the US as well as around the world. This "branding handbook" had set standards for Dell everywhere and particularly in places that had had none.

The most incredible part of this whole story was that our agency actually had received approval for, had produced, and was already running a branding campaign known as "Leaders" in a limited test area. We had been able to secure permission to tell the story of what Dell had achieved for such organizations as Mercedes-Benz and NASA, among others. These were organizations that were obsessed with reliability, performance, engineering, and quality. Just like Dell.

Mike Massaro had succeeded in getting this program implemented as a test long before Mike Miles was a twinkle in Michael Dell's eye. It was strategically potent and, in terms of the creative executions, extremely powerful. It was a pure branding effort executed primarily in TV but it translated well to print. It was the kind of advertising that was easily implemented on a global basis because of its flexibility in choosing each of the featured companies. Above all, the campaign was working on every metric, including qualitative and quantitative research results, anecdotal response, and hard sales data.

Unaided awareness had risen to 50 percent after only eight weeks in the test markets; the reliability gap between Dell and Compaq had dropped from 30 points to 10, and there was no longer any difference in customer consideration between the two brands. Most important, stunning actually, was that after such a short period of time, sales were up over 20 percent for every segment of Dell's business, with every one showing demonstrable increases. It all translated to an incremental revenue gain over $27 million in just a two-month test period alone behind a spending investment of only $3.3 million.

I relayed this compelling information to Michael Dell in a November 20, 1997, e-mail along with a discussion of the specter of the arguments being made against the indubitable results. Incredibly there were those at Dell arguing that the creative execution was unimportant and the results were simply the act of combining an endorsement strategy with brand spending dollars. The argument was extended to suggest that a large global advertising agency could somehow bring far better insight into the branding equation than we had with this campaign.

I threw back at Dell what he had always professed to us. Listen to the customer, who in this case was telling us to continue with the "Leaders" effort with their hearts and their wallets. Deal in fact and not opinion. It mattered little whether anyone liked or disliked the work because the facts said that it was working.

My last gasp was to suggest if he didn't buy any of this, then the least he should do was demand that any new effort by any new agency resource be implemented in a similar test market situation so that the two efforts could be compared on results and results alone.

Michael Dell and Dell had built a fantastic company on measurable results and return on investments. Instead, in this case they decided to ignore all of it and let an unknown quantity determine their future. They set the

"Leaders" campaign aside and plunged into trying to find a global resource that could do it "right."

Arguably this may have been one of the single worst decisions that Dell ever made. Had they allowed us to continue on as their primary agency resource and implement the successful "Leaders" campaign, the next 10 years of problems might have been avoided. Those problems included never being able to find the "right" agency and getting miserably beaten up in the personal computer market by competitors.

By a decade later Dell had gotten married and divorced to many advertising agencies, and to this day they do not have a clear, concise, or consistent brand image. They are now largely the price brand they started out being. They are no longer the number one PC maker in the world. In 2009 they were a business that was losing revenue, losing income, and floundering.

As a part of the whole review process exercise to identify an "international corporate branding" resource, we had to make a presentation to the European operations for Dell. Mike Massaro, Catrina McAuliffe, our planning director, and I met in an obscure town somewhere north of London at Dell's headquarters there.

Our parent agency at the time had become The Lowe Group and was supposed to provide us some significant resources to help with our "international" pitch. At the time Jerry Judge was the manager of Lowe Howard-Spink in London and he made all the appropriate promises until we got to London and we discovered they knew nothing about the personal computer business, less about our client Dell, and didn't care to. It wasn't considered their kind of client.

The last time I saw Jerry Judge was in Venice, Italy, where Lowe was holding a worldwide agency conference. Judge was lying on the floor of a vaporetto with a shit-ass grin on his face, drunk as a skunk . . . still making promises.

Our agency had logged 4,015 days of experience working on the Dell business, we had traveled 5,456 miles from San Francisco to England, and we were given 45 minutes to tell them why we were best qualified to be their corporate branding agency worldwide.

We gave a good presentation but it was like talking to the Moai Easter Island statues. Everyone in the room from Dell knew that we knew that they knew that we knew more about their business than even they knew. However, politics and personalities were at play and they were incredibly nonresponsive. A woman named Sarah J. Hammant, Dell's European marketing communications manager, was even quite hostile as she attempted to promote one of the other "global" agencies left in the review whom she favored.

There was some silver lining in this trip, and that was the week subsequently spent in London with my wife Jeri. We had a wonderful time taking a few days and exploring the city in a way we had never done before.

Unfortunately it ended in tragedy. That was the very week that Princess Diana was killed in a car accident and it was quite sad being there. They buried her the day we left London. That was also the day I concluded that we were going to be buried by Dell as well.

News of the Dell account goings-on ultimately reached Phil Geier, chairman at the Interpublic Group, the holding company that had bought Goldberg Moser O'Neill in 1996. We had become part of one of their "networks, The Lowe Group, headed by Frank Lowe. We were getting no satisfactory help from the "network" at Lowe in addressing the Dell situation. Part of the reason was that the "network" at Lowe was more a "notwork" of smoke and mirrors.

I received several calls during this period from Phil Geier expressing his eagerness to help with the situation and advising me of his personal friendship with Mike Miles. He asked if he should call him. I told him by all means please call and do whatever he could. He did and it didn't make a mouse turd of difference.

One of the criticisms that had been lodged against Goldberg Moser O'Neill was that we were not international. One of the reasons we had liked the idea of becoming part of The Lowe Group was so we could tap into their international network. But when it came time to use their global network, it really wasn't a network, and they were off busy pitching a directly competitive computer account, Gateway. They never told us and we spotted it in the trade press.

And so did Dell. This was something that Dell was not happy about at

all and it did not help better position us as a world resource for them. They also had not forgotten that a Lowe subsidiary, Lowe Direct, had done some work for Dell at one point and ended up threatening to sue the client.

Lowe also wanted to protect their interests with Sun Microsystems in the US, a Lowe New York client that had limited advertising potential and which they soon lost. This was a client that theoretically they should never have pitched, as we were part of Lowe and we represented Dell at the time.

We were even running some ads aimed directly at Sun. One ad appeared to be directed not only at Corporate America but at the Lowe organization as well.

Lowe shucked and jived and danced but refused to give us any commitments. They kept Sun, they continued to pursue Gateway, and they delivered no helpful resources. Frank Lowe did pirouettes and a pas de deux but offered no real help whatsoever, as he seemed only interested in protecting his interests at Lowe.

This part of the story would be incomplete in demonstrating just how screwed up advertising agencies can be without mentioning that a part of the Dell international agency search concerned having an outlet, office, or partner in the Far East. Of course we had none, but Lowe said they would identify one for us.

Months went by as we tried to pin down who that "partner" might be. Finally our people had to fly to Japan for the pitch meeting and while in the air still did not know who the Japanese partner agency was going to be. Exactly one day before the meeting Lowe provided the name of an agency to contact. It's unimaginable to me that they could run an organization in this manner. But they did.

There was one conversation that Mike Massaro had with Frank Lowe that stands out above all the others. When we were trying to garner some help from him with the Dell situation, Frank told Mike over the phone, "What the fuck am I wasting time talking to you about Dell when I've got Coke to worry about?"

Frank never really liked Mike. I don't think he thought he was cool enough to suit

Sir Frank Lowe

his tastes, maybe because he didn't ever wear yellow capes to work or scarves in the summer like he did. But Frank didn't worry quite enough about Coke as he ended up getting fired on that account.

Sir Frank seemed never to be held to any accountability in this whole affair as far as I know, although a few years later he made a very ungraceful exit out of IPG.

⊘ ⊘ ⊘

Phil Geier had another chance to help solve the problem as regards Dell and our agency. But he was unsuccessful. I spoke with Geier and briefed him on the entire situation a second time and he offered the McCann Erickson international network, run by John Dooner. He told me to call Dooner and he would set it up.

I received a fax from Geier on July 11, 1997, confirming the use of the McCann Erickson network. (And I'm a guy who saves important faxes and letters.) Unfortunately he seemed to have forgotten to mention it to the fellow who was running McCann, John Dooner. I called Dooner's office numerous times and left messages and yet he never returned any of my calls. I wondered how Geier, head of this huge holding company IPG, could put up with folks who seemingly didn't respond to what he told them. Or maybe Dooner just didn't care. Or maybe he never bothered to call Dooner. You think? I don't know.

More likely it's just that too many people in advertising are simply full of shit and not genuine. As far as I was concerned, it was Geier's last strike. I never spoke to the man again after that. Unfortunately I had to carry on with Frank Lowe for a while longer.

Frank Lowe himself was a key issue in all of this. Late in July of 1997 I got this cryptic fax from him advising me about the McCann possibility: "Dear Fred . . . the situation seems to have changed somewhat with regards to McCann which means it may not be workable."

The operating words here are *seems*, *somewhat*, and *may*. This response was before Frank became Sir Frank, but even then he had a hard time saying directly what he was saying.

Young & Rubicam was the first to present at Dell headquarters in Austin, Texas. Well, it's not really in Austin; it's kind of outside Austin in a 'burb called Round Rock. The day of their presentation a line of shiny black limos pulled up to one of the ugly, nondescript, virtually windowless concrete bunkers the Dell folks called home. Some would say these buildings are austere but functional. Many would agree that mental suicide from working inside these quarters was a strong possibility. There was nothing luxurious or inviting anywhere you looked and for good reason, as the design saved Dell a lot of money constructing and operating the buildings.

It didn't take more than a few minutes for a buzz to circulate the Dell campus. In fact it didn't take long for this news to reach us in San Francisco as various Dell folks called to report the happening. A dozen or so slick Madison Avenue ad guys from New York City, in dark suits and white shirts, and red or green solid ties, had arrived and were marching, big black bags in hand, into the building for their presentation. Among those included in the procession was Peter Georgescu, then CEO of Y&R, a man of impeccable taste in Brooks Brothers–like men's wear and in manners. I had worked with and for Peter during my Y&R days. He was a very bright guy but he did like the trappings of his office.

Clearly the Y&R folks didn't get that Dell was an understated austerity machine and Michael Dell was a guy who often flew coach to set an example. He could hardly have appreciated looking out his office window and seeing the limousines lined up outside the entrance to Dell like a funeral procession. He was basically really really bottom line orientated . . . er, cheap in a good business way. Cheap equals more profits, a concept that I shared on a number of occasions running my agency. However, in January 2013, it was reported in the *Wall Street Journal* that Michael had purchased a Boeing 787 Dreamliner. Per unit cost . . . in excess of $200 million. Oh well, as with most things, they change.

It turned out to be a funeral for Y&R, as they didn't ultimately get the business. It might have been the transportation they chose or it might have been that they presented an idea that was similar to one that Gateway, another large direct marketer of personal computers, had been using in a recent campaign. Actually it wasn't similar; it was the same. No one at that agency seemed aware of that fact, despite that the campaign had been running on national TV. The Dell folks were, however.

We made our presentation in Round Rock as well. It was quite good. We presented a highly creative and strategically relevant campaign: "Dell. Obsessed With Getting It Right." It expressed everything that Dell was and should be and I am confident it would have been immensely successful for Dell, maybe as successful as our "Leaders" campaign had been already.

But J. Walter Thompson was awarded the new corporate branding assignment. They may or may not have been Mike Miles's favorite choice but he wasn't left with many choices at that point after Leo Burnett and Y&R had both stepped on their weenies. We knew we weren't one of his choices so they had a choice of one.

It was reported to me that Miles was the one that apparently first recommended the need for a mega-global international monolithic agency to represent Dell and, guess what, just nine months later, alas, J. Walter Thompson was fired. They had spent all that time and lots of money giving birth to a television branding campaign that had very little to do with selling Dell computers. It did have to do with an elephant and a mouse and it did run a few times before it was pulled. And it did have a pretty good positioning line, which just happened to be one that we had presented to Dell a few years before, "Be Direct."

Dell president Kevin Rollins remarked in an e-mail before the JWT advertising began, "With this global campaign, we're really branding the way we do business."

I understood Michael Dell was not happy about the $4 million or so JWT had spent on the production of the advertising. After JWT was fired a nasty bunch of lawsuits and counter-suits ensued, which seemed to be the case in each of Dell's agency divorces that followed.

So now Dell was still without their "branding" campaign or a "real advertising agency." Mike Miles was still on the board. Kevin Rollins was still president and COO and we never heard from Michael Dell during all these goings-on. And the guy most recently placed in charge of the corporate branding, Scott Helbing, had just come from working with BBDO in New York.

It was only fair for Helbing to take the initiative and invite his previous agency at Pizza Hut out to make a presentation on our business. Somehow he "forgot" to tell us until a few days before they were to present. He actually called on a Thursday asking us for ideas due by the next Tuesday. No doubt he was thinking we wouldn't want to participate on such short notice so he had invited us to present as well. To his surprise we agreed to present our thinking anyway, and it was to my surprise as well since I was out of town at the time. After all this surprising, it was not surprising that BBDO was given the branding assignment and became the next Dell "brand agency."

The final insult for Goldberg Moser O'Neill came March 1, 1999, when we presented work to Paul Bell, the general manager of the Home and Small Business Group. This was an important division of Dell for which we were responsible. Dave Mathews, director of marketing, and our "good friend" Scott Helbing were also in attendance.

⊘ ⊘ ⊘

We had some truly wonderful and relevant creative work and a powerful presentation of the strategic rationale. After we presented we heard the sound of one hand clapping and Paul Bell took me aside and advised that his division's account was going to review other advertising agencies. It wouldn't have mattered if we had presented the best, most relevant thing since sliced bread.

To this point we had retained most of the business that we had before the branding and international agency searches had begun and which still constituted a large assignment, although mostly being made up of the ongoing product advertising. This work, however, was the fuel that made the Dell engine go, the stuff that had to get out every day, day after day, 24/7. Over the years these ads had become pretty mundane, straight at you product and price offers. The creative had very little creative about it. In fact there was nothing creative about it, and if there was, the little-minded folks at Dell made sure to pound out any remnants that might induce enhanced readership. It did, however, amount to about $60 million in billing to our agency.

Nevertheless, I decided that we had been abused once too often and that it was just a matter of time until someone at Dell would reduce our involvement still further. We decided it wasn't worth the continued loss of face. We weren't doing any good work. It was very hard grinding work out on these ads night after night. Frankly no one at the agency wanted to get near this business to work on these god-awful ads.

Around this time I looked back on a note that Mike Massaro had put together and sent to himself earlier. I read it aloud to everyone at the agency in making our resignation announcement.

It was entitled "Top reasons to resign Dell."

1. *We can't find any creative people to work on it.*
2. *The work is not improving.*
3. *The company is unwilling to commit to a strategy.*
4. *They think they have outgrown us.*
5. *The travel is brutal.*
6. *I've done it before.*
7. *They make me feel old.*
8. *Tom (Tom Martin VP Marketing) won't be around much longer.*
9. *It is better to find a job while you've already got one.*

I added number 10, as would David Letterman, just to accentuate number 2:

10. *The work is not improving.*

Dell had become very comfortable with bunt singles, whereas in the early days they were enthusiastic and demanding of going for home runs, as were we.

On April 26, 1999, after 11 years we had become what Hal Riney had accomplished in less than three. Irrelevant.

So we said good-bye as *Ad Age* noted on April 28, 1999. "After turbulent ride, Goldberg bids Dell adieu."

To explain why we decided to resign our largest, most important, and most successful client, I turned to my partner Mike Moser. This Mike had worked tirelessly and suffered in the later years more than most.

Part of our success with Dell was our "secret sauce" in assigning key senior experienced executives. It appeared that those whose name was Mike were best suited to work with Michael Dell. Mike Massaro in account management and Mike Moser as the creative force, neither of which was a run-of-the-mill Mike.

We ran an ad in the trades that Mike Moser created and which explained what had happened. We hoped it would attract some

new clients and maybe a personal computer client or two. It also helped us lick our very open wounds publicly. The headline was "What ad agency in their right mind would resign the most successful company in America?"

Joel Kocher pitching Dell in the early days.

Moser's visuals reflected well both Mikes' attitudes and emotions and said it all about our relationship with Dell from start to end.

Of course there was about a 99.9 percent certainty that we were going to catch a bullet as soon as Dell could figure out how to handle the tough day-to-day work that we knew so well. But why not make it a bit harder for them by forcing them to figure it out sooner? So we did and it felt good too. Yippee! (See the end figure in illustration on the previous page.)

We had much to offer any other computer company, having been the agency for Apple Computer, Intel, Cisco, Symantec, Quantum, 3M, and many other technology-oriented companies over the years. We had a powerful database of knowledge regarding the direct sale of personal computers from our years with Dell. After all we had taken Dell from 900 calls a day to 300,000. So we made up a short list of personal computer companies that we wanted to work with and which we thought might consider working with us.

At the top of the list was Micron. This was a company that was now headed by Joel Kocher, who had been the greatest champion of our work at Dell when he was there during our first six years of the relationship. He was a man who stuck with us when we bought ourselves out from Chiat/Day and allowed us to get the Goldberg Moser O'Neill agency off the ground successfully. He had enabled us to create and run work that got Dell and our agency acclaim both nationally and internationally.

We called Joel, we met, and we announced on April 30, 1999, four days after resigning Dell that we were going to work for Micron Electronics.

This may have been one of the truly finest moments in my entire career. Here was a man with whom we did some of the greatest work in the computer category and who also had parted with Dell. And now we were being reunited after being spurned by the people whose business we helped make such an enormous success. How sweet it was.

⊘ ⊘ ⊘

Dell (that is, the lower level echelons that had to get the work done) went ballistic when we told them we were leaving. It had taken our agency five or six years to perfect a system for producing the quantity of advertising and ads that were so detailed in the specifications and information that each carried. There was no room for error. We had refined this process to a very exacting level. It is estimated that we prepared over 5,000 ads for Dell during our tenure with them and we got our error level down to near zero.

The Dell folks asked us, "Who is gonna do all the shit work?" They didn't use that expletive actually. Day to day, night to night. 24/7. Sometimes ads were required overnight. We said JWT or BBDO or whoever was the "global brand agency du jour." They said they wouldn't know how and we were jeopardizing their business. And that they were going to sue us.

In these later years Dell did have a habit, it seemed, of threatening to sue their former agencies. Uh-oh! OK. OK. We agreed to continue on for a near-term timetable but insisted that we were going to work for Micron immediately. And we did.

We ended up working for both PC companies for several months. During this time we developed what were probably the worst ads we ever did for Dell. At the same time we did some wonderful ads for Micron right out of the box, compliments of two terrific creative people, Mike Gallagher, copywriter, and Eric McClellan, group creative director, and the enthusiastic encouragement and approvals of Joel Kocher.

The campaign tagline for Micron was brilliant both strategically and creatively. Micron was in the process of shifting their business model to sell over the Internet: "micronpc.com Think Beyond the Box."

We made a ton of money during this period of time. We were able to leverage our experience with Dell long after we parted ways. I can't say for sure just how much it mattered but it provided us with a very powerful story of effective advertising and sales relationships. It was like none that I had ever been involved with before and none afterward. We built an incredible compelling case study that we used hundreds of times in new business presentations, and to my knowledge it never failed to impress. Many times it meant the difference in our gaining a new account.

Dell was the single most defining relationship and experience that we had either as Chiat/Day San Francisco or as Goldberg Moser O'Neill, the successor agency. It was directly responsible for our becoming the $500 million–plus billing agency we ultimately achieved as GMO.

And we had experienced probably one of the most genuine and enduring agency/client relationships ever. It was the longest of any agency and a major computer manufacturer at that time.

Like so many of the relationships that we had over the years, the one with Dell started with something that was not very significant, and we were able to help build it into a very significant business. The experience with Dell is a powerful example of the importance of trust and commitment, of hard work, of relationships, and of the incredible power of creative advertising in establishing and sustaining a brand and a business.

There was one day when several of the senior Dell executives traveled from Austin to our offices in San Francisco just to present us with an award for being so responsive and so important to them. It was a hula hoop that had been spray-painted gold. It had a sentimental inscription of thanks for going beyond and jumping through hoops for them for so many years. I promptly hung it on the wall in our front lobby. It was the first thing everyone saw coming off the elevator bank and into our agency.

It is no exaggeration to say that most people in the personal computer business would agree just how great our contribution was to Dell's enormous success and that we were the ones who defined and built Dell's persona, the DNA, when it mattered during its formative years. I believe Michael Dell would even grant us this looking back, despite our ultimate quartering at the end.

I noted a recent ad for Dell that ran in March 2009 in the *Wall Street Journal*. A full-page black and red ad with the headline "GET MORE TECHNOLOGY FOR YOUR DOLLAR." Underneath was a picture of a Dell laptop and its price of $649 and copy indicating a savings of $309. The ad also included a range of bits and bytes and specs splattered around the page.

With my tongue stuck nearly through my cheek, I can say that besides the price, the only arresting aspect of the ad was the art director's "clever" use of the last three words of the headline, "FOR YOUR DOLLAR," appearing in red. Frankly I don't know why he didn't consider green for this important part, but what did I know?

What I do know in looking at this ad is that the quality and worth of Dell's advertising had reached new lows of engagement and in the building of their brand. They had come full circle back to price and item advertising. It was telling too that the business of selling Dell computers was hurting big time, as they have lost oodles of volume and market share and recently announced lower and lower profit numbers.

In the nine years after parting with Goldberg Moser O'Neill in 1999, Dell went through at least a half-dozen agency relationships. That computes to a new agency about once every 18 months.

They had one poor experience after the other, leading to the question of whether changing an agency is really a solution to unsatisfactory advertising. Usually not!

And the added side disadvantage, which most clients do not consider, is the enormous cost in making these changes. The time spent on reeducation alone, not to speak of the titanic impact on sales and branding that results from changing directions time after time. The result is a schizophrenic brand and company where the employees are as confused as the customer.

BBDO was given the global branding assignment after J. Walter Thompson flamed out. My partner Mike Moser was so moved by this event that he sent an e-mail to Michael Dell, Kevin Rollins, then president, and Scott Helbing, the marketing VP, and acknowledged BBDO as champion and mentor.

Whatever possessed him I don't know but he congratulated them on their new partnership and how BBDO was a much better choice than J. Walter Thompson, which was first picked but failed. He mused that BBDO would do a great job and offered Dell the best of luck. He further opined, "You deserve the best talent moving forward. I think you've got it."

Huh? (For a possible explanation see the discussion on "conscious unconsciousness" in the introduction.)

At the time we were still handling a lot of the Dell business. Only God and Mike Moser know why he sent this e-mail, but regardless both BBDO and Dell needed more than luck.

After BBDO inherited the global branding assignment, it was soon reported in the trades that they were scrambling and having trouble getting a "green light" from Dell top management for any of their efforts. So yet another "relationship" problem had emerged.

Even the "expert" ad man Mike Miles was said to be contributing by authoring scripts of advertising direction and ad copy that he gave to Scott Helbing with the challenge, "Have the agency beat this."

Apparently it was not too tough to beat, as the ad that emerged was able to combine both the boring and the forgettable. They did, however, make use of the angled letter "E" from the Dell logo by including it in the copy line "expect accountability."

And they may have saved a lot of money by running "two-color ads" instead of four-color ads. (Or is this a one-color ad, as black might not be considered a color.) Regardless,

they're presenting a true leadership-quality look and position, don't you think?

Along the path of hiring each new agency, at one point Dell remarkably hired The Lowe Group. This was truly amazing and showed how when organizations get large enough they really have absolutely no idea of what one hand or the other hand is doing. Lowe, an IPG company, had recently been merged with Ammirati to become Lowe Ammirati Puris or Ammirati Puris Lintas or something like that.

Ammirati had recently lost the Compaq Computer business so they looked like a good candidate to consider, forgetting that they helped drive Compaq into the ground. And Compaq was the company that was reported to want the very same advertising that we had been doing for Dell. Go figure.

However, someone forgot to mention that Lowe was also the IPG agency that had purchased Goldberg Moser O'Neill back in 1996 and had been a critical part of letting us and Dell down terribly when we needed them to help retain the account. On May 7, 1999, it was announced that Ammirati got hired to work on the Home and Small Business Group. Our ex-client Paul Bell, the senior VP of that division, remarked, "Ammirati shares that passion and has the creative and strategic talent to take us (to the next level)."

And Ammirati told everyone, "We are delighted to be working with Dell. We believe it is the most exciting brand in the technology category and one of the most exciting and truly innovative brands anywhere in the world. This is a partnership of like minds."

Martin Puris at Ammirati was "looking forward to a long and successful relationship."

Oh ooh! Just eight weeks later, on July 9, 1999, *AdWeek* reported that Ammirati had a problem: "Dell pulled everything and said go back to square one." The spots were in production. The campaign line was "Every relationship should be this good." Hopefully a tad better than it was with the new agency.

The partnership of like minds apparently was not "like" enough, as Ammirati was soon dismissed. Both Lowe and BBDO had caught bullets as well along the way. Dell next tried DDB out of Chicago. Other agencies had come and gone.

While the advertising agencies at Dell did not remain constant, one thing did. Mike Miles's position as a board member. Lest you forget, apparently he was the guy who started this entire thing with a cry for "branding" and a new, more internationally resourceful ad agency. In my opinion, this all resulted in significant turmoil and harm to Dell because of its distraction and the fact that it never really got resolved for years.

In July of 2009, Mike Miles finally stepped down from the board of directors.

One time Dell made an agency change, it was with a grand sweeping colossal announcement instigated by then chief marketing officer Mark Jarvis. This was in December of 2007, and they said they were awarding the assignment to WPP (the parent holding company of J. Walter Thompson, the agency that had done the $4 million elephant branding commercial) to form a one-stop shop for all of Dell's advertising and marketing requirements around the world.

The *Wall Street Journal* announced December 2, 2007, "WPP has triumphed over Interpublic Group in the seven-month holding company shootout for Dell's highly sought-after three-year $4.5 billion account and will be tasked to build a new agency staffed by 1,000-plus to serve the computer maker's global marketing needs."

The article went on to quote Casey Jones, VP of global marketing at Dell, "We will jointly develop what we hope is the greatest agency in the world."

And from Dell CMO Mark Jarvis, "We have been looking for an agency that is both an artist and a scientist."

They were to do this globally, and in less than a year. The new agency was to be operational by March 1, 2008. It seems, however, that they spent most of the first year just trying to come up with an appropriate name for this new enterprise. They decided on Enfatico.

I can report emphatically that Enfatico never succeeded. The *Wall Street Journal* announced that Enfatico had been plagued by problems since its inception. The grandiose design was never pulled together and so Dell called for a change yet again.

Now it so happens that one of the agencies that WPP owned, in addition to Enfatico, JWT, and others, was Y&R. Young & Rubicam, the very same that failed to impress when they arrived in a stream of long black limousines years ago to present a campaign already being used by Gateway, Dell's direct competitor. WPP announced in April of 2009 that it was going to fold Enfatico into Y&R brands.

Maybe it was that name Enfatico, meaning "play each note with emphasis." For me it sounded more like maybe fatigue . . . a tendency to break under repeated stress. Or possibly emphysema . . . a condition marked by abnormal enlargement and loss of pulmonary elasticity characterized by shortness of breath. Or maybe en passant . . . meaning "in passing."

To me, it is absolutely remarkable what Dell has gone through trying to find an agency. The fallout over a decade has been unbelievable. Can one even calculate the economic cost? I think not!

More amazing is the total scope of this part of the story. If I tried to make this up, I couldn't. People would say I was crazy. Maybe they still will.

When I think back on all the years that we worked with Dell and how many positive things we were able to achieve for them, it makes me kind of sad. Somehow we were able to deliver all that Dell required to keep its engine motoring along, reaching new plateaus every year in sales and profits.

We were not a huge agency and we went on to try time after time. But we cared, and because of that concern we were able to accomplish and deliver. Really this is just another example of bigger is not better. What matters is commitment.

Dell was a defining experience for our agency. When our work for Dell is combined with the earlier work with which we were involved for Apple Computer, surely there are no other people or agency that could say they helped revolutionize the personal computer business the way we did. Not just once, but twice. We changed the landscape of the industry and changed the world with our work for both clients.

The bell tolled three times for us on Dell. The first time we didn't hear it ringing. We were fortunate to answer the bell the second time. The third bell signaled the end of a fantastic agency and client relationship.

Ding ding dong!

Not very long after I founded Goldberg Moser O'Neill, an old client from Intel and a good friend of the agency, Pamela George, called. She actually wasn't old at all but just a past client. She was wondering whether we would come down for a meeting at the firm where she was now employed.

Mike Massaro, our COO, and I took the drive down the Peninsula to visit a Silicon Valley firm that was a fairly established but relatively unknown company. Pamela had arranged for us to meet with the then CEO and founder as well as the sales and marketing chief.

We didn't know too much about the company, which turned out to be Cisco Systems, and the two executives, who were John Morgridge, chief executive officer, and John Chambers, the head of sales and marketing.

We were under the impression that Cisco had decided to try some advertising and that we were there to tell them why we were the right choice of an ad agency to do that for them. However, when we walked in the room and had hardly taken a seat, Morgridge fired his first question at us, "Why the hell should we advertise?"

Morgridge had this scowling look on his face. It was a combination of intensity, anger, and defiance.

"Why the hell should we advertise?"

Like many successful people in the technology field, Morgridge didn't believe in it. Maybe it wasn't so much that he didn't believe in it as that he didn't really understand the power of it and how it might relate to their particular business. In this regard he was incredibly inexperienced and a novice.

They were like a couple of kids with no idea about this subject, which was completely foreign to them. And why not? After all, these "kids" had grown Cisco exponentially without any investment in advertising.

This was hardly the first time that I had happened upon this very same question and conversation. It had occurred before with several other well-known technology executives who really didn't believe in advertising, like Enzo Torresi, co-founder of Businessland, and Andy Grove, CEO at Intel. There were others.

In the early 1980s we had the Intel account at Chiat/Day San Francisco and I once received a 20-minute lecture on the uselessness of advertising from Andy. At the time Intel was spending less than one-tenth of 1 percent of their sales on advertising. This was woefully low by any measure.

I remember sharing a chart with him that showed a hundred major companies and their corresponding investment in advertising, ranging from a low of 2 percent to a high of 35 percent. But one-tenth of 1 percent really pushed the limit of uselessness.

Not meaning to be flip, I answered Morgridge, "Advertising works!"

Mike and I then began to fire off an explanation and justification to address the "why advertise" argument, but pretty soon into the discussion I sensed we were not making much headway and cut the meeting short. My clue came when I saw Morgridge pick up his latest copy of *Computer World* and start thumbing through the pages.

I offered at this point, "Well there are numerous reasons to advertise and we would be happy to discuss them further. But it would be a lot more efficient if we went away and came back another day and gave you a more focused response."

Morgridge looked up from his magazine and persisted, "OK, but why should we advertise?"

Morgridge reminded me of the one conversation regarding advertising that I had with Andy Grove. He too did not have much faith; actually he didn't believe in advertising at all and said it was a complete waste of money. During our six-year relationship with Intel they never spent more than $5 million and that was across 20 separate divisions. Years later Intel would become one of the most important advertisers of all time with their coop program behind "Intel Inside," spending at one point close to a billion dollars.

I said to the two Johns, "Look, this is a complicated question. We need to know more about Cisco. It would be more productive if we came back in a few days with a prepared point of view."

"OK. No problem."

A week later we were back and armed with an in-depth understanding of Cisco and its markets and a compelling story regarding the importance of advertising to their business.

This time Morgridge didn't pick up a magazine. He listened intently as did Chambers. They were incredibly engaged and asked pointed and relevant questions as we went through our discussion. We spent about 45 minutes and included some revealing insights into a number of our past and present clients, including Intel, Apple Computer, Oracle, Dell Computer, Ask Computer, and 3Com and their marketing and advertising programs.

When we were finished, both Johns were convinced they should be advertising and Morgridge turned to Chambers and said, "John, this looks like something we should be doing."

And Chambers said to Morgridge, "Absolutely, John."

And Morgridge said to Pamela, "Let's do it! Let's set a budget up. Say $100,000."

Oh well, we had something a little different in mind, like $2 million. But we had come this far and they had just de facto appointed us their ad agency without a review. At the time we really had no idea of the importance that Cisco would come to play as a technology company and leader over the next 10 years when we represented them.

Morgridge and Chambers had apparently been impressed with our arguments about advertising and with Mike and me. I suspect more with Mike since he was a person with both understanding and integrity and had very insightful perspectives on technology and technology businesses.

But for all I know, it may have been simply my suggestion that most people in America couldn't even spell Cisco and more likely than not thought that they provided restaurants with food service supplies. Sysco Corporation, a much smaller company, was far more widely known and had a larger ad budget than the one Cisco was now contemplating.

Over the course of our relationship with Cisco, we helped them grow from being a completely unknown and obscure tech company to a world-class dominating high-technology leading brand. As we persuaded Morgridge and Chambers to invest more and more in advertising, the more their growth was accelerated.

In every meeting we had with John Chambers, he would postulate how Cisco and the Internet would change the world in a way that no one could imagine. It took me awhile to fully grasp the enormity and validity of this vision. I had previously worked with another guy who espoused a similar evangelical philosophy about world change when he introduced the Macintosh: Steve Jobs. Both of these guys were indeed visionaries of the highest order. And I felt that both had incredible integrity in their beliefs as executives.

It was hard to imagine that when Chambers postulated his vision, Cisco would turn out to have a bigger impact on changing the world than Apple Computer. Having worked on and watched both companies, I personally believe that Cisco was the greater, more widespread global enabler for applications and communications, although invisible to most people. I say this knowing full well the impact that Apple subsequently had with the iPhone, iPod, and iPad and its impact on the telephone and music industries.

After we had the account for many years Cisco decided they really believed in advertising and doubled the budget, most of it dedicated to TV. We crafted a magnificent campaign that would run globally and was known as "Are you ready." It focused on the fact that virtually all Internet traffic traveled across "systems" of Cisco. It was all about empowering the Internet generation and the importance of Cisco in doing so.

To get a sense of the scope of this advertising, you only had to hear the announcer copy: "The Web has more users in its first five years than telephones did in their first 30 . . . a population the size of the United Kingdom joins the Internet every six months . . . Internet traffic doubles every 100 days . . . One day the Internet will make long distance calls a thing of the past." And then each of many kids from around the world asked into the camera, "Are you ready?" The spots ended with the announcer stating, "Virtually all Internet traffic travels along the systems of one company, Cisco Systems. Empowering the Internet generation."

It was brilliant and extremely powerful. And if you look back 15 years ago at what was being promised, it was quite accurately predicting the future.

In addition to John Chambers, the advertising had been championed at Cisco by Susan Bruijnes, senior manager of advertising, and Keith Fox, corporate marketing VP. They recognized well what the campaign could and would do by building brand image as an Internet leader, reinforcing brand values to their business partners, and making sure consumers knew of the Cisco brand.

Making Cisco synonymous with the Internet and the Internet synonymous with Cisco was achieved. Sales responded as the advertising took hold and the Cisco stock price mushroomed, an unexpected secondary advantage of the advertising and in my mind a great lesson for all would-be leadership companies.

Over 10 years, we did advertising for Cisco that to this day they have never duplicated and which made them true believers in the benefits of advertising. I heard that they issued orders to their current advertising agency to replicate what Goldberg Moser O'Neill had first done for them. The agency tried and failed, instead producing some inept and dated commercials that looked a bit like ours but didn't carry the empathy, understanding, or persuasiveness.

Cisco became a major advertiser and we did some of our best creative work for them. Working with Pamela George along with Susan and Keith, and John Chambers, who became CEO shortly after we became the Cisco agency, we made advertising history in the networking category with some astounding and outstanding ads. Cisco's budget swelled from the meager $100,000 start to over $60 million.

Cisco's sales meanwhile rose exponentially out of proportion to the increases in the advertising expenditures. When we started with them, they had revenues of $183 million, and when we parted they were a $12 billion company. At one point Cisco commanded the highest market cap of any company in the country. Today Cisco's sales are over $40 billion.

Unfortunately, as is often the case, size brings with it bureaucracy, and bureaucracy, constipation and politics. I left GMO in 2000 and Cisco moved their account soon after. There was little relation between these two events. Rather it had to do with a change in Cisco management resulting in the hiring of an individual who had a previous relationship with another agency.

But it also had to do with a concern on the part of a few at Cisco that in place of GMO they inherited an agency called Hill Holliday, an agency that they didn't know and never selected. This was complicated by the fact that some of the key people on the business, Mike Moser and Mike Massaro, had left and a few others were no longer to be seen. Brian Quennell, technology creative doyen, was perceived as an asset, but the people managing the account were generally not making the impact they should have been. Cisco moved their account to Ogilvy & Mather.

The agency that followed was never quite able to do any advertising that was remotely creative and had the impact that ours did. Of course they didn't have the benefit of working with people like Pamela George, Susan Bruijnes, and Keith Fox or directly with John Chambers to develop the ads and secure approvals. All of these great clients have long since left Cisco, except for John Chambers, who remains CEO.

Committees seem to have replaced individual responsibility and accountability. Cisco seems to be struggling and to this day is still looking for and in need of another great advertising campaign.

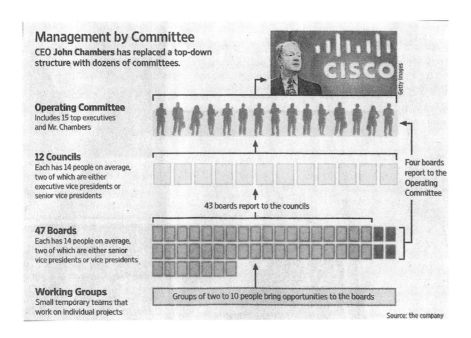

Management by Committee
CEO **John Chambers** has replaced a top-down structure with dozens of committees.

Operating Committee
Includes 15 top executives and Mr. Chambers

12 Councils
Each has 14 people on average, two of which are either executive vice presidents or senior vice presidents

Four boards report to the Operating Committee

43 boards report to the councils

47 Boards
Each has 14 people on average, two of which are either senior vice presidents or vice presidents

Working Groups
Small temporary teams that work on individual projects

Groups of two to 10 people bring opportunities to the boards

Source: the company

Getty Images

CHAPTER 16

MADE IN KOREA

"Paging Mr. Goldberg."

"Paging Mr. Fred Goldberg."

"Paging Mr. Fred Goldberg."

"Please pick up a white paging phone."

I had just landed at Las Vegas International Airport and was making my way through the baggage claim area with several other folks from Goldberg Moser O'Neill. We were on our way to a client meeting with the people at Ameristar Casinos who were based in Las Vegas.

I shouted "Wait up" to everyone and went over to pick up one of the white phones mounted on various of the pillars. My executive assistant Susan Brennan was on the line.

"He's dead."

"Who?"

"Greg."

"Greg who?"

"Greg Warner. Greg Warner is dead."

I immediately had a very sad and sick feeling come over me. Greg was our key client at Kia Motors America. He was a smart and sweet person. A genuinely nice guy. It was Greg who had been so often responsible for mediating many of the tough debates that occurred at the higher levels with the Korean management, as well as with the lower level American marketing people. It was Greg who may have been most responsible for our being awarded the account in the first place.

Greg had been at a dinner and had a cardiac arrest apparently triggered by an acute asthma attack. And just like that, that was it. They couldn't resuscitate him.

Beyond the personal loss of a good guy, this was a huge loss for the company and for our agency as well. It left us quite vulnerable because it was very difficult to establish really solid and reliable relationships with the Koreans. You never knew what they were thinking or how they were thinking. Sometimes I wondered if they were even thinking.

Half the time you didn't know whether they even had a clue as to what you were telling them. They had this habit of nodding their heads up and down, appearing to be in agreement with what you were saying, but actually were only indicating that they were receiving your sonant signal. Often they may have been in abject disagreement with what you might be saying but would not discuss it with you and, instead, left their American executives to pass on their interpretation and information at a later time.

Oddly, this was exactly my experience with Japanese clients years earlier. It may have been a cultural kind of thing. Keeping the cards close to the vest, so to speak.

The other big problem that immediately arose was who was going to be Greg's replacement. More than likely it would be marketing vice president Dick Macedo. We had worked with Dick from the beginning of our relationship in 1993 and he had proven to be a difficult client to deal with. To say the least!

There was a reason someone had circulated around the agency a photo of Macedo on a Popsicle stick: Dick-On-A-Stick! This man was a real piece of work. I'm being kind. He was a prick of the highest order. He brought "prickishness" to a new level. He may have even invented it.

Despite this we were able to do great work, and while the creative people might not always admit it, I felt that Dick was an important ingredient in our creative successes. He challenged the work and us and he bought into good ideas and then would help sell and protect them. Sometimes he actually improved them.

Our pursuit of the Kia business had begun when I first read that this huge Korean company was going to enter the American car market. This was 18 months before they had actually started up. I also learned that a fellow named Greg Warner was going to be named the top American executive. Greg had had much experience dealing with Asian car companies before.

I began a communication by mail with him to let him know about our agency and our interest in the Kia business. A few months later I asked him if I could come down and say hello in person. He agreed and I made the trip to Irvine in Orange County from San Francisco.

Greg was a gracious and hospitable host. I arrived at the Kia headquarters to be and he kept me waiting in the lobby no more than two minutes. After which he personally came out to greet me and usher me back into his office. As he approached me, he had a big smile on his face, his head was kind of tilted to one side, and his hand and arm were outstretched toward me. Very welcoming indeed. We had a nice chat but after 15 minutes of pleasantries I didn't want to overstay my visit and thanked him for his time.

That short meeting served as a very important bridge over the next year or so during which time I aggressively solicited the account. The selection of an advertising agency didn't take place until a year later and then only after

Greg had hired Dick Macedo to run marketing and advertising.

Macedo had been a senior executive at a number of advertising agencies including Wells Rich Greene and J. Walter Thompson. Rumor had it that he had been fired enough times that he finally found his calling on the client side. The Koreans at Kia didn't have a clue about him for six years. Or so it seemed.

I mean, Macedo was a man who would insult his Korean bosses directly to their faces, in front of any audience. Usually every audience. He played them like they were fools. And all that the Korean executives seemed to do was stare stoically ahead, appearing not to understand just how insulting some of the remarks were that were being flung at them.

His boss, Greg Warner, mostly kept Macedo in check. Greg had manners and a good knowledge of the car business, and he pretty well knew how to work with Korean management in the US as well as back in Korea. When he hired Macedo I suspect he had no idea what he was getting except a guy who had some advertising and some car experience.

Unfortunately, Greg's death left Macedo as the obvious heir apparent. And the Koreans wasted no time in anointing him to senior vice president marketing and sales director. Although Greg had been an executive vice president, they did not bless Macedo similarly.

I will say this about Dick Macedo. He was pretty smart in an intellectual way. He knew more than most clients about good advertising. He was willing to take risks with the ads. We were able to develop some absolutely terrific advertising that was extremely effective. Arguably it was the best car advertising in the business at the time.

We won many awards, including Effies, those ridiculous trophies given by the American Marketing Association for "advertising that had selling effectiveness." Ours surely did, but the glory of winning the Effie was considerably dampened by some of the other advertising for brands that received the award and clearly didn't deserve it. But we also won many real creative awards as well and these were far more meaningful and representative of the work, including Clio, One Show, and Communication Arts awards.

Macedo was a real workhorse or donkey. He worked long hours and was on the road very often visiting one market or another. It was this quality that no doubt most impressed the Koreans, who had an extremely high regard for work ethic, to the detriment of most other qualities like civility or manners. Hard work equals good performance. Good performance equals hard work.

In the advertising business an agency's winning and running a car account is maybe the most important measure of coming of age. We had had several chances to talk with an automotive company before Kia.

The first time was with a completely unknown start-up company called Rayton Fissore. This was an entrepreneurial group out of Oakland, California, who had come up with a very sexy, well-designed Italian SUV before SUVs were a twinkle in anyone's eyes. We got the business, but they got no money. So very shortly, we ended our first encounter in the car industry.

Then we had the fun chance not long after to travel to northern New Jersey and meet with Yugo. This was a Yugoslovian car selling for $3,990. We met at Yugo America headquarters late at night and it was dark. The air around us was permeated with the smell of burning gases belching from stacks and rigs of various refineries up and down the New Jersey Turnpike.

When we arrived at Yugo there were hardly any lights on in the building. Admittedly it was late but not that late. It looked like there wasn't anyone in the building.

We knocked on the glass front doors for quite a while. Finally the top Yugo executive opened the door, greeted us, and asked if we needed anything. We said a slide projector or an overhead projector would be nice. About 45 minutes later, after personally searching the premises, he came back and advised that neither could be found. I had a funny feeling that this meeting and this trip were rolling downhill and would turn out to be a total waste.

We had a less than productive meeting as we tried to talk through our presentation using paper decks. There was one American executive present who kind of understood some of what we were saying. The rest was completely and utterly lost on the Yugoslavians.

I was initially interested in talking with these folks for several reasons. First, we wanted a car account.

Second, I thought they had come up with a very neat name in Yugo. Turns out many people thought it meant simply a shortened Yugoslavia, not what I initially thought: "you go." Yugoslavia was a place where you definitely didn't want to announce your automobile was being manufactured.

Finally, I thought we had a brilliant strategy. At $3,990 per vehicle, the car was almost as disposable as diapers. The disposable car! Use it for a year or a year and a half and throw it away or kick it off a hill and get another.

The clients didn't like the idea as much as I did. And, it didn't matter to them that the cars had trouble lasting even six months. At the time these cars were rated lowest of any on the market on a quality basis.

We said adieu around 11 p.m., slept in a crappy motel on Route 80, drove to the Newark airport in the morning, and flew home to San Francisco never to hear from the Yugo folks again. And neither did anyone else, as they soon withdrew the car from the American market.

Chiat/Day had won the Nissan auto and truck account, and the client decided to review its new luxury sub-brand Infiniti for its introduction into the US. Of course we jumped at the opportunity and were able to get included in the review, which was intense.

Chiat/Day San Francisco invested a huge amount of time and money in putting our presentation together. Fortunately we did not have to present speculative creative, or it would have been even more. But we did end up with a really great presentation that we successfully gave to the Nissan Infiniti management group.

I left feeling very good about the job that we had done. However, from the start the client had trepidations about housing the Infiniti account at the same agency where the main Nissan business resided. And despite our assurances of separation, in the end they decided not to.

They ended up hiring Hill Holliday out of Boston. This, despite the expensive aluminum notebooks that I had custom-made and which contained our leave-behind materials. They were extremely handsome, indeed. We did get to learn a fair amount more about the car business regardless.

Ironies of ironies is that Hill Holliday got fired 13 months later. Chiat/Day Los Angeles was hired to work on Infiniti alongside its main Nissan assignment. We were now Goldberg Moser O'Neill and we would end up becoming Hill Holliday. What goes around comes around.

⊘ ⊘ ⊘

After we became GMO, we got into a car review for Oldsmobile, a brand that had been with the Leo Burnett agency for decades.

Just about everything was wrong at Oldsmobile: the models, the quality, the name, and the advertising. But what the heck, it was a car, and an ad agency with a car is better than one without.

Oldsmobile had been consistently losing sales and share year after year, but they had stayed with their advertising agency through it all. Now they had finally decided they wanted to hold an agency review.

Just about every agency in the country that didn't have a car account went after this business and tried to get into the review. And we took our shot as well and somehow made it in to become one of the 12 that were able to get a face-to-face meeting at General Motors in Detroit. Our ace in the hole was one of our senior executives, Pat Sherwood, who knew some of the General Motors people and something about the car business.

The meeting would take place at the General Motors building. There were six of us from the agency and we arrived on an overcast, cold, and ugly day. We were ushered into a waiting room on the ground floor of this really old, somber, oppressive, gray building. They put us into a waiting room that looked out on a main road, which passed right in front of the windows of the building.

It was curious, although not unexpected, to see virtually all Fords, Chryslers, and General Motors cars going by the window for the hour or so that they kept us in this holding pen. Coming from the West Coast, where import cars first made their mark and accounted for the majority of the automobiles on the road, it was very odd.

At one point, I excused myself to use the restroom. I had to walk down a long corridor that had these dark grayish marble slabs from floor to what were very high ceilings. My shoes echoed with each step and the sound reverberated up and down the totally empty hall. There was no one there but me. It kind of felt like we were back at Yugo headquarters where the smell of death had been in the air. As it turned out Oldsmobile did not have long to live.

Half a city block later I arrived at the door to the men's room and entered to find a huge bathroom filled with a long row of sinks and urinals and stalls. Again there wasn't anyone around.

It was immediately evident to me that whoever built this toilet was seemingly trying to emulate the bathroom at Penn Station, the railroad station in Manhattan, with which I was quite familiar from a previous life. Nobody was sleeping in there, however. In fact, I was the only soul taking a leak. It was eerie as the sound of my tinkle tinkled off the walls and ceiling.

I returned to the waiting room where my compatriots were pacing back and forth as one is wont to do prior to a new business meeting. Finally we were summoned to head out to a conference room on one of the upper floors. On the way up I noticed that the elevator was clad in what looked like that same granite or marble from the first floor. All and all the entire building reeked of an immovable force, one that would not easily change its ways.

Going into the meeting I felt that part of our agency's attraction was that we had at least one experienced and very good executive on our staff that had run the GM Saturn business at the Hal Riney agency. At the time GM looked favorably on their Saturn venture.

The other thing was, it seemed, they might actually have been attracted to the kind of breakthrough work that we were doing for our other clients. I was completely wrong about this, as it turned out. Most all of the 12 angry men and women, the General Motors and Oldsmobile executives with whom we met, were scared to death of our creative work, except for one. The guy who headed up all of GM's media, Phil Guarascio, was intrigued, but he was the only one.

We had a nasty meeting and headed back to San Francisco where we belonged. We were very lucky that we didn't make the next cut, as the remaining agencies that did had to spend gobs of money trying to win the account. In the end, GM left it at Leo Burnett, and it seemed like what they were trying to do was simply put a fire under their long-time agency's ass.

Advertising Age wrote an editorial expressing their compliments to General Motors and their congratulations to Leo Burnett on retaining the account. To the Oldsmobile group they offered felicitations for "running an agency review with such consideration, care and fairness." I felt obliged to write a letter to the editors. The review was a complete sham.

Indeed they did put a fire under Burnett. The agency quickly came up with some "new" advertising after retaining the account. However, it was just like the "old" advertising they had done in the past. Awful!

I received a letter from a consultant who had firsthand experience with General Motors. He professed to know fully the disingenuousness and arrogance of GM. He advised me that in fact, with the exception of one agency created from an existing GM agency, they had made only one agency change for all their car divisions in their entire history. I didn't know if this was true, but viewing the sameness of the advertising, year to year and decade to decade, one could presume that it carried some considerable validity.

And a short few years later the Oldsmobile brand faded to black anyway.

⊘ ⊘ ⊘

So, effectively when we started pitching the Kia account, we really had no car experience. And car experience is the usual prerequisite for including and excluding agencies from car agency reviews. In our case, we had found

some clients at a car company who actually admired our work, which helped open the door. It didn't hurt that Pat Sherwood of Saturn fame was on our team either. Pat had worked for me numerous times over the years and pissed me off every time he resigned to pursue some opportunity. But his stint on the Saturn business really provided important insight into the car business. And, my opening gambits with Greg Warner were quite useful too.

When it came time to finally have our first meeting, which was a credentials pitch where we mostly talked about ourselves, we did a less than glorious job than we usually did for some reason. Maybe it was nerves and the size and scope of the opportunity that presented itself. Or maybe we just had some bad food the night before at Brandy Ho's.

We received a letter from Dick Macedo, the marketing director, advising that Goldberg Moser O'Neill didn't make the cut for the next phase of the Kia agency search. He wrote, "The reality of the situation is that after comparing all submissions relative to size, creative reputation, services offered, available resources, strategic capability and media clout, and, relating them to our needs, it was a photo finish by all the contenders. Thus, no single considered criteria eliminated your agency, but a collective judgment and, damn, it was a difficult process."

I didn't accept the "photo finish" result. I thought the camera lied.

While we were cut from the long list, I continued on and we kept at both Greg Warner and Dick Macedo. We bombarded them with ads, thought pieces, materials, whatever seemed appropriate and relevant to have them at least question their decision to eliminate us so early on.

As it turned out the Kia review group of executives was in the process of reviewing their second-round agency picks, and one happened to be based in San Francisco. Turned out also that one of the agencies dropped out of the review and Kia decided to call us on the spur of the moment and see if we would meet with them in our offices when they visited the other San Francisco agency.

We didn't say no!

We met. We played our game at our usual very high level. We had a great meeting. We got re-included in the review and went on to make the cut to the final four.

We worked long and hard and invested a considerable amount of money in our final presentation, which was made at Kia headquarters in Irvine, California. As far as I was concerned, there was nothing more important than winning this account as I felt it would really put us on the map. I also felt we could do great work for them, something that was not likely with most other car companies.

I had our very best people help put our presentation together and the best of the best attend the final presentation. Mike Moser, Brian O'Neill, Catrina McAuliffe (account planning director), Camille Johnson (media director), myself, and of course Pat Sherwood.

The presentation was sensational. No one missed a beat. In addition to our credentials part, our thinking was highly strategic in positioning Kia to the American market. While other agencies in the review showed speculative creative work, we showed none. Instead we put together an insightful and wonderfully produced 15-minute film explaining how Kia's first car, the Sephia, should be announced to America.

This film was a big hit. I had gone to the bother of having the entire video translated with Korean subtitles to make sure that the Korean management "got" what we were saying, rather than leaving it to the American management to interpret it or to the Koreans' own poor translation. It worked so well that they later showed the film to a mass meeting back at Kia in Seoul to rave reviews.

Brian O'Neill did many wonderful things for our agency over the years and he worked extremely hard at all times, but his focus and dedication to putting this film together was truly beyond the call and a critical element in winning the account.

There were four agencies left competing in that final round. One of them was run by a guy named Jim Jordan, a fairly well-known New York copywriter.

Jordan was referred to in the business as an "advertising sloganeer." One of his claims to fame was that he invented "Ring Around the Collar" for Wisk detergent. This was something I remember as a kid and didn't like it then. I certainly wouldn't want to be remembered as the guy who came up with "Ring Around the Collar." How he got into the final review I'll never know. But there he was.

Jordan's agency was to make their final presentation just after we did. They were assembled in the lobby waiting their turn. I was told that Jordan decided to take a self-guided tour of the Kia workplace while he was waiting to present. He apparently had poked into each of the Kia executives' offices and discovered that our agency had left an elaborate leave behind including the presentation materials, a neat shirt, and a coffee cup, which was thematically tied to what we were presenting.

Well, toward the end of our presentation one of our group had to excuse himself to use the restroom. On the way, he walked past one of the executives' offices only to discover that there was one of the executives from a competing agency looking through the materials that we had left on everyone's desk. And worse, it was reported back that the coffee cup we had left had somehow found its way into the wastebasket. Whether the executive in question did these things or not I will never know. Frankly, I find it a little bit hard to believe, but then, ever since I had worked on the Gallo wine business, I never entered or left a conference room without first checking the wastebaskets. You'd be surprised what you can find there.

We did discover that some of our other coffee cups never made it to their intended recipients. I read sometime later that his agency, which was best known as Jordan, McGrath, Case & Taylor, had changed its name many times over the years, reflecting the comings and goings of various partners. And in celebrating each new name they had amassed over 20 different coffee cups to their credit. Why in the world they might have needed another cup I know not. Particularly one that had Goldberg Moser O'Neill on it.

We learned that during the agency selection process the five Kia executives ranked the four finalist agencies that were being considered to handle the business, and Dick Macedo was quoted as saying "all four agencies were ranked in the same order." Goldberg Moser O'Neill being first in everyone's opinion of course.

So, we won the account and it was a good feeling indeed. The clients flew up to San Francisco to tell me in person. I, in turn, immediately announced it to the agency and there was virtual pandemonium. You cannot imagine a more excited, enthusiastic, motivated group of people. Life was good.

On July 30, 1993, I sent an e-mail to the agency: "Well, we've done it. We're in the car business, and we have a chance to make some history. My hope is that we will be able to do some sensational car advertising, god knows that most of what's out there is the same old dribble. You can put just about any brand on any ad. Well, we won't be doing that kind of stuff. Rather the kind that Doyle Dane Bernbach did for VW in the 1960's; bright and fresh, the kind that gave the VW its own unique personality."

Just after winning the Kia account, I was interviewed for a major story by *AdWeek*, which ran January 17, 1994. I was quoted in that piece as saying, "I think we can make it a great success."

I was right. We did and it was and we were too.

I decided to celebrate the win that very day and arranged to have the entire agency take the rest of the day off and sail around San Francisco Bay with lots of beer and booze at the ready. I invited Greg Warner and Dick Macedo to join us for the celebration, and they did. We had a grand and glorious time.

Dick Macedo, Greg Warner, and me.

And we had a grand and glorious run on Kia. We did by far the best work in the automobile category at the time and arguably since Doyle Dane Bernbach had made the VW bug a household name back in the '60s. We were part of a huge marketing success, and it was importantly due to the creative work itself, which was very smart and inventive and engaging.

The work was smart because Dick Macedo and Greg Warner bought into the strategy and the creative almost all the time. But working with Dick Macedo on a day-to-day basis was like having a chronic liver disease that never stopped eating away at you. He had a way of making everyone, the agency people, the dealers and even his own management, really dislike him.

One day in early January 1998, I flew down to LA to have dinner with Macedo near his home in Manhattan Beach. We met at a nice Italian restaurant of his choice on the main strip of the town. I arrived at about 6:30, coming directly from the airport, and Dick was already there nursing his second drink. We said hello and had a really terrific time for the next four and half hours. We covered lots of topics, related and unrelated to the business, and consumed many see-throughs. When it was time to leave, I felt very good about having come down and spent the time. We had had a lot to drink. I know I had considerably more than I normally would. But Dick was regularly a big drinker, particularly when someone else was paying.

Nevertheless, it seemed like I had made some significant inroads in building my relationship with him further. It so happened that a few days earlier we had agreed to get together in the near future with our wives, Connie and Jeri, for dinner, and as he and I headed for the exit of the restaurant I reminded him of that.

To top off the evening I had purchased two expensive cigars, as I knew Dick enjoyed a good smoke, as did I once in a while. As we were leaving the restaurant I offered Dick the cigar, which he gladly accepted. We walked outside and lit up just in front of the restaurant. We stood there enjoying the aroma for a few minutes and then I said, "Well, thanks for the time, Dick. I really appreciate it. I think we accomplished a lot tonight."

There was no answer from him. I started to head toward my rented car and said, "Well, take it easy. Talk to you soon."

And then Dick blurted out, "Dinner's not a good idea. My wife doesn't really like you or your wife."

I thought he was joking. I turned around and looked at him as he was taking a long drag on the cigar. He tilted his head back and blew the smoke up and away into the air and then proceeded to walk in the other direction, got in his car, and drove off.

I was stunned. It seemed I had completely misread the camaraderie and the bonding that we had shared for the last four and a half hours. But this was indeed classic Macedo. Always trying to keep you off balance.

Well, even though I didn't blink when he made these remarks, inside it felt like he had delivered a bolo punch to my stomach and landed it squarely in the center. I got in my car and sat there for 10 minutes thinking about what had just occurred and how bizarre it was. I mean I had only met Dick's wife a few times and it always seemed to be a pleasant happening.

Finally I drove off to the hotel where I was staying and spent a sleepless night tossing around over the incident. I caught the first plane out of LAX early in the morning back to San Francisco and was in my office at 8:30.

I sat down and opened my bag to take out some papers, and the phone rang. It was Dick Macedo.

"How about having dinner on the 23rd. We'll come up to San Francisco and spend the night."

It was as if nothing had transpired last night. I said, "That sounds great, Dick. Just great."

I thought to myself, What a sick prick this guy is.

This was just one of many peculiar and curious ways that Macedo operated. I wondered whether he had that affliction where some people have split personalities and don't remember what the other personality is saying or doing. Or maybe he was just drunk. Or maybe it was a joke. Or maybe he was just a prick. Probably was just a joke delivered by a drunk who was a prick.

The end of our relationship came in 2000, seven years after we had first started working for Kia and launched the car. The last thing the American car market had needed was another brand when we introduced Kia to America. And even less so, one from Korea, which had a very similar perception as did "Made in Japan" after World War II. "Made in Korea" just didn't have a great ring to it.

When first introduced, Kia became the 37th car brand in the American market. But we had been able to grow Kia from zero to 186,000 units per year. And they have made good on the meaning of their name, Kia, "to arise to the world from Asia," with more than 356,000 units in the United States as recently as 2010. We had a budget dwarfed by almost every other car manufacturer. Furthermore, we had succeeded in all this despite Kia being, year after year, the absolute worst car in terms of quality in the country. According to J. D. Power and Associates' annual survey, it had more problems per 100 vehicles than any other. It was ranked at the bottom of the barrel in this regard.

What had been accomplished had been done because of a brilliant introductory advertising strategy and incredible breakthrough creative work from day one. But also the incentive of the low price.

Our introductory advertising strategy and creative work were completely fresh and unexpected and strategically brilliant. Mike Moser played an enormous role in the insightful strategic positioning, and in the creative as well. Ironically the campaign, "It's about time everyone had a well-made car," perfectly positioned the new Kia Sephia as a quality, affordable option to the intended target. And by comparing ourselves to Honda, the gold standard, we immediately elevated ourselves perceptually to a higher level. We had to when you consider all the negative imagery associated with Korean-made products and the fact that we were dead last in quality.

No one ever said advertising was a totally honest business but it's certainly better than being a lawyer or a politician. But not much.

The strategy was to credibly have the Kia Sephia perceived as offering Japanese quality and reliability at a more reasonable price. The strategic objective was "to convince prospects that the quality of the Kia Sephia rivals that of Toyota Corolla and Honda Civic, but at a more appealing price point."

We won many advertising awards for Kia. Notably the very first year at the American Marketing Association's Effie Awards we were given a bronze Effie. For whatever that was worth.

Much more importantly, that first year we won the top prize at the International Broadcasting Awards sponsored by the Hollywood Radio & Television Society. Selected from 336 finalists from 15 countries.

The local Ad Club in Southern California gave us seven awards for broadcast and print work while no other car company won more than one award.

Dick Macedo was quoted: "We did what we set out to do—produce unconventional advertising that is effective. It's not an accident that our advertising is noticeably different from every other car company's ads."

The campaign was based on the Kia proposition of "real-world testing" and the obsession to be as good as the Japanese competitors. We used a teaser introductory commercial called "Kia Monster" to dramatize the arrival of a better-priced competitor to Japan.

"There is only one thing more frightening to Japan . . . a well-made car for under $9,000. Aaaaaaaaaaaaaaagh!"

Dick Macedo was skeptical when we first showed him this idea.

He asked, "Is Godzilla an icon or a cliché?"

We said, "It's a genre."

He asked, "You're actually suggesting we introduce a new Korean car in America with a Japanese icon?"

Then he said, "I have no idea where this is going."

We said, "Customers need to see Kia as a Japanese-like car."

It was when we presented this idea along with others to Greg Warner that Macedo fully embraced it. Greg saw it and in his characteristic way poked his finger into the bottom of his chin. He was silent as he thought for a moment. And then he erupted in laughter. The idea was approved and became a critical element in the launch. Not only did we run full three-page newspaper and magazine ads, but we had a powerful :30 TV spot and giant wallscapes up on buildings in many cities. Across the country the dealers were clamoring to get hold of the inflatable 50-foot "Kia Monsters" to display outside the dealerships.

The real breakthrough in all of the advertising was making sure that prospective consumers saw Kia as a contender to the Japanese. Like a Japanese car but more affordable. In order to do this we cleverly started by putting the Kia directly up against a Honda Civic, in a real-life road test all over the country. We were actually able to sustain a competitive and documented performance for the entire 100,000 miles that the test ran.

The sagacity of presenting Kia in the context of Japanese quality was a powerful conclusion and not an obvious one. In my mind it was as important as was "radical" to the initial introductory Apple Macintosh advertising that we had created years earlier. Not just ease of use, but radical ease of use. We had to associate Kia as being Civic-like or Corolla-like in a highly believable and credible manner, which turned out to be both humble and likable.

Over time the campaign moved on to a series of dramatic and humorous demonstrations of "It's about time everyone had a well-made car." One commercial was the test where the Kia Sephia followed a Honda Civic everywhere around the country, except into the $10,000-plus price range. Other spots emphasized Kia's durability by portraying a Sephia as a rental car, a pizza delivery vehicle, and a driving school automobile.

Greg Warner said, "We have to be disruptive; we have to have different ads than every other car company." And, "These spots are different, no doubt, but they still convey an honest, humble message that Kia makes quality cars." We took a bit of creative license.

We all drank the Kool-Aid. Who cared that J. D. Power would rank Kia at the very bottom of the quality ratings? The advertising was strong enough to overcome even this disturbing long-term problem.

The media strategy was almost as critical as the creative given the extremely uncompetitive levels of planned spending. Toyota, Honda, Saturn, and Chrysler were spending $111 million, $35 million, $17 million, and $95 million, respectively. Our budget was set at $15.8 million.

Remarkably, there was no measurable dealer ad spending, which is a given for every car company and often adds 100 percent to the spending impact. We had virtually none.

It was interesting just how effective the positioning and advertising was in the marketplace. At the time there were over a thousand models from which consumers could choose. And in the subcompact category, which was in decline at minus 17.9 percent, there were 24 choices alone. Hyundai, also a Korean company, had years earlier poisoned the market for Korean-made automobiles with poor quality and particularly in this class of cars.

But the advertising created a valuable personality for Kia as honest, unpretentious, and likable, to overcome possible skepticism and to differentiate the new brand. It offset concerns that buyers might have had. Results were terrific, with broad awareness being generated among "import economy intenders" and high advertising recall. Awareness of the ads was ahead of Nissan, Toyota, Honda, Hyundai, Mitsubishi, and Mazda.

The advertising successfully positioned the car, gained purchase consideration, drove consumer traffic into dealerships, and helped dealers close the sale with a 20 percent closing rate versus the 9 percent the industry was experiencing. We sold every car they wanted to and more. This, despite the product suffering from serious quality issues from the very beginning of the introduction to America.

Anyone who says advertising doesn't work should rethink that concern. After just the initial wave of advertising, we had 70 percent of the target agreeing Kia "is similar in quality to Toyota and Honda"; 66 percent thinking that Kia was thoroughly tested; and 46 percent liking the advertising.

It was a huge success!

A few years later parent company Kia Motors Corporation in Seoul commissioned an advertising agency, MBC Advertising, to produce a commercial for some overseas markets. The commercial featured a Princess Diana look-alike being chased by paparazzi and emerging from a car crash unscathed. This was a very bad idea. The media had incorrectly identified Goldberg Moser O'Neill and Kia Motors America as the originators of this commercial, though we had absolutely nothing to do with it. We did our best to set the record straight but the damage had already been done.

I received a letter from Frank Lowe, head of the company that had recently acquired our agency, inquiring about the commercial and its taste level. This was understandable. Frank was based in London and was by this time known as Sir Frank Lowe, someone who wouldn't want his reputation sullied by association with this kind of thing.

However, we were not as sensitive as maybe we should have been all the time

Problems with '00 models

	Problems per 100 vehicles	'99 rank		Problems per 100 vehicles	'99 rank
Acura	95	4	Mazda	158	17
Lexus	107	6	**Indus. avg**	158	
Infiniti	110	3	Oldsmobile	161	23
BMW	121	5	Ford	166	19
Toyota	122	7	Mitsubishi	169	29
Porsche	125	15	Saturn	169	20
Honda	130	8	Pontiac	170	25
Buick	135	2	Chevrolet	171	27
Mercedes	137	13	GMC	178	29
Jaguar	139	1	Dodge	179	24
Plymouth	140	15	Jeep	191	33
Saab	140	20	Land Rover	195	31
Audi	144	17	Isuzu	196	34
Lincoln	144	12	Subaru	202	22
Mercury	148	25	Volkswagen	203	32
Cadillac	149	9	Hyundai	206	28
Volvo	154	14	Daewoo	214	-
Chrysler	155	10	Suzuki	228	35
Nissan	157	11	Kia	256	36

Sources: J.D. Power, USA TODAY research

J. D. Power research.

either. At one point the account group allowed the creative people to present a commercial targeted at 30-plus women. It had people in the automobile picking their noses and putting the stuff on the sun visor. For some reason the people at Kia frowned on this idea.

Kia sales went from 12,000 in 1994 to 83,000 in 1998 to 175,000 in 2000. And the advertising cost per unit kept getting lower and lower.

We had so many talented and hardworking people cycle through the Kia account over the years. This was largely due to the abusive and ugly behavior on the part of the client. More specifically, Dick Macedo.

Dick was a master at tailoring his abuse to the victim. He would give little credence to an individual because the person was new, or he might arbitrarily change due dates and project parameters. He would set ridiculous hurdles and then not even acknowledge the effort if the person succeeded. Usually he would complain that something had been overlooked. He just simply liked to eat people alive. Moby Dick.

The general thinking was that Macedo acted in this manner to maintain control. He would call late on a Friday afternoon insisting on changes in ads needed by Monday. He would utilize creative strategy only when it suited his needs or arguments, changing it when it didn't.

He would do stuff like call someone at the agency and leave a message to call him back but would purposely not mention the subject, so the person couldn't be prepared. He would often call one person and get some information and then call another person to give them a quiz to see if they knew the very same information he had just received.

Once he requested that an account person begin work and gave a detailed review of all the various things that were needed for an important upcoming dealer meeting. The next day he fired the agency.

One of the biggest issues for GMO people was his rudeness and the way he would say dreadful things about a person in front of other people. This certainly wasn't unexpected from a man who would do the same thing about his own Korean bosses and co-workers.

Some of these things could have been written off as gamesmanship, but the frequency with which he played these games led me to see them as something more.

Maybe the classic Macedo ruse was when he would call the agency on his speakerphone and ask a person if he or she wanted to keep their job. He might complain that the person had been rude to his secretary Becky, and she was hurt and devastated, and that this behavior would not be condoned and he was going to report this to me. On one occasion Becky called a few minutes later to let us know that she was sitting in Dick's office when he made the call and he was smiling and laughing at his "joke." Becky confided that she hadn't been insulted at all. What a guy!

Despite Dick Macedo and his MO, we succeeded wildly with Kia, and the automotive business is the toughest category in which to do effective advertising. In 1993, $5 billion was being spent annually, yet very little of the advertising was being remembered. Truth is, what makes powerful advertising in any category is what made powerful advertising here too. It just takes insight, sweat, and intestinal fortitude to get at it, to get it approved, and to get it on the air.

Automobile companies traditionally look over their shoulders developing ads. But you can't make history by emulating it, as I've said before. What worked in the past usually is not what will work in the future. If it's already worked, it won't work as well again. Or work at all. The environment keeps changing, requiring ongoing observation and modification and fresh, insightful solutions.

Car companies with competitive differences spend billions on mediocre, boring, and irrelevant ads. All remarkably similar. With most of the auto advertising you could put just about any model car in any ad and have the ad fit the model. Sometimes I think that is what they do.

Consumers complain about auto advertising. It re-creates exactly what they don't like about buying a car. The anxiety and confusion. They say car advertising fails to communicate what they do like: the experience of a new car. There is perhaps no other purchase so infused with emotion, history, and anticipation—right down to the smell of it.

How can someone begin to make an intelligent choice among the myriad of marques and models on the basis of advertising? They can't.

But wait. There is a small enlightened group that recognizes that the opportunity for increasing sales is directly and disproportionately related to the greatness of their advertising. A critical weapon in the marketing arsenal. The difference between success and failure. They're the ones with less to spend and who want to take advantage of every opportunity to leverage precious funds. They cannot outspend competition, so they outsmart them.

They demand smarter advertising. Advertising that stands out and is different. Sharp, cutting edge. Talked about. Relevant and empathetic. Often, ads like this carry a degree of risk. They generate controversy, comment, and criticism. It takes guts (often Rolaids) to run them.

Say you're employed by a traditional car company, working your way up to the executive suite. Got your sights on your boss's boss's job and you've got lots of folks to answer to. There's lots of history to demonstrate why doing what was done before is what you need to do now. Or at least what you need to do to stay on your career path. Oh and also to keep your job.

But it's the other kind of advertising that hasn't been done before that grabs people's attention. Imparts new information. That people want to see a second time. That dollar for dollar is vastly more efficient and explains why so many successful brands get established by stepping away from tradition. And why traditional car advertising just keeps rollin' rollin' rollin'. Introducing the new Oldschevilliac. It's got state-of-the-art stereo antilock braking power steering window door lock tires with rims.

With Kia we had the good fortune to have created advertising that went entirely against all of this history and baggage. Not one person in the United States had ever heard of Kia before 1993. They had a funny, hard to pronounce name (Kee-ah). A model name that was harder still, Sephia (Sef-fee-ah). From a country with a history of selling poorly manufactured products and particularly cars, Korea (Ko-ree-ah). Still Kia was a $6 billion giant selling cars in 90 countries around the world. Kia made the Sephia from Korea. Who cared in America?

Our advertising changed all of that. It was fresh and innovative and had impact. A bit daring. Fun and well liked. Most of all it was extremely relevant to intended customers. The theme "It's about time everyone had a well-made car" hit squarely at the issue that the economy car buyer most wrestles with. Dependability. And the advertising delivered the proof that this car, the Kia Sephia, was as good as the leader in the segment (Honda Civic) in a forth-right, competitive, and compelling way.

On a modest budget, Kia became the number two or number three best-selling car (cars per dealer) in every one of the initial 27 markets it entered. People liked the advertising more than any other in the category. They went in and checked out the cars. They bought the cars.

Although the cars were not anywhere near as good as the way the ads portrayed them, the lesson was clear. If your prospective customer likes the ads, they transfer that like to your product, sometimes ignoring just about everything else. That is what indeed happened with Kia.

Dick Macedo called on February 16, 2000. "Fred, I want to come up and see you."

"Why? What's this about?"

"I want to come up today."

"OK. What time?"

"I'll catch the next plane and be there by three."

"See you then."

I hung up the phone and knew what was coming. Macedo had decided to fire us. He had been making noises about saving money and using more promotional-oriented agencies. I also knew he had talked with some friends of his who had been trying to get into the account for a long time.

At three the receptionist rang, "Mr. Macedo from Kia is here."

"I'll be out in a minute."

I wanted my two partners to be a part of this so I called Brian and Mike and asked them to join me in the small conference room just inside the reception area on our sixth floor. I strolled out to the lobby to find Dick, ad manager Rick Weisehan, and Jim Sanfilippo, VP marketing, standing there. I ushered them into the conference room and sat down.

I said, "I've asked Brian and Mike to join us."

There was silence while we waited for them to arrive. I didn't offer the visitors coffee, a soft drink, or even water. I looked over at them and Rick and Jim were looking down at the conference table. Dick was rustling through some papers he had in front of him. Then Brian and Mike arrived and took seats.

Just as soon as they were seated Macedo said, "We're going with another advertising agency."

As soon as he said this, I stood up and said, "Fuck you."

I walked out of the conference room and left Brian and Mike and the three of them sitting there. I understand Brian and Mike then excused themselves a few moments later and the three Kia executives packed up their attachés and slipped quietly out of the conference room and went down the elevators never to be seen again.

So now we were without our largest and most important account. This was truly a body blow but one that ultimately could not have been avoided. I presumed that Macedo was a political snake and had engineered our undoing on the basis of saving money. He had likely convinced the Korean management that this was a good move, and if the Koreans could save 11 cents they were always for it.

We had spent the last 18 months negotiating a new contract and had only one week before signing the agreement. The Koreans focused largely on how to save money and Macedo knew full well that this fact alone would be fertile justification to change advertising agencies. We didn't have Greg Warner any longer to bring a reasonable perspective to the situation.

They didn't consider what we had accomplished over seven years for them. Nor the commitment that we had made to their business. It really didn't matter to them. I do know this, however: had Greg Warner still been alive, it would never have happened.

I was angry and decided the only thing I could do was at least to set the record straight. I waited until we had collected all of our outstanding receivables and then I sent a letter to the then Korean president of Kia Motors America at the time, Byung Mo Ahn.

The letter outlined what we had accomplished for Kia during our tenure and how we did this despite many obstacles. Obstacles like the inferior budget, the quality of the cars, and the

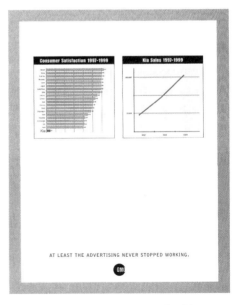

GMO house ad after getting fired by Kia Motors.

repugnant Dick Macedo. I included what an ex-employee of mine, Wayne Buder, had said to Macedo in an emotional and powerful letter he had felt obliged to send him on learning we had been fired. Thanks, Wayne.

I also ran an ad in *Advertising Age*. It had two charts. The one on the left showed several years of consumer satisfaction data for 20 popular automobiles with Kia registering the absolute worst on the chart, receiving hardly any positives. The chart on the right showed Kia sales for a similar several years with a red line indicating a 45-degree upward trajectory.

⊘ ⊘ ⊘

One year and a month later I read in the trades that Dick Macedo had resigned from Kia. The *Advertising Age* article mentioned that he was being forced out, although he denied that this was the case.

Our separation was described by *AdWeek* on April 24, 2000, as the "biggest diss" for the past year: "Kia Motors America to Goldberg Moser O'Neill. The carmaker watched the agency build its brand from scratch over six years, and then said it wanted a shop with greater resources. After firing GMO, Kia turned the $50 million account over to tiny startup David and Goliath."

The truth is that the group working on the Kia business at Goldberg Moser O'Neill was at least partially to blame for our losing the account, although not nearly as much as the client's behavior. Just about everyone had bad things to say about every client at Kia, and they didn't hide their feelings.

They would make fun of the products and the people. There was a constant bitching. I am not suggesting that it was not well deserved but it certainly didn't help ingratiate the clients to us. These relationship issues were in fact getting in the way of servicing and, in the end, retaining the account. People should have waited until reading these memoirs to vent.

The other thing that eventually led to our demise was that some of the very best people who were assigned to the business at the start had left the agency, including Pat Sherwood (account management), Mike Murphy (account planner), and Mike Moser (creative). Some physically left; others left mentally and emotionally. Some all of the above.

Complicating the situation further was that I had introduced a number of new players who failed miserably to contribute anything at all, and some of these people came at considerable cost to the agency. One senior former car guy, with more experience than anyone else we ever had on the account, stands out. He was hired as the top account guy, and his contributions were at the bottom.

But from the moment we were hired we were held under constant threat of being fired by Dick Macedo. It became like having arthritis: the pain becomes a part of your being and you continue on regardless.

I remember spending endless hours preparing a very detailed and well-crafted presentation and document and having to fly to New York to personally present, one on one, what was a "Process & Relationship Improvement Plan" to Macedo. It was a part of trying to manage and hold on to this important account at that time. I had done a similar thing several times before.

I met with Macedo, who was on a sales mission there. It was worth the trip, as it allowed us to hold on to the account (again). My only regret is that I never made the trip to Kia's headquarters in Seoul.

It might not have prevented us from getting fired, but I had always wanted to try *okdol bi bim bap*. Yum!

NOT THE ARMY, IT'S THE MARINES

GOLDBERG MOSER O'NEILL officially put their names up on the door on June 29, 1990. Unfortunately we had no doors, except on the restrooms, so the names went on the wall in the entrance lobby and outside on the building awning.

I wrote about our mission. Goldberg Moser O'Neill was "a bunch of really bright people with terrific client relationships making great ads that work." That's what we were and that's what we wanted to be.

Fulfilling this mission required a tough adherence regarding the kind of people we hired into the agency; the quality of the creative talent required to produce great work; and a grounding in the reality of why clients advertise in the first place.

Marines are and have been an elite fighting force. The Marines are the first to fight. People who join the Marines are not avoiding combat; they are essentially volunteering for it. Ronald Reagan once said, "Some people spend their entire lives wondering if they made a difference in the world. The Marines don't have to."

I always liked to say, "GMO wasn't the Army, we were the Marines." It was a heck of a lot harder to work at our agency than at most. We demanded more, much more, from everyone. Paying attention to the

Me, circa 1986.

details, no matter what your job was, mattered. Being able to withstand some of the added blows and pressure of the place was all in the line of duty. There were many rewards, emotional and financial, that proved just how much of a difference so many of the GMO people made on our product and on the way we did business. I am certain that it was a major part of why we were so successful.

Having a passion for what we did mattered. And, having a willingness to commit to long hours to achieve whatever it was you were responsible for mattered. I made sure that everyone who joined the agency received a copy of Tom Peters's *A Passion for Excellence* as well as an abbreviated version. I believed in much of what was preached in that book and tried to instill it throughout the organization. Not everyone was cut out for it—only the few and the proud. Managing our mission and keeping it on a track required a robust tenaciousness and passion that people weren't always able to deliver. It took a toll on people.

I received a memo from a creative person who was incredibly dedicated and hardworking. I often received memos from this person venting his frustrations. He was slightly unstable but did some really great work. His memo demonstrated how demanding the business is—that is, if you take it seriously.

> *I'm going to take the week off between Christmas and New Year's. I will be out of town. I will not break this vacation for new business or any other reason. Do not ask me to.*
>
> *You're asking why am I being so hostile in this memo?*
>
> *Here's why:*
>
> *I gave up two days of my honeymoon for a new business meeting. Not a great way to start a marriage. I cancelled a Thanksgiving trip due to workload last year. I made Christmas plans last year and was forced to cancel my flights. My wife went home alone. I showed up Christmas Eve and returned two days later. At great emotional cost to my wife. I had to cancel my vacation this year which had been scheduled for my wife's foot surgery. I couldn't be home to help her.*
>
> *December 23rd is more than two months away. That's plenty of warning. This year if forced to make a choice one more time, I will choose my wife. Please do not talk to me about this. Just know that I'm out that week and it is a very volatile issue with me. Thank you.*

I received many memos like this. The advertising business is not for the faint of heart. And given the standards and work ethic that we demanded, GMO was a much harder place to work for than your average ad agency. It was definitely tough and rigorous, and dealing with lots of subjective aspects made it all the more so.

I, for one, hired a number of executives to run account management who didn't understand that we were serious about our commitment to the creative and the creative product. They never got "it's the creative, stupid!"

Mike, Brian, and I had an unusually good working relationship. We believed mostly the same things when it came to the creative work and generally how the agency should be run to get the best. I may have been a little tougher in some areas than they were, but it all worked. I took the point of view with the press, in new business meetings, and with new employees that "Nothing comes between us . . . not even the punctuation."

Goldberg Moser O'Neill. It stood up to inspection. Goodby, Silverstein & Partners; Scali, McCabe, Sloves; Della Femina, Travisano & Partners; Young & Rubicam. My remark always got a smile and made an important point with prospects. It was clever, which reinforced, again, that we were clever.

⊘ ⊘ ⊘

Most advertising agencies have some kind of philosophy or credo other than they want to make a lot of money. Ours, in addition to the one about money, was focused on a real belief that creative advertising worked better than the other kind. And, worked better meant it worked harder in selling the product or service and in the end generated more business for the client.

Too many creative-oriented agencies only believe that they should be doing creative things without the restriction of these things having to work in the marketplace. This is how they give creative agencies a sullied name along with the stigma of being arrogant and having hubris.

Another thing about many agencies, particularly those that are creative oriented, is that they have a certain style or a look about their work. Even Chiat/Day, particularly in the early years, had a tendency to use the same typeface, to do a lot of "How to . . . " headlines, often to use only minimal copy, and so on. The work was great but it did have a similarity of sorts across many clients.

We always felt that this was wrong and that an agency's personality should never become a part of the brand for which we were creating the ads.

Hal Riney was possibly the greatest offender in this regard. While much of his work was beautiful and lyrical, it had a definite sameness. His folksy, down-home, low-key, repetitive mellow style and delivery made Henry Weinhard beer and MJB Coffee and Saturn and Perrier and even President Reagan's election campaign all sort of the same in a strange way. That his mellifluous and distinctive voice was the one delivering all the voice-over messages for all these clients added to the sameness. So, of course, any of these commercials could sometimes be mistaken for another: just put the other brand here . . . or there.

At GMO we didn't want look-alike or sound-alike. We wanted every piece of creative for each client to be fresh and different, distinctive and clever. That's a lot harder than doing formulaic ads.

Too many advertising agencies that call themselves "creative" are only interested in the being creative part. At GMO we really felt that the more creative the work, the more it would stand out, attract attention, and be seen. And, we felt by carefully targeting customers, the more they would relate to and remember, and feel good about and use the product or service we were advertising. We were able to prove that over and over again over the years.

It's a lot harder doing great creative work and being accountable for it than just doing great creative work. Some of our greatest successes on both these counts were for Dell, Cisco, Coca-Cola's Citra, and Dreyer's ice cream.

In 1988 when we went to work for Dell, their sales were around $200 million. Eleven years later they had grown to $25 billion. More importantly, since they were a direct marketing company, their calls per week rose from 900 to 70,000 during this time.

When we started with Cisco Systems in 1991, their sales were $183 million. When we parted nine years later, they were at $12 billion.

Dreyer's was even more spectacular given that it was a packaged goods company. In 1991 their dollar share of the ice cream business was less than 8 percent. Breyers, their most important competitor, was around 11 percent. Share for Dreyer's grew every year for the next nine years of our relationship to as high as 16 percent and exceeded Breyers.

There were many more examples of marketplace success, including Reebok's Pump shoe, Kia Motors America, Quantum, Teddy Ruxpin, Lazer Tag, Aerial Communications, California Cooler, and more.

To be sure, not all of these significant sales and marketplace successes were attributed to the advertising alone. But in every one of these cases the work was outstanding and distinctive and relevant and persuasive. Without the advertising, the extraordinary sales accomplishments would not have been possible.

Oh, and the list also included Goldberg Moser O'Neill. We had a hell of a run: we won a lot of business, we won a lot of awards, and we made a lot of money. We started the firm in June of 1990 with $58M in billings and nine years later had reached $500M.

We were successful because we demanded more from our people than anyone else. And even though we took pains to select only those who we felt belonged at our unique and elite company, we were able to convince them that they were in fact better than their peers at other agencies. They believed! GMO folks may well have been smarter. They were certainly more motivated and dedicated. An unusually high percentage of our employees looked at problems from an entrepreneurial perspective and therefore were able to capitalize on more opportunities. We tried to empower them as much as we could.

I used to relate this wonderful story about a large American shoe manufacturer that sent two sales reps out to different parts of the Australian outback to see if they could drum up some business among the Aborigines.

Sometime later the company received correspondence back from both agents. The first one said, "No business here . . . natives don't wear shoes." The second said, "Great opportunity here . . . natives don't wear shoes." That was the kind of thinking that was inspired at our agency and actually happened on a frequent basis.

So many advertising agencies had become commodities and were indistinguishable from one another. And it wasn't just their creative work. It was their offices. It was the way they did business. It was the people. We tried to build an elite group with an entrepreneurial mind-set. I kept telling everyone that the only authority they had at GMO was the power of their intellect, a phrase I believe was coined by Mike Massaro. And it worked. Most everyone felt empowered.

At the same time we tried to be really careful on our hires. We put them through many interviews with many people and always included both upper and lower level folks. It's amazing how many candidates fell out of consideration because they took offense at being interviewed by someone at GMO who was in a lower job. But the corollary of giving the wrong people authority is that if you empower dummies you get bad decisions faster.

I made sure that everyone had a constant reminder that we didn't suffer fools easily and didn't want dumb asses working at GMO. Everyone had to look at our "No Clown" logo that I had plastered just about everywhere. On writing pads, buttons, hats, umbrellas, T-shirts, sweatshirts, and the flag flying proudly, if a bit arrogantly, on our rooftop. I even had some cool Frisbees

made with the clown, which we distributed to everyone at the agency.

I insisted on personally giving a two-hour indoctrination about the agency and its philosophy to everyone who joined our firm. Attendance was mandatory for assistant account executives, associate creative directors, and media supervisors. For everyone.

The truth is that we had to have people who were smart. We had an unusually high percentage of clients who were entrepreneurial and entrepreneurial minded. They demanded far more smarts of the people who worked with them than the traditional corporate executive at, say, Transamerica or Clorox. We had to be fleet of foot, work smarter, and have a passion for what we did at the agency and what these clients were doing at their companies, and it was important to understand that results mattered.

Finally, it was essential that our people have a point of view and express it. There was absolutely no room for yes men or yes women. It was interesting how yes men outnumbered considerably the yes women back then, and we ended up with a disproportionate number of women in the agency and in critical executive positions. I believe about 70 percent of our employees were women and maybe a bit higher percentage of our management group. Tony Blair, former prime minister of Great Britain, mused, "The art of leadership is saying no, not yes. It is very easy to say yes." Amen!

Ready. Fire. Aim. This was a real-world model at the agency. And it was Steve Jobs down at Apple who pointed out to me one day that at IBM "the journey was the reward." This was true at so many corporations and ad agencies. I regularly pointed this out to my people so that we wouldn't get caught up in this kind of constipation at the agency. The journey was definitely not the reward.

When we were part of Chiat/Day, Jay used to say, "We want to see how big we can get before we get bad." I thought this was always a bit arrogant and dangerous. In fact, Chiat/Day did ultimately hit a wall of bigness and got bad. There was a period of time, maybe 18 months or so, where they lost more client businesses than most agencies ever hope to have in their lifetimes.

I modified our philosophy to say, "We want to see how good we can get before we get big." This allowed us to focus more on the work. It did not prevent us from working with smaller clients as long as we could do great work for them. And, frankly, getting big is really not the issue; it's how much money you take home at the end of the day.

I took on many small accounts at the agency for several reasons. First and above all, I knew we could do sensational work because the client wanted work that would be outstanding and would stand out. And they couldn't really afford to pay for it.

In most cases these were entrepreneurial-minded businesspeople and they valued the different, the new, the edgy because it enhanced their ability to have their company and products seen. They understood the inestimable worth of the free publicity garnered from the unexpected and newsworthy.

The smaller accounts were fodder to feed and nourish the creative hunger. They allowed for breakthrough opportunities. And despite what many people critical of taking on small, often unprofitable accounts would argue, they never calculated into the equation the worth of all of the things I've just mentioned. Rather, only the apparent amount of time spent on each of the smaller clients.

I never hired an additional person when I took on a small account, so in effect I had no real additional out-of-pocket costs. Yes, I may have been robbing a bit from Paul to pay for Peter, but it was a good trade-off in my mind. To be sure, people had to work harder but it had its rewards. And by the way, once in a while the small account actually turned into a big one. It happened at our agency an unusual number of times.

But the bottom line is the body of creative work, which is testament to my beliefs about small accounts. We did great work for smaller and/or start-up companies like Watermark (purified water), Businessland (computer retailer), Net Air (jet charter on demand), Interactive Network (interactive TV entertainment), Intelligy (educational learning system), Sea Legs (packaged foods), Levolor (window coverings), Casablanca Fan, Sun Valley Mall, Growing Healthy (baby foods), Catapult (video games), Oakland Raiders, Ameristar Casinos, Decibel Instruments (hearing devices), and Fat Brain (online books).

The focus was on doing really good stuff. It didn't matter whether it was a print ad or a billboard or a holiday card or a matchbook cover or planning a party or a new business solicitation poster or postcard. Or for that matter a media plan or an insight into the consumer. Or even the way the office looked or the way it was kept clean. I demanded everything be done at an unusually high level.

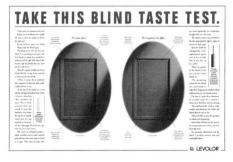

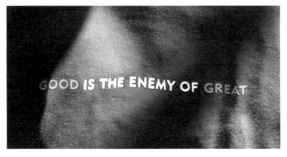

Of course, not everything we did was a success. But being part of our elite group definitely had an impact on most people's mentality about how they went about their respective jobs. And by and large those who didn't buy into the Kool-Aid ended up not being rewarded emotionally or financially. And they left. Which was OK! It was definitely a tough place for many people. Some couldn't handle the immediate authority that was vested in them and the expectations of their performance. I will say this was considerably less of a problem for the majority of the creative people who bathed in the environment.

Everyone was expected to immediately hit the beaches, some without any precombat training. Those who were smart and ambitious saw this as an opportunity. And it was. Those who didn't got left wriggling on the beach like a fish out of water.

I expected that anyone in the agency could talk with any one of our clients right up to the CEOs if need be. And many did. It was interesting how much better women were on average in this regard. Seeing young people able to accomplish this was one of the things that made me most proud of the agency as much as of them.

Winning was everything at GMO. I liked to win and I didn't like to lose. Winning could be gaining approval from a client to produce a truly unique creative ad or idea of any kind or gaining new business. Vince Lombardi was right when he said, "Winning is the only thing." And I believed him. He also said, "Practice does not make perfect. Perfect makes perfect." I believed that, too.

I liked to win new business and I won a lot of it. I had a street fighter mentality, one that didn't sit too well when I first arrived in San Francisco. Actually it never sat too well with a lot of people but I never really cared. All I cared about was making the agency a success, and winning was the fuel for achieving it.

I used to reward those folks that did special things. It may have been just a little thing like an extra day off, or an envelope with five or ten crisp $100 bills, or a Cartier watch.

Often we would give out gift certificates to folks who had extended themselves in some way. I received a thank-you once for a Kabuki spa certificate given to a group of deserving administrative assistants (known as secretaries elsewhere but having considerably less responsibility than at GMO).

I finally did something with the Kabuki gift certificate you kindly gave me (and some other assistants) for a full treatment of a sauna, back scrub and a shiatsu massage. The massage is actually quite powerful and it's a little hard to decide when you're on the table whether you're actually having a good time or not. Not unlike working at GMO. But the afterglow is pretty good, feeling pummeled, punched and very stretched. Not unlike working at GMO. It was great. Thanks very much.

We had the good fortune of being successful, enough so that we were always able to set aside a very significant amount of money to give back at the end of the year as bonuses. Bonuses went to the ones who really made a difference and who made major contributions to the philosophy of GMO. They were the ones who received the lion's share of the bonus money and I made sure these were generous shares indeed.

The alternative would have been to take those millions of dollars and divide them between Brian, Mike, and me. But I felt that we expected and demanded more from our people, and when we got it, we should handsomely recognize it. I don't know if the Marines get paid more than the general Army but they should.

This was quite counter to a philosophy held at many other agencies where, if there were profits, a chunk of money was set aside at year end and everyone received 1 percent or 5 percent, or somewhere in between, of their

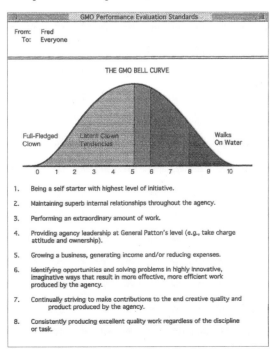

salary, regardless of their individual contribution. Not at GMO! The Marines who went beyond the call got the ribbon. The ones who didn't, didn't get.

My thinking was always that giving someone a Christmas bonus of 2 percent, the same as everyone else got, was not motivating and just became a part of their salary and was expected. It didn't recognize individual performance. It was very socialistic, contrary to my way of thinking. Contrast this with the person to whom you hand a 25 percent bonus and link it directly to the specific work that he or she did. Now that's motivation and appreciation. Somehow it soothed a lot of the hard work and abuse suffered in the previous 11 months.

The agency philosophy and treatment of our employees were communi-

Goldberg Moser O'Neill
Employee Handbook

cated not just to everyone who worked at GMO. I went out of my way to make sure clients and prospective clients understood what we stood for and what we expected out of everyone who worked at the agency. We spent a lot of time and effort developing an employee handbook that not only imparted all of this philosophical stuff, but also contained the traditional information, like how to fill out time sheets and how many vacation days one gets, that makes up your usual advertising agency handout.

This booklet became one of our most important and effective new business tools. Prospective clients read it cover to cover, and those who embraced the philosophical tenets that were everywhere in it became much more interested in hiring the agency than they would have otherwise. Many clients adopted a lot of the things that the handbook espoused.

Additionally they saw the booklet as a highly creative endeavor. The manual was a special promotional piece and said that we were a special agency. It reinforced all of the creative things that we claimed to do at the agency. It wasn't just about the television ads.

From the day we opened our doors we had much to be thankful for. As a result of our distinguished work in the world of business to business advertising and marketing, including campaigns for Dell, ROLM, and Interactive Network, Goldberg Moser O'Neill was chosen "Agency of the Year" in 1993 by *Business Marketing Magazine*.

We had built some truly unique relationships with many of our clients, which allowed us to perform at a high level, and because of the trust, our clients more often than not bought into more daring work. Most of us who worked at the agency genuinely liked our clients, unlike many in the advertising business who really don't like their clients. This fact alone let us develop far stronger relationships. But in fairness we really had some terrific clients.

Susan Gauff, senior director of marketing and corporate communications at ROLM, a division of Siemens Corporation, had this to say: "We needed to create a new strategy to develop a 'new' ROLM. We wanted an agency with solid high tech experience but with a consumer orientation. We wanted a strategic partner, not a creative partner. I can't speak highly enough of these folks."

One of the relationships of which we were most proud was with Dell Computer. Wonderful clients, including Michael Dell, Joel Kocher, Tom Martin, and M. J. Lawhon in the early years. Joel Kocher, Dell president, said, "It's been a real partnership which I've not experienced with another vendor." Tom Martin, VP marketing, said, "In this business, you either have arrogant SOBs who only talk or people who just listen and are risk-averse. These guys do both. Who wants an agency that just sucks up to the client all the time?"

I am particularly pleased and proud of almost all of the relationships that we had with those client people who initially hired us to work with them. Unfortunately in the advertising business there is a tremendous amount of personnel change on both the client and the agency sides. But it is generally the ones on the client side that end up ultimately leading to divorce.

Nevertheless, GMO had an unusual record of tenure with many of its clients over the years. The American Marketing Association reported at one point that the average agency/client relationship lasted about 3 years. I believe it has deteriorated more recently to something like 18 months, if that long. Yet we were able to work with Dell for 11 years, Dreyer's for 10 years, Cisco Systems for 10 years, and so on.

The end of our run came in 2000 not long after IPG decided to merge GMO with the Boston agency Hill Holliday, which they also owned. That was the stake in the heart and the GMO entity soon disappeared.

In April 2000, *Vanity Fair* published an article entitled "The New Establishment 2000." Of the 30 people they identified as those who had changed the world, we had had the remarkable opportunity to have worked with five either as Chiat/Day San Francisco or Goldberg Moser O'Neill: Steve Jobs (Apple), Andy Grove (Intel), John Chambers (Cisco), Larry Ellison (Oracle), and Michael Dell (Dell).

Furthermore, our people had the chance to work with others who may not have been selected by *Vanity Fair* but nonetheless had made enormous impacts on society and American business: Michael Crete (California

Cooler), Al Davis (Oakland Raiders), Gordon Eubanks (Symantec), Bruce Karatz (Kaufman & Broad), Don Kingsborough (Worlds of Wonder), Bill Krause (3Com), Sandy Kurtzig (Ask Computers), David Lockton (Interactive Network), George Lucas (LucasArts), David Norman and Enzo Torresi (Businessland), Ruth Owades (Calyx & Corolla), Howard Palefsky (Collagen), Gary Rogers and Rick Cronk (Dreyer's), Jack Tramiel (Atari), Roger Trinchero (Sutter Home Winery), Les Crane (Software Toolworks), and David and Riva Berelson (Sea Legs).

Pretty amazing when you think about the other 6,000-plus advertising agencies in the country who may never have gotten to work with even one of these kinds of businesspeople. All were entrepreneurial and ran businesses with an independent spirit and a view that is not often found in traditional Corporate America. We learned a lot from them, and working with them helped us build the agency substantially. I am certain that a part of our success in dealing with these kinds of people was directly related to our "Marines" mentality.

When I first started the agency in 1990, I had every intention of building it and selling it. As a result of our hard work and maybe some luck, I arrived at that position just six years later. We had grown the agency remarkably from $8.9 million in income to $26 million in 1996. We had hoped to be doing only $17.9 million at that point, but were 45 percent ahead of that goal.

I had a cartoon framed and hung on my office wall that said it all. It showed a man leaving for work and his wife in the doorway telling him, "Remember, Frederick, it's not if you win or lose. What counts is how much money you made!"

My name isn't Frederick and our work counted as much as the money, but in the end the money is what attracts suitors most.

I had been approached by several agencies before this time but wanted to get to a scale where the sale would mean something significant. With our having done so well to this point, by 1996 it seemed like a good time to test the waters. At the same time we were in need of some broader resources to service several of our clients, like Dell, who had grown enormously and globally.

I met with a number of agencies, most of whom I really didn't want to be a part of. They had little or no creative integrity. The only one that appeared to be a good fit with us creatively was The Lowe Group, which was a part of the holding company Interpublic. Frank Lowe had built his agency with a reputation of doing good creative work, and he ran Lowe. Lowe was large enough to provide us with some needed international and network resources. Lowe also claimed to be relatively autonomous within the IPG family, which had appeal as well.

One of my first meetings with Lowe was with Marvin Sloves, who had become a part of their management group when Lowe merged with his agency. He had been one of the founding partners of a great creative agency,

Scali, McCabe, Sloves. His presence was a big initial positive for me. Marvin was a delightful fellow and very encouraging of the acquisition possibility.

So it came to pass that I sold Lowe 49 percent of the agency outright with a "put to sell" the remainder at intervals over the next five years. In other words, this meant that they had to buy the rest when we said so, but we didn't have to sell it if we didn't want. This worked out very well for us and for them, as the agency grew over the next four years to $42.7 million in income and we both shared in the profits generated.

I have David Weiner, ex–Chiat/Day board member, financial consultant, and deal maker supreme, to thank for constructing the transaction with IPG. We did very well because of it. When I had asked David beforehand what his fee would be, all he said was, "You do what you think is fair."

David had told me some years earlier about another agency that he represented as seller and was about the same size as we were. In that case he told the seller the same thing and in return received a glass trophy with thanks. I hadn't forgotten.

One very smart deal maker: David Weiner.

So I went across the street from my Maiden Lane office to Christofle and personally picked out an exquisite crystal trophy that cost around $1,300. A lot of money back then. I had it carefully gift wrapped and packed up and sent off to David with a note of thanks.

When David received the piece, he called and offered his thank-you, which was considerable. I had inserted a check for $250,000 under the bucket in appreciation for his good work.

When I look back on the transaction, it is with some continued awe and pride. I say this because two years later, my previous agency, Young & Rubicam, the fifth largest agency at the time, filed for an IPO. The *Wall Street Journal* reported on February 27, 1998, that while their revenue was soaring to $1.38 billion, they had failed to make any money the previous two years. In 1996, they had a net loss of $238 million.

Who knew that Goldberg Moser O'Neill would ever make more profits than Young & Rubicam?

Lowe had said they wanted a West Coast presence. As Frank Lowe remarked to Stuart Elliott of the *New York Times*, "My view was never to do a start-up because one outpost makes me frightfully nervous—Fort Apache and all that."

He went on to say, "And America is a wonderful place to lose a lot of money opening offices. Rather, we wanted to find an agency with a good reputation and good, like-minded people."

I was quoted in the same article, saying, "I have the sense Frank is really sincere about trying to have each office doing great work. That's not to say he doesn't want them to be profitable, but the big reason he became the most attractive of all the people interested in us was that he convinced me and Mike and Brian he cared about the work."

How could I have been so wrong?

Things started to go from bad to worse in 2000. The global "network" operating in 28 countries was never made available to us. This had been an important reason we wanted the acquisition in the first place. And once they decided to merge Goldberg Moser O'Neill with Hill Holliday, everything went even further downhill.

When Lowe opened an office in San Francisco, a few hundred yards down Battery Street from ours, to service a client that competed with one of ours, I probably should have known that nothing that was said prior to the acquisition meant anything really.

I sat in my cubicle at 600 Battery Street reading the *New York Times* and the *Wall Street Journal* each day. I checked my stocks and did a bit of day trading. I was able to take all of my vacation days for the first time in my life. And I just generally wandered around the agency with not very much to do. They had their new management group who were taking care of things.

The most amazing thing was that the entire agency would disappear in just two years. And, no one at Hill Holliday or at Lowe or at IPG seemed ever to be held accountable. Frank's "frightful nervousness" about not starting an office and, rather, buying an established one turned out to be his Alamo and Fort Apache, and resulted in the removal of many scalps from the ad business in San Francisco.

One of the agencies that had been extremely interested in buying GMO was the French company Publicis. Maurice Lévy, the CEO, upon hearing that we were possibly for sale, wanted to meet with me. We had a pleasant dinner at the restaurant Rubicon in San Francisco.

At the time Lévy was embroiled in a major dispute with Foote, Cone & Belding and as such was unable to make any commitments to me. On the other hand, I was not impressed with the work that the Publicis agencies were doing and didn't really think we would be a good fit. But he argued to the contrary, and based on the way things ultimately turned out, he may have been right. One thing was for sure: we personally would have made even more money than we did if we had waited and sold to Publicis.

Maurice really wanted us. The day a small item appeared in the *Wall Street Journal* regarding Lowe's possible interest in GMO, I received a call from Maurice from Paris virtually begging me to wait and not to sell.

Who knows, maybe they would have cherished and nurtured the creative-oriented agency that we were and allowed it to grow by properly watering it and adding fertilizer? There might have even been a still bigger, much stronger Goldberg Moser O'Neill had we gone down the acquisition path with Publicis. But that's all water over the dam or piss down the drain.

Regardless, one of the proudest accomplishments for me was the ability to reward the GMO shareholders handsomely for their efforts over the years because of the deal we struck with Lowe and IPG. All but a few of the executives I started with were with me when we sold the agency in 1996.

The original shareholder group from the inception of the agency was made up of Brian O'Neill (co-creative director), Mike Moser (co-creative director), Mike Massaro (chief operating officer), Catrina McAuliffe (planning director), Camille Johnson (media director), Rosalinde Estes (office manager), Dennis O'Rourke (financial director), Tanya Stringham (art production director), MJ Rockers (print production manager), and Dave Woodside (associate creative director).

Along the way we added as shareholders a few other important players who had truly earned their bones: Sharon Rundberg (television production director), Yvonne Arnold (account management supervisor), Brian Quennell (associate creative director), Jim Noble (associate creative director), Hans Logie (associate media director), and Susan Pennel (associate media director).

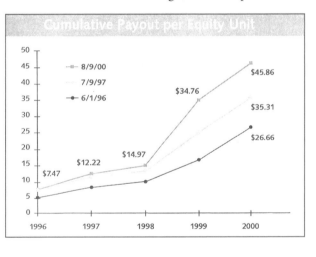

Of course the number of shares each of these people held varied dramatically but everyone received a quite unexpected reward. When we started the agency, we had projected that each share might be worth $26.66 a decade later if we achieved our goals. So, if an executive had, say, 3,000 shares, the stake would be worth about $80,000. However, we did better than that, delivering $45.86 per share, or in the example used here $138,000. All of the shareholders were smiling when I handed them their checks, which were 72 percent more than they had thought they were going to be. My final shareholders' dinner was held August 9, 2000, at Angelino's in Sausalito.

The last supper, or should I say my last supper, was held at Stars restaurant

Shareholders' dinner, clockwise from left: Yvonne Arnold, Catrina McAuliffe, Mike Massaro, Hans Logie, David Woodside, Tanya Hernandez, Susan Pennel, MJ Rockers, Mike Moser, Brian Quennell, Camille Johnson, FG, Rosalinde Estes, Sharon Rundberg, Brian O'Neill.

in San Francisco on December 7, 2000, with key executives and client friends. I had the rib-eye steak with foie gras butter, sherry-currant sauce, and white root purée. Delicious.

I was given a wonderful send-off speech from my indispensable chief operating officer Mike Massaro and an 18K gold Cartier watch with the inscription on the back "Good Enough 1982–2000."

Finally, Brian O'Neill prepared a video of some of the highlights of my 18-year career at Chiat/Day and Goldberg Moser O'Neill, entitled "The Fred Years." It was a bit tongue in cheek, but overall incredibly moving and greatly appreciated. I definitely had some lumps in my throat as the one-hour video played through. And now, when I occasionally watch it over again, the lumps are larger and last longer.

My last communication to this incredible group of talented and dedicated executives that I had had the pleasure of working with for all those years, and without whom I know that the agency would not have been nearly as successful, came on December 20, 2000. The subject was "That's That's That's All Folks."

> *Well guys this is it. Farewell . . . it's been swell. You have been*
> *a joy to work with and I'll miss the camaraderie, trust, energy,*
> *commitment and results that we all had in making our venture*
> *and adventure of GMO such a grand success.*

According to some the last thing a person says is how people will remember you. So try this on for size. Dennis will be distributing your final shareholder distribution checks. That's the bad news: it's the final one. But the good news is that there is included an incremental $.87 per share that hadn't been considered heretofore. One last hurrah!

Dennis will also be handing out the IPG shares which we have been waiting for along with your checks.

It was a good run. I wish you all the best in whatever you do from here on out. Thank you all again for your efforts.

Have a great holiday. Goodbye and love,

Fred

⊘ ⊘ ⊘

The following day I sent my "Very Last Email" to the entire organization. In it I expressed my surprise at how almost four decades had blown by since I had entered the advertising business.

I commented on how exciting and rewarding the business could be, and what made it so was the people. I had had the chance to work with more than an average number of exceptional beings, colleagues and clients alike. I was lucky enough to have hired, coached, collaborated with, and managed some of the best in the business. We had built a wonderful agency of scale: one that did some truly great advertising.

I urged everyone to stay focused on the goal of becoming known as a great national creative agency. Doing things, not just the ads, a bit more creatively than the next agency. Recognizing that it was a lot harder to be creative, and a creative agency, than the other kind.

Finally I expressed my principal regret in leaving, and that was having one unfulfilled expectation. The agency had done incredible creative work, first as Chiat/Day San Francisco and then as Goldberg Moser O'Neill. We did not, however, receive the full recognition deserved for a variety of reasons. It was my hope that going forward GMO would be in a position of creative leadership and recognized as such.

Unfortunately this was not to be, as the agency merged, changed its name, and closed its doors just a few years later.

GMO had become just another Army.

CHAPTER 18

LEAVING NOTHING TO CHANCE

In advertising the next most exciting and fun thing to work on after a Hollywood movie is working with a casino. In fact, my partner Brian O'Neill would do just about anything and go just about anywhere if there was a blackjack table, craps table, or one-armed bandit involved.

As for myself, I was destined to get involved in the casino industry, having spent a disproportionately large number of hours playing cards during my four years at the University of Vermont while everyone else was skiing. I ended up during my advertising years having the good fortune and good luck to have the opportunity to work with several gambling institutions.

My first experience was back when I was first promoted to account supervisor at Young & Rubicam New York and was assigned to the Commonwealth of Puerto Rico business. This account was composed of three parts, one of which was tourism and which relied heavily on the draw that the casinos at the hotels in San Juan provided. At the time Las Vegas was really the only other destination of importance as a competitor, as Atlantic City and the Indians hadn't come into their own yet.

I was excited to work on this account because it was interesting and exciting. It wasn't a Hollywood movie but it had its own cachet. And it was a lot of fun, at least for a while. The trips down to San Juan became a short-lived attraction and something I didn't look forward to after very long.

But I remember well my very first trip for my initial meetings with these clients. I had been booked into the Sheraton Hotel, which was not one of the newest but was still a relatively attractive place to stay. It was situated where the action was, on the strip between the ocean and the lagoon in downtown San Juan.

Our goal on this business was to attract people to come down to the lovely island. This was a challenge, as large areas of San Juan housed really poor people living in crates that were previously used to ship automobiles but now were covered with corrugated metal for roofs. And the ditches running in front of and behind these makeshift homes, filled with debris and other unspeakable matters, did not make for a tourism photo op. These kinds of pictures were regularly carried in the media in both San Juan and New York City, making Puerto Rico a less than ideal tourist destination. Except for the casinos and the gambling.

It didn't help either that as you strolled along the main streets you would pass cart vendor after cart vendor selling roasted meat of some kind. It was sort of like the Sabrett hot dog stands in New York City, which always made me wonder when was the last time the carts were cleaned. In Puerto Rico the answer was likely never, as everyone I knew who dared to sample this local fare came down with dysentery or something worse.

Yet the aroma of meat cooking emitted from these carts located every 30 yards or so was captivating. So much so that you would regularly see two or three people lined up ready to indulge. It was a wonderful demonstration of the real power of advertising in overcoming the most daunting issues, not dissimilar from trying to attract people to visit San Juan.

Somehow the government just couldn't focus on the negative effect that these kinds of things had on the ability to attract more tourists. Like the panoply of old car tires rising up in the lagoon like rubber tombstones, which many of the most luxurious hotels had as their front yards. The government preferred to look the other way.

Despite these enormous hurdles, we did some pretty good advertising over the years, and it definitely helped improve tourism to the island. Almost all of it relied heavily on the promise of the excitement and fortunes to be had with a bit of luck in the casinos. These clients did not want to take a chance on promoting very much more than the gambling the island offered.

One of the things I was most proud of was my creation of a Puerto Rico Tourism game. It was a board game that had the island laid out with all of the attractions you could visit: the rain forest, the surfing areas, El Dorado Country Club, the casinos, El Conquistador, and so forth. The idea was to roll dice and get from place to place, experiencing all the best tourism destinations. It was a wonderful promotional tool to reach the travel agent and the potential tourist as well.

When I first presented this idea as a part of one of our ad campaigns, everyone in the room loved it. These meetings tended to have scores of top to bottom bureaucrats, all of whom rose up from their chairs with accolades. "Brillante! Maravilloso! Estupendo!"

And when I presented the production estimate they all sat down. "Muy costoso! De mucho precio! También dinero!"

So much for my career as an inventor of games.

On my very first visit I arrived in San Juan at 1 a.m., checked in, and went directly to the casino. I had never been to a casino. I still had three hours to try my luck. The casino was fully packed and jumping. The crowd was buzzing and the slots were dinging. I grabbed a seat at a blackjack table and over the next two hours was able to amass what I considered a literal fortune:

$140. As luck would have it, I worked on this business for four years and never again walked away from a blackjack table a winner.

It wasn't until years later, at Goldberg Moser O'Neill, that we went to work for another gambling establishment, the Nugget Hotel and Casino. This was a client with whom we developed a particularly good relationship. It was with John Ascuaga, who owned the Nugget, located in Sparks, Nevada, a few minutes outside downtown Reno, in or possibly adjacent to a railroad-switching yard. We did his ads for five years.

John was quite a guy and personally ran his mega-hotel/casino along with his three grown children. We did some wonderful ads under the theme "Leave Nothing to Chance" where we utilized John as spokesman and representative for making sure everything was just so at the Nugget. It was a powerful idea because it came out of the reality of the situation.

We had John in the kitchen tasting the food to be certain it was excellent. He might be standing next to a customer who had just won a jackpot at a slot machine and he would be making sure all of the coins made it into the person's bucket. Or he might appear in one of the many swimming pools around the property. He would be taking the temperature of the water to be certain it was just right. In a business suit. Good ads all.

One of the reasons these ads got attention and motivated people was because, like many great advertising ideas, they were born of a truth that people could nod their heads and agree with. At the same time they were attention getting, humorous, and fun to watch.

The Nugget business expanded significantly as a result of these ads, and years and years after we had parted ways with John, the casino continued to use them. I actually think I saw an ad 15 years after the first one ran.

The reality was that John really did make sure things were the way they were, 24/7. He was relentless in his pursuit of excellence. He left absolutely nothing to chance.

John was also relentless in his pursuit of saving and/or making a dollar. I was at the casino one weekend, when the Sparks Hot August Nights was taking place as it did every year at that time. The classic cars and doo-wop music always drew a huge crowd to the area. At one point early in the evening, the power failed at the hotel. The lights flickered a few times and went out. People gasped. Some screamed. And there were those whose hands remained firmly glued onto the one-armed bandit they had been playing just when the lights went out.

The next thing I knew, there were 30 or so Nugget employees with dollies moving the slot machines that were located on the north side of the casino over to the south side. That is where some of the lights were still on, being powered by the hotel's own generator. The north side of the place had gone completely dark except for the myriad of flashlights beaming here and there as the workers toiled feverishly to move the machines.

They relocated approximately 150 machines, and hotel guests started again shoving coins in the slots just as soon as they could in the new locations. Some people stood by the slot machines they had been playing as the workmen lifted them onto dollies and marched side by side with them as they were being moved to their new location. Some even refused to remove their hands from the handles of the one-armed bandits they had been playing while the machines were being transported across the room.

It was then I knew for sure how inventive John Ascuaga really was and also just how profitable slot machines were. The average slot machine, which then cost around $5,000, paid itself back in about six weeks. John wanted to make sure they kept to that payback schedule.

I had heard that John had saved thousands of dollars by buying up some of the ugliest shiny violet comforters for all of the beds at the Nugget. So there was no way he was going to lose the revenue those slots produced when they went down even if just for a few hours.

⊘ ⊘ ⊘

Having had some considerable experience with casino advertising, we won another casino account, Ameristar Casinos, in 1997. It didn't hurt that my talented partner and creative director, Brian O'Neill, never lost his love of regularly testing his skills at blackjack, roulette, slots, and craps. Or any other form of gambling for that matter.

Ameristar was based in Las Vegas but had a half-dozen casinos around the country. They had only one in Vegas, which was 30 minutes from the Strip and catered mainly to locals. Its name was The Reserve. But the ones for which we were to advertise were located in places like Council Bluffs, Iowa, and Vicksburg, Mississippi.

A young, very hip fellow who was the number two guy, or acted like he was anyway, had briefed us. His name was John Raczka. John was very enthusiastic, energetic, and smart and had a terrific marketing sense. He gave us a complete background of the operation and its founder Craig Neilsen, whom we were soon to meet.

Neilsen was quite a guy. He had served as the Ameristar principal officer from its public inception in 1993 until his death in 2006. Before that, Ameristar had been a privately held casino hotel operation that consisted of two properties but which had now been grown to seven. Craig was a gifted executive in gaming, real estate development, and construction for over 25 years. He was honored as "Best Performing CEO" by the American Gaming Association one year and inducted into the Gaming Hall of Fame.

At our first meeting we met Raczka at the Ameristar corporate offices and were told that the meeting was going to take place at Craig's house. He ran all of his casinos from his large home in a gated community in a Las Vegas suburb.

So we packed everything up that we had already schlepped up to the corporate office and put it back into our rented cars and followed Raczka for 20 minutes through the side streets of Las Vegas to Neilsen's house. I had no idea Las Vegas even had any other streets except for the Strip.

We marched in, portfolios in hand, and were told to have a seat. We waited in the living room while various women went back and forth between what appeared to be a bedroom and the kitchen area. It was strange. This went on for an hour or more, when we were finally told that we should go in now.

There were five of us from the agency and we filed into what indeed was a bedroom, and a large one at that. There were half a dozen folding chairs arranged around the end and side of a large double bed. The room was uncomfortably warm and stuffy, and the air had a stale, almost foul odor that was pervasive.

In the bed, there was a head. That was all that was visible, as the sheets were pulled up to the head's chin. This was Craig Neilsen. We were taken aback, as we had been given little warning that this was what was in store.

We sat down and, uncomfortably and with a bit of awkwardness, said our hellos and introductions. Craig looked sideways and raised his left arm slightly to acknowledge each of us as we told him who we were.

We had a terrific meeting, as disconcerting as it was. Craig was only able to move his head a bit from left to right and back again and his one arm ever so little. He had been in a serious automobile accident years before, which left him paralyzed completely from the neck down. His brain was unaffected.

Craig was an extraordinarily bright and insightful person. During our time working together, I had some of the most rewarding conversations with him about advertising in general and what we were doing for Ameristar as well. He and John both responded well to our creative work and assigned us the account. In turn, they let us do some of the very best, award-winning advertising that we had ever done at the agency.

We maintained a strong business relationship for several years. Craig and John remain among the best clients with whom I was ever lucky enough to have worked. Brian O'Neill was ecstatically enthusiastic throughout the relationship. He won an unusual amount of times at his visits to Ameristar meetings. Or so he claims.

I was always very proud of the work we did for Ameristar and regularly showcased it whenever I could in new business and in any publicity about our agency. The campaign used outrageous people and situations to demonstrate that some things had no chance of success and others, like gambling at Ameristar, had a chance.

One example showed a pretty nine-year-old girl who was in a spelling bee and was given, by an off-camera voice, an absolutely impossible word to spell. She was dumbfounded and stared into the sky thinking for three-quarters of the commercial and then finally said very hesitantly, "T"? A card saying "No Chance!" flashed on the screen, replaced a moment later by another card saying "Chance!" The ad ended with the Ameristar logo.

Each of the commercials was designed to attract attention and generate awareness, and each one was more outrageous than the next. Another used X-ray photography of a school of sperm cells desperately swimming across the screen with some fast-paced western cattle drive–like music underneath. The tempo abruptly changed to a slow cowpoke meandering theme, and the screen panned over to one lone last sperm cell struggling along well behind all the others. Then the cards flashed "No Chance! Chance! Ameristar Casino."

The campaign had endless possibilities and we took advantage of them. We even had one with actual footage of Charlie Manson in prison performing a crazy lecture on camera, waving his arms and hands in karate-like motions in front of his face and speaking into the camera: "If you step into my circle, I will deal with you"! No Chance! Chance! Ameristar Casinos. We decided not to air this one.

We were able to significantly elevate awareness of Ameristar Casinos in the markets where we advertised with this work. That was the primary goal and also to give customers the confidence that they had a chance of winning. We won just about every creative award given for this work. And I had a doubly happy partner in Brian, indeed.

After we sold Goldberg Moser O'Neill to the Interpublic Group, I had a meeting in New York City with Phil Geier, then chairman of IPG. He expressed an interest in seeing our reel and I sent one on to him when I returned to San Francisco. A few days later the following letter arrived.

Fred

I loved your reel—although I had a bit of a hard time understanding the casino ones…

Nice job!
Phil

Whoever expected the CEO of an advertising company to understand great creative anyway?

⊘ ⊘ ⊘

My next encounter with casino advertising was very short, only one day. And that may have been one of the luckier times in my gambling and for that matter my ad career.

We flew to Las Vegas to meet with Sheldon G. Adelson. He's the fellow who made his first billion or so building and then selling Comdex, which was at the time the most important computer industry trade show.

A few years after my meeting with him, he was worth in the neighborhood of $28 billion and ranked third on the Forbes 400 richest Americans. This was a man who thought big. Really big. He had built Comdex into the premier computer trade show in the world. He had built the Venetian Resort Hotel Casino in Las Vegas, which opened with enough rooms to make it the largest in Vegas at the time. He built a humongous convention center that was attached to the Venetian. And more recently he opened a tower attached to the previous two facilities, bringing the rooms at the hotel to 8,000, plus making it the world's largest hotel.

Can you imagine going to your room 5678? And what if you had three martinis at dinner and ended up at 5768? You could get lost forever.

In 1999 when I met Sheldon, I went with a group of people including Brian O'Neill, who of course was very happy to be going to a casino; Nancy Hill, who was in charge of my new business; and Camille Johnson, our media director.

We were at Sheldon's place for the meeting. Sheldon's place was buried in the bowels of the massive Venetian hotel. And yet we were in a teeny-weeny, messy, and cluttered conference room situated adjacent to Sheldon's office, which I never got to compare.

We sat waiting for Sheldon to appear. His court arrived first, consisting of the three presidents, each of whom helped orchestrate various aspects of the casino operations: Mr. Goldstein, Mr. Weidner, and Mr. Stone. We made the obligatory introductions and handshakes and partook in small talk for half an hour, anticipating Adelson's arrival.

And then Sheldon appeared. He was a rather short and stocky fellow who was not dressed particularly well. His clothes were a bit rumpled and he had thinning orangey red hair that was askew. There were no trumpets when he entered the room and he didn't call for his pipe and he didn't call for his bowl, and there already were his fiddlers three, but as soon as he came in he called for his "tea."

"Where's my tea? Where's my tea?"

Say what? He wanted tea, iced tea. The tea soon appeared in a large glass pitcher filled with ice on a tray with one glass. Who would have thought that anyone else in the room might be thirsty?

The bearer of the tea set it down in front of Sheldon's chair at the end of the conference table, which looked a little like a throne. The chair, not the tea. It was a bit elevated above the rest of the chairs around the table. I presume that was so Sheldon could see more easily, and it provided him a perch from which he could look down at his devotees.

I opened the meeting and gave some introductory remarks about the agency and our philosophy and focus. Camille and Nancy followed and then Brian presented our creative work, some of which was outdoor, something it turned out that Sheldon was particularly interested in.

The formal presentation part of the meeting ended and Sheldon wanted to know what we thought of his ads. So Brian and I both gave our candid observations. But then Sheldon became defensive and explained why his ads were the way they were and particularly so with the outdoor. I ended up moving from one end of the table to sitting right next to Sheldon, albeit below him, as we continued to debate what was good outdoor and what was not.

I took umbrage with his headline, which was too long and boring. There was no creative concept. The colors used were garish. Another thing was the size of the type. Whoever did the Venetian outdoor used the same scale as if it were a print ad that you were holding 10 inches from your nose. It was impossible to read the copy from 10 feet much less from 100 feet on a road passing by at 30 miles an hour.

Sheldon didn't agree with any of this. And I refused to agree with his point of view and he refused to end the discussion with even a "let's agree to disagree." He wanted to continue to argue the finer points of outdoor advertising.

And argue we did. Our official meeting ended in less than two hours but I carried on with Sheldon for the rest of the day. All afternoon until Sheldon had to leave. During the course of which I noted that he consumed three full pitchers of iced tea. He never went to the bathroom even once and never offered any tea to me. After all there was only one glass.

Our debate was slowed numerous times by phone conversations with his wife. That evening they were traveling to Israel and she was concerned about this and that. They were going on one of his private planes. Just like John Travolta, he had a personal Boeing jet. Unlike John Travolta, he had three: a 767, a 747, and a 737.

The rest of the group from my agency and the other three Venetian executives got bored and one by one trickled out of the conference room as I sat nose to nose continuing the debate with Sheldon. It was no longer about getting an assignment and winning a piece of new business. Now it was simply about my integrity and defending a principle.

I can only surmise why Sheldon was inclined to spend the better part of a day arguing over the size of the type in an ad. The *New York Times* ran an article about him and calculated that his net worth increased in just a two-year period by $17.5 billion. That works out to $1 million an hour. That means he spent $6 million of his time arguing with me over some lousy print and outdoor ads. And they were lousy.

You might argue that in a relative way I wasted a similar amount of time, but it gave me some strange satisfaction carrying on in this manner knowing that it was highly unlikely that we were going to get a chance at an assignment. And if we ever did, it would surely be a nightmare trying to get approval for anything decent.

Gary Loveman, the CEO of Harrah's, was once quoted as saying, "Sheldon is a brilliant businessman, but he can be enormously difficult." He went on, "When he has a strong point of view, he pursues it very stridently."

I'll say!

If you take Sheldon's reported net worth, it was obvious that this man did not value his time, and he had some difficulty focusing on what the real issues facing him might be. Of course by the same token, on a relatively much lower plane, it seemed I didn't either.

At the end of 2008 the *Wall Street Journal* reported in an article entitled "Casino Empire Takes Fresh Hit" that Adelson lost a huge amount of his net worth and was now worth only $1.3 billion. At one point, it had been valued as high as $37 billion according to *Forbes*.

My last encounter with the casino industry happened when I got a call from Doug Sherfey, the gentleman who had been the advertising manager at the Nugget. We had had a very good relationship. He had moved on and wondered whether we had any interest in coming up to meet with his new employer, The Seven Feathers Casino in Canyonville, Oregon, located right there on Chief Miwaleta Lane.

This would be our first adventure with a casino owned by an Indian tribe. It had been originally the Oak Creek Bingo Hall and had morphed into this huge gaming hotel and resort.

With considerable interest and persuasion from Brian O'Neill, I agreed to meet with them. For some reason, if my memory is correct, and I know not why, I ended up being the only person that went to the first meeting. I remember, too, driving many hours, on roads that hardly had any sign of humanity or even animal life, to get to Miwaleta Lane.

When I arrived Doug greeted me and gave me a tour of the facility. It was impressive, particularly so being built in the middle of a giant forest. Even at two in the afternoon the parking lot was completely filled with trucks, cars, and RVs. And inside the action was going full steam. Lots of ding, ding, ding going on. Tons of people taking chances to win their fortunes.

I was to meet with a few of the marketing executives from the casino. I did and we had a pleasant enough meeting as I presented the agency, our philosophy, and some of the advertising and collateral work that we did. Of course I showed them our work for the Nugget and Ameristar.

I finished up and packed up my wares and headed back the long way I had come. I remember thinking that this could be a very long road to travel again.

When I got back to San Francisco I had a message on my desk from Doug saying, "Let's do some ads." Well OK! Brian was excited.

And we did some very clever ads, some of which were a little edgy, and none of which the Indians understood or liked or both. It may just as well have been that the head of the casino who attended the meeting didn't get it. She was a big, overbearing full-bodied Indian with a growl on her face from the get-go. And that face stayed with her for the entire creative presentation.

We thanked Doug, he said he was sorry, and we left as I saw him waving good-bye in the rearview mirror.

Last I saw, Seven Feathers had grown seven times. It had turned into a full-fledged resort with skiing, convention capabilities, and more. And they were running promotional materials using the line "Odds Are You'll Love Us."

This casino business didn't like to take many chances.

CHAPTER 19

SHORT BUT SWEET

My first experience with the ice cream category came when I attracted a local San Francisco retailer named Gelato Classico. They had nine stores and no money to advertise. Nevertheless, we did some really clever in-store posters and other promotional materials for them of which I was quite proud. We didn't learn much about the business except that the stuff tasted real good, having been given mostly free coupons for gelato in return for meaningful compensation.

Next, however, came Dreyer's Grand Ice Cream. Without a doubt one of the most important clients that I ever worked with. And yet in thinking about them I cannot find enough significant and amusing anecdotes to report in these memoirs. So this chapter on ice cream is short but sweet.

Dreyer's is a company that was started originally in 1928 but later on was purchased by two entrepreneurs, Rick Cronk and Gary Rogers. They maintained a hands-on approach even as the business grew to be a very substantial size. I had first pitched their business when I was with Chiat/Day and won a new product assignment.

Dreyer's was trying to develop a niche in the healthier yet indulgent arena and created this fruity good-tasting recipe, which they named Fruitola. The product's major point of difference was that it contained an abundance of fruit. We did some really terrific TV commercials that focused on the intense and bountiful fruitiness of the product.

One spot had an interview with a peach farmer whose crop had completely disappeared and he didn't know where it went. Another commercial had an interview with someone who grew blueberries and was being interviewed in an absolutely real situation. It was incredibly funny. In each of the commercials, all of the fruit always ended up being in the Fruitola.

All of the spots were somewhat outrageous and humorous and awareness generating. At the same time they drove home the strategic point of difference well and were fun. Apparently they or the product or both weren't fun enough.

The test markets for Fruitola turned out to be a failure for Dreyer's and resulted in a major loss of money for them and for the agency before the project was closed down. We only worked on it for 13 months.

I pleaded unsuccessfully with Dreyer's to compensate us somehow for the huge amount of time that we had spent. Of course, I had purposely over-invested given what I felt was a longer-term opportunity that this business represented for us. The fee that we had been given hardly covered the tolls for our people crossing the San Francisco–Oakland Bay Bridge to Dreyer's headquarters in Oakland.

I remember well my last plea bargain with Rick Cronk, sitting across from him at his desk, lodging every possible argument I could, to get some additional money out of him. Rick was very nice about it but he wouldn't agree to give us a nickel more.

No money but I did get a foothold. I think the effort with Rick paid off since we subsequently got another chance to work with Dreyer's when their entire business went up for review. Had it not been for our work on Fruitola and my begging for some compensation, we might not have been included. But we were, and we made it to the finals against Hal Riney & Partners but didn't win the business. And so once again we had invested still more money in Dreyer's.

Riney produced some pretty and pretty mushy and sweet advertising, nostalgic most would say. It was beautifully photographed, tugged hard at your heart and emotions, conjured up old-fashioned memories associated with ice cream eating, and of course had Hal Riney's mellifluous voice underneath as announcer, as did most of his other commercials for his clients. But it didn't work and Dreyer's got anxious for something that might.

Three times can be a charm. I had just formed Goldberg Moser O'Neill and after only a few months in business got still another chance to pitch the Dreyer's business that was put into review by their new marketing director, Bob Johnson. Bob was a very nice, smart, creative-oriented executive with considerable experience previously at Clorox, a place not well known for its acceptance of advertising creativity. I am guessing that Rick Cronk had put in a word for us to at least be considered in the review after our two previous encounters.

A very tough new business solicitation came down to Foote, Cone & Belding; Ketchum; and Goldberg Moser O'Neill, all of San Francisco. Without ever presenting a piece of creative work, we prevailed and ended up with our first major new business win as a new agency. I always treated Dreyer's with the greatest of respect and importance since it was our first "child," so to speak.

And Dreyer's treated us very well. They were nice clients, gentlemen at all times. They paid us a handsome compensation that soon more than made up for what we had lost on Fruitola. Importantly, the advertising was one of the top priorities for the company and therefore Bob, Gary Rogers, and Rick Cronk all participated in the process of development and approvals. They encouraged us to create fresh and edgy work and they approved it for production.

These entrepreneurial executives knew the power of advertising and believed in it. And they were willing to put their money where their mouth was, and they did. They kept a very high bar on the quality of the creative work, which was terrific. What was also great was that they made sure that the special freezer they provided at the agency was stocked full of Dreyer's flavors every week, 52 times a year.

In return for all this, we made sure that our best creative people gave every Dreyer's assignment the utmost priority. This wasn't really all that hard since this was a business that could score creative awards. All the work was carefully supervised and often refined by Brian O'Neill, creative partner supreme. The body of work was generally outstanding with just a few hiccups along the way.

Commercial after commercial broke new ground. We had a woman sinking her entire face into an open gallon of Dreyer's, expressing her incredible desire for it. We had an infant that was barely able to walk stand up and start break dancing over his excitement for the ice cream. We had a senior jumping for joy when it was announced that he was about to get a bowl of Dreyer's, and an old lady lifting up a car to retrieve a gallon that had rolled underneath. It went on from there.

Our strategic positioning was that the Dreyer's brand was not just your regular ice cream. This supported its premium price and the exquisite product quality. Most importantly it developed the emotional and psychological connection that so many people had with ice cream, ice cream memories, and eating ice cream. Our advertising oozed with emotional over- and undertones.

It separated us clearly from the competition, which was mainly the people from back East with a similar-sounding name.

That would be Breyers, which stayed tried and true to a narrow-minded rationale, a product-focused message, and equally dull and boring

commercials, which I believe emanated from my old agency, Young & Rubicam New York. "Breyers: Made with Real Vanilla Beans." Camera panning up and down the outside of the carton and over the ice cream. Snooze!

All of our commercials drove home the same point, having people do "un-normal" things when Dreyer's was going to be served. All were designed first to attract attention and generate awareness and then to support the consumer desire aspect. They also recognized a critical point that most ice cream advertising didn't. Eating ice cream was a huge reward, it was a pleasure, and it was fun. So why shouldn't the advertising be the same?

Interestingly, when we were pitching the account, we prepared a house ad that we sent over to Dreyer's, which asked the very same question. Wouldn't it be great if the people who saw your advertising got as excited as the people who ate your ice cream?

House ad created to pitch Dreyer's.

It all worked. It all worked incredibly well. Dreyer's sales took off not long after we began our campaign, "Evidently, it's not your normal ice cream," and didn't stop growing for years and years. Share of market continued to grow as well, mostly at Breyers' expense, and the company prospered. And so did we, as the advertising budget grew and so too did our revenue.

The campaign ended up on the *Wall Street Journal's* list of outstanding TV campaigns one quarter after the other, which was a real accomplishment when you consider the size of the budgets of the other companies that appeared on that top 10 list, including Budweiser, McDonald's, Nissan, and Coca-Cola. We were spending a fraction of what they were.

It was a great client/agency relationship that helped launch our agency at the start. And because of the sales success and the creative success, it allowed us to attract that many more clients who were interested in a different, more edgy creative product.

Our work for Dreyer's won virtually every creative award at one time or another: Cannes Lions, Clios, One Shows, and more. Somehow I ended up with two of the most important ones in my possession: two Lions from the International Advertising Film Festival in Cannes. They sit on my desk, now serving as wonderful bookends to *Webster's Dictionary* and *Webster's Thesaurus* as well as (not that I'm religious) a very old Hebrew bible that has been in the Goldberg family since the late 1800s and which I had recently restored.

The great partnership with Dreyer's went on for a decade. Ten productive years. But like most things in the ad business, situations change. For reasons never fully explained, Bob Johnson was pushed out and replaced by Tyler Johnston. The Johnston with a T then pushed us out and replaced us with another agency of his choice, a situation not uncommon in the business.

During our time with Dreyer's I always made sure to meet with CEO Gary Rogers regularly, usually over lunch. Maybe three or four times a year. It was pleasant, and I would always ask him how we were doing before each lunch ended and if there was anything else we could do or that we should do to make things better in any way. Gary inevitably said the same thing to me at every single lunch. And that was, "Fred, as long as sales keep going up everything is fine."

He fibbed! It turned out not to be quite true. Politics and backstabbing sometimes play a role. Actually all too often politics and backstabbing are the deciding factors in an agency/client relationship. And its demise.

In any event, when I look at the work before and after Goldberg Moser O'Neill, no other Dreyer's ad agency ever came close to producing the kind of work that we did or having the sales success as a direct result of the advertising as did we.

It was an incredible symbiotic relationship. We helped Dreyer's dramatically increase their sales and share of the ice cream business with our work. They in turn allowed Goldberg Moser O'Neill to do some of its very best work, which attracted many other clients to the agency and led to our own great sales success.

Dreyer's eventually sold out to Nestlé, and I suspect that Gary and Rick made gobs of money on the transaction. Goldberg Moser O'Neill eventually sold out to Interpublic and made gobs of money on the transaction, probably fewer gobs, however.

I always remembered that Rick Cronk used to say he couldn't imagine a better way to have to go to work every day and earn a living than making and selling ice cream. And I can't imagine anything too much better than having had to create ice cream advertising for the Dreyer's people.

And making money doing it.

CHAPTER 20

HELL HOLLIDAY

When I sold Goldberg Moser O'Neill in 1996, I had every intention of staying engaged in the ad business for the foreseeable future. And two years later, when we made the decision to move our headquarters from 77 Maiden Lane to 600 Battery Street, I still felt the same way.

Part of the incentive was that I wanted a chance to construct what was to be a unique architectural expression designed especially for Goldberg Moser O'Neill and the way we did business. And then to actually operate in what I hoped would be a spectacular environment. It turned out to be almost a two-year project from start to finish, but we succeeded in accomplishing something special in the end.

We moved into these new quarters in 2000. The excitement was evident throughout the agency. Everyone was psyched about having such a special and unique space in which to develop the kind of creative work that we did and to be able to operate as an unexampled advertising agency.

It wasn't until someone at IPG suggested that Goldberg Moser O'Neill be merged with Hill Holliday based in Boston that my interest in staying around began to wane. This took place soon after we moved into 600 Battery Street.

Hill Holliday was run by one of its founders, Jack Connors, and was another agency IPG had acquired. The benefits of the combination for Hill Holliday were obvious. They would gain a well-established highly creative agency with an established client base. They would have an instant presence on the West Coast and the accompanying potential that Connors sought.

The merged company would create a new agency with total billings of more than a billion dollars and a bicoastal operation with 900 employees. It would have greater creative firepower and resources, and the combination would allow both operations to be more competitive. There were few conflicts between existing clients.

The benefits for Goldberg Moser O'Neill were a bit more opaque. We already represented some big national clients and really didn't need any additional national resources. Our weakness was in serving a few clients internationally. In theory there would be a stronger management group, a succession plan, and an insurance policy in case I should get run over by a rickshaw or leave.

There was one obvious and significant hiccup with the marriage. Hill Holliday was not a particularly creative-oriented agency. They, however, thought of themselves as a highly creative one.

They had clients that we at GMO would largely not consider even talking to regardless of their size: Coopers & Lybrand, John Hancock, Lotus Development, among others. The advertising for these clients was mediocre. Their agency had a very different approach to client service (i.e., a wee bit more service oriented, a tad less product oriented). Their client management style was unlike ours in character and kind. Their CEO was a very different kind of guy than me to be sure. Their culture was way distinctly dissimilar.

Other than this, it was a marriage made in heaven.

Hill Holliday's most renowned creative work seemed to be what it did for Nissan's Infiniti when that automobile was first introduced. It featured :30 commercials using a locked-on camera focused on a rock. Nothing but 30 seconds of a rock. Motionless, nothing moving, not anything, just a rock sitting there. I'm not sure there was even music, maybe only the tweeting of a bird once every few seconds.

Or another with much more action and excitement. There was actually some motion to be detected. Tiny little waves on a very placid lake, lapping ever so gently, one after the other, against a beach for an excruciatingly long 30 seconds. That was it. Thirty seconds of lapping waves is a long time. There may have been some subtle peaceful Yanni-like music playing, but as I recall it was just the sound of the waves.

A rock, a beach, a wave. It was meant to reflect the strategic position of the Infiniti brand, which was Zen-like and spiritual. Buying an Infiniti was a quiet, comfortable, peaceful process. Haaaammmm. Haaaammmmmmm.

Well, at least they didn't have to use the running footage of cars that is mandated by most car manufacturers and/or the mandatory legal announcements crammed in at the end. They must have saved a fortune on producing the spots as well, and I wouldn't be surprised if that was one of the reasons the clients bought into the whole rock and wave idea to start, or lock and roll production.

I hated this campaign. It may have been different but it was not creative and was boring and it wasn't motivating in my opinion. More to the point it didn't move the metal. I mean, how could it? Buying a car is an exciting and extraordinary event for most everyone. This advertising wasn't exciting and didn't even show the car.

The client must have agreed, since they fired Hill Holliday not long after this campaign started running. Lo and behold they ended up giving the business to Chiat/Day Los Angeles, which was already responsible for the main Nissan auto account.

Ironically, too, we had unsuccessfully participated in the pitch for the Infiniti business when we were still Chiat/Day San Francisco. We had developed and made a really great presentation, but at the time the client decided they didn't want both car marques at the same agency regardless of our promises to completely keep the offices and personnel separate along with everything else except the moon. That was when they ended up selecting Hill Holliday. They changed their minds about having the same agency when the wave advertising went on the rocks.

The idea of getting Hill Holliday and Goldberg Moser O'Neill together overlooked that agency mergers have traditionally been proved to fail, time after time, as egos clash, agendas play out, and cultures collide. And that is certainly what ended up happening here.

Jack Connors seemed very eager to make the merger happen. He desperately wanted to be perceived as a bigger national agency player, and this representation in California accomplished that. And who wouldn't have wanted such a sweet deal. He didn't have to pay even a penny for GMO and all its billings.

It seemed he wanted the merger so much that someone from the Boston Hill Holliday office leaked the story to the *San Francisco Chronicle*, which in turn ran a long piece on April 18, 2000, that exposed the plot. No one at the paper ever contacted me or anyone else at GMO before running the story, and it caught us, and our clients, by complete surprise.

We, of course, hadn't alerted any of our clients or our employees to what was being contemplated. It was very bad form, and we looked really duncical to our clients. We also had a lot of employees who weren't enthralled about the way it was handled and what it meant for GMO.

The breach caused endless and unnecessary problems, and even after we put out the forest fire we had to deal with the continuation of many hot spots. We were on damage control for weeks. I sent a note out to the entire agency attempting to explain the situation, although I was clearly on the defensive. It covered the following issues.

- The union was a very positive thing and one that should help better compete and grow by better serving our clients with additional resources and more career opportunities for employees.

- Jack Connors of Hill Holliday was a man of his word and very much wanted the venture to be a success.

- GMO would become a creative beacon for the newly formed company.

- Our agency would not be considered an outpost.

- No "team" from Hill Holliday was to arrive from Boston to take over the agency.

- I was not retiring at the end of the year but this provided for a management succession for when I finally would.

Little of this turned out to be true, and I would leave the agency in a few months.

So then out came founder/chairman/CEO/president/king of Hill Holliday, Jack Connors, to meet me and to provide damage control about the arrangement. He and I were to meet for dinner at the San Francisco Ritz-Carlton, his hotel of choice. Jack was an hour late arriving at the table, for which he was unapologetic. He did, however, give me a huge energetic handshake when he arrived at the table.

"Fred, how are you? Great to see you."

Right!

Jack was an upbeat, smart, and likable enough fellow. It always felt a bit like he was running for office with his big grand smile, his firm and aggressive handshake, and the big bear hug that he reserved for a few.

Jack had proven he could build a good-size agency although they had had some troubles over the years. Unfortunately, he happened to be a guy that smiled a lot and appeared to stay discreetly away from firing ranges. Stray bullets can be harmful. It didn't matter which firing range. Instead, he sent in his lieutenants to do the dirty work on the front lines. In my short tenure of knowing him, I found him an intellectually dishonest chap. That aside, he might have made a splendid candidate for mayor of Boston.

We had a pleasant enough dinner once it got going, and I was reasonably convinced that when we merged I should stay on for at least a while. That would have been beyond 2000, which was the end of my five-year contractual obligation to IPG that had been part of the agreement in selling GMO.

With the GMO and Hill Holliday merger, the idea was for me to become the chairman of the combined companies and be based in San Francisco. Or so I thought. This was a role that would not require me to be involved in the day-to-day management, which is what I wanted. Jack was to be the CEO of the merged entity.

I decided to give the merger a chance and stay on in this new role as chairman. It was my understanding that they understood I no longer wanted to function as CEO and have that operational responsibility. While Connors was aware of this and needed to take on that role, he never flat-out agreed to or even acknowledged it.

He was always kind of slippin' and slidin' around the issue. I thought he was just humoring me to buy some time. He finally decided to leave the day-to-day management of the San Francisco agency to a woman I had hired to be a new business person.

In addition he decided to send in various people from Boston to "help" her do the job in finance and personnel and other areas as well. These people were to commute back and forth between San Francisco and Boston. He also identified a senior account gentleman, Terry Carleton, to "oversee" the efforts. Terry was a trusted soldier of Jack's. No Brutus he.

All of these folks provided Jack with an ongoing conduit and audit of "what was going on" information, which I believe was one of the prime reasons they were installed in the first place.

There was much hubris involved in all this. I mean, Mike Massaro, who was the key agency person responsible for two-thirds of the agency income and truly knew his accounts inside and out, never even received one call from Jack. And Terry Carleton spent a grand total of maybe 10 minutes with him before Mike retired officially from the agency and left.

This all turned out not to be a terribly effective way to run the agency, as you might imagine. And the politics of the situation with these knights out in the battlefield in San Francisco and King John on his throne back in Boston were remarkable, even laughable. Most of this scenario generally took place without any of my involvement, as I had become a footless chicken or, maybe more aptly, a castrated bull.

I wasn't pleased with the situation, as I effectively had lost virtually all of my influence and also frankly had little to do. Once the final details were put on the new space, what I was doing became even less. There were a lot of cooks in the new kitchen, and the stew was getting burnt and it started smelling bad. It was utterly painful for me to watch what was happening to a company I had built into a successful, quality, highly creative advertising agency.

One particularly colorful event was the catalyst that resulted in making up my mind to throw in the towel and leave. It turned out that my timing was impeccable, as it came just as the economy began peaking, and while technology and dot-com businesses were still important, they were beginning to blow up. Moreover, the advertising business, as we knew it for the past hundred years, was about to implode and change dramatically. I wish I could say I knew all of this, or any of this for that matter. All I knew was the agency wasn't being run very well any longer and I didn't want to be a part of it.

I was away on what turned out to be my last vacation. That's the one just before one takes the "ultimate vacation." Retirement! I was in Italy for three weeks with Jeri. I was deliberating whether to leave or not to leave. That was still a question. Upon returning to San Francisco and my first day back in the office, the question was answered. Leave!

In my absence King John had made a crusade to Babylon by the Bay accompanied by a few people from his Court at Boston. During the expedition John met with each of the key executives in the GMO office. In turn, and in all his wisdom and benevolent splendor, he blessed them and bestowed upon them all raises fit for a king.

Some of them were so large they weren't fit at all. But the GMO executives who received these tributes were happy and didn't want to look a gift horse in the face. And so, too, King John was happy and he returned to Boston from this evangelistic crusade triumphantly thinking he had effectively secured his second Court in the far lands in the West of his newly won kingdom.

When I discovered what had occurred, without my prior knowledge or consultation, my eyes widened and my eyebrows rose up to the front of my slowly receding hairline, and remained there. And when I heard the size of some of the tributes that had been granted, I was stunned.

They were obscene, exorbitant, stupid, and unnecessary. I felt they surely would disrupt the performance reward system we so successfully had in place for many years, and more importantly they ultimately had to seriously impact the profitability of the office. We had been a company that had achieved extraordinary margins and made extraordinary profits all along the way. The raises were not sustainable without a tsunami of new business gains, which never came.

Among the people who received these "king's ransoms" was one of the management supervisors. She was a very nice and hardworking lady, but far from an essential player in the grand scheme of things. She was not even in the GMO management group.

This gal had been responsible for three accounts, each of which was leaving or had left the agency. Why Jack decided to include her among his chosen subjects was a mystery. She was, however, a fairly attractive blonde with a nice pair of legs.

I rang Jack up on the tele and asked him what the hell he was doing and why hadn't he at least discussed it with me beforehand. I mean, I know he knew that I didn't want to continue on in the day-to-day operations but this seemed important enough to have included me at a minimum for consultation. He might have gotten some advice that was useful and he still could have ignored whatever I said to him.

Connors brushed off my concerns and my calamity when I said to him that what he was doing could single-handedly possibly wreck the profitability of the office for the foreseeable future. I asked him, too, what he was going to do for his next act with these people, and I told him whatever it was he would be doing it by himself. With that I said good luck and good-bye and hung up.

When Jack realized I was leaving for real, he scrambled and promptly made two critical decisions. He put Terry Carleton in charge of the GMO operation and he promoted Nancy Hill, GMO new businessperson, to president. He had her report directly to him, sort of, with Terry in charge of the operation. Both of these decisions would come back to haunt him and the agency.

Terry Carleton, one of Jack's Boston gang members, would commute from Boston every week, arriving in San Francisco Monday morning and leaving Friday. This wasn't a terrible plan, as I had commuted several times in my career in the past and knew it was doable. However, it took fortitude and motivation, neither of which Terry had. He began to shorten his stays not very long after he started the routine.

Even when Terry started making the trips each week, in my opinion he was never truly committed and never stepped into a leadership role. His main concern was catching that flight back to Boston.

And who could blame him? That's where his wife, kids, and, I was told, a nice large house were situated. Not to speak of his "real" job at Hill Holliday in Boston where he was still actively responsible for several accounts and various managerial duties.

Every now and then Terry would cruise by my office and stick his head in, interrupting my reading of the *New York Times*, and say, "Hello, how are you?"

And I would say, "Hello, how are you?"

We never discussed anything that had to do with the agency that I had built and knew something about. This may sound like sour grapes but it really wasn't. I just thought it was kind of chuckleheaded not to at least hear what my point of view might have been on some of the issues that they were facing. But he and Jack wanted to run the Kingdom their way. And they did just that.

Before all the merger talk I didn't know Jack Connors at all. And I had met him only on three subsequent occasions once the idea of merging started percolating and thereafter. The first time was the aforementioned dinner at the Ritz. The second time, after the merger became public, was when he wanted to assemble and address the entire office in San Francisco. The final time was my uninvited and unexpected appearance in Boston at a meeting he had called.

I had, however, done some background checking with people who knew him. It turns out he had a history of strange and odd behavior.

For example, after it had been agreed to move forward with the merger, Jack asked me if it would be appropriate for him to call our clients. One of the few times he asked my advice. I assured him absolutely, a good idea. He asked for a recommended list, which I provided for each client with all the appropriate contact information. As far as I knew, he never made one single call to any one of those clients for as long as I was still at the agency.

At another point Jack decided to invite a bunch of the GMO executives to a gathering in Boston at Hill Holliday. This was a nice gesture to be sure but he invited 18 people. I asked him who was going to pay for this and he told me that it would be an office expense, meaning a San Francisco office expense. Jack didn't cotton too well to my pesky questions.

I wasn't one of the 18 people who were invited but I showed up anyway. Jack was quite surprised to see me and I got a much better insight into his character than I would have otherwise. He seemed to always have an agenda, and his actions during this visit confirmed a lot of what I had read about him in the press and heard from others in the industry that knew him. He belonged in politics. Most of his behavior was, in addition to being strange, rather political.

Fortune magazine a few years earlier had done a review of America's toughest bosses, and Jack was named one of the featured seven. It was reported that he could be a bit bizarre and calculating: "At one meeting in the mid-1980's, an executive gave him some sales projections that Connors didn't like. Connors started kicking the man's chair violently—with the executive still in it. Recalls a manager who was present: 'There was Jack kicking the chair while this guy hung on like a fighter pilot.'" In the same article employees pointed out that he was a thoroughgoing SOB—"cold, calculating, and mean."

The press also provided insight from Hill Holliday ex-executives regarding a standard and recurring theme, in Jack's own words: "I do everything and no one else does anything around here."

Thus explaining completely why I wasn't supposed to have questioned him about giving out all those raises.

Then one day a command arrived from across the land, and it was made known that a reduction in the number of executive heads would be required because of poor profit expectations. In other words a mass beheading was required.

Some of those to face the guillotine were the very same executive knaves who had not very long ago been so generously enriched and who had pledged their allegiance to King John. The business had begun to falter. After this purge, those who had not been executed but had also received earlier humongous tributes were asked to take reductions in their take-home pay. And they did, albeit unwillingly.

Fortunately I had left the Kingdom before having to witness firsthand the effects of this pogrom.

From the beginning of the merger talk, it was quite apparent that one of the most important things to Hill Holliday, that is, Jack Connors, was to get the Hill Holliday name up on the marquee in San Francisco, on Battery Street. The first indication of this was the preliminary discussions I had regarding what the name of the newly merged office was to be once it was decided to combine the two operations.

I felt Goldberg Moser O'Neill/HHCC was a good and fair choice. Or Goldberg Moser O'Neill/HH. He felt Hill Holliday Connors Cosmopulos/GMO was better, if even a larger mouthful. Simply listing everyone's name alphabetically seemed to be another fair alternative, although it didn't solve the problem of which entity was more recognizable in San Francisco by any means. Connors Cosmopulos Goldberg Hill Holliday Moser O'Neill.

And what a mouthful some of these names would have been. "We have to meet at Connors Cosmopulos Goldberg Hill Holliday Moser O'Neill this afternoon." I don't think so.

Over time, many advertising agencies seem to get reduced to just a series of initials and letters: Y&R, JWT, DDB, BBDO. And so we might have become CCGHHMO. KaKaGuhhMo!

Some of the other names kicked around included Goldberg Moser O'Neill/Hill Holliday Connors Cosmopulos; Hill Holliday Connors Cosmopulos/Goldberg Moser O'Neill; Goldberg Moser O'Neill/Hill Holliday; Hill Holliday/Goldberg Moser O'Neill; Goldberg Moser O'Neill Hill Holliday Connors Cosmopulos; GMO/HH; HH/GMO; Velocity GMO; Velocity HH.

I have no idea where the ones with "Velocity" came from but I assure you not from San Francisco. In hindsight maybe Velocity would have been a good name, as it foreshadowed just how fast the new Hill Holliday office could disappear from the Bay Area.

We settled on GMO/Hill Holliday. This retained the thing that most people on the West Coast were familiar with, GMO, and added the new element, Hill Holliday. From my point of view the agency would continue to be known as GMO, which I presumed they realized too, as they would soon surgically remove that vestigial appendage from the name and become simply Hill Holliday.

There was never any discussion about changing the agency name back in Boston, which was to remain Hill Holliday Connors Cosmopulos. The entire discussion about the name was just a short-term appeasement, it seemed.

So the new signage went up over the front door in 2000 as GMO/Hill Holliday. It was soon changed again in 2001, after I had left the company, slicing off the GMO.

I thought this was one incredibly stupid move since it was GMO that had established the major advertising presence and reputation over a long period of time on the West Coast and even nationally. But King John wanted it otherwise, sacrificing the smart business decision for a dumb emotional one.

And while I thought it was the wrong move, it didn't bother me really as they had already removed or lost most of the good things that Goldberg Moser O'Neill had stood for and which had been built up over the years, as well as most of the clients.

When the sign outside the building was first changed to broadcast the new name, GMO/Hill Holliday, no doubt Nancy Hill took some unanticipated pride in this development since she was to be the president of the agency. Not every hired executive gets to have his or her name included on the door of an established firm. Nevertheless, I suspect that her euphoria faded somewhat quickly, as did the agency.

Nancy Hill as the anointed "president" was faced with many issues with which she was unable to cope in moving the agency forward. Plus who knew what her real authority was and to whom she actually reported?

In my opinion one of the most important reasons why agency mergers and acquisitions fail is that the acquiring entity will always put itself ahead of the "acquiree." In this case Hill Holliday wasn't even buying the entity; it was a Lowe and IPG decision to merge them with GMO and it didn't cost Hill Holliday anything. So it's my opinion that the merger was treated with about as much concern and respect as most things you get for free.

Retired from the agency for a year but still occasionally looking at *AdWeek*, I came upon a short piece headlined "'Bidder Days': Hill Holliday Makes Like eBay." Nancy Hill, then still president of what became of the agency, decided to have an employee auction to rid the place of "stuff" no longer felt of use.

This was a strange way of announcing the move to the much smaller office space of what was formerly Lowe & Partners in San Francisco, which had recently disappeared from the San Francisco ad scene, leaving that space unoccupied and available.

In effect the auction was a public celebration of the deconstruction of an ad agency. Dan Bellack, the old-time San Francisco adman, once wrote about how agencies were committing "cultricide." Well, here was one great example of it. If there was a time to whisper, this might have been it. Whoever said there is no such thing as bad publicity was wrong.

Some of the things auctioned off were parts of the Goldberg Moser O'Neill culture and heritage no longer considered vital or even useful. They had already gotten rid of the GMO part of what started out as GMO/Hill Holliday. Now they were dispensing the remnants.

Among the items was a stunning Helmut Newton photography book entitled *SUMO* that had formerly sat just outside the main conference room on a special rack, as an art piece. When I bought it, I felt it was a wonderful reflection and inspiration of the level of creativity that Newton brought to his craft and a reminder for all of us at the agency. The book was $1,500 new and sold for a song.

They also auctioned off a pool table that I had originally bought and paid $10,000 for, for my home, but which I had brought to Goldberg Moser O'Neill when we first moved into the new 600 Battery Street space. Someone should have asked if I wanted it back or at least offered a 6 percent "commish" on the item when they sold it.

Other articles were auctioned off, many of which had comprised elements of the special GMO culture that had been built over the years and were now being publicly eliminated one by one.

When I read about all this, I had a sad feeling but should have expected it. During my very last week at the agency I was sitting in my office doing nothing. I had become like the GMO name, an appendix, a vestigial organ. But I had already come to terms with leaving and it was actually OK with me.

I had time to devote toward constructing my leisure plans, and for the first time in my business life I was able to regularly leave the agency at 3:30 every day. And I did.

They raised a grand total of $3,500 from the auction that day. And they got some "ink" in *AdWeek* celebrating their virtual implosion. They gave the money to charity, which was a nice gesture. Not very long later they closed down Hill Holliday in San Francisco for good, which was not so nice.

One day I was having lunch at the Globe Restaurant located directly across the street from the entrance to 600 Battery Street. I was looking out the window at the then sign for Hill Holliday, and lo and behold it appeared that the GMO/Hill Holliday name seemingly had been returned. Not!

Turns out that the previous name on the signage had never been completely removed but rather, no doubt to save a few dollars, they had pasted or painted over the old one. With the weather and such, the surface had given way, causing the old Goldberg Moser O'Neill initials to bleed through. And there it was, GMO/Hill Holliday.

Was this a spiritual message of some sort? I think so.

Hill Holliday San Francisco was forced to give up the wonderful building and space as they suffered client loss after client loss. We had originally designed the building to accommodate about 350 people and had almost 300 at the time we moved into the space, leaving a cushion for growth.

It turned out there was no need to ever worry about where to put any additional people. Hill Holliday went the other way. They shrank down to about 60 people, vacated 600 Battery Street, and moved down a few blocks into the old Lowe San Francisco offices. Once there, they went to 40 people, then 10, and then . . . poof!

In 2003 John Geoghegan, who had become president of Hill Holliday San Francisco, announced they would cease being a full-service agency and would concentrate only on media planning and buying. The only accounts that remained from the GMO days were Silicon Graphics, Quantum, and Beringer wines. What had been GMO was almost all gone.

After 33 years in the advertising business, I was at a point where I was truly not unhappy about leaving. The entire situation with Hill Holliday had helped me accelerate my departure, but I recall how it really depressed me when I walked out the front entrance at the end of 2000 for the last time.

Ad Age reported on my departure, September 11, 2000: "Goodbye to helm of good Bay agency."

On June 18, 2001, *AdWeek* reported that a Gallup Poll ranked advertising the lowest of all professions in

Goodbye to helm of good Bay agency

Fred Goldberg, the irascible gadfly of San Francisco advertising, exits at yearend as chairman of **GMO/Hill, Holliday**. "It's about time," Goldberg says, and some of his rivals and former employees would agree, though Goldberg actually meant he's going to be savoring the moment. Goldberg—the account guy on creative landmarks such as **Apple's** "1984" spot as well as financial successes including **Teddy Ruxpin**, **Dell** and **Cisco**—is one of a group of movers who put San Francisco creative on the map. Others such as **Jack**

terms of truth and honesty. It was good to be smelling the roses, which I was literally doing in my backyard, where 30 varieties were in bloom.

Our name disappeared from the ad scene, but Goldberg Moser O'Neill left a great legacy. We had taken something and we had shaped it and we grew it into something very unique. We had attracted an extraordinary group of talented people who had produced an incredible body of superb creative work. We had been unusually successful in growing to over $500 million in client billings. We generated tons of profit. We made our key executives far wealthier than they would have been otherwise. And we were able to do some outstanding advertising that really worked in the marketplace.

If someone else were to make these claims, particularly in the ad business, I would call it company "wee-wee." But in this case I know it's all true.

Just a few years after the merger of Goldberg Moser O'Neill and Hill Holliday, what started out as a $500-plus million billing agency went to zero. The agency that had at its peak almost 300 people went to zippo. The Goldberg Moser O'Neill flag (No Clown) that had so proudly flown first at Maiden Lane and then at 600 Battery had been lowered many months ago but still hangs in my garage in Belvedere, California. And my final payment from IPG for the purchase of the agency remains in my bank account.

The Hill Holliday folks in San Francisco had one hell of a ride. A long run for a short slide. Or, maybe better said, a short run for a short slide. There were some good clients and hundreds of good employees lost along the way. As the agency played out the end of its last year gasping in San Francisco, it must have been a "Hell of a Holliday."

Goldberg Moser O'Neill had had a highly unique culture where we celebrated the intellectual level of individuals regardless of their station at the organization. We had created an atmosphere where most people truly did strive for excellence. We had the majority of our people believing that they were actually smarter and better than those that worked at other agencies. And they may well have been.

Over the years we produced a body of work that rivaled that of the very best creative agencies in the country, including even our predecessor parent Chiat/Day. We had won many awards for our work at Cannes, the One Show, the Clios, the San Francisco Show, and more. Our work helped build some of what became the most important businesses in America and even the world. Companies like Dell, Dreyer's, Oracle, Cisco, and Kia.

In the advertising business the work speaks for itself. All you have to do is look at it and make an assessment. I was very proud of our work and what we had achieved.

And I still am.

My final executive action was to sign the official Certificate of Dissolution for Goldberg Moser O'Neill, required by the State of California. I packed up the remaining personal items in my office, picked my Ghurka shoulder bag off my desk for the very last time, and walked quietly toward the front door. I said good-bye to the receptionist. No one else saw me leave.

And so ended my career in advertising.

00636033

CERTIFICATE OF DISSOLUTION

Fred Goldberg and Brian O'Neill certify that:

1. We constitute all of the directors now in office of Goldberg Moser O'Neill, a California corporation.

2. The corporation has been completely wound up.

3. The corporation's known debts and liabilities have actually been paid.

4. The corporation's known assets have been distributed to the persons entitled thereto.

5. The tax liability will be paid on a taxes paid basis.

6. The corporation is dissolved.

We further declare under penalty of perjury under the laws of the State of California that the matters set forth in this certificate are true and correct of our own knowledge. Executed on December 21, 2000.

Fred Goldberg

Brian O'Neill

PART II

THE BELIEFS,

THE OBSERVATIONS,

THE DERANGEMENTS

CHAPTER 21

THE HOUSE THAT FRED BUILT

I JOINED CHIAT/DAY IN 1982, and Jay Chiat had not very long before that purchased two San Francisco agencies: Hoefer Dieterich & Brown and Regis McKenna.

The latter was based down in Silicon Valley and was primarily a technology public relations company that happened to have a few bothersome advertising accounts they had inherited and didn't really know what to do with.

Hoefer Dieterich & Brown was an established blue-blood San Francisco ad agency with very traditional old-line accounts like Transamerica and the California Brandy Advisory Board.

It had been decided that all the accounts would be consolidated at the Hoefer Dieterich & Brown building in San Francisco, where the merged agencies were to be situated. It was a quaint old red brick building at 414 Jackson Street, the typical structure that advertising and design firms in San Francisco seek out.

The building had a lot of charm dating from the turn of the century. It had once been a brothel situated in what was then the Barbary Coast area of San Francisco. All of the land for blocks in every direction had been filled in largely with the debris left from the 1906 earthquake. The consolidated Chiat/Day office was in the center of this wonderful quaint historic area. Right next door was the cutest little tiny Sharper Image store.

Holiday card, 1983, showing 414 Jackson Street building.

You knew that the place had been a house of ill repute because just about every one of the rooms (now offices) was long and narrow. It had a darling, diminutive little narrow elevator, which was able to hold no more than three and half people and moved from floor to floor at a snail's pace.

It had two conference rooms, one of which was quite small but had a wall of windows overlooking Gold Street and Bix Restaurant at the rear of the building. This room was situated halfway between the first and second floors and was charming but stifling, as it received none of the air-conditioning from the rest of the building.

More recently, the entire building has been restored and retrofitted for earthquakes and today houses an array of antique and art dealers. Unfortunately the building is also now filled with crisscrossed 12-inch brown steel beams, 40 feet long, effectively destroying the uniqueness of the original interior. And when you see the building from outside, it looks a little like a penitentiary with thick iron bars apparent throughout.

Apple Computer was the most important account in the office but the revenue was shared with the Chiat/Day Los Angeles office, as they contributed significantly to the work that was being done.

When I joined, we didn't have all that much other business even considering the newly acquired agencies, but we were able to grow significantly over the next two years to a point where we had totally outgrown the 40 or so offices in our eccentric little building.

This was the impetus for Jay Chiat to make a major statement and investment in the San Francisco community. After going through a horrendous debate over where new and larger space might be located, I prevailed for the wrong reasons.

Jay had us searching all over the Bay Area for space, even down in South San Francisco, which would have meant a difficult commute for many, an out-of-the-way and ugly geographic location, and little redeeming value except that the space was cheap. Oh, and it was only a few minutes from the San Francisco airport, which could be seen from one of the buildings that Jay expressed an interest in and which looked like it was designed specifically for a life insurance company. Space and spaces for many desks in itsy-bitsy cubicles.

But we finally settled, or should I say Jay settled, on some space known as the Ice House in downtown San Francisco. It was right next to where Foote, Cone & Belding advertising and Levi Strauss were located in the Embarcadero area. It was a terrific part of the city, near the water and surrounded by a wonderful park with a brook running through it.

The buildings were very old, probably turn of the century, but it was a unique space, with a bridge connecting two of the buildings right across Sansome Street. The bridge was kind of neat to walk across and was enclosed, with windows on either side, running ceiling to floor. It was elevated way above the road, so when you looked down, you saw the traffic whizzing by below.

There were lots of interesting windows of different shapes and sizes, some like Roman arches, and old wood floors and many brick walls on the inside throughout. But frankly, other than the view from the bridge, there was no other place where one could see outside to speak of. Despite the location being so close to the waterfront. There was no water in sight.

Jay personally wanted to negotiate with the landlord for the space, and after many months of doing so he got frustrated and blew the guy off. The situation had been inflamed by the fact that the landlord who owned the Chiat/Day building in New York had been a constant source of pain for Jay. He was an Arab. Luckily for me, the landlord in San Francisco happened to be an Arab as well. There was nothing that couldn't be haggled. And there wasn't. Jay threw in the towel.

He washed his hands of the whole thing and we walked away from considering that space. This meant that we fell back to the site that I really wanted in the first place, which thankfully was still available. It was a building I had found just off the center of San Francisco at Union Square. It was a wonderful, bright space with large interesting arched windows and plenty of room in the building for expansion. It had skylights and an upper floor that had immense possibilities from an architectural and functional standpoint.

I particularly liked the energy that the downtown area brought to the agency and to our people. This building was located at 77 Maiden Lane, a narrow street, two short blocks long, a great place with gates at either end that were closed off most of the day, making the street a pedestrian mall.

Oddly enough Maiden Lane was aptly named and was similar in ways to the 414 Jackson Street office. Both were places that had housed ladies of ill repute for many years, back when San Francisco was wild and woolly. Situating an advertising business in either of these buildings seemed particularly appropriate, as it is a business filled with many "whores."

Coincidentally, or maybe not, Chiat/Day in New York ended up with offices on a street in Manhattan similarly named (Maiden Lane), possibly proving the thesis regarding advertising agencies and the people that work in them. Or maybe not.

Jay must have warmed to the Maiden Lane space because he decided to invest a fortune. Millions of dollars. And this was kind of odd for a guy who admittedly hated San Francisco and later on only wanted to get rid of the San Francisco office. Chiat/Day had first opened an office in 1979 and shut it down before 1980 was over. Here he was back again trying to make a mark.

I guessed that he may have been going through a period of boredom or possibly just wanted to be distracted from one of his five or six marriages. This became a pet project for him for a brief period of time.

At any rate, he bought the most expensive furniture of its kind to construct offices within an open space environment. There were to be no closed offices, that is, no doors, which was kind of a revolutionary idea, at least in San Francisco at the time. The Chiat/Day LA office already had such a configuration.

We announced our new offices with great fanfare in a postcard sent to several hundred people. It had the headline "Chiat/Day isn't going very far." Next to it was a map of San Francisco with a line drawn from the old 414 Jackson Street office to the new one at 77 Maiden Lane. Clever.

The offices (i.e., cubicles) were manufactured in Sweden by Dux. Jay

 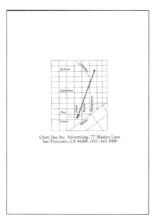

hired a friend of his, Eric Erickson, to do the interior architecture design and decorating and paid him handsomely. Eric and his wife Sammye Jean had extremely expensive tastes. But then, they had an unlimited budget and were still able to exceed it. For example, they bought Edward Fields area rugs and custom leather furniture from Saporiti Italia. And this was just the beginning of a long list of extravagances.

There were two bedrooms, a kitchen, a living room, and a dining room on the penthouse floor. We built a deck on the roof for various important affairs like barbecues and watching the Blue Angels fly over the city during Fleet Week. It was also the only place left, for people who had to smoke, to smoke.

When all was said and done, however, I made good use of the space and most of the lavish accoutrements. I owe Jay for all his lavish expenditures. We stayed at 77 Maiden Lane for 15 years as the agency ultimately grew to be a $500 million shop. We expanded from the original fifth, sixth, and penthouse floors to include the second and then fourth floors as well. Then we had to take additional space a few doors down from 77 Maiden Lane at 27 Maiden Lane, and soon after at 25 Maiden Lane.

While the offices at Maiden Lane were unique and kind of shocking, I never really cared for some of the elements like the ultra-contemporary "art" from Jay's artist friends Charlie White III and Laddie John Dill and others. I particularly abhorred the stuff that Charlie did with materials that could have easily been found in a landfill or an auto wrecking establishment. Maybe they were. Plastic, neon, aluminum strips and circles, spray paint.

On October 8, 1985, not very long after the main "wall sculpture" (I mean "art") had been installed in the lobby, some of the neon lights, which were part of the structure, went out. Charlie had actually told me these neon lights were good for life. Turns out, not measured in my life, but a considerably shortened one, like a housefly's maybe.

There was no way the lights could be changed by a normal person so I called the artist himself. He advised that he would require $3,500 to come up from LA to change the bulbs. That was not including his travel expenses, which he requested as well. He had already received $125,000 from Jay for his contributions to the "art" collection we had acquired.

I wrote Jay a note suggesting we shouldn't have to pay for the bulb change and, if we did, certainly not the exorbitant amount that was being requested. He wrote me back: "Don't fuck with the art" and "Just pay the bill." What's a good patron for anyway?

Main lobby with Charlie White installation. Photograph courtesy of designer Eric Erickson.

Maybe the most lavish and incredible expenditures that Eric and Sammye Jean made were up in the penthouse meeting area where they created a living room. The idea was to have clients come up there, and we could screen commercials in the space. Nobody bothered to ask me, or anyone else who actually had to use the place, for input about the design.

Turns out that the monitors were way too small to make any impact. You had to sit 4 feet from the screen in a room that was 40 by 40, and you had to sit sideways to view the monitors because the sofas were facing one another, not the monitors. The electronic systems that were installed regularly failed. Inevitably clients got neck aches from having to sit on the edge of the couches and turn their heads.

The sofas were made of the softest most luxurious black leather available possibly in the world, and they had possibly the most uncomfortable softest black leather cushions from which it was nearly impossible to extricate your body unless you were a regular gym frequenter well practiced in performing stomach crunches. At the same time, if you perched only on the edge of a sofa, you had to concentrate on not slipping and sliding right off the damn thing.

The sofas had custom red leather piping to match the embroidered

Penthouse client viewing area. Photograph courtesy of designer Eric Erickson.

thin red line in the Edward Fields black area rugs, which lay beneath them.

This little touch of red cost an extra 30 percent touch of green.

Another problem with this part of our office space, which was conceived as a conference/viewing room, was that an adjacent sitting area across from the two sofas had four oversized cushy light tan armchairs, arranged in sort of a square. This area could accommodate no more than four people, each facing one another. If you had five people, one had to sit on one of the sofas in the adjacent area across the room. Or vice versa, with six people sitting on the sofas and the rest in the chairs, 20 feet away. It was a tough way to carry on a conversation, much less a meeting, in what was supposed to be an intimate setting.

The easy chairs had two other notable things. First, the upper part of the back of each chair was flexible and was intended to potentially move up and down or be shaped in any manner the "sitter" might like. This meant that the four chairs inevitably ended up looking weird at the end of each day. Some up, some down, some half up, and some half down. No one ever bothered to put them back the way they found them.

The other thing about these chairs was the incredible way that they attracted grease and coffee stains. And once the stains were there, it was virtually impossible to remove them because the color of the fabric was so light. No one ever said the chairs or the space had to be functional. The wood-burning fireplace in front of the easy chairs was very nice, however.

All in all, the room design was completely and utterly useless as a serious place to have a meeting or for viewing commercials. It was virtually impossible to hold a new business meeting. But the room definitely looked grand when you first entered it through large black double doors. Spectacular actually. And that was worth something to some prospects.

The funniest thing about this incredibly sumptuous and lavish setting was Jay's insistence at the start of the project and his primary request to Eric Erickson that "the total environment of the office provide equal status among all workers." Like communism. In defying Jay's dictate, I made sure that only a few people had access to the penthouse area. They would have just left their used coffee cups, gum wrappers, and crap all around anyway.

Another design element for the other floors was to have each person's open workspace separated by five-foot-high storage closets and a small work-table between what became two side-by-side offices. The design was meant to provide each creative team (copywriter and art director) with a place to face off and work together over the teeny-tiny table set between their two office spaces at the end of the row of closets. It was such a bad idea.

Constructing this setup was done at considerable expense, and the tables ultimately served only as a storage area for videotapes, stuffed animals of different sorts, coffee cups with an inch of coffee left in them with grayish stuff growing on the surface, and just about anything else including coats, jackets, and even shoes. In fairness there was no place provided to hang a jacket.

To my knowledge these tables were never used to create any ads by any creative team. Ever! It simply was not the way two creative people "worked" together. And, it would have been uncomfortable besides. Instead, a copywriter or an art director would simply step around the storage cabinets that separated the office spaces and sit down in a chair and work with his or her partner. Side by side, next to one another. Duh!

The pièce de résistance of the design was the atrium. An area that was part of the living room penthouse, created seemingly for no other purpose than to impress. While it was impressive, it was also oppressively ugly. And a very dysfunctional setup as well.

After the atrium was completed, it became apparent that something was needed to keep the sun and heat out. The glass roof made the space unbearably hot and uninhabitable. Shades were then ordered custom made and electrified to keep the sun from pouring in when the rain wasn't. The glass roof leaked from day one.

These electrified shades were so delicate that they required regular repairs since they needed to be closed every sunny day or the place heated to 110-plus degrees with the air-conditioning on full blast. And remember, San Francisco doesn't really need air-conditioning all that often. But we did, just about every day in the atrium.

On a really hot day it was possible to annihilate all the plants and any human beings who happened to be up there. We never suffered a human failure but were constantly replacing the various plantings, again at considerable cost.

However, I discovered an unexpected side benefit from the glass roof. When it was raining, buckets were needed in strategic areas to catch the water that leaked through the seams in the roof. Some of the leaking water dripped directly into several of the pots that held the various exotic plantings.

Penthouse atrium. Photograph courtesy of designer Eric Erickson.

The fake rock–like planters were pretty awful, too, as were the Fred Flintstone table and benches that filled the area. They had no redeeming features, being ugly, fragile, and uncomfortable.

In my opinion, one particular design element bordered on genius. Seriously, and it had to do with the tops of all the separating walls of each office cubicle and partition. These were fabricated triangular panels with the pointy part facing upward. As a result no one could put their "stuff" on the edges, making the entire office appear a lot neater than it would have otherwise. The tops of office partitions normally act as a magnet for papers, books, cups, creative awards if one had any, and just about anything and everything else.

Typical workstation. Photograph courtesy of designer Eric Erickson.

Jay was given and took all the credit for the design of the space. He reminded me of that on a number of occasions when I wanted to change the position of a plant or whatever. Nevertheless, despite all of my criticisms I was still generally happy since the office served us well over many years. The entire design was in so many ways very impractical, and it got fatigued and dated quickly. It was like many things that Jay did with irrational exuberance. It didn't wear well.

As soon as I bought the San Francisco Chiat/Day office in 1990, I gradually implemented changes in some of the architectural elements around the office. I tried to make it more contemporary but warmer; I got rid of a lot of the "art." One of the very first things I did was raze the main lobby wall of the "plastique" pink and blue fluorescent-lighted thing that had been hung there by Charlie White back in 1984.

Charlie always referred to the piece as his "wall sculpture." To me it was a conglomeration of metals and plastic and neon lights, predominantly shiny pink and blue, colors that were definitely 1950-ish. I deconstructed "the wall" and replaced it with a much more appealing idea, which then confronted anyone coming off the elevator banks.

I had the wall painted entirely black and hung large six-by-four-foot blowups of a few of the most provocative and memorable images from some

New GMO redesigned lobby. Photograph courtesy of architect Dirk Stennick.

of our ads. After all it was the first impression of Goldberg Moser O'Neill. They looked great and made a great statement.

I had an architect that Jeri had found and who had done some wonderful work for us at our house in Sausalito and subsequently in Belvedere, named Dirk Stennick. He had a wonderful eye for details and design. His taste level was impeccable. He collaborated with me on making some modifications around the agency, the first of which was the aforementioned lobby and the main entrance area.

I was very pleased with the new look of the lobby. The only vestigial element from the original lobby was a small metal piece that I had hung at the end of the elevator bank between the men's room and women's room. You could see it as you emerged from each elevator. It was a small part of the installation that Charlie White had put up. An attractive but odd-shaped chunk of brushed stainless steel I had sawed off the main structure and hung up by itself. I thought it looked hugely better than the archetype, particularly set off against the black wall. Charlie didn't.

Most all of the changes we made at this time turned out to be exceptional, except for one. And that was the light tan carpet that Dirk recommended be installed on the fifth floor. The trail of coffee stains from the mini kitchen to virtually everyone's offices made it a disaster after only a few weeks. It looked like rodents had gone to and fro from every office on the floor. There was a maze of little streams and brown spots this way and that. I needed to have the entire floor carpeting replaced almost immediately at a cost of $20,000. We used a dark color the second time around, which hid the rodent stains henceforth.

Redesigned art production area. Photograph courtesy of architect Dirk Stennick.

Oh, and I almost forgot about the unpainted unsealed concrete floor we installed on the fourth level. This looked absolutely terrific but ended up crumbling as folks regularly shuffled across it. There were times when a dust cloud hung a foot off the floor over the entire space from people rushing here and there. We ended up sealing it and painting it black. It looked better that way anyway.

A final touch in the main entrance area was the "Wall of Fame." Here, on three curved metal ledges, was an assortment of ads arrayed and displayed. Those ads represented the best

Redesigned conference rooms. Photograph courtesy of architect Dirk Stennick.

work being created at the agency. Brian O'Neill mainly selected the work but occasionally I had something to say about what went up.

The wall was a clever idea. It was a wonderful way to reinforce what our product was and show it off. It was a terrific design element as a part of the interior space. And it was highly motivational for those whose work made it to the ledge.

By 1998 we had totally run out of space. We had three, sometimes more people stacked up in office spaces meant for two, and two in spaces meant for one. Sort of like the California prison system: overcrowded.

Still more importantly our landlord at 77 Maiden Lane was being forced by the city to retrofit the building, and he wanted us to leave during this time and then come back after the work was done. This would have been virtually impossible to do, and incredibly disruptive, and we really needed more space anyway, as we now had around 285 people crammed into the three Maiden Lane buildings we occupied.

Where only the best work showed up. Photograph courtesy of architect Dirk Stennick.

It also occurred to me that whenever the government, in this case the city, gets involved, you can be sure of endless and thoughtless complications, which surely would have delayed the process of getting back in the building.

After all, it was the city that in-- sisted we install, in addition to regular men's and women's restrooms, a handicapped bathroom on every floor when we first moved into 77 Maiden Lane. This was no problem for Eric Erickson since he had an unlimited budget, but each of those bathrooms cost $50,000.

Worse still, in the 15 years that we occupied the space, those bathrooms were used by the occasional druggie, by a few people who got drunk, as a place to change clothing, and for some sexual encounters but never by a handicapped person.

At any rate we made the decision to look for space and I began a search for a suitable new home and environment for Goldberg Moser O'Neill. Since I had just about two years left on my contract with IPG and was contemplating retirement at that point, I was hoping to make this project a swan song and legacy of sorts.

After an incredible amount of scouting around San Francisco, we came upon an old lithography plant dating back to 1929, located as it turns out just one block from where we had started out at Jackson Square as Chiat/Day. The building had most recently housed a bank that used it as a back-office facility. As such it had lots of tiny rooms, only a few of which were long and narrow, however.

I had in my mind to make this a major investment and design commitment, one in which I wanted to be very personally involved. I liked this 1929 space and saw its potential for us. I decided to go for it. We signed a deal and leased the entire building, which was located at 600 Battery Street. It was over 100,000 square feet of potential office space. The building ran a full city block in two directions, from the corner of Battery Street and Pacific on one side to Front Street, and on the other side to Jackson Street.

It was a wonderful space with huge windows, lots of skylights, and many possibilities. The high ceilings were spectacular, as was the potential to take advantage of the open spaces. It was an architectural challenge and opportunity to do something really special. And I did.

We gutted the entire place so that we could start with nothing but bare floors and windows: a completely blank canvas.

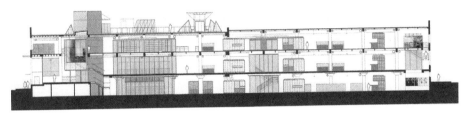

Leddy Maytum Stacy architectural drawing of future 600 Battery Street.

Nobody had told us that in order to house the printing presses just before Prohibition, the floors in the building required an exceptional amount of strength. Thus they poured three feet of concrete to make sure the floors were strong enough. We discovered this when we wanted to install a stairway connecting two of the floors. It took a few more weeks and considerably more dollars just to make that hole.

All in all I decided to do everything possible to make this a very unique and special place for Goldberg Moser O'Neill. I hoped it would look and feel like no other advertising agency. You might say I approached the project a little like Jay Chiat might have. I was extremely hands-on, and the endeavor consumed a good part of my final two years with the agency.

I budgeted a considerable amount of money for the project and, as had happened with Jay before me with Maiden Lane, some of it became irrational

Gutted areas, 600 Battery Street building.

exuberance. I felt the money that I was investing was being well spent. However, the folks at the Interpublic Group, who had bought our agency a few years earlier, not so much!

Our rent nut alone was going up from $1.8 million per year at Maiden Lane to almost $3 million in the new space. But we needed the extra space to house all of our employees, and we had to vacate from Maiden Lane because of the earthquake retrofit. It was justified.

We had another $1.4 million in construction build-out costs. Then, just as I was about to give the final go-ahead, a bureaucrat at IPG raised issues on our anticipated costs. For example, he objected to connecting the floors with the stairway.

Main entrance.

To me this was an essential element, although it was quite expensive given the three-foot concrete floor we ran into. Funny, that was one of the major arguments I had with Jay over at the Maiden Lane site and in which I prevailed. We ended up there with a wonderful open connecting stairway between the fifth and sixth floors, which really helped from a functional standpoint, and also in the spectacular way it looked. At 600 Battery our stairway was not going to be quite as aesthetically pleasing, but the open-air bridge I was going to build from the main conference room to the office space area turned out to be incredible.

This fellow at IPG also objected to the number of skylights we had planned, and he wanted to remove the bridges inside the space that connected various work areas. He didn't like the indoor/outdoor back porch overlooking the park at the rear of the building and the decking on the roof housing a large barbecue and gathering area. He didn't like the workstations that we had selected and the extra bathroom and shower for runners. He wanted dropped particleboard ceilings instead of open high ones as we planned. He even objected to the number of projectors we had included in the estimates for each of the conference rooms. I wondered how sitting in New York City he could even remotely know how many projectors we required for our purposes 3,000 miles away in San Francisco.

The agency was doing very well at this time and it certainly looked like things would continue their upward trajectory. In the end I went ahead and did everything that I wanted to do, and it all turned out just splendid. What didn't turn out so splendid was the way IPG and Hill Holliday managed the agency post-2000, and that the building ultimately became a huge albatross for them.

But what a building it was.

I interviewed 12 architectural firms in San Francisco, large and small, narrowed my search down to four, and ended up selecting a relatively small one where I had the chance to work directly with its key principal, Bill Leddy, of Tanner Leddy Maytum Stacy Architects. He was deeply involved and did a marvelous job of executing our vision—or, should I say, my vision for the building.

There were four primary concepts that drove the development of the space.

1. We were technology driven and technology was what drove the business, so we wanted to turn the technology outward so everyone who entered the space could see it.

2. Color was not as important as texture and inter-texture. We wanted to achieve a tactile feeling with the use of unusual materials throughout for interest and contrast, like copper mesh, brushed steel and aluminum, glass, and even crushed sunflower seeds, which made up some panels. We wanted a simplicity and cleanness in everything and did not want to junk it up with lots of plants, for example. We tried to maintain a monochromatic feeling throughout and let the various textures provide contrast and interest with what color there was to be.

3. We wanted to be able to see outside, no matter where you stood, and to be able to see inside, through and through. We used lots of glass for see-through conference rooms, copy rooms, and coffee stations. You could even see through the translucent ad images that we placed at the main lobby stairwell. We used perforated office partitions to further achieve this sense of openness and glass and/or perforated stairs, so as to allow a visual experience of the greenery and park just outside the rear of the building. We even were able to turn the walls of some of the conference rooms out into the corridors to display the work so everyone in the agency could share in it.

4. The last thing we wanted was something robotic, or anything close to a rat's maze, so we used curves instead of squares and rectangles. We built five curved "streets" or corridors; we used curves in the office partitions; and we had curved conference room walls, curved glass stairwell enclosures, and even curved glass walls for a spectacular server/router room, which kind of represented the engine of the agency.

All of this added immensely in providing a different and unique dimension and perspective when walking through the space. It was meant to be fun and an exciting experience. It was sort of like walking down a real street to the park or past a coffee shop.

There was signage for each of the coffee stations with foot-long clear Lucite containers mounted on the corridor walls at the appropriate strategic places and filled with coffee beans. The signage for the copy stations was also see-through containers but filled with crumpled-up pieces of paper. And so on.

Main stairway. Photograph by Richard Barnes.

Curved corridors cost more than straight ones . . . lots more. Photograph by Richard Barnes.

The entire design was highly functional as well as pleasingly aesthetic. We turned the technology inside out by leaving exposed the many wired and computerized aspects of the building functions. You could see all the innards. We built special racks in the open ceilings throughout to hold the wiring for the entire agency. In a way expressing just how connected everyone and everything really was.

There were lots of windows; three-quarters of the outside walls were glass; and there was an all-glass lobby and glass conference rooms. We made use of translucent and opaque materials so even if you couldn't clearly see through to an area, you could see movement behind the luminescent walls and partitions. In many areas, if you looked up or down, you could see the activity happening on another floor in a different part of the agency. The curved lines everywhere softened the entire environment.

I had another debate with the IPG accountant mentality regarding a second stairwell that was being constructed at the rear of the building. This was situated just in front of a glass wall that looked out upon a beautiful park sprinkled with many trees and numerous unique sculptures. I wanted the stairs to be glass so as you approached them you would see through them and

Wall panels open up to corridors. Photograph by Richard Barnes.

right out to the park. When we finished, you could see right out to the park.

We had some hiccups with the construction company besides trying to burrow through 3 feet of concrete. There were some spaces where the walls were 20 and 30 feet high, like the main entrance. This space was to be clad with textured copper sheeting. It was extremely rich and elegant looking and had a lovely sheen that picked up lots of the reflected light from the inside fixtures but also the light outside streaming through the windows. The use of copper was, I admit, a bit indulgent but it looked great.

Unfortunately, when the copper went up on the walls, the workmen didn't think to wear gloves and left hand- and fingerprints all over, which you could see remarkably clearly. They forgot to seal the material. I talked to Sharon Rundberg, my office manager, with whom I had collaborated on this entire project. I said to her that the copper needed to be cleaned.

She called the appropriate people and they came and cleaned it, but with something that caused the copper to end up looking like brownish mud. I told Sharon they had to fix it. Sharon talked to the appropriate people, who said they had done all they could. No, they were going to have to do more.

Finally they were persuaded to come back, as I hadn't approved payment for the installation. So they came back and used some really strong chemical to rid the walls of the brownish mud, but now it turned into brackish black. And I told Sharon no good. Got to get it fixed.

The company refused. I got the architect, Bill Leddy, involved in the discussions since he had recommended the use of copper to begin with. The company refused to do anything more. I got our attorneys involved. The company refused. They had spent a lot on the additional labor to try to repair the situation and now I refused to pay them at all.

The company finally agreed to replace all of the copper on the walls. This time they put the proper sealer on it before it went up. And this time they had their workers wear white gloves during the installation. The copper walls turned out to be a highlight of the entire design experience.

All of these elements helped refine and accentuate the fully open environment, with no doors and no walls, a concept that we had inherited from Chiat/Day days but now took to a new level of elegance and functionality. It encouraged people to engage. It didn't allow them to shut anyone out. More communication: more productivity. Less secrets: less fear.

If people wanted or needed privacy, there were 45 conference rooms scattered throughout the space. These rooms were put to good use for all sorts of things. They were not very good for anyone who might want to fool around, however, as there were no shades. Every conference room was named after a creative inspiration, like Jobs, Mapplethorpe, Duchamp, Lucas, Dylan, Marley, Leibovitz, and so on. Somehow Stephanopoulos got on the list but was soon removed as not being quite inspirational enough, if at all.

Main conference room. Photograph by Richard Barnes.

The space ended up having lots of natural light throughout. Almost every office space received some. This resulted in an airy, ethereal, open, creative, and energized feeling throughout. You could see outside the building from virtually everywhere, even from the main conference room, which was buried in the center of the space.

The main conference room was spectacular and dramatic. It had several large TV monitors at one end; a completely hidden one-way mirrored presentation control booth; walls that could be opened to enlarge or closed to reduce the area; and a huge drop-down presentation screen. I had selected a beautiful wood table with highly contemporary chrome chairs. There were two additional elements that put the room over the top.

The first was a hole in the center of the ceiling, to bring in daylight, but which could be closed electronically just like the eye of a camera shutter. And, then there were the curved movable walls that could be pulled shut to close off the main part of the room containing the conference room table and encircle the clients or anyone else sitting at the table. The insides of these walls were pushpin boards upon which creative work could be hung and displayed.

One of the new business presentation techniques I found particularly effective over the years was to expose all the work that we were presenting right at the beginning of the meeting without any explanations. This was often overwhelming in a positive way, and had great impact. It allowed clients to pick and choose what they wanted to look at and talk about.

It got them immersed in a dialogue about the work. It had everyone focused on the work. It also allowed clients not to have to react on the spot to a particular piece of advertising before moving on to seeing the next one, which in my experience inevitably led to less constructive dialogue about the work.

The technique also avoided the traditional way in which ad agencies present creative work. That would be in a serial-like fashion usually leading up to what was supposed to be a climax with the last idea and the one favored and recommended by the agency. It didn't always work out that way, I found.

All of this architectural planning and design again demonstrated that we were focused on the creative work and that we approached the business in a very different way than a traditional agency.

Unfortunately, I never got to make even one new business presentation in that room that I had so carefully designed and built expressly for that purpose. I am not sure that the successor agency Hill Holliday was able to make effective use of the room since they ended up unable to afford to remain in the building, a result of not generating enough new business and losing most of their clients.

This 600 Battery Street project was a marvelous challenge for me. I had lots of discussions, made a few compromises, and experienced some extra costs. I had no idea how much more curves cost than squares or rectangles. A lot more, I know now. I also know that I might have made a pretty good architect, as I had harbored some thoughts in that direction at one time long ago.

I felt a real sense of accomplishment in planning and bringing this building to fruition. But after we moved in, I sat in my office cubicle and never made use of most of the things that I had planned so hard to incorporate. I did, however, make frequent trips to the coffee station and the restroom, both of which I enjoyed.

After I had left the Battery Street space, and so had Hill Holliday, the newest tenant, Foote, Cone & Belding, decided to hold the San Francisco Awards Show at their office, which they affectionately now referred to as "The Fredifice, in honor of Fred Goldberg, retired chairman of Goldberg Moser O'Neill, who built it to house his agency." At least I assume that was meant affectionately.

Four years after I left, *Advertising Age* reported that there might have been a curse on what many were saying might be the most architecturally acclaimed of spaces for advertising agencies.

Hill Holliday had taken over Goldberg Moser O'Neill and not very long afterward was forced to move out of the space into smaller quarters. Foote, Cone & Belding, another IPG agency, replaced Hill Holliday and in a short time fell on hard times. They, too, were soon forced to relocate to smaller quarters.

Then came giant McCann Erickson, still another IPG agency, who took over the space from Foote Cone. The then executive VP and general manager, Courtney Beuchert, said he didn't believe in ghosts or curses but to be on the safe side he "might want to kill a chicken in the lobby."

Courtney left to form his own agency and McCann Erickson fell on hard times, losing most of their largest account, Microsoft. The last I heard there were a number of IPG firms now sharing the space, but you can hear echoes throughout the considerable empty parts of the building. The space definitely had a curse upon it.

The 600 Battery Street space was designed for a creative-oriented agency that believed in doing really good work. The space started as Goldberg Moser O'Neill, and each of these successive agencies was increasingly removed from the focus on the creative work. The building was simply reacting in a most natural manner like when a human body receives an unsuitable donor implant. The space was rejecting what was foreign to it.

Maybe Courtney should have killed two chickens.

CHAPTER 22
CULTRICIDE

DAN BELLACK, OF TYCER FULTZ BELLACK, a successful technology agency located in Silicon Valley during the 1980s, to my knowledge coined the word *cultricide*. He was referring to the loss of the culture of a company and in particular that of an advertising agency.

I had the good fortune of having a number of clients who had created really unique cultures. So much so that the culture became an asset of the company and in most cases a competitive weapon.

One of the most effective cultures ever built was that of my client Apple Computer. Not unlike many technology companies, it expected people to work their butts off until all hours of the night and day, and it insisted on doing "insanely great" things not just with the products it developed but with things related to them, including the ads, the collateral, and just about everything else.

And Chiat/Day had one of the absolute strongest and defining cultures, built by Jay Chiat, Guy Day, and Lee Clow. They knew clearly what they wanted to be and how to differentiate the agency from all the rest. They worked hard at maintaining the culture, particularly in their early more formative years.

It was remarkable and rewarding that I found the Chiat/Day culture incredibly in sync with my own beliefs and feelings about advertising. This was confirmed not too long after I joined the agency and sent a note to Jay, Guy, and Lee regarding my insights as to why the Nike and Apple advertising was so powerful and effective. I received a note back from Guy, and he sent my memo to the entire agency.

I viewed both Apple and Chiat as superb learning experiences and gained much from working with both of these companies. I took a lot of what I considered the best from each and applied it to my own firm in later years.

When I founded Goldberg Moser O'Neill in 1990, we had as a part of our philosophy trying to hire only the smartest people. And at the same time I tried to make the people we had on staff always feel as though they were smarter than the folks working at all the other competitive advertising agencies. Very often they were, because of the care we took in hiring and the empowerment we offered individuals as well as the reinforcement for smart behavior.

We developed a mascot, emblematic of our philosophical beliefs and practices. It was the face of a clown with a line drawn all the way across it like an international "NO" sign. It was created and designed by my very talented partner Mike Moser, the creative director but also an insightful and clever art director.

The "you/we are smarter" inculcation became an essential part of our culture. Most of our people believed that they were indeed smarter than their peers at other agencies and that we did smarter work than our competitors. Clients and prospects bought into this evangelistic thinking. And speaking of believing, I believe this was an extremely important element in our great success as an agency.

For years we used the symbol on sweatshirts, memo pads, T-shirts, hats, coffee cups, umbrellas, and our own giant flag that we proudly flew on the roof of our buildings. However, when I retired and the successive management group took over the agency, one of the very first things they did was purge the company of anything clown-like. This did not necessarily apply to individuals, however.

This was a first step toward committing cultricide. They didn't understand the clown or his value to the agency. Sure, they may have saved a few bucks over the next two years, but that was only before closing the agency down for good. Er, I mean, for bad.

I experienced cultricide firsthand numerous times throughout my career. In the advertising business, it can happen when new management wants to wipe the slate clean and they throw out the baby with the bath water. It also happens when large holding companies decide to buy and then combine one or more entities for whatever reasons.

One of the hardest things is to retain a company culture as management, staff, clients, and situations change. So much so that my experience proves that the acquisition and/or merging of advertising agencies is sort of like two heavenly bodies hurling themselves directly at each other until they collide.

YOUNG & RUBICAM NEW YORK

My first exposure to this anomaly was at Young & Rubicam in New York during the 1960s and 1970s. Y&R was a successful agency in its own right, having been in existence since the early 1900s. It was one of the first agencies to search for and acquire a range of specialty companies in the interest of growth and service opportunities. These included such established and successful firms as Wunderman, Ricotta & Kline, the leading direct marketing ad company; Sudler & Hennessey, the largest pharmaceutical advertising company; Landor & Associates, a design firm; and many others.

And after they had acquired these specialty companies, which were arguably the most successful and largest firms in their respective fields, they decided they should pursue a strategy of acquiring successful, but small, more regional and local advertising agencies around the United States.

They did this and acquired somewhere in the neighborhood of 20 or so of what were again arguably some of the very best localized firms.

Now all of this would have been swell and dandy, except that when it came time to maximize the interaction of these firms with Y&R, the parent advertising firm, and interchange and exploit the respective client bases and expertise, problems appeared.

Specifically, the folks at Y&R did not feel that their work was on the same plane as these other lesser and "inferior" agencies. This was particularly true for the specialty agencies, who had developed a genuine and unique understanding of their respective clients and their marketing and advertising requirements. Direct marketing was something else, and it wasn't considered "real advertising." Advertising to the medical community, with all its technical jargon and requirements, was not considered "real advertising." And so on.

In other words the elitist folks at the "real advertising agency" did not embrace what these experts did.

"We do television spots. And we do print and radio ads. We don't do 2- or 10- or 30-minute infomercials hawking vacuums, exercise equipment, vitamins, or Clappers. We don't do detailed restrictive type-laden medical or pharmaceutical ads with pages of mandatory requirements, directed at doctors. We do real ads."

So there you had it. The creation of huge conflicts and a general resistance to meaningful collaboration with the Y&R people, and a heightened sensitivity to their "inferiority" on the part of just about everyone else at the acquired specialty firms. The thinking and the cultures were so dramatically different that it's little wonder this happened.

The other thing that occurred was the decision to take people from the parent company and insert them into the acquired ones. This was done at both the specialty firms and the traditional but smaller local ad shops. This action caused numerous problems across the board mostly because the thinking and cultures were so different to begin with. The way the work was developed and the way management was undertaken.

Nowhere was this difference in management philosophy more apparent than in the smaller regional agencies scattered around the country that had been acquired by Y&R. Almost all of these were entrepreneurial in nature. Many were still run by their founders. They were all successful in their own right and local and/or regional forces. In fact they knew what they were doing.

The impact of all of this was exacerbated significantly at those agencies that happened to be west of the Mississippi. It was not unlike trying to get a New York City born-and-bred copywriter writing an ad for Jell-O to think that there actually was a world to the west of the Hudson River with real live humanoids who possibly had some different values and lifestyles than he had.

And so those agencies to the west had to suffer with the attitude that the "only real advertising happens in New York City." This and an attraction to things like limousines, long lunches, and country clubs helped drive major wedges through establishing appropriate relationships.

And over time the weight of the requirement to send bags of money back to the New York City headquarters, combined with the insertion of New York Y&R personnel, led to the destruction of one after the other of these firms. At least that's my opinion.

One example with which I was somewhat familiar had to do with the assignment of a fellow for whom I had worked and who was sent to Phoenix to help "run" the acquired firm in that market. He walked in with a swagger and a penchant for three or four martinis at lunch.

"These hayseeds don't know how to develop advertising and how to manage client relationships the way we do at Y&R New York."

The founder of this agency was still there and actively trying to continue to do what he had always done, although he was a lot richer now that the cash from the sale of his agency was in his savings account.

When my ex-boss arrived, he knew exactly how to take the reins and show them how it was to be done. This created a bit of friction.

The same scenario was repeated over and over with many of the other acquired firms, so much so that if you reviewed the roster a decade or so later on, you would find that all but one of these firms were no longer in existence.

This was a proven way of committing cultricide.

YOUNG & RUBICAM/DENTSU LOS ANGELES

In 1978 I was sent to Los Angeles to manage the Gallo wine client and then became the general manager of that office. About two years into my assignment, word came from New York that an exciting opportunity had arisen and that we were going to merge the office with another agency.

That other agency was a company called Dentsu. At the time Dentsu was a huge advertising agency and they were extremely successful. However, 95 percent of their total revenue came from their operation in Tokyo, from Japanese clients. They effectively had no real business outside Japan and so they were looking to expand into the United States.

Y&R on the other hand viewed the partnership as an avenue to long sought-after Japanese accounts that were growing dramatically in the 1970s and 1980s in the United States and around the world. Clients like Yamaha, Toyota, Sanyo, Toshiba, Suzuki, Honda, and the list went on and on.

So the Young & Rubicam Los Angeles office was picked as the guinea pig, so to speak, probably because of its location as a major gateway to Japan. The office was renamed Y&R Dentsu and three executives from Dentsu Japan were sent from the mother ship in Tokyo to join me and the executive to whom I reported, Sid Marshall, in setting up and running the new agency.

The three Japanese men were delightful: Meg Nimuro, John Okazaki, and Shinzo Ueno. They were smart and gentle people. They were always accommodating and concerned. And they were able to generate some significant new business leads, all from Japanese clients.

Dentsu was an incredible force in Japan. They were much more than an ad agency. They really were a multifaceted communications juggernaut. They did absolutely everything for their clients. They would develop television commercials but they would also go to Peoria and take pictures of some new rice soup in a supermarket there. And anything else that a client asked for without any hesitation.

And so, some of this philosophy was imported into the new Y&R Dentsu operation. At the top of the list was taking the long view. We would do lots of favors for existing clients in Japan, most of whom we would never ever have a chance to work for.

We would do presentations to visiting Japanese clients on how American companies operated; case studies of successful marketing and advertising campaigns; tours of Los Angeles and beyond. Guided visits to Disneyland. Everything was seemingly directed at establishing and maintaining a relationship that someday might yield some payback to Dentsu.

On the other hand it did open up some reviews of Japanese companies, which were conducted in the United States. We became an almost automatic consideration because of the Japanese link. Not only due to the Dentsu importance in Japan but due to the fact that we were at the time the only real Japanese/American agency in the US.

We took on a lot of small accounts because the Japanese did not discriminate by size. It was about the relationship and the long term. This was a concept that Y&R executives back in New York had some difficulty dealing with, as each office was measured at the end of the year by the amount of profit it sent back East. End of discussion.

Nevertheless, the Y&R and Dentsu relationship did pay some big dividends. We got the chance to pitch for the Suzuki motorcycle business and won it. We acquired the Sanyo Electronics business and Nissin Foods account. And even Aderans, a maker of high-quality wigs sold through a chain of retail stores. You can imagine the size of this account with only seven stores contemplated.

The thing was that we still had a lot of other accounts at the agency like Security Pacific Bank, Ralph's Grocery Stores, and Mattel among others. And we managed those in our traditional fashion.

The Japanese accounts required a different and "foreign" process. Most of the Japanese businesses had Americans in the second level jobs like marketing or advertising directors.

So the way it worked was that the American executives at the agency would meet with the American executives at the respective clients. We rarely got to present above their level, and when we did, the senior Japanese management of these companies generally sat in the meetings with their eyes closed. I was told that this was their way of maintaining intense concentration. I was also told that the top guy was expected to do this. Frankly, I think they just liked nodding off for a little nap during the day. I mean most of it was pretty boring. And maybe they knew then what we are now learning about taking small naps at regular intervals being healthy.

All in all, it was definitely a different way of doing business.

The process was mind-boggling. The Americans would meet, most of the time with one of our Japanese colleagues present. We would do whatever we had to do and discuss whatever we had to discuss. We would reach decisions about next steps. Gain approvals or rejections.

You know how the Japanese are always taking pictures. Picture here, picture there. Snap! Snap! Snap! In front of the Golden Gate Bridge, on the Golden Gate Bridge, below the south tower of the Golden Gate Bridge. And so on.

Well, our Japanese colleagues also took copious notes. No matter what we were talking about, they were writing it down. Notes and notes. And they did this in every meeting we had with and without the clients. They would seemingly take notes even when we weren't talking about anything except last night's Frisbee scores.

At the end of each meeting everyone would stand up, bow a bit to each person, and shake his hand: two people facing one another, clasping hands firmly followed by one sharp jerk downward done simultaneously with a short maybe five-inch tip of the upper body forward from the waist. This would be repeated with everyone in the room. Firm handshake, jerk down, bow head with bend at waist. And repeat with the next person, and so on . . . The next tradition was that our Japanese colleagues would meet with their Japanese clients and discuss what we had discussed. And a day or so later, we would be called into another meeting at the agency and be told what they had discussed about what we had discussed. And then were advised what was to be the next steps.

The pitch we made for Suzuki was another chasm of cultures. As with all new business pitches, you try to truly understand the market and the competitive landscape. We had never had a motorcycle client and needed to learn as much as we could.

My Japanese colleague John Okazaki told me, "No problem."

"What do you mean?"

"We know motorcycle business."

"How?"

"Dentsu represent four motorcycle client in Tokyo."

"Really?"

"We get information."

Sure enough, it turned out that in addition to representing Suzuki, Dentsu also represented Honda, Kawasaki, and Yamaha motorcycles. And unlike in the United States, where client conflict is a real issue among clients and agencies alike, they don't have that problem there. Or didn't then.

The Denstu headquarters was a huge building in Tokyo and they devoted a separate floor to Honda, and one to Kawasaki, and one to Yamaha, and another to Suzuki. Conflict problem solved.

Then during one of our preparation meetings for the new business pitch to Suzuki, in walked John Okazaki with two cardboard file boxes he had just received from Japan, one under each arm. He placed them on the table among all of the other materials we had assembled and were referencing.

I asked, "What's that, John?"

"Motorcycle information."

"Where'd you get it?"

"Tokyo."

"Great. What have you got?"

And to my great surprise, and pleasure, there were the full-fledged complete marketing plans for each of the competitive motorcycles: Honda, Kawasaki, Yamaha, and Suzuki. And not for the Japanese market but rather for here in America.

So much for client conflict. We won the Suzuki business, but the business of Dentsu and Y&R was never a success.

The culture differences were incredibly disparate. But I think it really boiled down to Dentsu's willingness to wait to make their profits over the long term, or none at all, in the interest of establishing a relationship. And, Y&R always looking at the profit (or loss) for the current 12 months. It was a major culture difference and clash. In this case you might say the cultricide was hara-kiri.

I actually enjoyed my time working with the three gentlemen from

Dentsu, despite all of our differences. I became particularly friendly with the senior Dentsu executive stationed in our office, Shinzo Ueno. He later was called back to Tokyo and went on to hold a very high position at the parent Dentsu. In my opinion he deserved it. He was a superb executive.

I considered the three Japanese good friends, and when I decided to leave Y&R, they graciously treated me to a farewell dinner at the Winter Garden Chinese restaurant in downtown Los Angeles. I discovered that Japanese love Chinese food. At least the ones who crossed my path. No culture difference there.

It was bittersweet. We had lots to talk and laugh about, a great meal of many dishes, and way too much sake. The last was probably the reason for the restaurant selection.

After we opened fortune cookies, they presented me with a stylish blue-faced Seiko watch, which I still have and cherish today, unlike the combination of Y&R and Dentsu, which is long gone.

CHIAT/DAY AND HOEFER DIETERICH & BROWN—SAN FRANCISCO

When I joined Chiat/Day in 1982, they had not very long before that purchased an old-line established advertising agency in San Francisco called Hoefer Dieterich & Brown.

Hoefer had been run by John Hoefer, a likable enough fellow, but clearly not in the Chiat/Day mode. He had his office done up sort of like the inside of a sailboat. He had ship lamps scattered around here and there. Red and green ones. A life ring was propped up in the window bay. Lots of pictures of his boats. He was a sailor.

The agency was very successful but had all these very traditional clients. For Chiat/Day it was a foothold back into San Francisco. They had unsuccessfully tried to enter the market a few years earlier.

At the same time, Chiat/Day purchased another advertising agency, located down in Silicon Valley. Actually they purchased the clients who advertised from Regis McKenna, which was basically a high-tech public relations firm. They had been trying to do the advertising as a sidebar without much success.

These two agencies and the clients were merged into one at 414 Jackson Street in San Francisco. This had been the Hoefer Dieterich & Brown offices. A lovely little four-story brick building on a quiet tree-lined street with upscale antique stores one after the other.

So they mixed the Hoefer people up with the McKenna folks and stirred in some Chiat/Day kindred all together with the Transamerica client and the California Brandy Advisory Board client and the Intel, Shugart, Fafco, and GE Calma clients. Oy gevalt!

What did they end up with? Bouillabaisse. And instead of a two-dimensional culture clash, this one was like an obtuse triangle and, as you might expect, resulted in triangulation. Or strangulation.

The Hoefer people and the McKenna people and their respective accounts were as different as you can imagine. Not just in who they were, but in their interests. The McKenna folks were techies who really enjoyed the technology they represented for their clients; the Hoefer folks were very much the traditional ad agency folk who worked on packaged goods accounts.

The client mix was radically different and required radically different skill sets among the radically different agency people. A high-tech media person was a far cry from a person that knew packaged goods.

And creatively it was a similar but worse problem. To write technology ads, creative people had to really know the products. The people that were working on the California Brandy Advisory Board or Saffola margarine or Wienerschnitzel did not. And it also happened that most of these creative folk didn't want to have anything to do with the technology clients or their products or with doing the ads.

So into this unharmonious atmosphere were dropped a bunch of Chiat/Day people. Chiat/Day where the work comes first. Nothing matters but the work. The goal is to do award-winning work. We want to see how big we can get without being bad. This was a philosophy foreign to both Hoefer and McKenna.

I arrived on the scene as all of this was percolating. People were leaving and so were accounts. Just about all of the Hoefer clients departed, having wanted nothing to do with Chiat/Day. I was only in the office a few weeks when Transamerica, one of the largest remaining clients, told us good-bye.

The office survived because we were able to hold on to most all of the technology businesses that came from McKenna, but it changed the focus of the agency much more toward technology than would otherwise have been the case. Of course, history would have been a lot different if one of those technology clients hadn't been Apple Computer.

All in all it was a culture clash of earth-shattering magnitude. About an 8.0 on the Richter scale.

CHIAT/DAY AND MOJO

Frustrated in the quest to make Chiat/Day more of an international company, and acting somewhat I think on impulse, at great expense Jay Chiat decided to purchase Mojo.

Mojo was a leading and established agency of scale from down under. They were billed in Australia as, and perceived as, a creative agency. They had 15 or so offices scattered around different places in the world. They had made their fame primarily by developing jingles, some clever and some not, for their clients.

Mo (Alan Morris) and Jo (Allan Johnston) had established the agency in 1979, riding on the coattails of one of their biggest successes without a jingle: having Paul Hogan pitching "I'll slip an extra shrimp on the barbie" for the Australian Tourist Commission.

And therein lay the first problem. Mojo was based in Australia and had four locations, in Sydney, Brisbane, Melbourne, and Perth. Chiat/Day did not need any of these places to further its international ambitions. Some could argue, and did, that in fact the merger may have damaged the goal.

With the exception of San Francisco, all the other Mojo locations were more like small service offices in London and Houston and elsewhere.

Now, while the Aussies were genuinely lovely and nice people, there was a definite difference between their culture and that of America. So this was a potential immediate problem.

For example, Mike Massaro was in his very first meeting after the merger with the creative director assigned to the Australian Tourist Commission account, which was serviced from both Sydney and San Francisco. The better part of the morning was spent doing a very thorough review of the business and the account. Among the topics covered was some detailed discussion of target segmentation. We also presented a 16-page insert that we were planning to recommend to the client in the US. After all this taking place over four hours, the creative guy from Mojo offered a singular comment, "Make the tits on the women bigger."

Yes, there was a cultural divide.

But it went both ways.

Down under Mo and Jo liked to do jingles. They really liked doing jingles. They thought it was a very clever way to solve just about any advertising problem. The two partners would sit down in their office, strum a tune or two on their guitars, and knock down a few bits of lyric. Voilà! There you have it. An advertising campaign was born.

Chiat/Day didn't develop its award-winning advertising that way and Chiat/Day didn't do jingles. They never did one. And they frowned on their use. It was beneath a Chiat/Day creative person to even consider it. Even the company Christmas card one year announced that Chiat/Day didn't do jingles.

Do ya think there might have been a problem with this merger? There was. A few years later Mojo was sold off to another agency at a huge loss.

CHIAT/DAY SAN FRANCISCO AND MOJO (NÉE ALLEN & DORWARD)

One result of the overall Chiat/Day purchase of and merger with Mojo was the integration of the Chiat/Day San Francisco office with the San Francisco Mojo office, which had previously been an agency known as Allen & Dorward.

Allen & Dorward had been a successful local San Francisco agency with an array of really terrific clients. And they had been doing some quite excellent creative work. Mojo had ferreted them out and bought them earlier. Among their clients were Rainier Beer, Lone Star Beer, and Beringer wines. With the purchase by Mojo they added the Australian Tourist Commission, Koala Springs Beverages, and Qantas airlines.

After the Chiat/Day/Mojo merger was announced, we moved all the people from Mojo's Front Street office into the Chiat/Day San Francisco offices at Maiden Lane. Some good people and some not so.

The mentality of many of the Mojo people was immediately at odds with what we were trying to do at Chiat/Day San Francisco. We wanted to grow. We wanted to do great creative work. We were aggressive in both regards and it scared a lot of Mojo people and it scared a lot of their clients.

Most of the employees who had come over from Mojo were not used to the work ethic demands or the work environment and either went away or were asked to leave. The same thing happened with most of the clients.

In little more than a year, hardly any of the people or the clients were left at the merged agency.

Another failed combination arising out of two very dissimilar organizations trying to act like one.

GOLDBERG MOSER O'NEILL AND THE LOWE GROUP

After five years, in 1996 we had reached a scale that made it worthwhile to attempt to sell the agency. And we did. But first I tried to scope out those firms that might be the best fit for us. I talked with a dozen or so agencies, and while I received interest from many, it was usually fairly obvious that the fit was not quite right.

Except for The Lowe Group. Marvin Sloves and Frank Lowe appeared to offer an agency network that we desired and one that was truly embracing of our ideals and our work and the way we worked.

I had a number of delightful premarital rehearsal dinners along the way to our marriage. Each of those dinners ended with much embracing, holding high glasses filled with the finest bubbly, and celebrations of whatever was the latest and greatest creative accomplishment for Goldberg Moser O'Neill at the time.

It was too good to be true, and when the rubber hit the road, the line indicating just how worn the tires were came shining right through. All Lowe really cared about was how much profit we would deliver back at the end of each year. If we did some good work, well that was fine, but the bottom line was that it was always about the bottom line.

They promised us that they had a priority commitment to the creative product. But our performance was totally about the profits that we sent back. And when the agency sought new business, just about any client who knocked on the door and had some money in their wallet became a target. They promised us help in servicing our clients internationally, which was an important defensive measure we were seeking. They never delivered. And, we had a no smoking policy in the office that Frank Lowe regularly violated.

The funny thing about it all was just how important our profits were to them. We were having one of our regular operational reviews with Frank and a guy named Peter Minnium. They were trying to get us to reduce some of our expense items in the budget and squeeze a few more dollars out of our bottom line and into theirs. In the middle of these intense disagreements, Peter leaned over to Mike Massaro and whispered in his ear, "Mike, you haven't flown until you've flown private."

GOLDBERG MOSER O'NEILL AND HILL HOLLIDAY

My last fateful involvement watching two disparate bodies trying to integrate came as I was deciding to retire or not in 2000. The Interpublic Group and The Lowe Group had decided to merge Goldberg Moser O'Neill San Francisco with another IPG shop in Boston known as Hill Holliday and run by one of its founders, Jack Connors.

Two things converged to make this happening a fatal misadventure.

First, they put some people in charge that had no sense of why and how GMO had become so successful. They had no understanding or sense of the cultural aspects that we had worked so hard to develop and instill in our employees and even in our clients. I was partially to blame.

One of these executives I had mistakenly hired to run account management. He came up with what he called a "crazy thought." I agreed. It was insane and stupid. In order to improve face-to-face communication he recommended that we should have one day per month where e-mail was outlawed. This was to me just one more example of improper and inadequate management. I expected that people would have face-to-face communications as a part of being effective executives. If you had to pass a "law" to accomplish that, it was a sad situation.

This same fellow recommended that we take away bonuses from people who didn't do performance reviews of their people. I believed that if you have to punish people for not performing their jobs, we were in a sorry state. Fire them, but don't make them stand in a corner with a dunce cap on.

Just a few months before I was to permanently leave the agency, an e-mail was circulated from a top management person asking everyone to help find a portfolio bag that had been delivered and somehow misplaced. Not only was everyone asked to try to find it, which was certainly a fair request, but this person was compelled to offer a reward in asking people to do so. A Razor scooter. Having to reward your own people for doing something that is expected and in the interest of the company seemed perverse to me. It was a violation of the culture we had built over almost 20 years.

And on one of my final days at the agency, I was sitting in my office reading the newspaper. No one bothered me anymore for anything. I looked up and I saw Gary Korpi, my long-time mailroom manager, pushing a trolley filled with cartons on it. The cartons were filled with No Clown pads that we used to provide to everyone as a reminder of a critical part of our culture: be smart.

Gary had instructions to get rid of 800 brand-new five-by-seven memo pads with our signature No Clown image at the top.

A fitting end to one critical element of a unique culture nurtured over 10 years at Goldberg Moser O'Neill.

Jamie Brown, my superb MIS manager for years, put it this way in describing what had happened to a great advertising agency: "Was GMO, then bought by the Interpublic Group, squirreled under the Lowe Partners umbrella, shuffled off to Hill Holliday, became GMO/Hill Holliday, the partners all left, we spent about three years laying everyone off and moving offices a bunch, then it died a horrible yet grating death. I blame everything on moving to Lotus Notes." Jamie went off to purchase and run a bar in San Francisco. Fittingly.

My partner Brian O'Neill said it best when he described what happened: "Two disparate cultures clashing together in disharmony." And it was the same for every other merger that I had the occasion to witness and, I am sure, holds true for those that I haven't.

THE GREATEST EFFECTUATION OF ADVERTISING CULTRICIDE THAT DIDN'T HAPPEN

What would have surely been the absolute greatest big bang of clashing cultures and lethal degradation fortunately didn't happen to Chiat/Day or to me.

At the end of 1985, Jay Chiat came up with one of his largest and most grandiose ideas. Why not buy two great creative advertising agencies, Ally & Gargano and Hal Riney, and create a new entity to be known as Ally Chiat Riney? This naming would likely be the only thing that the three companies might amicably agree upon since the names were in alphabetical order, thereby removing some of the political and emotional tension.

In many ways, this combination, Ally Chiat Riney, was a brilliant thought since it would have brought together arguably the three most creative agencies of the time, each a key player in an important advertising market: New York, Los Angeles, and San Francisco, respectively.

Not too much thought was given as to how Ally and Chiat and Riney might work together, well or not, but Jay offered that he would "run it." Uh-huh.

For years Hal Riney, the well-known ad guy in San Francisco, had maintained that he would never sell his agency and that he was not considering it and that he would never consider it. The truth was that he was regularly carrying on discussions with us for many months. David Weiner, a Chiat/Day board member, held several direct meetings with Riney's financial manager Lyn Muegge. But Riney denied it all even after the talks were over.

Information of all kinds was exchanged back and forth. This was beneficial, as I got to see what Riney's accounts were really billing as opposed to what they claimed in the press. On the other hand he got to see mine.

One day, at Jay's direction, I sat at lunch across from Hal at the then San Francisco institution, Jack's Restaurant on Sacramento Street. It was one of only two times I met him. We were there to discuss the contemplated merger of Chiat/Day and Hal Riney & Partners. And I had the extra pleasure of watching him consume four bourbons and rocks over lunch.

Riney phoned Jay the next day to tell him what a negative guy I was. Now I might be a negative guy or, put more diplomatically, cautious and conservative, but the truth is I hadn't said hardly a word during the entire lunch. Rather I sat and respectfully listened to him blather on about his various accomplishments, while he reloaded shots of the aforementioned whiskey.

Well, what can you expect from the fellow who when asked by the *San Francisco Business Times* (January, 28, 2000) to name the most important person in the Bay Area advertising community answered himself. "Much as I hate to say it, I think I am." No demur here.

I met Riney one other time, and it was at the Quaker Oats corporate offices in Chicago. We were both pitching some Quaker business, and Jay Chiat, Lee Clow, Jane Newman, and I were on our way into the meeting while Riney was waiting in the lobby sitting with several Riney executives waiting their turn.

Among them was John Yost, who was a smart and very nice person but who for a number of reasons I had recently had to relieve of his duties at Chiat/Day San Francisco.

Yost had been involved with a few executives in trying to unseat the then creative director, Ross Van Dusen. But Jay got wind of the plot and publicly skinned Yost alive. And, then privately told me to get rid of him.

As our group of four paraded past the Riney people in the lobby, Hal shouted out to me, "Hey, I just hired one of your flunkies." It didn't dawn on me immediately that he was referring to John Yost, who was sitting just to his left.

Don't know why he did this, but it was odd. I didn't consider my two meetings with Hal successful in any way and was quite happy that Chiat/Riney never came to be.

As for Ally & Gargano, the negotiations for buying them were well under way when at the last moment they decided to sell to another firm for 50 cents a share more. Now that's when you know a creative agency has a real commitment to the creative work. Chiat/Day was by far the greatest creative shop for most of the 1980s, and being a partner should have been worth 50 cents.

Had the partnership of Chiat and Riney and Ally ever come to be, it is unlikely that I would have been an important part or even a part of it, given the personalities involved and the incredibly variant cultures of the agencies.

Three distinctive and divergent personalities and three dissimilar and disparate cultures compressed into one, coming together in discord and disunity.

It would have been the incomparable model of extreme and rabid cultricide.

SOME OF MY BEST FRIENDS WERE CLIENTS

I THINK THE SAYING GOES "Some of my best friends are Jewish." Often announced in a defensive mode. And so, too, with "Some of my best friends are clients." Too many people in the advertising business don't really like their clients; they put up with them.

I always felt different about any client that was willing to entrust their marketing or advertising to me. I was particularly fortunate in that many had an entrepreneurial spirit about them along with an inventive idea for a product or a service.

One thing was common to all of these people. They were mostly terrific folks whom I genuinely liked, and because of that I over-committed my time and my resources to try to help them succeed. I tried to be personally available and involved in their businesses because they respected what we did and were grateful and complimentary of our efforts. After all they were handing me their "baby" and asking me to hold it and nurture it and help it grow. In turn I always felt a personal obligation and very much valued that trust they gave to me.

Therefore, I always tried to put their best interests first. As a result some regularly invited us to their business meetings, some asked us to their company parties, and some opened up their homes as well.

It was interesting that these clients knew well how to motivate a talented group of creative people. Maybe it was because they all knew a good creative idea when they saw one and they embraced it without hesitation. This was not a group of Procter & Gamble or Kraft brand or product managers applying the rules of marketing and advertising history by looking over their shoulders.

On many of my clients I never made much, if any, profit, but we were without exception able to develop great creative ideas and work that was enthusiastically endorsed and approved. Some of the very best ideas that we produced were for them. I am certain it was because they were creative in their own right and intelligent, adventurous, enthusiastic, and willing to take risks.

I remain in touch with many of this group of wonderful ex-client people today. Many of them I consider to be among my good friends. They are indeed the bacon bits in the salad.

In 1967 I first went to work at Young & Rubicam in New York in the marketing department. A year later I ended up in account management working on the General Foods business and specifically the desserts division, which included such products as Jell-O Pudding, Jell-O Cream Pies, Whip 'n Chill, Minute Rice, and Jell-O Gelatin. The last was the oldest and most important brand at the agency, dating back to around 1902. It was the agency's second client after Postum, which no longer advertised.

The Jell-O product manager was a guy named Dick Mayer. Dick was a smart, fun-loving person who really was an anomaly at General Foods and not just because of his red hair. He didn't fit the stereotypical GF executive in looks or in actions. He was willing to take on the establishment for what he believed in and to satisfy his ego as well. For a corporate executive he was very entrepreneurial in an environment that did not encourage that kind of thinking. It rather discouraged it.

The Jell-O Gelatin business had softened and GF management was concerned, as were the top folks at Young & Rubicam. Dick Mayer had been newly installed as product manager to try to turn around the business after having had a very successful run on Dream Whip, a dry-packaged ersatz sort of whipped cream topping that came in a cardboard box. Dick had achieved something of a miracle by tripling the sales of a brand in deep decline with an inspired, insightful, aggressive, and unusual strategy.

Now on Jell-O, he had identified what he thought was the turnaround strategy. It was referred to as "Reminder to Prepare." It emerged out of the understanding that the limitation to increased consumption of Jell-O was the requirement of having to remember to make it the evening before because of its four-hour setting time. So, the idea was to utilize advertising to remind women so they would prepare it the night before, or early the next day, in time for the next dinner. The message and the media was all to be geared to accomplishing this.

No one at Young & Rubicam was buying into this strategy except my boss, Mike Russell, who was the account supervisor, and me. We both thought it was a brilliant solution to a very mechanical problem that could not be solved without a major product innovation, which was not on the horizon. Everyone else thought it was the wrong way to go.

We struggled and lost a battle with the agency's Strategic Review Board. This was a group of very senior Y&R executives that sat around and reviewed various client strategies and passed judgment on them and the people presenting them as well. The forum was used to intimidate the presenters as much as possible, too. It actually helped me grow a steel lining in my stomach and prepared me for later battles I would have in my career.

The "Reminder to Prepare" strategy was deemed far too rational for an emotional product like Jell-O Gelatin. The Y&R board ordered the account group not to proceed. In rejecting the strategy, they set up a major dispute between the agency and the client, so much so that it resulted in a situation where the agency was put "on notice" to develop advertising against this strategy, or else.

And in the end, since "money talks and shit walks," we went forward with creative development against the "Reminder to Prepare" strategy.

Despite all the adversity and angst within the agency, we were able to develop advertising that was fun and arresting and delivered the message that you shouldn't forget to make this great-tasting dessert for the next dinner. Mike Becker, a talented copywriter, developed the campaign "Put a Jell-O Out Tonight" (and you'll remember to make something delicious tomorrow).

The General Foods people liked it and approved it and we produced it and it went on air. In fact, the only problem the clients had was using Jell-O in a generic fashion (Jell-O and not Jell-O brand gelatin) and the possible weakening of the trademark, which they held very dear to their heart. But "Put a Jell-O brand gelatin out tonight" didn't quite have the same ring as "Put a Jell-O out tonight" and we prevailed, due to Dick Mayer's support. Maybe it was a bit logical and rational but it almost immediately started to work. Jell-O, I mean Jell-O brand gelatin, sales and share responded positively.

Unfortunately, not long after the campaign launched, Dick Mayer was replaced, and the new product manager, Bill Dordelman, immediately abandoned the effort. It was customary that every product manager wanted to do his own thing and Bill was no exception.

Dick and I had been the main players defending the approach, and he and I became extremely close business and personal friends. We spent many hours talking business and also spending time socially together, with and without our wives Diane and Jeri and the rest of our families. I visited at Dick's house on several occasions in Simsbury, Connecticut, and he at mine. With and without our children.

We remained good friends for many years, long after Dick got forced out of GF. They had a problem with pesky entrepreneurial inventive free-thinking minds. He went on to become president of Heublein and after that head of Kentucky Fried Chicken. We stayed in touch, off and on, for many years but then drifted apart.

Years later we met for breakfast at the Hyatt Hotel in San Francisco, where Dick was staying while attending a business meeting. His wife Diane joined us and we had a nice time remembering days gone by.

I never saw Dick again, however, and most unfortunately never had the pleasure of working for him at either Chiat/Day or Goldberg Moser O'Neill. He would have greatly appreciated the creativity of both organizations and we would have been able to do much good work. Of that I am certain.

Unfortunately, too, I never got to ask him how on earth he kept the Kentucky Fried Chicken business at Young & Rubicam after the tribulations we had gone through on Jell-O. I can only guess that he didn't really understand the depth of resistance to his genius strategy among the top Y&R executives.

⊘ ⊘ ⊘

In 1969 I was asked to host one of General Foods' sales executives and give him an orientation to Young & Rubicam and what we did and how we did it. His name was Lynn Jordon.

Lynn and I spent three days together and we immediately liked one another, as did our wives. We all began to socialize away from the business. As luck would have it, over the years our paths would cross over and over and over.

When Lynn left General Foods, he ended up at E&J Gallo, an account that I took over in 1977. Lynn and I renewed our relationship once again and strengthened it further under the rigors of the Gallo management style.

Some years later Lynn was working for La Victoria Salsa and he helped me win that business for Chiat/Day. He was head of Trader Vic's food service for a time and we did some very clever creative work for that brand, as we did for Indian Summer vinegar products when he joined that company in 1994.

Lynn was always an insightful marketing executive and championed the unique and clever advertising idea. We did wonderful work for him time after time. Unfortunately there was never a significant budget, but the work served us well and I am certain helped win other clients we shared it with.

Jeri and I have been friends with Lynn and his wife Jeanette for now over 40 years. We have had many dinners together; we have gone to Europe together several times; we have slept at their house and they at ours numerous times. We have been to their sons' marriages and they to our daughter's. We never miss the opportunity to get together when we can.

What a great client. Lynn was always so supportive and accepting and encouraging. And what great friends Lynn and Jeanette have been these many years. They are truly lifetime friends. We number them among our very best.

⊘ ⊘ ⊘

In 1978 when I relocated to the West Coast to work at the Young & Rubicam Los Angeles office, I was introduced to a young man named Simon Sherman. Simon was a Brit and was trying to get a high-quality line of soccer shoes off the ground in the United States, where soccer was a nascent industry and just beginning to become popular. He was a lone voice at the time, doing tireless groundwork to develop the soccer market as well as sell his line of shoes named Kudos.

I acted as marketing counselor to Simon and we spent many hours together. He and his wife Rhonda and Jeri and I all became quite close friends. Simon had a wonderful mother and father with whom we became friendly with as well and spent many happy times together.

Sadly, I was playing squash with Simon at the San Francisco Tennis Club one day and he dropped dead on the court, the result of an aneurysm. One of the hardest things I ever had to do was drive out to his home in Piedmont and tell Rhonda what had happened. When I pulled the car up to the house, she was waiting at the front door and it was as if she already knew. She knew something bad had happened. She was there, with her two children, and it was a very tough time.

I always counted Simon as a client even though I was never paid for any of the work I did for him. It was mostly marketing consultation, as we never prepared even a single ad. Simon was a smart, hardworking entrepreneur and I was blessed to have known him even if for a much shorter time than I would have liked.

Simon never saw the substantial growth of soccer here in the United States but he played an important role in seeding it in its earliest beginning stages. The Soccer Industry Council of America created a special award called the Simon Sherman Leadership Award.

Simon would be very proud and pleased at just how popular soccer has finally become in the United States, not so much as a spectator sport but rather as one that millions of boys and girls now participate in.

If Simon were here today, he would still be among my very best "client" friends.

⊘ ⊘ ⊘

In 1987 a fellow called and said he had heard that I had a successful record with entrepreneurial ventures. He pointed to our great success with the toy company Worlds of Wonder, and he wondered whether I might be willing to spare him some time just to chat. I said sure and we met up a few days later at the agency.

When this gentleman arrived, my receptionist called back and said, "There is a Mr. Jim Lavelle here to see you." I told her to send him back.

A few moments later, into my office space walked this big, tall, good-looking guy with a close-cropped stylish beard and mustache and a full head of curly hair. He was dressed meticulously, and as he placed his attaché on the edge of my desk I couldn't help but notice that it was made of some quite unique skin.

I asked him, "What's that case made of?"

"Eel skin!"

"Oh."

He proceeded to open the top of the elegant eel skin attaché and I saw that it was filled with all sorts of shoelaces. Green ones, yellow ones, red ones, bright and light, dark and patterned. Different lengths, styles, tips, and whatnot. He told me he had a product idea and he wanted to know what I thought about it and possibly give him some direction.

"I have a patent on lighted shoelaces."

"Say what?"

"Yeah, lighted shoelaces like these."

With that he pulled out a pair and dangled them in front of me. As he shook them, they started to twinkle like little tiny Christmas lights. They flashed on and off each time they were moved. So the idea was if a kid, or anyone for that matter, had them in their shoes, the laces would start twinkling with every movement of their feet.

I said, "Hey, that's a terrific idea. I like it. I think you can do something with it."

Jim broke into a big smile. I offered to spend some more time with him and subsequently visited his house in Tiburon, where we spent the better part of a day talking about the idea mostly from a marketing point of view and some of the ways he might start to develop the business.

The lighted shoelaces never got off the ground, but a few years later lighted, twinkling shoes became all the rage. Unfortunately someone else had figured out how to use a similar technology in the heel and other parts of a shoe, avoiding the shoelaces altogether.

Fast-forward to 1998, years later, when sitting in my office one early morning, I answered my phone and heard a booming voice on the other end.

"Fred, it's Jim Lavelle."

"Huh! It's been seven years, hasn't it?"

"No, more like 10."

"Well where the hell have you been?"

"I know. I know. But I've been busy. I run a company now called Cotelligent."

"No kidding. What do they do?"

He explained that Cotelligent was an information technology company with $500 million in sales and I don't remember how many hundreds of employees, and that he wanted to talk about doing some advertising.

And so we developed some really good but edgy advertising, advertising that had some of the people at Cotelligent scared to death. That's the thing about new and different. It makes people nervous, particularly those who are warm and comfortable doing what has been done before.

But, Jim had the guts to go forward with the work anyway. Had the market situation for Cotelligent not changed for the worse, I believe that advertising would have helped build the company dramatically. But that was not to be, as the computer consulting business went the way of the dot-coms.

Regardless, ever since then I have been close friends with Jim and his wife Barbara. We have dinners often with our wives and we have had some great one-on-one breakfasts together, as Jim explains whatever his current venture is that he is involved in. He has the true entrepreneurial spirit about him.

Jim is one of the most enthusiastic and likable people I have ever met, and it is a joy having him as a friend. I am so glad I didn't get frightened away by the eel skin bag.

⊘ ⊘ ⊘

In 1985, not very long after meeting Jim Lavelle, I received a similar call from Jonathan Rosenthal. He had heard about us and admired some of our work. Would I spend a few minutes with him to hear about his venture?

He too had an unusual and unique idea. Alas, it too would turn out to be another one that was just ahead of its time, like soccer shoes and lighted shoelaces.

Jonathan's company was for on-demand private jet air service. It was a heck of an idea but the economics at the time were off. Jonathan was a real entrepreneur and he worked at trying to get the company off the ground for years.

During this time we were able, with his encouragement, to create some really great advertising along with other promotional ideas. One of which became a very important tool for us as an agency and for some of our other clients who couldn't afford big advertising dollars. It was the five-by-seven postcard ad. An inexpensive way to deliver a message with impact to a very specific target.

My friendship with Jonathan resulted in helping me win one of the most important businesses of my career, Worlds of Wonder. It so happened that the day I was pitching the Worlds of Wonder clients, Don Kingsborough and Paul Rago, Jonathan was using one of our conference rooms next to the one I was having the new business meeting in. We took a break at a point and I introduced the prospects to Jonathan, who in turn spent the next hour selling them on our agency.

I don't see Jonathan that often now, but I am pleased to have known him and know that he has done extremely well in his ventures since Net Air. And I am sure he takes some pleasure in knowing that his idea was a good one and that Warren Buffett thought so too, having successfully launched Net Jets.

⊘ ⊘ ⊘

Two of the very best clients, and now friends, I have had are Kathy and David Lockton. Truly two of the classiest, smartest, and nicest people I have ever met.

And it was a very close call that I even ever got to work with them. I had crossed paths with Kathy Lockton while working on Apple Computer, where she worked. Frankly, despite her good looks and wonderful persona, I didn't put the name and person together on the day when she popped into the agency at 77 Maiden Lane without calling.

This was in the fall of 1991, and I got a call from the front desk advising that a Kathy Lockton from Interactive Network was in the lobby and would like to see me. Without thinking too much about it and after hearing "network," I told the receptionist that I would have someone come out and meet with her, believing that she must be representing some computer or network-related firm trying to sell us a system or software or something.

I had Harold Mann, my MIS guru, go and meet with her. Harold was one of the smartest folks who ever worked for me and handled himself extremely well for such a young fellow. He took her into a small conference room.

A few minutes later he rang and said, "Fred, maybe you should come in here. I think this is a new business opportunity."

Oops!

I immediately went over to the conference room, recognized Kathy, and shook hands. Without any remarks, Kathy proceeded to explain (again) about the new company that she and her husband David had started. It was an exciting idea, a unique patent, for which they had considerable funding and they needed an advertising agency to help with the communications.

Despite the way I had shuffled off the meeting initially, Kathy was gracious and enthusiastic about having us involved. She never even mentioned the slight. Had the tables been reversed, I would have been gone long beforehand. But she didn't and we had a splendid meeting and she hired us, and together we did some absolutely sensational marketing and advertising programs that broke new ground.

Interactive Network had developed and patented a system that allowed customers to play along in real time with various programs that were being broadcast on television like *Jeopardy!* or *Wheel of Fortune* or an NFL football game. The neat thing was that it was capable of doing this simultaneously, in real time, as shows were being broadcast and therefore allowed a level of interaction by viewers at home that had heretofore not been possible.

Both Kathy and David were among the most creative clients I had ever worked with and were very supportive of anything that had a creative edge. More importantly they were willing to put their money up to implement a good idea.

Of the many inventive ideas that got approved, one involved producing and broadcasting what would be the first live TV commercials in 30 or so years to help launch the Interactive Network service. This was done from the Oakland A's stadium during an actual televised baseball game. We had people at the stadium playing in real time on Interactive Network along with the ball game as it was being played and televised.

This was pretty risky stuff but highly innovative and clever, and it had enormous impact. It was not so much the impact that the advertising would have but rather the potential to generate considerable free publicity, something that was not lost at all on David Lockton.

No one had gone live with commercials since Toro started their lawn mowers to demonstrate that they always did. Not since John Cameron Swayze kept Timex ticking while it took various lickings.

Unfortunately Interactive Network was another one of those ideas ahead of its time. Communicating in real time today is a given, but just 20 years ago it was not.

I worked with Kathy and David for many years and we did lots of good things together. I spent many dinners with them and we have stayed at their house and they at ours on several occasions. They remain good friends.

⊘ ⊘ ⊘

I had met another husband and wife team, also with an entrepreneurial mentality. Two of the nicest, most gracious clients who ran a food company. Both of these folks were meticulously and fashionably dressed. Our first meeting was in my offices on Maiden Lane in San Francisco in 1985. They were looking for some help in building their brand.

The company was the Berelson Company and David and Riva Berelson were the two people who ran the firm.

They had created and successfully built a brand called Sea Legs, which was at that point sold only direct to food suppliers and not the end consumer. The product was a fish called pollack that underwent an established Japanese process that turned it into something called surimi. This in turn was then extruded to look something like lobster claws or crabmeat. It actually tasted quite good and most people didn't know the difference from the real thing when they were buying lobster or shrimp salad in the deli or supermarket or even being served in a restaurant.

We did some wonderful work for the Berelsons largely because they were such inventive and accepting clients. In true entrepreneurial fashion they encouraged us and approved some pretty innovative creative work, especially for a packaged food.

Print ads for "The Great Pretender" and "Little White Lies" were clever and beautifully shot so as to make the food appear as good as the real thing: "delicious deception in the grocer's fresh seafood section."

In addition we developed a television campaign along the same lines with gorgeous food photography of the products with an underlying music track that used the Platters' "Great Pretender" song.

After this initial campaign we were looking for a new direction and we came upon one. The idea emerged from our real-life interactions with David and Riva, both of whom were very bright and quite opinionated. Often, even when they disagreed on something, kind of a wonderful, almost comical banter went back and forth between the two. It was entertaining and often fun. It was the stuff of today's reality programming but done for real.

So the idea was to use the two of them in a television campaign and capture that smart, engaging, whimsical dialogue between them as they acted as spokespeople for Sea Legs. Their passion for their products and the product quality would exude from their dialogue. And if done right, the "reality" of it all would be very believable. It would be engaging and awareness generating, as much as motivating and enhancing the quality of the products and the brand.

Everyone at the agency that worked on the account got a real kick out of being in the meetings and interacting with the Berelsons. They were always a lot of fun, particularly when they were at odds with one another on some issue or other. They also were always very complimentary and sweet to their agency people.

I will admit here there was a bit of resistance on both David's and Riva's part at first to the idea of appearing in the commercials. But our creative person, Ross Van Dusen, and I convinced them of the merit of the idea and they acquiesced and agreed to go ahead. We set a day for the shooting.

While I wasn't at the shoot, it was reported to me that David and Riva arrived, as usual dressed beautifully and in very good spirits. However, as soon as they were asked to sit on the two stools set up in front of the cameras, traces of fear began to creep into each of them.

They sat down, the director reviewed what he hoped could happen, then he sat down and said "Action." And with that they froze.

Six hours later, like frozen surimi, they hadn't thawed. We had lots and lots of footage in the can, and none of it was usable. We were unable to capture on the film any of the marvelous energy and personality that these two passionate and intelligent individuals otherwise exuded. They simply didn't come off as "real" and these were really real people. Salt of the earth.

It was an ironic result, and of course the last thing we wanted to do was to put Sea Legs, this "semi-fake fish" that was pretending to be something other than what it was, in an unbelievable or unreal situation.

Well, we left all the footage on the cutting room floor, as they say in Hollywood. It was an unfortunate experiment. But in a way it brought us all together even more in our relationship. Everyone at the agency would jump through burning hoops for these two people. And after this mishap, they jumped even higher.

The Berelsons ultimately sold their company to a Japanese firm that managed to destroy what was a really great enterprise.

I am still friendly with David and Riva and see them often. They live in Tiburon, California, about a mile and a half from my home in Belvedere. They are good and dear friends. Jeri and I are particularly proud to be godfather to their son Serj, who has grown into a splendid Berelson as well.

And so all of these clients and others, as Julie Andrews crowed, are a few of my favorite things.

CHAPTER 24

THE ONLY THING HARDER THAN CREATING A GREAT AD IS SELLING IT

THE GREATEST FAILING OF AN AD is that is doesn't get seen. And ads don't get seen for a variety of reasons, including that they are boring and run-of-the-mill and don't attract attention. Or they are irrelevant and do not motivate the intended audience. Or they are placed in obscure media that have a small or inattentive or uninterested or disinterested audience. Or the client hasn't got the balls to run something that is bold and provocative and pushes the edge of the envelope. By far it's the last situation that is the nemesis of so many of the great ads and breakthrough concepts. Those that don't get to run, and even some of those that do.

There is a metaphysical tension that exists between a client's search for advertising that will drive their business forward and the level of willingness to take chances with the creative. Yin and yang. Generally these are inversely correlated, and even the most entrepreneurial and daring client sometimes suffers cold feet. I experienced this with Worlds of Wonder, California Cooler, Apple Computer, Jell-O Gelatin, and even Dell Computer, the last of which was among my most daring clients, at least in their early formative years.

It's an issue that plagues all advertising agencies, creative or not. The more conservative monolithic ones are bothered less because they are happy to just run advertising that the client approves and bank their fees or commissions.

But those agencies that honestly strive to do great or even good creative work suffer far more. The better creative people regularly feel this pain. It requires a special resiliency to withstand this kind of rejection. It also requires a fiscal philosophy that does not put just making a profit ahead of producing good work. At the end of the day it costs a lot more in emotion and time to generate outstanding ads.

Of course an agency needs exceptional creative talent in order to manufacture great ads. It also needs a focus on greatness since good ads are clearly the enemy of great ones. When you settle for less, it shows.

Most of all, getting the exceptional kind of creative requires an extraordinary level of salesmanship and of trust. The agency has to have people who are willing to fight in an uncommon manner for the great ideas that they produce no matter who they are or what their position is at the agency.

It's a matter not of being obstinate but rather of garnering the trust of the client, putting forth well-thought-out arguments in defending the work, and being passionate and believable in one's convictions. Unfortunately all too often this gets interpreted as "creative arrogance." And all too often it is, particularly from the least creative agencies and individuals, which is odd.

People who are not to be trusted have long sullied the advertising business and made it considerably harder to sell good work. I have a cartoon that portrayed the situation so well that I kept it hanging in my office over the years. It had a little tiny bird sitting on the inside of the lower jaw of a huge alligator whose mouth was wide open, ready to snap shut. The caption over the alligator read, "Trust me." The only thing missing from the cartoon was the words "advertising executives" across the alligator's tail.

At one point, according to Gallup, advertising was ranked as the least trusted profession. Another, different survey was maybe more kind, placing ad execs just above the lowest category, that being used car salesmen, but behind lawyers and politicians. There is a reason.

The situation makes getting clients to buy into the work much more difficult than it might otherwise have to be. But the truth is it's a lot easier for someone at an advertising agency to say an ad is exactly what a client should be doing since it's not their business at risk or their money being spent. I believe you'll find similar phenomena with stockbrokers and money managers.

One of my first experiences with defending a good creative idea came early in my career back in 1975 while working on the Bristol-Myers Excedrin PM account. Excedrin PM was a nighttime pain reliever that also acted as a mild sleeping aid.

We had worked for 12 months producing a commercial, which used what was then a new and complicated imaging technique. It had a nude man lying on his back photographed in a dark gray-blue X-ray-like image. As the announcer talked about nighttime pain, various parts of the man's body would begin to light up and glow in red and pulsate to suggest pain points.

The spot wasn't even close to a great commercial, but it used a novel and arresting technique to demonstrate the pain problem that people suffered and how it could interfere with sleeping. Given the television network and FDA restrictions placed on analgesic commercials, it was a considerable creative step forward compared with the Anacin hammer hammering and the Bufferin buffer buffering. The spot turned out to be effective and sophisticated, and it used this innovative animation process called rotoscoping in a dramatic and attention-getting manner.

We were quite pleased and proud of the effort we had made and what we had produced. The two creative people on the business, copywriter John Ferrell and art director Don Ross, and I marched the few blocks from Y&R at 285 Madison Avenue to Bristol-Myers headquarters at 345 Park Avenue to share the result. We were all psyched up in a positive way.

Our meeting was with one of the product management executives, and upon entering his office, before we even sat down, it was clear he was preparing us for his rejection in the event he would "need" to do that. He was such an arrogant little shit. Actually he was over six feet tall, but still.

He was sitting in his office behind his desk when we arrived. He looked up at us, not even saying hello, and began tapping the tips of his fat fingers together. All this body language was being emanated while John Ferrell was getting ready to run the rough cut of the spot on the videotape machine that had been rolled into the office. (This is actually one of the techniques that clients unsure of their creative evaluative skills frequently use to put an agency on the defensive.)

We didn't say much more. John just pushed the button and let it play. The commercial ended 30 seconds later and there were a few moments of silence, but then the client just shook his head slowly from left to right and then again from left to right. He had this affected smile, that is, "shit-eating grin," and then he said, "I don't think we got it."

And then he repeated it. "I don't think we got it."

I was sitting in a chair directly in front of his desk across from him, and without missing a beat I reached across the desk, grabbed him by his tie, pulled on it, looked directly into his face, nose to nose, and said, "I don't give a shit what you think. We worked a goddamn year on this thing and think it's great. We're showing it to Sheedy."

"I wouldn't do that," he said.

And then he repeated himself. "I wouldn't do that."

I shouted, "Watch me!"

John Sheedy was the VP advertising director and final authority on all advertising matters. I grabbed the tape out of the machine and told John and Don to follow me, and we marched down the hall to Sheedy's office. The product manager traipsed along a few feet behind us.

I knocked on the open door and said, "John, we've got the rough cut of the Excedrin PM spot we've been working on and we'd like you to take a look at it."

He said, "Sure. Great. Come on in."

I shoved the tape in his video machine and, without any preamble or qualifications, pushed the button and ran the spot. He watched the commercial and then said, "Great! That's great. Let's see it again."

I rewound the tape and played it again.

"That's just great. Congratulations. Good job. A really good job."

He turned to the product guy and said, "What do you think?"

"Yeah. It's good. It's good."

It was hardly a brilliant commercial and maybe didn't deserve my over-the-top reaction, but what happened is illustrative of what so often happened during the advertising process. It's about people not really knowing the difference between good and bad advertising in the first place. And it's too often about authority, power, politics, and manipulation.

For me it was an important lesson learned. I admit I may have acted a bit irrationally and somewhat irresponsibly. I risked my relationship on the account. But it demonstrated that if you want to get unique and better ads through the system, you've got to be tough and stand up for what you believe. That means you often need to risk giving up "relationship currency" in exchange for integrity. It's extremely important in a business that suffers from anemia in this territory.

The Excedrin PM commercial story took on near-epic proportions and was of huge benefit to my career and to me henceforth. The story went around the agency in New York like wildfire, allowing me to garner a great deal of the creative people's admiration and respect. As these things often do, it took on a life of its own and became larger with each subsequent telling. There were some who believed that I grabbed the client around the neck with both hands and shook his head back and forth until he cried uncle.

The incident preceded me to the West Coast before I was transferred to the Y&R Los Angeles office. And when I walked into the office for the very first time, I was a rock star.

"We definitely need account people who know what good advertising is."

"Hey, it's great to have someone here that will finally stick up for the ads."

"Did you really strangle that Excedrin client?"

"Did he actually pass out?"

"Is it true he spent several days in the intensive care ward at New York Presbyterian Hospital?"

I had become bigger than life, and maybe I was.

⊘ ⊘ ⊘

While at Y&R Los Angeles I won the Twentieth Century Fox TV advertising account. They had a range of popular shows for which we did TV and radio commercials in promoting them.

The thing about Hollywood and its studios is that absolutely everyone believes they know more about how to do the advertising than anyone at the advertising agencies. They also believe that they have the authority to make the decision on what is done and what isn't. Usually what goes on is that the lower level folks exercise their "no" vote but rarely their "yes" vote.

And the truth of the matter is that there is always a man or woman at the top that is the final decision maker, and everyone at the studio lives in mortal fear of upsetting that person. As a result, a huge amount of energy is expended by people trying to second-guess what that person might want, will want, does want. Yes sir! Yes ma'am! Yes-siree-Bob-sir-ma'am!

We had done some really terrific and edgy radio commercials for one of the Fox shows and were previewing them for the brand manager on the show.

"Gosh, I don't know."

"Gee, it's a bit controversial."

"Not sure about these."

"Don't know if Harris will go for this."

So he called in a few secretaries to see what they thought.

"Gosh, I don't know."

"Gee, it's a bit controversial."

"Not sure about these."

"Don't know if Harris will go for this."

So I suggested that we let Jerry have a listen to them. Jerry Greenberg was the ad manager and we called him in.

"Gosh, I don't know."

"Gee, it's a bit controversial."

"Not sure about these. Don't know if Harris will go for this."

So I said, "Well, let's see what Harris has to say." Harris being the head at the top of the Twentieth Century TV totem.

"No, no, we don't want to do that. We don't want to do that."

The reason "we don't want to do that" is that when you are in the second-guessing business, it requires that you are always correct, and since advertising is a pretty arbitrary and judgmental thing, open to many interpretations and personal biases, it makes the advertising decision-making process incredibly sensitive particularly to guessing.

"Let's just forget about these and do some others."

I said, "Huh?"

"Yeah, let's just do some new ones and we won't have to deal with these questions."

"No, let's let Harris hear them and decide for himself."

Harris was Harris Katleman, who was the tip-top banana at the Fox studio overseeing all the television programming and whom everyone lived in fear of. I insisted that we let Harris hear the spots before deciding whether to do new ones. After all, they cost a fair amount of time and money to produce and were ready to go on the air. And the fact of the matter was that they were very good.

In the middle of what became a heated discussion, it so happened that Harris walked in to ask an unrelated question and queried what was going on.

Before anyone could say "nothing," I said "something."

"We've got some new radio commercials that we're presenting and we'd like your opinion."

Without a hesitation Harris said, "Let's hear them."

I proceeded to run the cassette. There were three spots, and after he heard them, Harris, still laughing, said, "Those are just fantastic. Congratulations. They are terrific. When do they go on the air?"

And then everyone else in the room chimed in, "Yeah. Fantastic. Terrific. Good job."

"They'll be on the air next week. For sure!"

And so more good advertising was saved from the jaws of ego, hubris, politics, and fear.

⊘ ⊘ ⊘

One of the strangest ironies of the ad business is that there are those clients who are very much attracted to a truly creative advertising agency. One that has done breakthrough work for clients with demonstrable results in the marketplace. Some clients don't even have to have the results part.

They hire this kind of agency, but when the time comes to belly up and say "yes" to a creative concept that may be a bit more daring, their product becomes different from all those other clients' products whose ads they had so admired. Indeed it is a scary thing and requires considerable courage to embark on groundbreaking turf for your own brands and business.

There was a time when Reebok decided that the Chiat/Day office in New York couldn't deliver the creative they sought any longer. The client wanted to put the business in review but was persuaded by Jay Chiat to let each of the Chiat/Day offices, in New York, Los Angeles, and San Francisco, compete and pitch the account against one another. It was a smart move to stave off a competitive review involving other agencies.

All three offices made separate presentations to Paul Fireman, CEO, and other senior Reebok executives. Chiat/Day San Francisco emerged with the only winning concept that Reebok embraced. My partner, Mike Moser, and copywriter Jeff Billig created it.

It was a brilliant but very daring commercial. In order to demonstrate how the new Reebok Pump shoe worked, how it fit better, a product comparison was set up between the Pump and Nike. Two men were selected; one wore the Reebok Pumps and the other wore the Nikes. Both men were then shown bungee jumping off a bridge over Puget Sound up in Washington.

The commercial was shot with incredible drama in slow motion and followed the men ever so slowly and quietly floating down, down, down. And then whap! With a loud sound of the rubber rope snapping, the man wearing the Reebok Pumps was shown bouncing upside down, up and down at the end of the rope. Then the camera slowly panned over to one side to see only the rope left slowly swinging and a pair of empty Nikes. It was fantastic. It was powerful. It made the point about fit in an incredible way.

The client loved it. It went on the air. There was a firestorm of related publicity on all the networks and news programs as well as other shows across the country. Arsenio Hall showed it to his audience for a five-minute segment where he interviewed the two guys that actually did the bungee jump. His audience stood up and wildly cheered and applauded.

Just about every soul in the country knew immediately about the Reebok Pump after the commercial ran. Every Reebok Pump in the country was sold quickly. The commercial appeared on the *Wall Street Journal* list of "Most Popular Commercials" in the number 11 slot up against others like Pepsi-Cola, Nike, Miller Life, and Budweiser who were spending millions and millions on their advertising. The "bungee" commercial never had more than $500,000 in paid media behind it.

Alas, the commercial only ran for a few days and was taken off the air. People complained to Reebok and to the networks that it was encouraging people to commit suicide. Oh my God! What a warped interpretation. No sense of humor at all.

Reebok had none either. They couldn't stand the pressure of the critics despite their original love for the commercial. And despite that they benefited mightily from the enormous amount of free publicity that it had caused and the widespread exposure of the new product.

Sometime later I had occasion to screen the Reebok spot for my Celestial Seasonings tea client. They had asked me to speak about advertising to a gathering of all of their employees. Immediately after I showed the spot, the auditorium erupted into a frenzy of laughing, clapping, and shouting with great appreciation. This was a younger group of people who "got it" and they responded to it. Suicide never crossed their minds.

The Reebok Pump commercial was one of the very best commercials ever produced, in my opinion. It stands up today as an incredible piece of creative work. It attracted attention, it announced a new product, it featured the product's benefit, and it was a joke and fun. It worked even with only a few days' exposure, but there was no way we could get it back on air. And Chiat/Day ended up getting fired.

At 3M we first went to work for their data diskette products division. They were attracted to us because of our good work at Chiat/Day San Francisco for several other technology companies, including Intel, Shugart, Apple Computer, and Businessland.

For 3M we were able to develop and get approved some really great advertising for what arguably is one of the dullest and most uninteresting and mundane categories that ever existed: data storage diskettes. It didn't help either that diskettes were commodities virtually identical for all manufacturers. But the 3M clients hired us to differentiate their brand from all the others. And we didn't disappoint.

Someone once said, "A brand is like a shining beacon in the sea of ambiguity and complexity." Truly we delivered that beacon for 3M.

We developed TV and print. One ad was better than the next. These ads helped drive awareness and brand quality and differentiate 3M diskettes. The business went up and we won many creative awards for the work.

The ads were unusual in that they were all black-and-white with a very distinctive treatment of the 3M diskette logo jutting up as a triangle from the bottom of each page, with headlines like "3M introduces one less thing to worry about," "You should live so long," and "The cure for worry warts."

We were asked to present our credentials to several others at 3M. One of the other divisions we went to work for was the personal products division. They were attracted to what we had done and to our creative work in general. Or so they said when they hired us.

We were assigned a product called Buf-Puf, a facial cleaning product. We presented numerous campaigns, one after the other, all clever and relevant to what we were trying to say about the product. The product manager and the division president had come down with a sudden impairment resulting in consternation, trepidation, misgiving, and a general inability to make a decision to approve anything. Their angst level grew greater with each new campaign that was presented. And our patience diminished with each subsequent one.

This was a big and important company, and having 3M as a client was an important and prestigious asset. But the clients in this division were so constipated and afraid that I finally made a decision to tell them to go away. This was extremely difficult, as I did not like to give up business and because we had relationships with several other divisions.

But we had spent an enormous amount of time and creative energy trying to please them over many months with nothing to show for it. I was angry because we had presented much good work and they couldn't find a way to approve anything. It was also one of those situations where regardless of the number of valid arguments that may be put forth, including positive ad research results, you just can't budge a client.

So I wrote a letter to the division president resigning the account. I was frustrated and it showed up in my letter. It was a classic example of clients who just couldn't bring themselves to approve innovative and clever advertising no matter how relevant it may have been. This was also one of those times where I wished I had not committed my feelings to the written word and put a postage stamp on it.

The craziest thing was that 3M had a reputation for being true innovators in everything they did. In order to do that, they had to inculcate the entire organization with the desire and need to seek out innovative solutions. Turns out in the case of Buf-Pufs that innovation did not extend beyond product development.

While I didn't regret resigning the account over these creative issues, my letter came back to haunt me. Alice Cuneo of *Ad Age* wrote an article entitled "Chiat's Goldberg Makes His Move." It had to do with my breakaway from Chiat/Day/Mojo and the purchase of the San Francisco operation and the founding of Goldberg Moser O'Neill.

In keeping with the media's need to generate sensationalism, Alice, who was West Coast editor, dredged up some things to make the article more controversial. Or, as she always used to say, "more balanced."

Somehow she had gotten her hands on the letter that I had sent to the president of the Consumer Specialties Division at 3M. She decided to include and quote parts of it in her article.

> *I have worked with some of the most demanding and visionary entrepreneurial people. And I have worked with the most sophisticated of the packaged goods companies. At neither end of the spectrum have I seen such constipation and inability to apply sound judgment. As such we do not wish to be associated with a client that has such little regard for marketing innovation and is unwilling to accept any risks. We will find another who does!*

I wasn't really happy that the letter had found its way to *Ad Age* and that they had published parts of it. Turns out, however, it became a tremendous morale booster and motivator for the entire agency and publicly reinforced our commitment to the creative product and to our culture. It also may have contributed to my image, which you can read about in the next chapter, entitled "Sandpaper."

I am certain it added to our credentials as a creative agency and resulted in attracting more of those clients who desired inventive ads. It definitely reinforced my reputation as a tough and committed advertising executive. Which I was.

We had the Sutter Home Winery business for many years and did exceptional creative work for them during that time. The clients were pretty savvy when it came to the need to break through and make sure their advertising stood out and was seen or heard as its first priority.

They believed that if an ad wasn't seen or heard, it wasn't going to do any good. Seems like such a simple thought but it's amazing how few clients actually embrace it. It seems even more so when a client has untold amounts of money to spend on media. But most clients don't, and particularly smaller clients who like to try to maximize their efforts.

Our work for Sutter Home was always edgy. It stood out and it made an impact. One year we were running a radio campaign that in one ad made a bit of fun of the purple birthmark on Russian president Gorbachev's head. Another went after used car salesmen. And so on.

The campaign was very humorous and made excellent points about Sutter Home in terms of what we were trying to communicate. But our clients, all of them, suddenly got frozen feet. They had a difficult time approving the ads. By being strong and argumentative, we prevailed largely on the basis that they didn't have a lot of money and they needed to generate awareness and cut through and stand out from all the other wines that were advertising at the time. It was that argument that hit closest to home for them.

The campaign ran. It drove Sutter Home awareness up significantly along with its sales. Used car salesmen from all over the country called to complain, as did the Russian consulate. All proof that the advertising was being heard and working well. It also generated much added positive publicity for Sutter Home and their wines along the way.

On a similar note we produced a radio ad for Round Table Pizza, which featured a situation that everyone who ever went to the dentist can relate to. In the commercial the dentist told his patient, "Sit back, relax, you won't feel a thing." But in the background you heard the sound of a drill whirring away diabolically. Then the announcer delivered the line, "Get real. Get Round Table."

So the Round Table clients got a call from the American Dental Association demanding a cease and desist of the commercial. I mean lighten up. Isn't that what actually happens when you're in that dental chair? And moreover it was a joke. People nodded their heads and laughed.

You never know where "ad killers" can come from, or when, but you have to be strong and fight them off. This ad kept running over the ADA protestations because of a strong and creatively committed client. Maybe also because they received a lot of positive feedback. Having an agency that fought for the work to stay on the air helped too.

Maybe the perfect environment for creating great advertising without any hiccups or roadblocks happened when we went to work for Al Davis, owner of the Oakland Raiders. We were on an incredible timetable where we had to create and get ads on air in five days. Time is the great enemy of great work unless there is little of it. But obviously with less time, the ads had to be simple from a production standpoint.

The creative team, Brian O'Neill, Paul Carek, and Terry Rietta, came up with a cool and compelling TV campaign in 24 hours. Brian flew down to LA the next day with some rough tissues and met with Davis in his all-white house, with his all-white furniture, in his all-white jumpsuit. Davis approved everything with enthusiasm. We produced the work over the next three days and it aired the next week on time.

That's often how good advertising makes it through. An entrepreneurial mentality; a client who can say yes; a creative team that's creative; an agency that's committed to doing good work. And no time to dick around with the work. Al Davis was all "white" with me.

⊘ ⊘ ⊘

One day after I had a one-on-one meeting with Steve Jobs, he asked me to visit John Lassiter over at Pixar, where Jobs had begun to get involved. He wanted me to talk with Lassiter about advertising. So I set up a meeting and drove across the bay to see him. I spent an hour with him, after which he said he had no interest whatsoever, confirming my beliefs that selling advertising is hard. Of course, his lack of interest might have been fully justified since he ultimately wound up producing the highest grossing animated film ever, *Finding Nemo*. The film generated its own publicity and advertising and went on to win an Oscar.

⊘ ⊘ ⊘

There is another situation where you don't have to worry about getting client approval for a great concept. That is when the agency does self-promotion advertising.

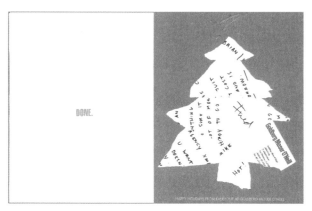

I did this pretty regularly and it included the preparation of a holiday card every year. This was a project that I took very seriously and had the creative people start working on January 2 of the year of the card. Why? Because I was the client, and most of the creative people that worked on our holiday card will tell you that "clients" don't come any tougher. I insisted that the card be absolutely great. Every year. Year after year.

I felt it was an extremely important affirmation of our creativity as an agency and I had a long list of recipients to whom I sent the card each year, including current clients, past clients, prospects, friends, enemies, recruiters, venture capitalists, competitive agencies, the press, and members of my family. It always generated positive responses and goodwill for Goldberg Moser O'Neill.

My last year-end card effort was in 1999 and the creative folks did not let me down. This was an almost impossible challenge since we had done incredibly great cards almost every year before.

For this final card we tried to exploit the fact that just about everyone in Corporate America was crazed over the problems with what was called Y2K,

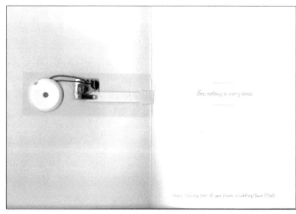

the change in the calendar to the new millennium and the potential it had for creating chaos with computers and network systems around the world.

Sparing no expense (literally), the creative group designed a card that said on the front, "To help ease your fears about the millennium bug, this card contains a small computer chip which will play for you the familiar and comforting New Year's Eve song 'Auld Lang Syne.'"

When the card was opened, a tiny computer chip started playing the song "Take Me Out to the Ball Game."

At the bottom of the card was the message, "See, nothing to worry about. Happy Holidays from your friends at Goldberg Moser O'Neill."

It was without doubt one of our most clever endeavors in the holiday card arena. Actually in any arena. The timing was so perfect, coming at year-end just before the year 2000 was upon us. I thought it was so brilliant that I approved it and its production on first seeing it, despite what was a very expensive production cost.

After all, it was my last holiday card. It did such a great job reinforcing our creativity and inventiveness. I was always screeching for the more creative solutions to our clients' problems and felt obliged to put my money where my mouth was. But it was brilliant.

We received tons of positive response and feedback. The one that stood out the most was from Mickey Mouse himself, Michael Eisner, at the time the head of Disney.

He personally called and said, "Out of the probably 10,000 cards I've gotten, yours was by far the most creative I've seen. I just felt compelled to pick up the phone and tell you that."

We never did get any Disney business.

There are many situations in other chapters in this book that revolve around the issue of just how difficult the advertising business is because of how hard it is to sell innovation. And even when you get it sold, making sure it sticks is a challenge. I experienced this knotty problem repeatedly in somewhat different ways with Apple Computer, California Cooler, Dell Computer, Worlds of Wonder, Jell-O Gelatin, and many other clients.

One lesson emerges from it all, and clients would do well to think about it when they ask an advertising agency to develop their advertising.

You can't make history by looking over your shoulder.

CHAPTER 25

SANDPAPER

WHEN I WAS A PRE-MED FRESHMAN at the University of Vermont, I joined the Tau Epsilon Phi fraternity. During hazing week some of the senior "brothers" of the fraternity in charge of this insidious and imbecilic activity selected me to carry a coffee can tied under my chin for days.

Of course that wouldn't have been too bad, but they directed that it be filled with fresh dog excrement. I had to suffer this repulsive and humiliating exercise for three days, including sleeping with the can at night. They required that the can be filled up "fresh" each morning.

As a result of my attitude or simply as an addition to the pleasant coffee can experience, the "brothers" gave me the nickname of "Sandpaper." For the next three years they referred to me in this manner and addressed me as such. Sandpaper. As in "Hey, Sandpaper!" or "Where you going, Sandpaper?"

They came upon this name because of my low, kind of scratchy, abrasive voice. That's the one I still have today. They had no idea that it might have been a descriptive precursor, or at least a part of one, that helped shape the personality that I would develop over time. Or maybe it was carrying around the coffee can that did that to me.

When I first came to San Francisco in 1982 and 18 years later when I retired from the business, I was referred to as a gadfly. In fact, I was identified in this way many times in between. And I guess that is a pretty good observation of me. I had this nasty habit of trying to keep and set the records straight.

A year after taking over the Chiat/Day San Francisco office, I attended what would be my first 4A meeting (American Association of Advertising Agencies). It was held on the 52nd floor at the very top of the Bank of America building on California Street in the Carnelian Room. A pretentious French restaurant, with spectacular views of San Francisco, that has long since gone out of business.

I walked into the room, and there were maybe 25 or 30 of the local senior advertising executives milling around with a scotch or a martini, and most with a cigarette, in hand. These were the people who were running the branch offices for the big national agencies like Y&R, Ketchum, J. Walter Thompson, and BBDO and some of the smaller independent ones like Allen & Dorward and Dailey. It felt like they felt they were a very important group indeed.

The San Francisco ad community was a pretty tight-knit circle and most of that bunch was in the room. There was an understood back-scratching philosophy and a certain gentlemanly approach to the business back then. That's code for there was not a lot of open honesty and directness between competitors. And while a lot of what went on was "gentlemanly," it was laden with considerable backstabbing, in my opinion.

Eventually we sat down for dinner, and over coffee and/or brandy or both, just about everyone lit up cigars and began puffing away, filling the room with smoke and harrumphing, as the topic of the evening was debated.

That topic was why and how these 4A agencies could attract a limited number of college students as interns. It seemed from the exasperation of the aggregation that the agencies represented in the room were having no success despite offering a nice stipend to potential candidates. The discussion went on for 45 minutes and no meaningful solutions emerged. It was really just a lot of grousing and complaining, as the room grew hazier and hazier. And so did I.

Finally, I stood up. I didn't bother introducing myself, although I hardly knew anyone there. I didn't have to, as they would all remember me well.

I said, "I don't understand why you all have this problem. I never had the problem when I ran Young & Rubicam Los Angeles and I don't have the problem now at Chiat/Day."

I continued, "You might want to look at your outreach program—that is, if you even have one—at the colleges of your interest. We have a list of target schools across the country. You might want to look at what makes your agency attractive, if anything, to a young person interested in learning about advertising. You might want to review who you have reviewing and recruiting these candidates. I am personally involved in doing that with our intern program.

"And you might want to decide whether you are willing to offer these people a chance to get engaged in real work at your agency and not be there just to make copies and run errands. Can an intern who is interested in media actually help develop media plans? Can one who is interested in film production work side by side with your TV producers? Can an intern who wants to be a copywriter actually get to write ads and, if they are good enough, present them to the client?"

I concluded, "We have no trouble whatsoever finding six new interns to join our agency for three months every quarter. We have an abundance of candidates and turn away far more than we take on. We don't offer them any stipend. All we mainly offer is a chance to have some real responsibility and actually learn the advertising business. If you let me know, I will be happy to forward those candidates that we decide not to take on. Gentlemen, good night."

With that I walked out of the smoked-filled brandy-sniffing harrumph-ing group of advertising executives and never went to another 4A meeting for the rest of my days in advertising. Clearly I did not endear myself to the community with brazen in-your-face preaching.

By the way, some of the very best executives who worked for me over the years had been our interns.

My 4A meeting surely established my presence in the Bay Area ad com-munity and was certainly the source of many conclusions drawn about my particular personality and me. Some turned out to be true and some not.

There was another situation I found myself in during my early days in San Francisco that shaped the perception of me as well. When the Apple Computer "1984" commercial made history, it seemed I was always trying to keep the media honest regarding the circumstances of its development, production, and utilization. The media and the community, in trying to sen-sationalize the situation, disseminated all sorts of misinformation.

I can remember dozens of times when I tried to set the record straight on some of the most preposterous exaggerations and misinterpretations that the media kept propagating. Since I was the senior account person managing the business at the time we produced the commercial, I felt it was important to have the record accurate. It also simply bothered me intellectually to have the story so twisted. I wrote letters, and when I had an opportunity during an interview, I would express the facts.

Despite all this, my efforts were mostly to no avail except to reinforce my gadfly image. The media were not interested in anything that would diminish the sensationalism of the story behind this great commercial and its success. Almost 30 years later, they still aren't.

I sent a letter to the editor of *Business Week* 15 years after the commercial had run regarding their cover story "The Fall of an American Icon," in which they made a number of completely inaccurate statements.

> *I was managing the Apple Computer account when the now famous "1984" television commercial was produced. In fact, I personally had the production estimate signed by then Apple Marketing Vice President, Floyd Kvamme. It included the production of a second commercial for the now defunct Lisa computer, in a :30 and :60 version. In other words, three com-mercials were actually produced at a cost of $650K. A far cry from the $1.6M reported.*

> *The notion that the "1984" commercial "was shown only once" is a myth. It actually ran a week prior to the Super Bowl in 13 spot markets. One of these, by design, was Boca Raton where the IBM PC division was situated.*

The suggestion that the commercial was a part of some super public relations effort by Apple is nonsense. The concept for the commercial was actually created two years earlier for the Apple III by Mike Moser, then Art Director. It was not approved then, but re-surfaced as one of many ads that were to launch Macintosh. Steve Jobs championed the concept and it was produced, but later rejected by Apple's Board of Directors.

The commercial was originally to have run twice on the Super Bowl but we were unable to sell off the second time slot. So history was made. And it had nothing to do with Apple's "well oiled image making machine." In fact, it had only to do with a guy named Steve Jobs thinking it was great. And a bit of fate.

This was just one of the many times I endeared myself to the media by attempting to keep them honest in their journalistic endeavors. At least regarding the things I knew something about.

They were wrong about the history of the famous "1984" commercial. And boy were they more recently so wrong about reporting and predicting the fall of Apple. I only hoped that those few people who read my letter might adjust their thinking on *BusinessWeek*'s credibility and that of the media in general.

I had started my business career in marketing research and I knew a fair amount about it, and particularly so in the area of copy research. This became a flash point for me over the years and I am sure contributed also to my gadfly image. That is, one who "annoys by persistent criticism." Too many people in the business did not understand the limitations that are inherent in trying to test advertising ideas, particularly the great creative ones.

My crusade in this area started way back at Ballantine Beer when the ad manager tried to conduct some copy research that was designed to make the ads appear effective regardless of whether they were or not. He eventually got fired.

My evangelistic efforts continued when I worked on General Foods and exposed the fact that their companywide on-air day-after recall system, which they totally relied upon for airing or not airing finished commercials, was fraught with inconsistencies and errors. They tested hundreds of commercials in this manner every year. When I exposed the inherent flaws of their system, they did nothing except get angry.

Over at Bristol-Myers I discovered 30 different flagrant deficiencies in their theater-testing model, which they used for testing advertising across most of their divisions. As a result of my initiatives, they actually abandoned the system for a while but soon reinstated it for lack of any other acceptable copy testing procedure.

When the Apple board of directors tried to kill the "1984" ad, I had it copy tested and discovered that ASI (Audience Surveys Inc.) concluded the spot was the single worst business to business commercial that had ever been tested in their system, as it received the absolute lowest score ever. So much for the validity of quantitative copy testing procedures.

But maybe the most prevalent misuse of a research tool was that of qualitative focus groups in determining the worth of advertising ideas. I was so upset by the lack of understanding of the limitations that I once sent a memo to everyone at Chiat/Day on the subject.

> *In the past several days I've sat in a number of client meetings where focus group research has been discussed. Frankly I'm disgusted. It sounds like we base our advertising decisions on the fact that "the focused groups said this, or the groups said that." If any of you think that's what we do around here then maybe we should just hold focused groups on every issue that comes up and get rid of half of our people.*
>
> *To set the record straight. It's the insights and interpretations that we as marketing and communications experts put on information that matters. It's not that some guy doesn't like a tagline or some woman is offended by a photograph. Qualitative research is only a stimulus to expand your thinking horizons. It can improve directions and ideas. It can provide fodder for additional and new directions. It can make you think twice and re-think what we have concluded. It is not to be used or presented as a black and white decision tool.*
>
> *You get paid to work at this agency for bringing your own thinking, your digestion of all the data that exists around a problem or opportunity, and coming up with a logical, well-thought-out point of view. And probably more than half of that point of view should be derived from judgmental conclusions and beliefs and prior experiences.*
>
> *I don't want to hear anyone using focused group research as the reasoning for killing, or accepting for that matter, any marketing or advertising idea. Believe it or not there's more to the identification of great advertising ideas than seven people sitting around a table in a dimly lit room eating stale dried-out ham and Swiss sandwiches. At least at this agency there is.*

As you might imagine, my point of view was quite offensive to all those who had made a career out of using small groups of dim-witted consumers who fancy themselves advertising experts, have nothing better to do for two hours on a Wednesday night, and are asked to sit in judgment of advertising.

Incredibly the experienced creative talent, getting paid often hundreds of thousands of dollars, often had less to say about the ad ideas than the consumer volunteers at a focus group getting paid $40 for 90 minutes of gabbing off the top of their heads. They also got a free roast beef or ham and cheese sandwich and coleslaw.

I successfully pissed off many marketing and advertising research people at the various agencies at which I worked, along with research firms and even clients. Maybe more than any, however, were all those account planners in the business who had made the focus group research an "infallible" method of assessing ideas that generally are highly emotional in the way they might affect an individual. Having consumers talk about ideas in front of others simply was a very blunt tool and one that should generally be taken with many grains of salt.

One reporter referred to me as the "industry outsider." I liked that. I always wanted to challenge the establishment. Frankly, I didn't care at all about being on the inside. The fact is that I was a cynic and questioned just about everything. People tend not to like that and I understand why. It doesn't radiate a lot of trust when one does that. But my cynicism served me well over the years and acted as an intellectual gatekeeper on so many issues and particularly when it came to creative ideas.

Thank goodness for my associate Mike Massaro, who relieved me of bearing this burden in total. If there was anyone who was more cynical about just about everything, it was Mike. God bless him. By the way, it is one thing to be cynical. It's quite another to be cynical and smart. Mike was the latter.

Another time, I was publicly in the media accused of being a perfectionist. Guilty! I've been denounced for working too hard. Guilty! I've been blamed for being relentless in the pursuit of the right idea and right solution. Guilty again!

Writing in the *San Francisco Examiner*, Carla Marinucci reported that employees at my agency described me as "driven, often demanding, occasionally explosive, but they also laud his warm sense of humor and fierce devotion to his troops and his two younger partners." Yet again—guilty!

Rosalinde Estes, my office manager for many years, once said for attribution in a magazine, "I know Fred has a tough reputation in the industry, but he loves rewarding people. He practically rubs his hands together when he gives people bonuses."

There was a story that circulated that I once threw a pot at Rosalinde out of frustration during an argument we were having. That wasn't true. I accidentally hit the flowerpot on her desk while I was wildly gesticulating with my hands and somehow it took off from the desktop in the air and toward her and landed in the windowsill behind her. Some wanted to believe that I would actually have done that, and the incident added to my infamous reputation.

I admit that I expected more than most from my employees, but I did love giving the good ones, the ones that broke their asses and did great work, rewards. I tried to do that as much as I could.

The truth is I never expected more of anyone than I did of myself. I was a relentless nitpicker when it came to many things, but not all things. But the ones I really cared about received my considerable attention. Things like crafting business memos and reports; delivering profits; having great creative ideas, be they space design, year-end parties, promotional ideas, or break-through advertising; the quality of the fresh flowers that populated various areas and my desk at our agency; and providing well for my wife and children.

But being insistent can drive others to the Golden Gate Bridge or off it. They don't fully understand the necessity and the benefits, nor do they nec-essarily agree with either. I, on the other hand, was infatuated enough with details and quality to purchase and hand out a copy of Tom Peters's *A Passion for Excellence* to everyone who was hired at the agency.

I am sure that some part of this temperament had to do with basic inse-curities. I was not a confident kid back in elementary and high school. When I went off to college, I gained considerable self-confidence and intrepidness. This did not come from doing well in class in the early years at university but rather from nonstop rounds of poker, gin, and, my favorite, hearts for stakes that I couldn't really afford. A lot of my insecurities were solved by winning, which I did far more frequently than losing. In fact, I can't remember ever losing a game of hearts in my four years at UVM.

While this certainly helped my esteem immensely and resulted in a very competitive desire to win, it did not interest everyone. Just because you want to win doesn't mean you're going to, unless you determine to go the extra mile. That certainly is the case in advertising, in winning new business or get-ting a great ad on the air.

Some generally perceived me as tough and a real son of a bitch. I admit I was really tough on the dumb ones. And on the political ones. Less so on the smart ones and the trusted and faithful. And less so on the totally inept, whom I just fired. Sometimes not soon enough, however.

I had my principles as we all do. But mine were cast in granite and I tried always to be faithful to them. I practiced them at the office and at home. And in keeping them I am certain it resulted in the perception and reality of the way I was viewed.

For example, I worked hard. I came in early and stayed late. I worked at home at night and on vacations. Most people didn't do this. And that was OK with me as long as their performance was maintained and the results were great.

For me, the hard work was an essential part of my being and of my suc-cess. I would always be thinking of the next thing and then try to do it. This was true when I started out as a clerk at my first job and was still true when I was running my successful agency.

I never stopped thinking of the next thing that would make a situation or a proposal or an ad better. I used to love to run and would use the time alone to think out issues, opportunities, and problems alike. I would look forward to a long plane ride so I would have the quiet time to cogitate on new solutions.

I always kept three-by-five cards on my person in order to jot down thoughts that would come to me and about which I wanted to think further. I had a pad and pencil next to my bed and would often wake up and jot down thoughts through the night so I wouldn't forget them in the morning. At one stage I had a tiny little recording device that I used for this purpose. I thought it was good enough to purchase several dozen and give them to my key executives and managers.

I demanded absolute trust from the people who mattered. And when someone violated that, it didn't sit well with me. It sullied my view of that person from then on. Maybe "trust" was the single most important differentiating factor that I used to evaluate one person from the next. And I think it may have been a critical reason that we had such a successful agency. I felt it was an absolutely essential ingredient in our managers and executive staff as much as their professional skill set.

Several times I let an untrustworthy (e.g., political, self-promoting, intellectually dishonest) person into the executive group. This failed and caused problems until I was able to remedy the situation by removal or execution.

If I said I would do something, I made sure I did it. I expected that behavior of others as well, and when they didn't, it reflected again on trusting that person or not. This was a very important thing for me and I am reminded how too often people say things just for the sake of the moment or to assuage a situation. But then they don't deliver. I made it a point all my life to deliver and I know that it added to my credibility and to my success. Clients and employees and friends know well that if I said something, then I would do it if I could. At least I wouldn't say it and then forget about it.

I always believed in extraordinary, maybe absurd preparation. I am certain that this was a result of insecurity and lack of confidence in myself from earlier days. I still have a scar from an early grade speech I had to give in an English class. I was sick to my stomach the night before with fear. I gave an absolutely awful presentation and received a terrible grade. And most of all I was embarrassed about my inabilities beyond expression. I never forgot that incident and preparation became critical for me.

I rehearsed all my business meetings beforehand. I kept a cheat sheet of notes in my pocket before a client lunch. I used copious outlines of my remarks for new business presentations. I wrote and rewrote speeches I might be giving and always relied on my notes. All of this may have not resulted in as eloquent a delivery as it might have been, but it served me very well and gave me needed added confidence.

Jay Chiat used to chastise me regularly for using notes in meetings. He was a natural off-the-cuff presenter. He was really excellent at spontaneous delivery and ad-libs. On the other hand, I saw him make some incredible faux pas, which were always costly because of his lack of formal preparation.

Whenever he started in on me, my response was always the same. Whatever works! I never changed this part of my preparation procedure.

I rarely forgot a key point because I had it written down and could refer to it. Frankly, though, since I rehearsed and reread my material so many times, I ended up knowing it almost by heart anyway.

I have always been a very direct person. To the point of people rolling their eyes at some remark I might have made. I always felt my demeanor in this regard had to do with being brutally honest. Too many people do not want to hear the truth for whatever reasons. In hindsight it may well be that I was overly direct on certain occasions or in certain situations. I would do it all over again exactly the same way.

Some have joked that my demeanor was something like Larry David's. I don't believe I ever approached the level he does in *Curb Your Enthusiasm*. But I may have. Most people get very uncomfortable dealing with people who are direct. They can't handle the truth. I have a hard time myself sometimes.

We once did a great ad for Dell, which may or may not have come out of the way we dealt with issues at the agency. Dell was at the time one of only a few direct marketers of personal computers and people didn't really understand the benefits of buying from them. The particular ad explained all of those benefits below the headline "It Pays to Be Direct."

It was a really great ad. I thought then and still think now that it's a really great personal philosophy. However, being older and maybe wiser now, I admit to being somewhat softer and less direct.

Someone once gave me a gift of a bullhorn as a joke. We had open offices with no doors or walls and so I was often prone to shouting to people across various partitions. The bullhorn became a fixture in my office and I used it quite frequently.

I would see someone walking down a corridor maybe 40 feet away and would grab the horn and give a shout.

"Hey, Ross, have you got a minute?"

"Mike, can you join us in here?"

"Camille, how ya' doing?"

It was quick. It was easy. I didn't have to dial a phone number. It worked for me. Some people didn't like it.

One of the things that most pleased me when I finally decided to leave the business in 2000 was an article that appeared in *Advertising Age* entitled "Goodbye to helm of good Bay agency." The national recognition, that Goldberg Moser O'Neill had achieved something significant as a creative shop, was satisfying.

The writer referred to me as an "irascible gadfly." According to Webster, *gadfly* means any of various flies that bite or annoy livestock. Yep, I guess that was me. I'm not as sure about the "angry, hot-tempered" part, which is also included in the dictionary definition. Well, maybe that too.

A plaque was presented to me just before I walked out of the agency front door for the last time. And Nancy Hill, who was then running the office, established a scholarship for young individuals who demonstrated they could deliver great creative ideas and work. The plaque said, "THE FRED LIFETIME ACHIEVEMENT AWARD. Presented to Fred Goldberg from all who will think of you before all others when hearing the name Fred. December 2000."

Very nice and much appreciated. Both of these were touching gestures. I learned later that the scholarships were canceled without anyone ever receiving even the first one. So much for delivering on promises. I used the wood plaque to start a fire on a chilly evening in my den fireplace.

My retirement dinner was organized by my first hire at Chiat/Day: technology guru par excellence, preeminent account person, marketing and advertising intellectual, superlative chief operating officer, essential board member and shareholder, and good friend Mike Massaro. He flattered me with his words speaking for all of the key GMO executives as he presented me with an exquisite gold Cartier watch.

He said, "It was a difficult process, ripe with bias and intrigue. In the end, however, the old phrase 'good enough is not enough' kept coming back. You've been our leader from 1982 to 2000. You've built Chiat/Day San Francisco and Goldberg Moser O'Neill. You've led the brand building of innumerable important companies—Apple, Dell, Intel, Cisco, Dreyer's, Kia, California Cooler, and others. And most importantly you've built a lot of us in this room as businesspeople, as advertising people, and as adults. We think that's good enough for any one career. So that's what we put on the back: 'Good Enough. 1982–2000.' Thanks, Fred."

EPILOGUE

HAVING COMPLETED THE LION'S SHARE of the writing of this book, I was paging through *The Ark*, the local town newspaper, when I chanced upon an announcement asking for volunteers who might be able to help the town of Tiburon better "brand" and market itself. It wasn't clear to me exactly what reason they had for doing this or what they actually wanted to accomplish, but I decided that since I had some time on my hands, it might be a worthwhile and interesting project in which to get involved.

I admit I had some reluctance, having worked with a number of nonprofit situations before and suffered the consequential committee mentality and tiny-minded process that seems a genetic part of these kinds of organizations. Particularly problematic is where the status quo seems always to have the major share of supporters, making for a not very rewarding or productive situation or solution.

Nevertheless, I sent in a short note expressing my interest to help, along with my background and credentials, to the selection committee, which consisted of the Tiburon town manager, a woman named Peggy Curran, and two of her fellow council members.

I was subsequently invited to "interview" with them at the Town Hall, which I did a few weeks later. While my résumé contained many of the marketing challenges I had been involved in over my 30-some years in the business, I touched on a few of them specifically in our meeting. In fact, one of my greatest strengths had been my strategic and marketing prowess for many of my clients, some of whom are portrayed in this book.

If I were to highlight a few of the positioning and branding successes specifically, they would include but not be limited to the Apple Macintosh introduction, Jell-O Gelatin, the Commonwealth of Puerto Rico, California Cooler, Security Pacific Bank, Dreyer's Grand Ice Cream, Sutter Home Winery, E&J Gallo, Rice-A-Roni, Dell Computer, Kia Motors America, Calyx & Corolla, Boston Market, Beringer wines, and scores of others.

At any rate, I soon received a letter from Ms. Curran advising me how they had had an overwhelming response to their call for help on this branding project. Fully 17 people had volunteered.

She continued on: "After much consideration, in the end we concluded that this Task Force needs to be very small to be successful, no more than six general members plus the Council Committee and myself." The note went on to explain that "despite your excellent qualifications and willingness to serve, we were not able to include you in the group."

OMG!

Clearly the ironic and painful finale to my marketing and advertising career. Rejected for a volunteer nonpaying job, working with a committee of at least nine, for a civic body. I didn't even make the top third.

It begs the question that I ask too frequently these days: Does any government group know what it is doing? I'm afraid the answer is no.

Fortunately, only a day later redemption arrived and my ego was made whole again.

I received a note from the president of a nonprofit with which I had been working for several years. The company is called Cleanerific, a nonsectarian, nonprofit social enterprise helping to create jobs for people in need and provide them with above-industry-average living wages and health benefits. Cleanerific is a cleaning and janitorial service company that is partially underwritten and managed by the Jewish Family and Children's Services.

My challenge for Cleanerific was, with little to no funds, to identify a branding position and build it into something that would define the company versus a myriad of other competitive cleaning businesses.

I was happily rewarded with the following letter from Michael Berke, CEO of Cleanerific.

> *I hope that you are having a great summer. I know that this e-mail is way overdue, but the fact is, because of your marketing expertise, Cleanerific is booming! Last month was our best on record and this month we have already surpassed last month. As always, thank you for the generosity of your time and expertise. We are up to 26 cleaners who are now receiving a living wage plus full medical benefits.*
>
> *We are now in the process of hiring more cleaners. Once that is completed, I would love to get together again and do some planning on future marketing campaigns.*
>
> *Again, the staff of Cleanerific and myself thank you.*

And as fate would have it, coincidentally on the same day I received the note from Michael Berke, I also received an e-mail from another Michael, Michael Dell. He wondered how I was doing and was seeking my thoughts on how Dell might take advantage of a recent situation that arose as Hewlett-Packard had announced the divestment of their PC business. A critical part of this occurrence of course had to do with the impact on the Dell brand.

Beyond any branding and marketing skills that I may or may not have, when all is said and done, maybe the most important things that I retain and cherish are some of the comments that the people who worked with me over the years had to offer.

Gary Korpi–Mail Room
"I have been working for you for seven years and seen high times and low, but my loyalty has always been with you. I have also seen lots of people come and lots go. That's why when I told you it's been a 'pleasure' I meant just that."

Jim Noble–Creative
"Without sounding like too much of a brown nose I want to tell you that you have been the best boss I have ever had. Period. Ever since I came to Chiat/Day in 1987, I have felt like you were always looking out for me. Creatively. And financially. Especially when it came time to buy my first house. Anyway, I think we did some exceptional work while I was here and I'm sure it will continue long into the future at GMO. I will miss you. This place. And will always look back on it with a great deal of pride."

Wayne Buder–Account Management
"You're always the one passing out kudos. This one's for you. While you were in your office accepting your congratulations from our new clients, I was among the masses hovering outside taking in the moment. Fred, I wish you could have seen what was going on with your troops. The smiles, the high-fives, the hugging, and even tears of joy were everywhere you turned. I have never seen such camaraderie and spirit in any of the agencies I've worked at. There was this sense of awe at having 'arrived.'"

Camille Johnson–Media
"A mere thank-you seems pathetically inadequate for your generous trust in us. You took an incredible risk four years ago which not only provided us with jobs but also gave us the rare opportunity to build something ourselves. For that I am truly grateful. I hope we continue to reward that initial leap of faith you so generously took."

David Weiner–Financial Manager/Board Director/Deal Maker
"The ice bucket is great. Your wishes are appreciated. I was proud and delighted to help. And the check is much more than money—it's a class action by a class guy and company."

Marilee Brusaschetti–Media
"I wanted to leave you with my personal top 10 reasons why GMO is a great place to work:

10. CC Mail is back up!

9. Work we can all point to and say: 'My agency did that'

8. Co-workers we can call friends

7. The hours (just KIDDING)

6. No Clowns

5. No Shit!

4. It's a place 'where everybody knows your name'

3. Pat is back!

2. Grossman is gone!

and the number one reason GMO is a great place to work:

1. One word: Fred."

Dave Woodside–Creative
"I want to thank you once again for the time I spent here. I feel like I grew up here. GMO has been a part of my life so long, it's been a way of explaining to myself who I am. We had exciting times, and I'm feeling like I'm leaving my safety net behind. You guys have treated me well by accommodating my idiosyncrasies. And you've given me that rare option of taking time to pursue my daydreams."

Mark Bilfield–Sales Promotion
"I'd be remiss if I didn't send you a note to wish you well on your retirement. It's well deserved. You're one of the really great ad guys and your brand of advertising and management will be missed by a lot of people. Good luck."

Tony Bennett–Creative
"You know, I talk to people all the time. Ex GMO-ers. East coast folks. And one thing that always comes up is how great a place it was and how awesome the culture was. People always say to me that it was the best agency they ever worked for. And I have to say that I agree. It was a lot of work and hard work, but I always felt like I was valued and appreciated by you and Brian and I can't tell you how rare that is. I had a great time while I was there and did some of the best work I have done in my career. It was truly a wonderful place to be. I'm sure people tell you this kind of thing all the time, but I thought you should hear it again."

Some of the most meaningful comments came from my management group at GMO, some of whom I had worked with for 18 years. My enormous thanks to the absolute best executive group that could have been assembled and without whom I couldn't have succeeded. Camille Johnson, Rosalinde Estes, Mike Moser, Brian O'Neill, Tanya Stringham, MJ Rockers, Dennis O'Rourke, Sharon Rundberg, and Mike Massaro.

Brian O'Neill–Creative and Partner and GMO Founder
"The number one query I get from the gazillions of ex-GMOers I hear from on LinkedIn is: Have you talked to Fred lately? You have garnered an amazing amount of respect and admiration (especially from my wife)—but for the life of me I don't know why."

And one of the most appreciated of all . . .

Paul Carek–Creative
"Well, according to my résumé it's simply been: 'Goldberg Moser O'Neill, September '92 to October '99.' But the last seven years have been much more than that. In that time, I've learned what it's like to work at a real agency, had the opportunity to grow professionally, met the love of my life, and became a son-in-law. Of course, none of these things would have been possible without you.

"Thanks for creating a place where smart, nice people can work. And thanks for being such a good, generous father-in-law. It's been (and continues to be) a pleasure getting to know you better. Love, Paul"

ACKNOWLEDGMENTS

THERE ARE A NUMBER OF PEOPLE I WOULD LIKE TO THANK, without whom these memoirs would never have been written.

My gratitude and thanks to the late Professor Grief of the University of Vermont, who saved me from drowning in pre-med studies after my first two years. He ignited an interest in marketing and advertising and was also responsible for helping me go on to graduate school to secure my MBA.

To the late Professor Hector Lazo, my advisor at the Stern Graduate School of Business at New York University, who was incredibly motivating and supportive of my academic endeavors during those years. He encouraged me to continue on academically, and while I was accepted into the doctoral program, I was in need of an income and decided not to pursue the advanced degree. Thank goodness.

Next is John McMennamin, my first boss, who hired me at P. Ballantine & Sons into the Marketing Research Department and promoted me several times and whom I replaced as marketing research manager when he left for Young & Rubicam. John is really the one responsible for my entering advertising, since he recommended that they hire me at Y&R as a marketing executive, which was the start of my career in the business. I also learned a heck of a lot about integrity and insight from John.

I had a number of wonderful mentors during my years at Young & Rubicam, including Joe Dedeo, Bob Walsh, John Hathaway, Jack Klein, Mike Russell, Bob Gleckler, Jim Makrianes, and Ed Ney, all of whom proved to be excellent teachers and models each in many and different ways.

At Chiat/Day I was blessed with a good friendship and business relations with both Guy Day and Lee Clow. I learned so much from both of these executives. And I owe so much more of what I learned about the "real" advertising business to Jay Chiat. I also am indebted to him for giving me the opportunity to build my own advertising agency and for the success in which it resulted. My creative director at Chiat/Day San Francisco, Ross Van Dusen, was a critical part of our success in those days. He brought a special creative talent and work ethic for which I am extremely grateful. Ditto for the great copy writer and associate creative director Dave "Woodie" Woodside. I also thank all the other great creative talent that was attracted to Chiat/Day during those heady years and for the incredible body of work that they produced under Lee Clow's guidance. They made selling advertising immensely easier.

At Goldberg Moser O'Neill our fabulous success would not have been possible without the creative talents of my two partners: Brian O'Neill and Mike Moser. These two individuals, while dramatically different from one another, shared a similar creative brilliance that resulted in a phenomenal collection of great advertising. And unlike a lot of creative advertising, most of ours actually worked. Brian's and Mike's brilliant strategic insights and creativity, hard work, and dedication over the years to the agency and to the work attracted so many clients and made them both famous and rich. The clients, that is.

A special note of thanks to my very first hire at Chiat/Day San Francisco, Mike Massaro, who became chief operating officer of Goldberg Moser O'Neill. Mike was a very unique and exceptionally talented executive without whom I doubt Goldberg Moser O'Neill would have been nearly as successful. He had a unique understanding of marketing and particularly technology that few others had. He brought objective insight and creativity to every issue and challenge. He was most dedicated and committed to the agency and to the work. That he was an incredible devil's advocate served me extraordinarily well. I consider him a great businessman and a good friend.

And to the very special group of senior executives, most of whom were with me for my 17 years in San Francisco, which included the founding and running of Goldberg Moser O'Neill. They made up a unique management group and were each in their own way responsible for the excellence and meritorious performance of their respective disciplines and for the incredible success of the agency: Camille Johnson, media director; MJ Rockers, print production manager; Tanya Stringham, art production manager; Rosalinde Estes, office manager; Sharon Rundberg, TV production manager; and Catrina McAuliffe, account planning director. Oh, and also Dennis O'Rourke, CFO, whom I spent an entire day interviewing before hiring and who made many significant contributions to our profitability and saved me lots of money. Including by not attending my final farewell dinner.

There were a number of other executives over the years whose work and efforts I well remember and who directly and indirectly contributed to my successes in one way or another. Creatives: Brian Quennell, Jim Noble, Paul Carek, and Randy Hibbitts were all standouts. And there were so many more. In media: Hans Logie and Susan Pennel, and my very first encounter with an account planner, M. T. Rainey. Special thanks to Pat Sherwood, who worked with me at Young & Rubicam, Chiat/Day Los Angeles, Chiat/Day San Francisco, and Goldberg Moser O'Neill in between his jobs at a multitude of other ad shops. He was exceptional nonetheless.

Special thanks to David Weiner, who was on the board at Chiat/Day and was always an excellent source of counsel and a friend. He represented Chiat when I purchased the San Francisco agency and he represented Goldberg Moser O'Neill when I sold the agency to Interpublic. He did a superb job. Both times.

And to my attorney Richard Greene who provided wise guidance over many years and through both the purchase and the sale of the agency, along with the myriad of other matters, like getting sued by an employee who lifted a coffee cup and hurt his back.

Thanks to my neighbor and publisher John Owen, who gave me valuable advice when I started down the path to publishing these memoirs and to whom I have to give thanks for ultimately connecting me with the fellow who edited the book and provided conceptual oversight, Jay Schaefer. Jay has been a wonderful and positive influence on bringing these memoirs to fruition. His counsel and creative contributions are reflected throughout the pages. His observations and recommendations were astute and made for a substantially better read than it might have been otherwise.

Thanks to Judith Dunham for a fine job copyediting and fact checking. And a special nod to Pamela Geismar, who designed the book and cover, and truly contributed wonderfully and so creatively to many of the various design elements. And to Owen Prell, who vetted the book and provided important guidance on presenting the material in a fully truthful and legal manner.

My thanks and appreciation to Council Oak Books and its publisher, James Connolly.

And a big thank-you to my mom, Birdie, and my dad, Sydney Goldberg, the latter of whom was a dedicated, hardworking, and successful executive at Decca Records for almost his entire business life. He set a standard of commitment to and engagement with his business that left an indelible mark on me and my entire career. I was incredibly proud of his accomplishments. And of course to my mother, who along with my dad was responsible for getting me here in the first place after all and making it all happen.

Finally, blessings and commendations to all of these wonderful people, and the ones I haven't mentioned as well, who were part of my journey through the crazy world of advertising and without whom I might very well have gone insane.

INDEX